The best of
Dilemma
&
Decision

The best of
Dilemma
& Decision
from
International Management

Compiled by the editors
of International Management

INTERNATIONAL
MANAGEMENT

McGraw-Hill International Publications Company Limited
London · New York

Published by INTERNATIONAL MANAGEMENT
McGraw-Hill International Publications Company Limited
McGraw-Hill House Maidenhead Berkshire England

British Library Cataloguing in Publication Data

The Best of Dilemma and Decision from International Management

1. Managment   2. Decision-making
I. International Management

658.4'03   HD30.23

ISBN 0-07-084731-2

Designed by **Frank Fry**

Printed and bound in Great Britain by
Oxford University Press, Walton Street, Oxford, England.

Contents

Introduction

For years, Dilemma & Decision has been among the most popular and widely read columns in *International Management* magazine. Month after month, *International Management* writers have dreamed up fanciful problems that senior managers might face. And month after month, consultants and practising managers have stolen a few hours from their real jobs and responsibilities to imagine what they would do if they were the man on the spot in each dilemma.

Now the best of the dilemmas and the decisions are published together for the first time. The dilemmas are grouped broadly under functional management labels – marketing; production, computers and finance; industrial relations; human resources; corporate strategy and social responsibility.

Inevitably, the choice of category is often arbitrary. All of the dilemmas have at least two things in common. First, they cannot be answered by formula, but involve difficult choices between conflicting people, policies and situations. Second, they cannot be answered by convening a committee or calling for a report. Most of them call for decisions to be made immediately, in a crisis situation, by a single individual.

As author of many of the dilemmas, I have been amazed at the quality of the analysis and the penetrating but commonsense nature of the solutions offered by deciders of many different nationalities. True, it is easier to make decisions when nothing is at stake should they prove to be wrong, which would not be the case in a real-life situation. But most of the decisions have been made by men whose livelihoods depend on their being right most of the time, and the quality of their thinking shines through.

No attempt has been made in this book to update the deciders. If Mr. Smith or Mr. Dupont was managing director of the ABC Consultancy when he provided his decision, he is still credited with that position even though he may, by now, have moved on to other things. I hope and believe that every manager will find in these pages, which are meant for browsing through, something not only entertaining but also challenging and useful.

ROY HILL, Senior Editor, International Management
January 1985,
Maidenhead, England.

Chapter 1

Marketing

The deciders in this section are mostly consultants advising on problems of selling strategy, product launch, sales force management and pricing. Should a perfume company follow a new scent? Should a new sales chief sack a third of his sales force? Some of these dilemmas, although fictionalized by International Management, *are painfully akin to those encountered in the real world.*

Should new sales chief sack a third of his sales force?

" **I**'ve got a problem," Alan Landry sighed as he slumped down on the couch in managing director Colin Straughan's office. Straughan quickly guessed what the problem was. The energetic 37-year-old sales manager still hadn't revitalized the sales force after four months on the job.

The pleasant after-glow of a two-hour lunch began to fade as Straughan recalled the high hopes the board had placed on Landry. When the previous sales manager had retired it seemed a golden opportunity to bring the sales force up to par with the modernized production facilities and the innovative research team. The only difficulty was that it meant by-passing the number two man in the sales force, affable, 58-year-old Geoffrey Duggan. But a hard look at the stagnant sales figures for the past three years had convinced even Duggan's friends that the company needed a new man.

Landry described how he had tried to win the support of the firm's 20-man sales force. He had talked to them individually. They listened in sullen silence. He held meetings to air problems in selling the company's latest products. There were plenty of wisecracks and complaints, but no helpful suggestions. When he pointed out that overseas licensees were selling the new line well, he had been informed how different things were in the home market. He had explained in detail the need for the new system of reporting sales calls that he had instituted. "They just don't want to know," he told Straughan. "And some of them are deliberately obstructive, as these reports show." He tossed a sheaf of papers on to the managing director's desk.

Unfolding the grand plan

Glancing through the single-page forms made out by the field salesmen, Straughan noted that none had been completed properly. Some questions about customer acceptability of new products had received near-abusive answers from the salesmen. One man had written across the form: "Form-filling or selling: cross out which does not apply."

Then Landry proceeded to unfold his grand plan. He wanted to fire the six salesmen who had ridiculed his reporting system and otherwise obstructed his efforts. He also recommended letting Duggan go, or as he put it, "making his retirement official." He wanted to reduce the average age of the sales force to about 40 from its present 50 by hiring aggressive young replacements.

"Don't you think that's a bit drastic, Alan?" Straughan interrupted. "You can't just cut off 30% of your sales force in one swoop. Why not hire two new sales trainees and build up gradually? I'll authorize the additional manpower. Anyway, their salaries wouldn't approach what your idea would cost us in severance pay."

1

"My plan would cost a lot more than severance pay," Landry persisted. "To attract the kind of people I need, commissions should be boosted by 50%. In fact, our problem right now is a direct result of underpaying salesmen. All the good men we've hired and trained have left for better money. Through the years you've accumulated a sales force made up of men who aren't good enough to get another job."

Landry then produced a detailed report. It calculated that firing the seven men, hiring and training their replacements, and increasing the commission by half would boost his department's costs by 40% over the next 12 months. He forecast only a 5% sales increase for the period. But he added: "If sales aren't up by 30% the following year, I'll resign."

That evening Straughan met Duggan by chance. After a brief chat about their families, he asked: "How's the sales team?" "Not too good," Duggan responded with a frown. "We're slowed down by all this new paperwork." He hesitated, then went on: "Between us, young Landry has turned all the men against him. Some of the salesmen are threatening to leave. If they go, you'll see some big accounts go with them. You have to face it we are in a slowly declining industry. We've improved our market share simply because of the personal contacts our men have built up over the years."

The next day Straughan summoned his financial director to go over Landry's plan. His cost estimates were quite accurate. And Landry had been hired largely on the basis of his record for hitting sales targets. But was he right to place so much reliance on the new product line? Duggan had confided that the men didn't push the new products because they could be substituted for the older, higher priced ones.

Also Landry's plan would mean a small loss for the year, instead of the budgeted profit. But if the sales manager were right it would mean higher profits in the years ahead. Straughan felt that if the turnaround didn't come in the second year, his job would also be forfeit. He also reasoned that if he didn't back Landry, he would have to fire him and put Duggan in charge lest he wind up with the worst of both worlds.

DECISION

Straughan should support Landry, or fire him

Straughan has a bigger problem than whether to support or to fire Landry, and he is wise to start worrying about his own future. As managing director, one of his most important responsibilities is planning the future of the company, and it appears that he hasn't done it well. If Duggan is right in saying that the company is in a slowly declining industry and the new products are displacing the older, higher priced ones, then planning should have foreseen it and devised the sales strategy accordingly.

Despite Landry's low opinion of his sales force, it appears that they know more about their business than he does. Rather than invoking the success of the overseas licensees, he would have been better advised to forego his new call-reporting system and get down to fundamentals with his staff.

Straughan was probably right in passing over 58-year-old Duggan in favour of a younger man, but his basis of selection of the new man was superficial. To have hired Landry largely because of his record for hitting sales targets is akin to backing a golfer because he can sink putts, without much regard for the length of his drives or his ability to get out of traps. Landry obviously never broke par on his management of people and it would appear that he had never played this particular industry course before.

Some of the current trouble arises from Straughan's failure to deal positively with the Duggan situation. If Duggan had really lost all his effectiveness then a "golden handshake" would have been in order, but he seems to know more about the sales situation than Straughan or Landry and is well worth retaining.

The managing director should certainly not approve Landry's "grand plan". To avoid embarrassing Landry he should admit his own incomplete knowledge of the market situation and propose that he, Landry, and Duggan launch a fact-gathering campaign. They should try to find out – for it appears that they don't know – the size of their market, their share of it and whether their share is increasing, as Duggan says it is. From their customers they will readily learn how their salesmen are regarded and how they compare with the competition.

Their trade association should be able to give them useful comparative information about salesmen's salaries and commissions. Likewise, the company's personnel department should be able to follow up on the good salesmen who have left over the past few years to determine whether they did, in fact, command more money in the jobs they went to.

A visit to some of the overseas licensees and their customers should also be arranged as part of the fact-gathering effort. Useful ideas might be obtained, particularly if the successes are occurring in advanced countries. But if the company is in a declining industry, one suspects that the good results are coming from the less developed countries where older products may still be in strong demand.

Since it would appear that Straughan and Landry, and probably affable Duggan as well, have not burdened themselves with marketing facts, they therefore might have difficulty in getting the answers needed to formulate a proper marketing plan. So Straughan should consider seeking outside advice on market research and in developing a market strategy. This would be a much more prudent expenditure than to approve Landry's 40% increase in his department's costs.

Improving human relations

When the facts are known. Straughan might well consider naming Duggan field sales manager, with direct responsibility over the salesmen with whom he has good rapport. In that case Landry should be charged with setting sales policy, working with the research and development team to provide more modern products, devising better advertising and sales promotion programmes, and improving after-sales services.

In the meantime Straughan should send Landry on a short course on human relations and motivation. He should also persuade Landry to lay less stress on his salesmen's reports and spend more time out in the field with them.

When the smoke has cleared Straughan will have solved more than his dilemma over Landry's rash and immature plan. He should have at least made a start toward the development of a proper long-range business plan. He will have to develop all the other parts of the plan and then revise

3

and refine it almost continuously. But if he does it right he will be able to manage better, his company will have a future and he may even be able to get back to his two-hour lunches.

This decision was provided by Lynn A. Brua in his capacity as head of international operations of U.S.-based executive recruiting firm Heidrick & Struggles.

DILEMMA

Ought the technical director to delay product launch?

All day the factory of Chauliet SA had been buzzing with rumours that the company's new line of chain-saws had suddenly failed during the testing cycle. Then, late in the afternoon, managing director François Lefort called his top managers together. He explained that technical director Bernard Bonnier had called for the meeting, and asked the obviously tense Bonnier to outline the situation as he saw it.

"I'm afraid we are going to have to stop production of the new model," Bonnier stated flatly. Shouts of protest immediately erupted. The company had spent over a year in developing the new saw for introduction late in the current year. Then suddenly the firm's leading competitor splashed out with a marketing campaign for a closely similar product to be introduced in September. The move had galvanized Chauliet into action. Marketing executives prepared an instant advertising campaign for the new product. Manufacturing cleared floor space, put through rush orders on machinery, and went on a crash hiring and training programme. There was a pent-up demand for a more efficient hand chain-saw. It was a near certainty that if Chauliet didn't get its product to the market at the same time as its competitor, it would stand to lose a large portion of the business.

As the protests died down Bonnier explained that, as agreed, he had authorized full production after 250 hours trouble-free testing of the six prototypes off the production line. But after only another 50 hours, four of the saws had suffered main bearing seizures. Bonnier pointed out that the firm could not risk having that happen in the hands of customers. The only answer was to stop production until the fault had been overcome.

Facing double trouble

Sales director Jean Delahaye objected: "It would be disastrous to stop production now. If our competitors get established in the new market before us, we'll have the devil of a job to break their hold."

"If you stop production now, we'll still have to pay all the extra men we've just hired," added works manager Philippe Seurat. Lefort brought the meeting to order. He asked each member to outline his case.

Bonnier began by reminding his audience that the pre-production testing programme had been reduced from the normal 500 hours to 250, under pressure from the marketing department. The latest results showed that over half the saws now coming off the production line would probably seize their main bearings after about 300 hours' use. Bonnier estimated that, using all available facilities, he needed three weeks to produce enough specially-made parts to support production until a reliable standard part could be brought into service. Meanwhile, research into the cause of the failures was already under way but the results would not be known for some days.

Keeping production going

"Why not keep production going, carry out the urgent deliveries, and then replace the faulty parts in a month, at the time of the free service?" asked Delahaye. "Less than 10% of the models in normal service will have been running for 300 hours by that time. That way, we'd have the initial sales and be able to maintain our reputation for reliability."

Seurat supported Delahaye. He wanted to keep production going at all costs, and he pointed out that the factory had no facilities to store the saws, either finished or unfinished. Further, he questioned the validity of Bonnier's gloomy predictions. He thought that normal on-off use would allow the bearings to cool down so they would last longer than in the development department's flat-out tests. And he suggested that the problem might lie with just one batch of poor material. He contended: "You'll probably find that the bearings don't need modifying. In the unlikely event that they do, we can do the work in the distributors' workshops. There'll be plenty of time after we have the modified parts."

Delahaye put in a final word: "At the worst, failures in service will go up by 7% for a few months. I think it's a risk worth taking."

Lefort is impressed by Delahaye's plan for pressing on with shipments. A successful launch could mean the new saw would generate 20% of Chauliet's total sales within a year. However, if Lefort waits until the fault is overcome, the new product probably won't reach the market until a month after its rival. This in turn would mean a smaller than projected market share, and a longer period to offset the increasing start-up costs.

On the other hand, Lefort has worked hard to build Chauliet's reputation for reliability. It is almost certain that the trade will eventually find out that he allowed potentially defective products to be sold. In addition, at the back of his mind is the worry that Bonnier's men may not be able to produce a reliable bearing in time. Massive failures in service could permanently damage the reputation of all the company's products.

DECISION

Lefort should sell two different models

Chauliet SA has been driven into a corner. The management faces two alternatives, depending on whether Lefort is right in his fear that Bonnier's men may not be able to produce a reliable bearing in time to prevent "massive failures in service". If Lefort's apprehension turns out to be unfounded, it will be simple to modify the bearing and the production and marketing effort need not be delayed. Minor alterations will have to be carried out to the finished products on the shop floor and the saws already delivered to the wholesalers will have to be replaced by modified models.

But if the apprehension is well-founded, it will be necessary to wait for a month or more to obtain a product reliable for more than 300 hours' use. And until the fear is proved groundless, the company must take action on the assumption that the worst may happen. Management needs to find out the relative costs of each course of action. As no figures are available, we shall pass over this important aspect of the problem.

However, the most vital factor for the future of any firm is to satisfy its customers. This should become management's main worry.

Amateurs and professionals

The customers of a given product are seldom homogeneous in their use of the product. In this case, there are likely to be at least two categories of user. Those we could call "amateurs" will use the saw only periodically, and will take many months to build up 300 hours' use. "Professionals", on the other hand, will be those for whom 300 hours' use will be reached over a relatively short time. The proportion of these two categories should be determined by the marketing department.

Then the sales promotion service will have to plan the very quick launching of two different models for the initially forecast date. One, the currently produced model, will be immediately available for the amateurs. The other model, giving the desired reliability for professionals, will be available in one or two months' time, allowing for modification and build-up of production.

It will be necessary to use two different colours for the models. And minor technical changes, such as stronger handles, should be made to the professional model to justify a higher price. Production can be kept going at a lower rate by reducing working hours and storing as many components as possible.

Thus a commercial campaign can be started very quickly for the two models. It will show the customers that Chauliet is anxious to satisfy their needs. Chauliet will have the time to prepare a strong model justifying the company's reputation. And it will minimize the risk of trouble with customers. (If a professional buys an amateur model, the eventual seizure of the bearing could be partially attributable to him.)

There ought to be only a small loss of customers because the professionals would already have their own tools. A waiting time of one to two months ought not to reduce their desire to buy, providing Chauliet's sales force is aggressive enough in promoting their new model against the rival chain-saw.

Abandoning the amateur model

If the customer is in a hurry, he can be sold an amateur model, but Chauliet should insist that it be replaced by a professional one when these are available. This would involve reconditioning the amateur models sent back to the factory. And Chauliet will have to create a special commercial network for second-hand or hired chain-saws.

Clearly, the above proposals are only palliative. As soon as a stronger model is ready to sell, all the publicity for the amateur model should be abandoned. By monitoring the sales rate the company will be able to decide in the coming months whether it can stop production of the amateur model without taking any risks with total sales volume.

This course of action is forced on the company by the urgent situation. But it should also help the firm's management to get to know customer reactions and develop more systematic product design methods.

Study of the case leads to two suggestions for the long-term management of the company. Before launching a new product on the market, management should use a well-prepared network planning analysis to find the shortest time in which the product can be designed and produced. And the firm's managers need to be trained in the practice of creativity, value analysis and decision-making. Only in this way will they be able to avoid being overcome by such problems in the future.

This decision was provided by Henri Bonnafy in his capacity as managing director of PA Conseiller de Direction SA, the French subsidiary of PA International Management Consultants Ltd. of the U.K.

DILEMMA

Is risking the U.S. market, to win in Europe, a good idea?

When the designers at Galway Prints Ltd. first heard about marketing director Frank O'Rourke's proposal, they assumed he was joking. But once they found that the managing director was seriously considering the idea, they then became very distressed and worried.

O'Rourke had put forth a plan that would mean reducing shipments to the big, profitable U.S. market in order to establish a position in the continental European market. At present the Irish firm was selling 90% of its output to the U.S. market. Over the years the designers felt they had developed a "feel" for the American market. The material they produced was specially designed to cater to U.S. tastes. Indeed, it was so U.S.-oriented that previous efforts to sell on the Continent had proved largely unsuccessful. So a completely new line would have to be designed, and probably sold at a loss in the first year, to establish a European market.

A recent trip to the U.S. had made O'Rourke nervous of leaving all his eggs in one basket. He returned home with a feeling that booming sales in the U.S. were likely to dip sharply in the coming year. "Other clothing firms whose sales have paralleled ours have recently found demand slackening," he argued. "Customers have begun to bargain harder over prices, and two of our larger clients have told me that they might not be able to take up their commitment for this year. In themselves these changes are not serious, but I think we should prepare ourselves for the possibility of a sharp downturn."

Galway Prints' chief executive, Desmond Nolan, pointed out that it was already doing its best to expand sales in other areas, "but this takes time. Our products have always been aimed at the U.S. market". All but two of the designers had until now worked full-time for the U.S.

O'Rourke felt that the time had come to speed up the programme of market diversification, even at the expense of the currently steady U.S. market. His plan entailed expanding the plant and recruiting more designers so that the firm could develop full ranges for the other markets, instead of the present piecemeal work. But there would be no time to extend the factory for the current year's design and production cycle.

Lower profits

So O'Rourke felt that a further five of the 20 designers, and a proportionate number of machines, should be detailed immediately to work on designs for European countries. "It might mean much lower profits for this year," he agreed, "but if we can get a foothold on the Continent it will put us in a much better position to withstand a big drop in the American market later on. If we wait, a collapse of our U.S. business might leave us too weak to launch an effective campaign on the Continent. Besides, Europe is bound to become more important to us now we've joined the Common Market."

Senior designer Liam Murphy accused O'Rourke of "overreacting to gloom and doom talk by buyers and competitors. Sure, our friends in the industry would like to see us get out and leave the field for themselves. I'm not saying that we shouldn't look toward Europe, but why be in such a hurry? The U.S. market is not going to change overnight. In fact, if we throw away all those profits and sales, some of our shareholders may well think we've taken leave of our senses".

Continental expansion

Another designer noted that O'Rourke's conviction that there would be a drop in U.S. business still had to be borne out by the facts. "The only way we can be certain that we will lose this business is if we voluntarily give it away to our competitors," he argued. "And once it is lost, we'll never get it back. Why not channel all our expansion towards the Continental market? That way we'll get the best of both worlds."

After the meeting, chief executive Nolan considered O'Rourke's plan and the widespread opposition to it. O'Rourke's feel for market trends had been consistently accurate, and had led to successful introduction of new ranges in the past. Nolan now accepted that the present methods did not seem to be penetrating new markets. And he was confident that O'Rourke would be able to sell the new ranges outside the U.S. But, if he followed O'Rourke's plan, would the present designers produce acceptable work when having to change their styles against their will?

Reduced orders

As he was pondering the problem his secretary came in with an urgent memo from O'Rourke. Galway Prints, third largest customer in the U.S. had just notified the firm it was reducing a tentative order it had placed by 35% "due to market uncertainties". Should Nolan gamble that the U.S. market might taper off but would not collapse over the next year or two? Then the diversification could be achieved without losing established business in the U.S.

Nolan should organize for changes in both markets

Desmond Nolan's problem is due to uncertainty over the rate of change of the market. Some important information is lacking and the existing information is not very reliable. However, a slump in demand must be regarded as probable, though this does not necessarily mean a falling off in market share.

The necessary reduction in uncertainty can be achieved in three ways. Firstly, one can wait until information is more up-to-date and so more reliable before acting. This method has obvious disadvantages. The cost of reliable information is the inability to take timely action, which could dangerously reduce effectiveness.

Secondly, one can take action on either the "gamble that the U.S. market might taper off, but would not collapse", or on a gamble the other way, that it would drop suddenly within the next year. The disadvantages of this method are just as obvious. There are no established reasons for saying that either decision is the right one. It is possible to make the right decision by *chance*, but only by chance, just as it is equally possible to make the wrong one. The risks involved cannot be estimated.

Finally, one can regard both alternative market changes as equally probable and simultaneously introduce appropriate measures for each eventuality. This solution also has its disadvantages. Costs of implementing one course of action will be lost, as the market will change according to only one alternative.

Considering three possible solutions

An evaluation of the three possible solutions shows that the decision depends basically on Nolan's readiness to take risks. Assuming the firm is aiming at long-term growth with appropriate profits, then the decision must fall in favour of the third possibility. At all events the first possibility would cause a curtailment in production and a loss in turnover, because of the long time-lag. The second possibility *can* cause the same, just as it *can* bring no turnover loss, but it is impossible to estimate which. Such a decision is merely a question of luck and so cannot be taken seriously.

The third solution is the only one that *guarantees* no major curtailment in production and turnover loss. It allows costs to be minimized while dealing with the threatening crisis. In order to determine the necessary short-term proportions of production for the U.S. and European markets, one must have more information over the cost structure of Galway Prints. This could at present lie between 60% and 80% for the U.S. market and 20% and 40% for the European market. As soon as new information is available – such as further cut-backs in expected contracts – then the respective proportions must be modified.

Apart from the cost considerations mentioned above, several other arguments speak in favour of the third solution. The most important of these is its flexibility. It takes into account the market fluctuations and provides a suitable foundation for enabling the firm to adapt quickly to a changing environment. This can place a burden on short-term profits. But in the long term it leads to profit optimization. Galway Prints would then not be so subject to future changes in national markets.

What form does this analytical solution take in concrete terms? Nolan should follow O'Rourke's plan, but instead of setting five U.S. designers to design for the European market, he should recruit five European designers. At the same time sales promotion for the European market should be greatly expanded. Designs for the European market should be prepared and then immediately come into production replacing production for the U.S. as necessary. Meanwhile, some of the U.S. designers should now be preparing reserve designs for Europe.

This solution means that the company will be overstaffed until total production can be increased. Also, the U.S. designers will have to work overtime until the new designers have established themselves with successful designs for European markets. The long-term aim should be to have a third group of designers who could work equally well with the specialist designers who have a feel for either the U.S. or the European markets.

This decision was provided by Dr. Horst Schmelzer in his capacity as managing director of the Cologne-based European consulting group Wema Institut KG.

DILEMMA

Ought 'group interests' hold back an effective product?

Richard Volter, the chief executive officer of Brelperk SA., a large Swiss chemical and pharmaceutical company, was troubled by a long and distraught letter he had received from the general manager of a company located in Australia. He had at first assumed that the letter might be from a customer, but before he'd read far he realized it was from the managing director of a small patent medicine company that Brelperk now owned. The company, Rodgers Cough Drops Pty., was a subsidiary of a substantial Australian chemical company that Brelperk had acquired three years earlier.

The substance of the complaint from Rodgers' general manager Harry Smithers was that internal company politics were standing in the way of Rodgers making a major sales gain in the current year.

A month earlier a major scientific journal had reported on the findings of an exhaustive research effort on the effectiveness of cough drops. The article, which Smithers had enclosed, showed that Rodgers' cough drops were the most effective of all those tested in relieving sore throats and reducing coughs. Smithers and his marketing manager had geared a major promotional campaign based on these findings. They had ordered 5,000 reprints of the article to be sent to chemists across the country. And they had approached the advertising agency that handled Brelperk's account in Australia, asking them to help draft a consumer advertising campaign to promote the survey. Smithers was anxious to put most of his promotional budget for the year into this campaign, which he was certain could not fail to boost sales dramatically for Rodgers' cough drops.

However, no sooner had Smithers' marketing manager presented his plans to the agency than the account executive was on the telephone to the marketing director for Brelperk Throat Lozenges. Brelperk Throat Lozenges was currently in the midst of a major advertising campaign attempting to enlarge the share of this popular European product in the Australian market. Since the lozenges had been introduced in Australia three years earlier they had climbed to a sales level approaching $800,000 a year. This represented only 5% of Brelperk's worldwide sales for this product. Even so, its Australian sales exceeded those of Rodgers' cough drops.

Dropping the campaign

When the Brelperk marketing director in Australia discovered the results of the survey he became alarmed. Brelperk throat lozenges were rated fifth most effective of a dozen lozenges tested. But they were outranked by the market leader as well as the front runner, Rodgers.

Smithers' letter recounted how the Brelperk marketing director in Australia had called his counterpart for continental Europe. He, in turn, had taken the case to Karl Sontag, the board director responsible for non-prescription medicines. Shortly thereafter Sontag had telephoned Smithers from Switzerland. Sontag began by trying to explain that "over-all corporate interests must be taken into account". He advised Smithers not to proceed with his campaign. At first Smithers had resisted altogether. But during the course of the conversation he offered to cancel all the mailings of the reprints and delete all mention of Brelperk lozenges in his advertising campaign. However, he recounted, even this compromise did not satisfy Sontag. This Swiss executive had brusquely ended the telephone conversation by saying: "I want this advertising campaign dropped completely. Now do as you are told!"

It was this that had prompted Smithers to sit down and write the angry letter to Volter. He was enraged that the corporation was sacrificing great growth opportunity for Rodgers' cough drops in favour of promoting "a second-rate Swiss product". He even went so far as to suggest that by suppressing the advertising campaign the Swiss parent company "was cheating the Australian consumer".

Despite the extreme remarks, Volter carried out an investigation. He discovered from Sontag that Smithers' account was substantially correct. Sontag argued that such an advertising campaign would even have reper-cussions in Europe. Besides, he explained, Rodgers' cough drops tasted "awful". The Brelperk lozenges, he insisted, were much more palatable. And even if you believed the survey, they were only slightly less effective in soothing throats. He also insisted that Rodgers' advertising campaign would mean spending corporate money to undermine Brelperk's sizeable investment in establishing its own product in Australia.

Then Sontag added: "By the way, I've been thinking it might be a good idea, so long as we have a facility in Australia, to phase out Rodgers' cough drops altogether and manufacture Brelperk lozenges on the spot."

"Before we make a move like that," Volter responded, "I'd like to think it over, along with this whole situation."

The company-wide product is backed against the local maverick

The three key executives in the Brelperk case have varying degrees of responsibility and involvement in the dilemma. Volter has two problems. He must take an immediate decision about the promotional campaigns for the two cough lozenges and decide between two courses of action with conflicting interests. Both campaigns are already under way with consequential investment and their concurrent running was only revealed by chance. In the longer term, Volter must resolve the problem of being chief executive of an organization with partly functional, partly geographical, partly result-oriented units: a typical traditional structure.

Smithers' outburst is understandable, for he is in an extremely difficult position. He is a manager of a subsidiary of a geographical unit of a multinational, multi-product assembly of functions and firms without a clearly defined corporate strategy.

There are no problems as far as Sontag is concerned. He has one of those healthy functional roles which carry status symbols, great titles and fascinating activities – but no profit accountability.

Volter must immediately take two crucial steps. Smithers of Rodgers' Cough Drops Pty., should be given permission to proceed with the planned, and already commenced, sales campaign for his "front runner" product. And Brelperk should continue with its advertising campaign for the European product in Australia.

At the end of twelve months, the results of the sales campaigns should be evaluated in terms of expenditure, increase in market share, and profit (the most important aspect, yet one which was not mentioned by any of the executives). The total market should also be reviewed again.

It should be made clear to Sontag that in any future similar cases he must give instructions to his direct subordinates only if he is talking about "overall corporate interests." In any such case, he should quantify these interests in terms of future profit potential and ask for a decision from the man responsible for this profit.

It is of paramount importance that Smithers should receive wholehearted support. Personnel must never be demotivated or discouraged. However, longer term decisions must take into account the possibility of new competitive products being brought on to the market.

Over-emphasizing coordination

In organizing and managing any multi-product, multinational and, therefore, automatically multifunctional organization, the normal but economically obsolete tendency is to over-emphasize coordination. In this approach, every little action in Australia would be coordinated with any other activity directly or indirectly connected with it. This is theoretically right, but practically impossible. It kills motivation and accountability on the lower but decisive hierarchical levels.

In a profit-oriented multinational organization there is no need for a central board director to have responsibility for non-prescription medicines, as does Sontag. But clearly the central board can and should oversee the development of standards, qualifications and requirements by respective specialists in line with company policy.

Volter's rethinking of the situation should be based on the realization that his responsibility is not to find solutions for such problems, which may occur every week. His job is to repair the basic structural mistakes, the sources of such negative symptoms. The source of the problem in this case is clearly the total organization structure of the worldwide concern.

Consider the company structure

The particular solution must flow from the following criteria: Every employee should have one – and only one – boss; responsibility and authority must be coordinated. The company must be structured into profit-oriented units with clearly defined objectives. And if overall company policy in a particular case will work to the disadvantage of one of the units, a suitable compensation for the "loser" must be agreed and taken into account in the plan. Functions should be centralized only if clear economic reasons justify it. Most central services should be sold to the profit-oriented units, who will have the right to buy the services elsewhere if that is more economic. And staff and control functions such as that exercised by Sontag in this case should be kept to a minimum.

If Volter does not realize this main responsibility and does not develop a plan of campaign to design a new structure, the administrative board has to replace him with a man who is not one of many pharmaceutical specialists of the company but an experienced top manager.

This decision was provided by Willy O. Wegenstein in his capacity as chairman of the Swiss-based international consultancy Knight Wegenstein.

DILEMMA

How can luxury goods company make up sales revenue loss?

Horst Hetzner, managing director of Marschallin AG, reached for the telephone to call marketing director Regina Woitusch into his office. He had just been reviewing preliminary first-half sales figures with finance director Udi Kapeller.

Sales of the company's line of bath essence were running 12% below budget, and had declined in each of the past three months. The company would be in a loss position by the end of the year if the present trend persisted.

When Woitusch entered the office she had a ready explanation for the falling sales. She blamed them squarely on the 25% price increase that had been instituted in late 1974 over her heated objections. "That cost us thousands of customers that we'd just convinced to step up to Marschallin products," she said. "I think it is essential to reduce prices, or at least come back with some widely advertised special offers."

Kapeller slapped his forehead with his palm. "That would only make things worse," he exclaimed. "We could not hope to get enough extra business to compensate for the reduced revenues from our present volume. We could reduce the contents in the bottle slightly, but that would not really amount to much of a saving. I am afraid the only answer is another price increase."

Facing up to recession and inflation

"Maybe you haven't heard," retorted Woitusch, "but there is a recession going on. People are becoming very reluctant to buy very high-priced luxury items. But I think that if we trim our prices and step up advertising we can still recapture some of the customers we have lost, and perhaps increase our share of the market. As you know, our main competitors are feeling the pinch, too."

"Don't forget the inflation is as bad as the recession," Kapeller argued. "Our main costs are all going up, advertising, salesmen's salaries and distribution costs. But before we go on, I would like to show you something very interesting when the actual sales figures are broken down by territory.

"Now look at the urban areas; Düsseldorf, Cologne, Munich. Sales are all up, despite increased prices. And here, look at Hamburg! Sales up 14% over the second quarter of 1974."

Kapeller went on to show that sales had declined mostly in smaller cities and towns, although some larger cities, such as Stuttgart and Hannover, showed modest reductions in turnover.

"The outlying areas were where we have made the most gains in the past two years," said Kapeller. "They would naturally be the first to fall away. Now we are left with a hard core of loyal customers, who are relatively insensitive to a price increase. If you will pay DM16 a bottle for bath oil, you will pay DM19 or DM21 for the same bottle."

He went on to propose that the company radically alter its marketing policy. It should concentrate all its efforts in major urban areas. It should further concentrate on large department stores and try to place its own staff behind the counters.

"This would enable us to cut out a number of salesmen who are now covering outlying regions. It would also save considerably on distribution costs," said Kapeller. "And perhaps we could even cut back on some of that expensive television advertising, too."

Rejecting financial interference

Woitusch's stunned silence was only momentary. "That is the most incredible thing I've ever heard," she retorted. "I thought I was supposed to be the marketing expert in this company. How can you still interfere in my department after what your price increase has done to us?"

Then she turned to Hetzner: "If you even considered following that sort of advice you will be condemning this company to remain small for ever. We've fought hard to become a national brand, and now he wants to throw this all away," she argued.

"Even Kapeller admits that we are a luxury line. And if we want to keep that image we have to promote it, and that does cost money. But if we concentrate sales in big cities, then a lot of our national magazine and television advertising will be wasted going to areas where the product is not available."

Hetzner puffed on his pipe and then broke his long silence. "I know it is a difficult decision to make," he said. "But we have to do something right away to try to keep the company profitable. Frankly, even if we could cut the cost of the product by 20% it would have very little impact on our situation. I think the answer must lie in the marketing area."

Company should base its strategy on market research

Marschallin AG is typical of the companies suffering at present from the market recession and high inflation. But this is only half its problem. The other half is due to poor planning and the unnecessarily long time being taken in reaching decisions. Management is reacting instead of planning.

Planning is obviously weak and incomplete. Management appears to be more concerned with past trends in the industry as a whole, and the effects on the company and its competitors, than in establishing any sort of strategy. Moreover, the company does not seem to have any proper market research. Certainly the senior managers do not perceive the market very accurately.

To add to these problems the working relationships in the company leave a lot to be desired. The managing director seems inclined to follow his intuition rather than depend on systematic planning in solving his problems. He is paying more attention to the advice of his financial manager rather than his marketing manager in forming his marketing strategy. This is quite wrong. He is also wrong in blaming the cause of the drop in sales entirely on the market recession and inflation. The company badly needs to establish for itself a marketing policy and strategy based on detailed market research.

Rejecting the short term solution

The question remains however: whether the company should increase or decrease its prices as a way out of this unhappy situation. To make a quick decision will resolve the problem only on a short term if at all.

My advice, therefore, is that there should be no price change, either up or down; any change would create further unrest in the company and in the market. It would only serve as a short-term solution.

The company might consider raising the product price at the end of the year. But this should only be done if the price of other products of equal quality has been raised and only in order to keep in line with them.

The company should continue to push its sales in the regions where the products are not selling well. It should increase its sales distribution force and put its most qualified and able sales personnel in these areas to boost declining sales.

I also suggest that the company continue to advertise on television, radio and in women's magazines and perhaps even increase its advertising budget to increase awareness.

Find out why market has shrunk

It is essential that the company immediately initiate a market analysis of the cosmetics business as a whole and of bath essences in particular, on which to base its medium and long term plans. It is no good planning for the short term alone. The company has got to establish its ultimate goal.

Among other things the company should investigate carefully the reasons for the drop in the market, analyse the competition, and estimate the potential market loss. It could perhaps also analyse its own image in the market and consumer reaction to the company's product.

It may be necessary to enlist outside advisers or specialist consultants to do this properly.

In establishing its marketing concept or strategy the company will have to decide for itself several important questions.

Does it wish to operate in the market with bath essence as its only product? Or should it market other products, with higher distribution, advertising and other costs, to put things on a broader basis? It may wish to market its own products exclusively but at a higher price to a very select market. Alternatively the company could market quite separately a cheaper product under a different name that could be sold in department stores, chain stores and even grocery stores. In this way the company could preserve the high image of its existing products.

The company might also consider marketing an assortment of products from other companies. It is possible to get these in advance without requiring a large cash investment.

The company should also consider its distribution arrangements. Does it wish to maintain its own distribution centre? It could employ outside distributors already marketing other products. This would save on distribution costs. It could take in a partner to share distribution costs, perhaps cutting such costs by up to 50%.

Many of these choices would mean a drastic change in the type and organization of the company. But it is better to take action than to remain at the mercy of an erratic market.

This decision was provided by H.W. Jaeger in his capacity as managing director of Jaeger & Partner BDU, German management consultants, based in Frankfurt-am-Main.

DILEMMA

Should home market be put at risk to gain in exports?

Anatol Seebohm, chairman of J.V. Mandela SA, had that sinking feeling as he put the telephone down. From the tone of Martin Garfeld's voice when he asked for an immediate interview, it was clear that the volatile marketing director was on the rampage again. Seebohm wondered whether he and the other board members would tolerate Garfeld's outbursts if he were not so undeniably brilliant at his job. Over the past six years, the 39-year-old marketing director had pushed exports up from only 15% of the company's production to nearly 40%. Twice in that period the company had won the national exporter of the year award as a result of his efforts.

Garfeld came right to the point. "It is this memo from the production department," he explained. "It says the production capacity for Q-design electric irons will be 20% below the capacity forecasted. What the hell is production up to?"

Q-design was a special economy design intended for the developing countries. Lacking the streamlining of the European and North American designs, it was more robust, with less gadgetry to be damaged by ill-use. The company had not the resources to invest in large repair and maintenance facilities in thinly spread markets.

Shortfall had been accurately predicted

With Q-design, which had been largely Garfeld's idea, Mandela could make do with an arrangement of one good agent in a region of up to four or five developing countries. The idea had worked so well that Q-design now accounted for nearly half of all export sales to 23 countries in Asia, Africa and South America.

Seebohm explained that he had asked Peter Strich, the production director, to send the memorandum to all directors so that the matter could be discussed at the board meeting in a couple of days' time. Strich had done well in predicting the shortfall so far ahead of time. He had personally visited the company that was building one of the major units in the new assembly line only to find out that they would be six months late in delivery and installation. Had Strich not taken the trouble to check up, Mandela probably would not have known of the delay until shortly before the contracted delivery date, some three months away.

"As it is," said Seebohm, "we have time to prepare ourselves. Strich is seeing if he can farm out some of the production to sub-contractors, although he does not hold out much hope. In the main he is worried about quality control. We would do ourselves immeasurable harm if we put out inferior irons. What you will have to do is get together with the distribution department to work out how we are to spread the cuts."

Only slightly mollified, Garfeld agreed to look into the effects of the production shortfall before he grumbled about it any more.

At the board meeting, Garfeld was well prepared with a stack of computer print-outs and sales charts. He was openly scornful when Strich declared that he had been unable to find a suitable sub-contractor.

"I don't think you realize the mess that this leaves my department in," ranted Garfeld. "By restricting supplies to all of our established markets I can cope with about half of the shortfall. But that still leaves me with nothing for our new markets in Africa. It has taken me 18 months to establish a network in Chad and now we may lose it."

"Who cares about Chad?" retorted Strich. "It cannot possibly account for more than five per cent of Q-design sales."

Realizing the importance of Chad

"No, but it is right next door to Nigeria, one of the biggest markets in Africa," said Garfeld. "Once we get established in Chad, we can export to Nigeria, which has always been a closed market to us. If we abandon our agent in Chad now, sales will be picked up by one of our competitors and we can say farewell to the Nigerian market for ever. Why can't you just switch over one of the home production lines to Q-design?"

Strich explained that this would be expensive, both in re-training and re-tooling, and would put the line in question out of production for three weeks. The company faced fierce competition at home and in North America, so profit margins were pared down as far as was safe. To take one line out of production for so long would eat up most of the profits from the home design.

"That just proves my point," said Garfeld. "It is exports that provide most of our profits. The Chad market is more important than the home market."

Seebohm found himself torn between the two points of view. There were risks in cutting back home production, because the competition might fill in any market gaps the company left. On the other hand, Garfeld's solution was certainly tempting.

DECISION

Six months' production would eliminate sales loss

Mandela's basic problem is a lack of long-term marketing strategy and planning which is brought to light by a relatively minor issue. What is really important is to put things into proper perspective and not be distracted by the tip of the iceberg alone, when far greater dangers loom below the surface.

What is really at stake? According to Garfeld, his marketing "strategy" is about to be ruined by a production shortfall of 20% over six months of the Q-design. Since this model represents 50% of exports, that is, 20% of company sales, the real loss in company sales on an annual basis would be 10% of 20%, which amounts to 2%.

This drop can be compensated for in the six months following resumption of planned production. In addition, the distribution set-up should make it easier to spread the cuts in supply relatively evenly. The situation can be personally explained to the five or six agents who represent the 23 countries. They can then advise how best to share the shortfall within their respective areas. In this way loss of goodwill can be minimized. The Chad market should be supplied and plans made for penetrating the Nigerian market as soon as production is back to normal.

Don't forget the home market
Garfeld is right in fighting for the Nigerian market. But surely he is acting more like an export manager than a marketing director. It would seem that he is giving too little attention to the domestic market, which, after all, provides 60% of company sales. If the choice now has to be made between the home and the export markets, should this choice not have been included in an overall marketing strategy which Mandela seems to be badly lacking? No reference is made to a strategy plan or even objectives.

On the production side, hopes of finding a suitable subcontractor should not be given up so easily by the production director. Strich is understandably sensitive about quality control and reluctant to farm out production. But surely, Mandela is not the only manufacturer capable of producing the unsophisticated Q-design? After all there are several competitors in the whole market. Seebohm should convince his production director of the vital importance of urgently finding suitable manufacturers to overcome the immediate supply problem and to develop a network of subcontractors for the future.

Profitability is the key point
The actual cost of switching one of the home production lines to Q-design, plus the delay incurred and loss of sales on the domestic market, should be looked into and weighed against the loss of 2% of total company sales due to the shortfall.

The profitability of the domestic market is a key point in this issue. Why is it so low and should production not be subcontracted or reduced in favour of export models? These are basic questions to be worked out and for which a clear and consistent strategy must be developed and implemented. If home production is to be sub-contracted, reduced or phased out, this should not be done on the spur of the moment and under pressure of day-to-day problems. It should, on the contrary, result from a carefully thought-out plan and be implemented according to an agreed schedule. Redeployment of production and marketing efforts cannot be improvised.

But perhaps Strich was not adequately informed of the marketing director's plans and Garfeld not sufficiently aware of the production director's difficulties. This raises the problem of communication between executives which seems to be another of Mandela's key problems.

It is clear that one of Seebohm's major tasks will be to improve relationships at the board level. There are indications that the hatchet has only been half buried by the production and marketing directors. The former possibly suffers from over-cautiousness, while the latter's behaviour and sweeping statements are far from meeting with general approval.

Reduce surprises by circulating information
Again, if an over-all marketing strategy had been developed and approved by all concerned, the risk of personal friction would be considerably decreased. It is the managing director's responsibility to see that a regular flow of information circulates between departments and that unpleasant surprises are reduced to a minimum.

Looking back, it seems that Seebohm himself could have avoided a confrontation. He could have asked the production director to expose the supply problem at the board meeting rather than circulate a memo beforehand abruptly announcing a 20% shortfall.

More planning and better communication should see Mandela out of its dilemma.

This decision was provided by Bruno Simma in his capacity as managing director of Industrial Consulting and Management Engineering Co. (ICME), a Swiss management consultancy, based in Zurich.

Should key salesmen move to boost firm's sales?

The second day of Vespucci SpA's annual sales conference in Milan threatened to end in uproar. The business equipment manufacturer's 28 salesmen had received sales manager Guido Tulli's proposals to reassign them to new territories with a great deal of angry condemnation.

Explaining the reasons behind the drastic measures, Tulli had reminded the salesmen that the company was suffering from declining sales and had a serious cash flow problem. This was mainly due to slow payments by customers. Accounts receivable were increasing at an alarming rate, he had told them.

Under Tulli's plan, the company's top salesmen were to be switched from the areas with high sales to areas that currently yielded low sales. He had explained that this would mean the more experienced salesmen could concentrate on building up sales in the less productive regions. The less experienced salesmen could easily handle the well-developed territories.

Some of the firm's leading salesmen immediately started to object. "I have spent years building up my territory," one of them protested. "I do not see why I should have to hand that over to a novice, and then have to start all over again in a new region."

Tulli pointed out that he felt that the firm's best salesmen were being wasted in these well-developed sales regions. "You are simply going to well-established customers and taking orders," he argued.

Are the salesmen becoming stale?

An experienced salesmen contested this view, observing he had greatly increased sales in his territory the previous year by persuading existing customers to expand their amount of orders in business stationery.

This supported his view, retorted Tulli, that the salesmen in the well-established territories were becoming stale, and were failing to uncover new customers. "This is only natural," he added. "When I was promoted sales manager, I was amazed how successful my successor was in getting new orders in my old territory. The company badly needs your experience to develop the weaker regions."

Another experienced salesman asked if the new plan would mean salesmen would get an extra bonus or higher commission rates for establishing new accounts. Tulli began to explain why he thought this was impractical, when he was interrupted by one of the younger salesmen who had been sitting at the back of the room quietly fuming. He told Tulli that he felt completely demotivated by the proposal to remove them from the undeveloped terrritories.

Tulli tried to reassure the young salesmen that the company did not regard them as failures. The changes were being made simply because the company was having difficulties, and needed to boost sales quickly, he pointed out.

Tulli swallowed hard before announcing another new policy he knew was likely to upset the gathered salesmen. "The management board has also decided that in future sales commissions will be paid quarterly and only on those orders for which payments have been received from customers," he announced nervously. "As from today it will be your responsibility to raise the subject of slow payments with customers. Moreover, no new orders will be acepted from customers until all overdue payments are received."

This was too much for the salesmen to take and the meeting erupted into a noisy uproar. "Why shouldn't we be paid for orders we have succeeded in getting?" demanded one salesman furiously. "It is not our job to collect debts," protested another.

Proposals meet a hostile reception

"This contravenes our employment contract," shouted yet another.

The salesmen were all talking agitatedly at once when Tulli decided to close the proceedings for that day. He rushed to a nearby hotel where group managing director Leon Cavallo was staying overnight. He was due to address the conference the following morning.

"Our proposals have met with even more hostility than we expected," Tulli told Cavallo, relating how the meeting had broken up in disorder. "I'm afraid you will have a hard time of it tomorrow convincing them that the proposals are in everybody's interest. But I don't think we can dodge the issue now. We have to tackle it while we have them all together."

Cavallo nodded gravely. His first inclination was to proceed with the proposals whether or not the salesmen approved. On the other hand, he reflected, salesmen are the key to a company's success. It might be unwise to impose a new system on them without their consent.

DECISION

Set sales quotas with special incentives

Like some aeroplane crashes, most business failures are a result of "pilot error."

Riding out a turbulent period, Vespucci SpA is in serious trouble. Cavallo, in the cockpit, is having second thoughts about a board directive to boost cash flow by tightening credit.

As if these orders from the control tower are not bad enough, he has just learned that Tulli, at the back of the aeroplane, is trying to stabilize the situation by instructing the cabin crew to get up and switch places.

Lack of critical judgment in letting others do his thinking and planning for him is Cavallo's error. He faces a well-deserved sleepless night. While he is awake, he might reflect that at least Tulli had the good sense to thrust this problem on him with still some time left. He has a few more hours before he addresses the convention.

A well-defined problem is already half-solved. Thus, the way to a decision is to distinguish the causes from the symptoms of Vespucci's malaise.

Evidently, a severe cash shortage is uppermost in management's mind, to the exclusion of almost everything else. So far, this is good. It is certainly responsible to worry about keeping enough working capital around to meet current obligations. Should this mean refusing to sell to slow-paying customers? Shutting off credit can reduce accounts receivable, but it will not ncessarily bring in more cash – not to Vespucci anyway. This is like reducing traffic congestion by refusing passage rights.

An alarmingly high level of accounts receivable is one cause of the cash flow deficiency. But both these problems are, in fact, symptoms of a more fundamental weakness: declining sales. If, as Tulli believes, the marketing effort is flagging, any action to tinker with the sales plan by holding back commissions and shifting successful salesmen from producing territories is not going to work. Unilateral action to revise territories is dangerous in good times or bad, particularly where management is clearly not closely informed about individual performance data and market statistics.

One possibility might be to let the territories stand, but add manpower, giving the senior man a continuing role. The drawback here is that unless the senior man has a stake in what the junior man does, an equitable division of the territory is almost impossible. Headquarters' control over sales activities is lessened as well.

The solution, I believe is to establish a sales quota system.

By assigning quotas, Vespucci could measure individual performance and motivate salesmen towards a predetermined level of achievement. Annual quotas based on expected sales also help in planning production, inventory and working capital needs. Territory changes are more palatable under a quota system because quotas can be easily adjusted to reflect the area's potential.

Companies sometimes set lower quotas for less able salesmen, but this can be demoralizing – as Tulli discovered.

A better method is to set quotas on an objective market base, and to offer special incentives, such as a new account bonus or higher commission rates for sales over 100% of quota.

Vespucci's insistence on a straight commission plan is outmoded. This works for agency and contract-type sales, but modern industrial firms have discarded it in favour of a combination of salary and commissions. Salesmen drawing even nominal salaries tend to think as company men and they have less reason to resist sales plan changes that are justified in terms of company goals. Loyalty is strengthened, and with it acceptance of the obligation to service and follow up accounts – not just take orders.

Cavallo and Tulli must devise a proper quota-based plan incorporating fixed and incentive compensation components. To do so, Cavallo must define two important factors: geographical market potential and criteria for what constitutes a good selling job. The latter should include, for example, new accounts versus repeat business, preferred product mix and target customers, retailers and end-users. Moreover, business equipment companies must always ask themselves whether they sell hardware or systems, and then reward their best producers accordingly.

Cavallo's immediate job is to get the salesforce moving with fresh vigour. He has waited long enough. Now he has to write a rousing speech for the morning meeting.

This decision was provided by Dudley C. Smith Jr. in his capacity as president of Archer, Smith & Associates, management consultants based in Brussels, Belgium.

Can U.K. subsidiary help to remove serious sales discrepancy?

For some months retail and consumer audits had indicated a lower market share for Pandora Specialty Products in the U.K. than Charles Smith, the marketing director in Britain, was willing to contemplate or believe.

Pandora's ex-factory sales were some 20% over the retail sales figures indicated by research. Meanwhile the international company's young U.S. subsidiary, Pandora Inc., which had some 12 months earlier opened a plant in upper New York State, was having a rough time. Sales had declined sharply a month ago and showed no sign of recovery.

Jack Haldane, managing director of the U.K. company and a director of the international board, did not connect the two circumstances. The U.K. was doing well, so clearly the market research initiated by Smith was wrong.

Smith was concerned by the U.K. situation, although he would not admit it to Haldane. There had to be a reason for the difference between factory output in the U.K. and what was sold after passing through the independent wholesalers.

Smith's suspicions are confirmed

Smith now ran parallel samples and conducted further research in the U.K. All the figures tended to bear out the audit data.

A close examination of individual accounts revealed that much of the discrepancy could be traced to several large and medium-sized wholesalers. Visits to these companies revealed nothing untoward, however; their levels of stock had not appreciably increased.

A month or two later, Haldane received a confidential memo from the president of the U.S. company. It stated that, quite by accident, some U.K.-manufactured Pandora products had been found in a U.S. wholesaler. The man had been reticent about their source.

Haldane immediately called Smith in to his office. Without comment he passed across the memo.

Smith grimaced. "I had my suspicions," he said, handing the memo back. "After all, the sales volume unaccounted for in the U.K. almost exactly matches the sales lost in the U.S."

"So what has been going on?" Haldane demanded.

"I have examined the price structure in the U.S. in detail," Smith replied, "and I have found that even allowing for freight and duty it would be possible for an efficient single distributor to undercut our U.S. company's distributors by some 15% or even 20%."

Haldane frowned. "So the evidence points strongly to heavy unofficial exports to the U.S.," he said.

Smith nodded.

"Which no doubt has been made possible," Haldane continued, "by the fact that the U.S. company's pricing strategy placed their leading brand at the top end of the market."

"As you will recall," Smith said drily, "I voiced my objections to that policy at the time. I thought the product was over-priced. But in the end the accountants and the agency convinced me that, with the heavy cost of distribution and advertising, it was the only hope they believed for a quick return on the plant."

"Well, it seems to have backfired," Haldane observed.

He got up from behind his desk and started pacing his office. "As managing director of the U.K. company I'm more than happy to see our plant here running to capacity," he said. "But as a member of the international board I'm also acutely aware of the growing problems of Pandora Inc. So what do we do? Any ideas?"

"Well, one thing is certain," Smith replied. "I don't see how we can stop our independent wholesalers exporting to the U.S. if they want to. And you can't really blame any wholesaler taking advantage of the exchange rates."

"That may be true but it is not much help to our U.S. company," Haldane said.

Smith felt like saying: "It's all very well saying that, but you ought to have sorted out the whole pricing strategy, at international board level, long ago."

Instead, he gave Haldane another unpalatable truth. "If the U.S. company alters its pricing strategy now," he said, "it's going to make nonsense of a very expensive advertising and promotion campaign. But if they don't do anything, can we tighten things up at this end?"

DECISION

U.K. company should switch to a more aggressive marketing strategy

What Haldane must do is go through the process which should have been explored before the U.S. venture was started. By studying the competitive brands on the U.S. market he could get an idea of the kinds of volumes that he might be able to sell at different price levels. He would also be made aware of the extra quality, value or luxury that he would need to build into the product itself, if he wanted to charge a high premium price for it.

He could construct several price structures and their corresponding profit and losses. He would soon see that the company had only three choices:

● Pull out altogether and close down the U.S. operation, leaving the U.K. company to earn its normal profit margin on the goods which British wholesalers would then sell over to the U.S.

● Change the U.S. company's strategy to a low-risk, low volume, high-margin business based on exports from Britain.

● Choose an aggressive marketing plan which, if it succeeded, would produce a much larger business with a bigger profit measured in absolute money – even though the profit as a percentage of sales would be smaller than in either of the other two cases.

Assuming that Pandora is a company with good resources, I think it is the last of these possibilities that Haldane should choose.

24

The trouble with taking the first course, and pulling out of the U.S., would be that the people smuggling British-made products into that country would soon cease their activities, since they need the consumer demand created by the U.S. company's activities in selling, promoting and advertising. Moreover, their attraction to U.S. buyers is their discount, which ceases to have meaning when no business is being done at the "full price".

So although this withdrawal plan would eliminate the headaches, it would soon eliminate the U.S. business as well.

If he adopted the second possibility, the U.S. factory would be closed, thus eliminating its overhead expenses and its inefficient, low-volume, high-unit-cost production. The retail price would be raised further, the product made correspondingly smarter and the advertising strategy altered to one based on "exclusive, imported, rare" appeals. The smugglers would then not be able to compete because the special de luxe product would not be available to them at all.

Using an aggressive marketing strategy

However, if the company has the stomach for a fight, and the cash and manpower to back it up, Haldane could switch to a much more aggressive marketing strategy. This would involve more risk, more advertising investment and a delay until profits were made.

Volume would need to be trebled, or more, and to achieve this the price would have to be lowered and the advertising budget increased. Happily, this is a synergistic possibility, because the more competitive price would put the brand into a bigger segment of the market. The increased advertising would help to procure a bigger share of the bigger segment. The extra volume would enable unit manufacturing costs to be reduced and percentage overheads would fall. Thus, in turn, funds would be provided to finance the extra advertising. Meanwhile, the price reduction would have squeezed out the smugglers.

Standing by a bold plan

But the plan would have to be bold. Losses would be made initially, until the volume was built up to beyond the threshold levels.

Of course, the international board should have taken a longer-term view in the first place. Then the subsequent problem would not have arisen. Just because their costs of administration and advertising were high in the U.S., that was no reason to suppose that U.S. consumers would pay an unusually high price for a product which sold at a moderate price in Britain.

Competition in the U.S. is fiercer than in Britain and a wider range of brand choice is open to the American consumer. If the standard product was offered at a premium price it would be unlikely to sell in the kind of volume that would be essential to permit low unit costs of production and low percentage overheads. Even without the smugglers, the U.S. company would have been in trouble.

This decision was provided by Eric Morgan in his capacity as managing director of British American Cosmetics Ltd.

How to prevent a brand manager endangering the product?

The memo which landed on the desk of Karl Hottinger, marketing director of Heinz Bockler, a Swiss manufacturer of high-class confectionery, was brief and explicit. "As from the first of November," it read, "the transparent gold filigree outer wrapping of our Desirée chocolates will be discontinued." The memo was signed "Hans."

Hottinger frowned. Used as he had become to the high-handed manner of brand managers, he found the arrogance of Hans Staub, favourite nephew of the firm's founder, increasingly difficult.

He called Staub on the phone. "This is a major step, Hans," he said. "On what grounds have you decided to dispense with the traditional gold wrapping?"

"On cost grounds, of course," Staub replied. "The product can afford to stand on its own feet."

"That is a debatable statement," Hottinger objected. "You have been making a lot of savings lately. I think you are in danger of downgrading this product to a point where the cachet of Swiss-made chocolates will be lost."

"I am in charge of this brand," Staub replied. "I built it up into its present position. Don't forget that." Then he rang off.

As Hottinger stared at the phone he reflected on how things had changed since the founder had ceased to be chairman and chief executive. Bockler had made all the big decisions himself, but only after personal investigation and always with Hottinger by his side. For example, the decision to enter the U.K. market many years ago had been taken only after Bockler had visited the country several times and had observed confectionery buying habits in many large U.K. cities.

In 1972, Bockler had retired. He still visited the company headquarters in Zurich from time to time, but he was a sick man. He had been succeeded by Konrad Koch, a banker who was not a member of the family and who, lacking experience in confectionery and consumer-goods marketing, had introduced brand managers to handle Bockler's three main confectionery lines.

Hottinger had argued in vain that since the brands were well-established and complementary, central strategic marketing control was all that was needed. Brand managers would tend to be divisive, he said, and could lead to "overkill" in well-defined markets.

"Nonsense, Karl," Koch had replied. "Even I, a mere banker, can see that the modern trend is to have brand managers. You will have to concern yourself less with tactical matters and more with grand strategy."

Bockler's nephew Staub was a business administration graduate from a U.S. university. He had been brought back from the U.S., where he had been a brand manager for a leading company in the toiletries field. He was put in charge of Desirée, a middle-range brand of chocolate. He had built it up into market leader in its price category in the home market, as well as achieving very respectable sales overseas.

By the end of 1976, however, Desirée sales had reached a plateau. Then, in 1977 and throughout 1978, Hottinger had watched with growing concern as Staub began cutting corners on the product always with the excuse of "trimming off the fat."

First he had had some of the chocolates in the assortment that were individually wrapped stripped of their silver paper. Then he began experimenting with different styles of packaging, finally introducing one that was considerably cheaper to produce but less substantial and inviting.

He also began to pressurize the technical people to reduce the cost of the fillings in some of the chocolates. The company's U.K. advertising agency became irritated by constant criticism of a proposed campaign to reinforce Desirée's image against encroaching rivals. The campaign was abandoned at the last minute.

Although it was not evident from Staub's sales figures or from his optimistic forecasts, Hottinger heard rumblings from several sources that the brand was beginning to lose ground.

When the U.K. agency resigned the account, Staub merely shrugged it off. But the account executive told Hottinger that Desirée was no longer a product that did the agency's image any good when seeking other clients.

Unable to get anywhere with Staub and feeling totally impotent, Hottinger commissioned a consumer survey of the brand without telling Staub. However, the brand manager soon got to hear of it and complained bitterly to Koch, who ruled that the survey could go ahead only if it was placed in the brand manager's hands.

Hottinger said he had no faith that Staub would push the survey through or would accept its findings. He pointed out that Desirée now accounted for nearly half of the firm's turnover. Any slide in the product could do the company irreparable harm.

Koch listened politely but distantly. "Where is this catastrophic sales slide?" he asked. "I can see no sign of it. And I don't share your distrust of Staub. I think you have your knife into him."

Suddenly Hottinger saw the game that Staub was playing. He understood why Staub was risking the brand by cutting costs to such an extent. He wanted to prove to his uncle, now becoming increasingly senile, that he was a financial as well as a marketing expert. He wanted to stake his claim to the chief executive's chair before the old man died.

But what could Hottinger do? If he pressed his fears about the brand, his motives would be even more suspect than they already were. If, however, he let the brand collapse, possibly the company too would be submerged.

DECISION

Ambitious brand manager threatens both product and company

The Desirée dilemma at Heinz Bockler is the manifestation of greater corporate problems. These have now been brought into the open. There is the problem of marketing management and control. There is also a problem of personalities, of lack of adequate management in general and, ultimately, of who will succeed to the top job in the company. It is not clear, from the dilemma, whether Hottinger himself has ambitions in that direction.

What Hottinger should do is clear, however. He must do his job. He must present Konrad Koch with such an impressive amount of relevant, rational evidence that he cannot avoid giving proper consideration to the matter, so that Koch fully understands, with a view to taking appropriate action. These arguments should be supported by expert opinion from others, such as Hottinger's technical colleagues and the advertising agency.

Hottinger should not be deterred from doing this by his previous failure to make Koch see his point of view. Indeed, he has to assert himself, since the lack of respect shown to him by Hans Staub is so blatant. For Hottinger to take no action would amount to surrender to Staub.

Hottinger, it must be said, demonstrates that he falls short of the ability to manage the company's affairs as a chief executive. He probably half realizes this. There appears to be no good reason why he would be any better than Koch. Indeed, by their actions, and still more by their inactivity, Koch and Hottinger appear weak and inefficient.

But Hottinger at least recognizes the shortcomings of Staub's brand management performance. It should not matter greatly to him that his motives are questioned by Koch. He should leave Koch in no doubt that the company must come first and that who takes over comes second.

If the worst comes to the worst, he must be prepared to present Koch with an ultimatum that either Staub goes or he goes. But it need not necessarily come to that.

Hottinger should analyse the respective attitudes of those involved.

Koch seems to want an easy and undemanding life until his retirement. Staub is rash and ambitious and appears to dominate his colleagues. Hottinger wants to do his duty by the company but has been ineffective.

Remedy the lack of trust

But are things precisely as they seem? If Hottinger looks at things objectively he may wonder whether Koch can really be so blind. After all, he has been a successful banker. Despite the gaps in his marketing knowledge, presumably he has been discharging the major duties of a chief executive to the satisfaction of the founder.

Maybe he is hedging. Maybe he knows more than he is willing to admit about Desirée's market position and the reasons for it. He may even be giving Staub enough rope to hang himself.

There seems to be a lack of trust and confidence between Hottinger and Koch which the former must remedy. Koch has not indicated when he will retire or who will succeed him. Nothing is finally decided. So Hottinger must assume that Koch is open to persuasion.

So far as Staub is concerned, Hottinger should recognize that maybe the brand manager's position is not as strong as it seems at first sight. There are three points against him.

Product stripping cannot be covered up indefinitely.

The company's U.K. advertising agency has already resigned.

Events may catch up with Staub at any time. That gentleman is much more vulnerable than he appears to think.

In common with bad brand management practices everywhere, Staub's decisions and actions are superficial, short-term and too oriented to impressing those around him.

The diligent brand manager's nightmare is the flattening sales and profits curve which goes into a plateau and then into a decline. The anticipation and prevention of a sales decline is achieved by effort, judgment, experience and research.

Brand managers operate most effectively if they have the ability to know when, how and why to apply the specialist skills available both inside and outside a company. Staub appears to be either mishandling specialists, such as the advertising agency, or ignoring them. These people are valuable allies for Hottinger.

It is true that "trimming off the fat" is part of brand marketing responsibility. But to recognize what is fat, and to know the difference between cost savings and product enhancement, is a lesson that Staub has still to learn.

While cultivating Koch, Hottinger must launch a two-pronged attack on Staub. First, he must make an effort to be friends, to secure his co-operation in positive steps which Hottinger will suggest. And even Staub, who after all is not stupid, may be brought to appreciate that power, deviousnes and enthusiasm are poor substitutes for ability, knowledge and wisdom.

Hottinger should tell him frankly that he appreciates that Staub is going for immediate returns. But he should point out the need for a potential chief executive to take a longer-term view.

Hottinger, however, must also do his duty by the company. He should pursue his own research, regardless of Koch's injunction not to. Then he can present Koch, or the full board, with an assessment of the situation that he, or they, will have to listen to.

This decision was provided by Philip Turner in his capacity as managing director of Eurographic Ltd., a U.K. consultancy that specializes in design, packaging and marketing.

DILEMMA

Must sales force be cut to meet marketing budget?

John Hepple was marketing director with Beano Products Ltd., which made packaged snacks aimed mainly at children and the youth market and sold through supermarket outlets. The company had prospered and had been taken over by a bigger company, Hygiena Foods Ltd., which was not in the snacks market but had been looking for the best means of entry for some time.

Hepple, who was 52, had wondered about his future with Beano. However, it was his boss, with whom he had worked for many years, who unexpectedly had been retired. In his place, Hygiena had appointed as managing director one of their young, brash and ambitious executives, Ross Vernon.

Vernon made it plain from the start that Hepple had been retained not entirely with his approval. "I'm in favour of a young team and you are the oldest executive we have," Vernon had said. "However, I must admit you have a good track record. And it's results that really count."

Hepple's first battle with Vernon had come when the latter had suggested that it might not be necessary for Beano to have a sales force at all. "You have 60 salesmen regularly visiting outlets in this country," he said. "That's a hell of a lot, especially since the cost of employing a single salesman now runs at around $40,000 a year."

Vernon had suggested that Hygiena's own salesmen, who visited the same supermarkets, could take over the selling and display of Beano's packaged snacks. Hepple had disagreed. Hygiena's salesmen, he pointed out, had little, if any, experience of pushing lines that were aimed at the young, had to be attractively displayed and essentially were impulse buys.

"I accept that one of the advantages of the takeover could well be some rationalization of the two sales forces," he had told Vernon. "But it needs to be carefully planned, with adequate training. And all the sacrifices cannot come from our people."

Growing sense of insecurity

Vernon had appeared to accept the point. At any rate, he had let the matter drop. But through the indefinable communications channels that exist in all companies, news of the supposedly secret board level discussion soon got out. Harold Ryan, the sales manager, told Hepple of a growing sense of insecurity in the sales force which, if allowed to continue, could adversely affect results.

Hepple had reassured Ryan. Although he and Vernon did not see eye to eye on quite a few matters, he confided, the record of Beano's salesmen was one the new managing director could not dispute. Ryan could go back and tell his salesmen that, provided they continued to perform as effectively as in the past, they had nothing to worry about.

Soon after making this rather rash statement, Hepple was told by Vernon that his total marketing budget for the following year could not be increased by one cent. Since inflation was high and the salesmen expected comparable salary increases, the news amounted to a substantial budget cut. "I am under pressure from corporate headquarters to improve the bottom line straight away," Vernon said. "We have to demonstrate to shareholders that there is synergy in our take-over of Beano."

Vernon added pointedly: "We all know your dedication to keep your sales force intact, Jack. Indeed, I hear you have almost promised them indefinite security of tenure. So your savings will have to come from other areas, presumably. The best of luck."

No hope of a budget increase

Hepple was not so much dismayed as inwardly seething. He was angry with himself for having shown his hand to Vernon so early in the game. If Vernon was gunning for him, he had been handed useful ammunition.

Hepple sat down to look at his budget of $5 million, which was not going to be increased although he had been hoping for at least $6 million during the next financial year. The sales force accounted for $2.4 million of the $5 million. That left $2.6 million for everything else on the marketing side of the business.

In the current year, Beano had spent $1.6 million of this on advertising. One million dollars had been spent on television, $500,000 on press and $100,000 on trade advertising. Hepple's plans had projected a considerable increase in the advertising budget.

In addition, Beano had spent $500,000 promoting its Instant Sparkle vitamin snack through sports sponsorship.

The company had spent $300,000 on miscellaneous promotions and the remaining $200,000 in the budget represented administrative costs.

Hepple frowned. Any cutback in advertising and promotion would have to be considered very carefully indeed. So far as administrative costs were concerned, Hepple thought, even if savings could be made they would be of little real help compared with the cost of maintaining the salesmen in the field.

Was he, therefore, bound to make big savings in the sales force? If so, what kind of savings? And how could he find a solution that did not represent himself as a man who supported one policy one day and happily scuppered it the next?

DECISION

Budget standstill threatens future of sales force

The marketing director's dilemma at Beano Products Ltd. appears, at first sight, to be the direct result of the company's takeover by Hygiena Foods Ltd. However, it in fact mirrors a problem facing all fast-moving consumer goods companies at one time or another.

In the U.K. recently, for example, the concentration of grocery purchases in a few large supermarketing chains led to more than 5,000 grocery and provisions shops closing. Such a trend is forcing manufacturers to assess the viability of a large sales force.

Far from resisting demands upon his sales force, marketing director John Hepple should already have been reviewing his marketing and sales costs and searching for ways in which they could be pruned. Or, if that proved impossible, he should have looked at how he could produce a better return on an investment of $5 million, instead of offering a hostage to fortune – and his own future – by making rash promises about the future security of sales force jobs.

What should he do now? First, he should analyse the profitability of Beano's top 20 key accounts. These customers probably produce 70% to 80% of the company's sales, give rise to most of the costs and contribute too little profit compared with the problems they create, and the time invested in them by the sales force, He should then look hard at such principal costs factors as:

● Levels of back-up stock and by how much they can be reduced.

● Salesmen/servicing call frequencies. Can these be reduced? Major customers are often over-serviced.

● How discounts are allowed. A change in the mix of discount allowances could increase the size of each delivery and thus reduce the cost of distribution.

● Annual sales volume compared with forecast. Perhaps major customers could be set targeted sales against which Beano could negotiate prices, discounts and promotional support.

From the analysis, Hepple should be able to develop with his product managers key customer strategies which will produce a higher profit contribution, with costs that are identified, reduced and capable of being policed precisely and regularly.

Second, Hepple should analyse the tasks of the sales force and identify those which could either be eliminated or done more cheaply.

For example, he could look at how much time is taken up in sales administration, particularly in collecting and transmitting orders from customers. Without incurring any outlay, he could pilot test in three areas, giving the salesmen hand-held computer terminals from three different manufacturers. This would enable him to evaluate the effectiveness of transmitting orders via the telephone system to the company computer.

He could evaluate how many customer calls on both key major customers and others are made only to collect routine orders. If there are a large number of these, then he should pilot test telephone selling in one sales area for a six-month period.

Third, he should review the training given to the sales force. It is likely that most of Beano's key major customers no longer have to be persuaded that Beano makes mouth-watering snacks that are in great demand. So the sales force must be skilled in sales negotiation based upon a fluent, accurate knowledge of the financial deals to be struck and the concessions to be traded.

No new sales staff to be recruited

Fourth, Hepple should analyse sales force turnover for the last three years due to such factors as retirements, resignations and dismissals. It will probably exceed 10% a year. He should decide not to recruit any new staff to fill sales positions falling vacant during the next two years. The saving on his sales force budget will yield a minimum of $120,000 and a maximum of $240,000 per year.

With this money he can achieve a number of objectives that will have a pronounced and favourable impact on sales force productivity and future costs. It will pay for the cost of a six-month test and evaluation of telephone selling and a test of the impact on sales of subcontracting merchandising and sales promotion operations now carried out by the sales force.

If it is successful, he might be able to encourage some of his present sales force to become Beano's merchandising and sales promotion brokers on an annual contract. This will motivate those with a wish to do their own thing while at the same time removing from Hepple's sales force budget about $20,000 for each man who decides to join the broking company.

Hepple could also try a sales force incentive scheme linked to the achievement of minimum profit contribution targets being achieved from sales to Beano's top 20 customers.

Finally, he should tell the sales force the hard facts of life – the effect that market factors are having on the company and the changes and economies that must be introduced if the company is to have a profitable future. He will be surprised by the uplift in morale that will flow from such a blunt statement.

This decision was provided by John Lidstone in his capacity as deputy managing director of Marketing Improvements Ltd., a U.K. marketing consultancy which numbers among its clients many multinational companies.

Should perfume company decide to follow new scent?

T he facts, gathered from market and consumer attitude surveys and from the accountants, were clear, Camelot Inc.'s old-established perfume brand, *Pure Lace,* was still a brand leader. It had been so since before World War II. But, particularly at the younger end of the market, it had slipped.

Its longevity, its up-market image and its name had kept it at the top for a long time. But in the last six or seven years new brands, projecting brighter images, had nibbled into the market.

Just over a year ago, at great cost, the company had launched its new perfume brand, *Slinky.* It was aimed specifically at young, independent women.

The company's technical team was particularly proud of the scent – so light as to be barely noticed, yet definitely there. Its light blue, angular pack, research indicated, was the one most favoured by the women at whom it was aimed.

There had been difficulties, however, on the production side. Gary Stevens, who was production manager, had wanted from the outset to put in a brand new, fully-automated bottling line that would handle both *Pure Lace,* with its round bottle, and *Slinky's* triangular-shaped bottle. However, Paul Chambers, the managing director, had asked him to bring his technical ingenuity to bear to adapt the existing *Pure Lace* line to handle the new bottle, as this would be less costly than installing a new bottling line.

In this, Chambers was strongly supported by the financial director, Vincent Gregory, who had pointed out that the recession had hit the sales and profitability of a number of Camelot's products, and that large capital expenditure at this time could not be justified.

The new brand fails

The modification was made. But the long delays involved in shutting the line down for alterations and cleaning the machinery between runs of the two products proved quite costly.

Although the test marketing of *Slinky* had been successful, within a few months it became clear that the company had a loser on its hands. The sales graph which had seemed so promising, based on early sales, soon flattened out and then turned down. Seven months after the launch, the product was withdrawn.

In other circumstances, Chambers might have congratulated himself on his foresight in preventing big capital investment on a separate production line for *Slinky.* However, some of the marketing people were blaming the production difficulties for contributing to the failure by creating local shortages of *Slinky* in the stores at the time of the most intensive TV advertising.

Stevens now presented Chambers with a memorandum which said that the existing bottling line was nearing the end of its life due to the extra wear and tear resulting from the modifications. Unless it was replaced, production of the original best seller, *Pure Lace,* could not be guaranteed. He favoured putting in a fully automated line, numerically controlled so that production could alternate between batches of different bottle shapes at will, without a single bottle being touched by human hand.

The finance director was aghast at the expenditure involved, which he said would be at least 75% more than putting in a straightforward product line to handle *Pure Lace.* "Even if we put in a needlessly sophisticated line," he asked, "what else will it produce? We have just tried a new product launch and it has failed. Let's not rush into another failure."

Simon D'Arcy, brand manager for *Pure Lace,* who had masterminded the *Slinky* launch, argued that although they had not got the product and its pack quite right, there was still a need at that end of the market for a new scent. They had learned a lot from the *Slinky* launch. If flexible production facilities were provided he was certain he could now come up with a market winner.

Chambers, meanwhile, his faith in D'Arcy somewhat shaken by the *Slinky* failure, had commissioned another independent research firm to look at the fragrance market, and the position of *Pure Lace* in it, with a fresh eye. They were more pessimistic about the future of *Pure Lace* than other researchers had been. They forecast that what was now a gentle downhill slope could become a precipice, and that it was better to abandon *Pure Lace* altogether and develop a new product aimed at a wide market spectrum.

When Chambers produced this report at an executive meeting, Gregory, the finance director, was in favour because it fitted in with the idea of one new production line for one new product. D'Arcy was strongly against it, saying they would be throwing the baby out with the bath water if they abandoned *Pure Lace* totally, in its present form, when they had no proof that any alternative would work. As for Stevens the production man, he warned that a decision on a new line would have to be taken very soon, if production breakdowns were not to proliferate.

Chambers wondered what to do. After one recent product failure, another product could not be produced just like a rabbit from a hat, and anyway there was conflicting advice about which marketing direction to take. But the production decision could not wait.

DECISION

Fragrance market requires special approach

Paul Chambers would be reckless to abandon the best selling *Pure Lace* before having a proven new product with which to replace it. In fact he should get rid of the research company that made this recommendation. Chambers should bear in mind that the failure rate of new fragrances is notoriously high, and that a successful fragrance does not die overnight but over a period of years. There's still a lot of profit to be taken on a brand leader even if it is beginning to decline in sales.

Chamber's first concern must be to ensure the continued production availability of *Pure Lace*. This means taking a decision to replace the old bottling line. But he should reject Gary Steven's proposal to install a line which is capable of handling different bottle sizes. The extra flexibility that this would give is not worth the 70% extra cost compared with a straightforward line for *Pure Lace* alone.

Consider contract filling and outside help

Future new product development should try to take account of existing bottling line limitations. If this is not possible for marketing reasons, contract filling and packing may be the answer. Additional capital expenditure can only be justified once the new product is established.

Chambers is right to have doubts about the competence of Simon D'Arcy. A brand manager should know that his first priority must be to investigate all the options in an attempt to revitalize the image and market position of *Pure Lace*. These might include updating the product presentation, broadening the advertising platform to appeal more to younger women and looking at new promotional ideas to draw attention to the product in the stores. It may be necessary to increase advertising expenditure.

If none of these steps work, all marketing expenditure on *Pure Lace* should be terminated. Most likely the product will go on delivering profits for the next ten years or so.

The purchase and use of perfumes is highly personal. So any attitudinal findings from market research must be treated with extreme caution. I don't think consumer tastes change as frequently as they do in other product areas. This may explain why major brands like *Chanel No. 5, Christian Dior, Fidji, Joy, Madame Rochas* and *l'Aire du Temps* have been on the market for such a long time and continue to dominate the international fragrance scene. In my opinion, the only really successful new product launch in recent years has been *Opium* by Yves St. Laurent. However, there have been many resounding failures. One must remember that the ultimate success of a perfume is largely dictated by emotional factors beyond the marketer's control.

Test the market with several choices

I don't believe that the failure of *Slinky* can be blamed on production difficulties. In fact, an out-of-stock situation can often stimulate demand by creating the illusion that the product is moving off the shelves. I think it's wrong to launch a new perfume by mass marketing, which is what Camelot did with *Slinky*. I would prefer to put three new products on the market on a very limited basis in the hope that one of them will take off. If one of them is a success, your financial problems are solved. And that's the time to put money behind it.

With fragrances you just can't interpret in advance how consumers will respond.

This decision was provided by Neil Cochrane in his capacity as general manager of Burke Egan & Co., one of Ireland's leading distributors of cosmetics and perfumes.

What solution to the problems of matrix management?

It has been a long, exhausting day for Martin Simon, area marketing director, Europe, for the toiletries division of Diamond Laboratories. On the plane to Paris he balances a drink on his open briefcase and prepares to shift mental gears from the pleasant sales meeting with the Danes he has just left, to the somewhat more combative session with the French that he expects when he attends the executive committee the following day.

Last night, Jacques Chevalier, general manager of Diamond's French subsidiary, had called him at his hotel. "Martin, we've got a problem. I've just seen the third quarter figures. Sales for both the medical and dairy divisions are tracking pretty well on latest forecast. But your sales are 15% down. Now, if I'm going to make the profit plan for France I have to get another $100,000 from your operations. At this late date the only realistic solution is to eliminate the advertising for Neptune bath oil over the next three months."

Simon had protested that to lose consumer advertising pressure now with the peak Christmas season approaching could seriously prejudice the future of the brand. To which Chevalier had replied: "We can worry about that when we've made the budget."

Neptune was launched two years ago into a highly competitive market. According to the Nielsen store audit, consumer sales are growing, but at a slower rate than Simon had projected. The advertising agency in Paris has warned that they are already spending close to the lower limits of viable reach and frequency.

Consider the problems of a matrix organization

Simon knows that even if the toiletries division misses its target in France, he can easily compensate by taking the money from Germany where Neptune and other products are comfortably over plan. He has already agreed with Klaus Engelbert, general manager of Diamond GmbH, that the income generated by these extra sales would be shown as a profit in the German company's books at the end of the year. So this solves Simon's problem from the product division's profit point of view. But it is unlikely to convince Chevalier to support continued advertising for Neptune in France. Engelbert and Chevalier are rivals for promotion. Few general managers are prepared to sacrifice their profit plans to help an area marketing director.

Simon is familiar with this kind of conflict. Diamond has a matrix type of organization in which the area marketing directors share profit and loss responsibility for their respective divisions with the local general managers. At the same time they have line responsibility for the division across the entire area. The general managers, on the other hand, have responsibility for all three divisions but only within their territories.

The problem would not be so bad, Simon feels, if Chevalier and he had the same boss. But Chevalier reports to the vice-president, international, at corporate headquarters in Stockholm, while Simon reports to the group vice president in charge of his division. Local profit plans and any corrective action needed to accomplish them are discussed at the quarterly executive committees held in each country. These committees comprise the local general manager, his financial director and the three divisional area marketing directors. Stockholm is the ultimate court of appeal in the event of a deadlock. But Simon knows that his boss expects this possibility to be used sparingly.

Try persuasion rather than legislation

Christer Larssen, Diamond's president, describes the inherent conflict in the organization as "kinetic equilibrium". He believes that managers should not expect to have their accountability matched by authority. This means that they must get things done by persuading rather than legislating. "The business will benefit," he said at last year's shareholders' meeting, "by reconciling local corporate priorities in each market with those of the operating divisions at the area level. Shared responsibility is the best means of achieving this."

Simon gathers his thoughts for the next morning's meeting. What arguments can he use to persuade Chevalier to maintain Neptune advertising at the almost certain expense of his profit plan? Has he examined all the marketing alternatives? How far should he be prepared to compromise? And what form might a compromise take? Is the issue sufficiently crucial for him to take it to Stockholm for resolution? And if so, how should he handle this?

DECISION

Simon must seek a negotiated solution

For profit or for loss, for better or for worse, the shared responsibility marketing matrix is firmly entrenched at Diamond Laboratories and Martin Simon must live and function effectively within it.

The situation with which he is faced probably occurred several times within his organization and Simon himself should be no stranger to these marketing problems as well as the negotiated solutions.

In his meeting the following morning with Jacques Chevalier, Martin should have two key objectives in his mind. First, he must do everything possible to keep the new product growing in the highly competitive French market. Second, he must help Chevalier solve his own problem and thereby create a better working relationship between the French general manager and himself, not only for the immediate future, but more importantly for the long term.

The sales shortfall is occurring primarily because the forecast is probably too optimistic. The optimism, most likely, is based upon more positive results in Germany, Denmark and other areas. Simon should freely admit his inaccuracy in projection to Chevalier. Then, Simon must earnestly attempt to persuade Chevalier to keep the advertising budget intact. He should point out that if the advertising budget should be eliminated for the fourth quarter, assuming that Simon can get out of some probably firm French media commitments, consumer sales projections for the fourth quarter would suffer in the highly competitive marketplace. Most likely, however, the relatively small advertising budget is being used primarily for merchandising to the retail trade. If the promised advertising were withdrawn, Diamond Laboratories could tarnish its image with the trade.

If consumer buying declined, Chevalier could expect product returns occurring primarily in the first quarter. At best, Chevalier could probably expect reduced factory sales during the first quarter of the following year.

Even if Simon and Chevalier agreed on a crash trade-loading programme to save the fourth quarter advertising budget, the first quarter factory sales would still suffer. This could lead to a continuation of the advertising hiatus and a premature plateauing or decline of the brand.

Examine other areas for profits

Clearly, budget saving help must come from another quarter, and Simon must be prepared to offer at least part of it.

Simon should immediately examine with Chevalier all other areas of the Neptune budget and other toiletries of the division in France.

If Simon is unable to cover the entire $100,000 within his own French budgets, he should ask Chevalier to see if he can cover Neptune's shortfall with division money from the other divisions.

In order to gain more readily Chevalier's co-operation, Simon should offer to return the favour, if at all possible, in the future if and when the other divisions in France get into trouble.

Of course, in the extreme short term Simon personally is covered quite comfortably from a division financial standpoint.

He doesn't really need Chevalier's cooperation, and can put all the blame on Chevalier's intransigence for any French problem that may occur in the first quarter.

But if Simon plans to remain a successful marketing director and move up within his company, he should keep the continued development of Neptune as his number one goal.

If Chevalier, however, is in an uncompromising mood, and if Simon cannot find any sacrificial funds in his other French budgets he should refer the matter back to Stockholm. Simon should explore at the executive committee level the possibility of the other two area marketing directors for the dairy and medical divisions generating more profit to compensate for Neptune's shortfall.

If the executive committee apparatus is unable to help Simon keep his advertising budget for Neptune, then he can give in to Chevalier, knowing that he has done just about everything possible and practical within the framework of the shared responsibility matrix.

His last step then becomes communicating the entire sequence of events through proper channels to his boss, to corporate headquarters in Stockholm and, most importantly, to Christer Larssen, the president, to let him know subtly that his "kinetic equilibrium" is not functioning as he intended.

This decision was provided by Mitchell B. Streicker in his capacity as vice-president, marketing services, for the Health Care Products Division of Miles Laboratories Inc., Elkhart, Indiana, U.S.

How should a jeans manufacturer improve its service to retailers?

Roger Defoe sat looking around his comfortable modern office on the seventh floor of the Grantley Tower. The room was filled with mementos of two decades of success as the world's largest and most successful jeanswear producer. Always stressing quality in its advertising and promotion, Grantley had stormed ahead of its rivals and, indeed, had become the generic name in jeans.

In northern Europe, the area over which Defoe was president, sales growth had been astronomical in the 1960s and 1970s. It simply had not been possible to produce jeans fast enough. All the management were young, and the professionalism they brought to merchandising made them world leaders in brand management.

Certainly they had problems; but these were very much the problems of growth and success. For example, in the years following the oil crisis of 1973, there had to be a dramatic intervention to cut stock levels, reorganize, and streamline a business that had been growing like Topsy.

Basic problem

But today Defoe was concerned about something much more fundamental. It was a problem he had been dwelling on for some time, and given a lot of thought to each evening, as he ran home from the office, preparing for the London Marathon. He had reached the conclusion that the world had fundamentally changed, and that Grantley had to find a radically new way of responding.

Defoe's passion for running had given him the physical and mental strength to overcome stressful problems in his job before. Privately, he knew that running was his salvation. It was the only place the telephone couldn't reach him – the only place he could get enough peace to put his thoughts in order.

Today, he needed as much time as he could get to think things through to a conclusion.

Growth began to slow

In the early 1960s, supply had always been less than demand. One of the biggest constraints had been the availability of top quality denim. But this situation had now changed completely. For the first time, market growth had begun to slow down. Denim was in good supply, many producers having established themselves overseas, particularly in Hong Kong.

Even more of a problem was the fact that more than 200 small, innovative, flexible brands had developed in Britain.

At the three-mile mark, Roger Defoe felt the "runner's high" coming on. But jogging past a commercial block, he counted window displays of nine of those competing brands – all of them less than three years in the market. His high turned into a depression.

"Of course we couldn't keep this boom all to ourselves," he muttered under his breath. "I've seen it before in a dozen industries. Boom, overcrowding, bust – that's the cycle."

What Defoe could not forgive himself for was failing to see the "enemy" coming over the horizon, and not being ready for demand to level off.

In the past, Grantley had put its major efforts on to the end-consumer, both in terms of quality products and of image promotion. And, as the largest clothing manufacturer in the world, it had developed advanced technology in the area of mass manufacturing. Retailers had not always got the service they would ideally have liked; but this had never been a really big issue. They were just so happy to get Grantley products, which they could always sell profitably. So not getting the complete order on time could easily be forgiven.

But now the situation was very different. Cost pressures and tough competition in the retail industry meant that service was extremely important to Grantley's leading customers. They needed the right goods at precisely the right time, to minimise their own inventories and slot in with their own promotional programmes. Goods not delivered on time represented a lost sales and profit opportunity.

Equally, both Grantley's traditional competitors and the aggressive small brands were ever present, looking for opportunities to grab market share in, at best, a static market.

Price-cutting had become rampant, and although this might well be attractive to some of the smaller producers, Defoe firmly believed that Grantley must remain the brand and price leader.

In the last two years, the company had made considerable strides in getting away from its image as an inflexible giant. Defoe's dilemma was how to change the culture, which traditionally had been highly biased towards high volume, standardized mass production, and which was end-consumer oriented, towards one which recognized that retailers were now the key to continued market dominance.

In supplying these retailers, quality products were no longer enough. Defoe's organization had to give them, as he felt they rightly deserved, an excellent service to support their retail activities.

Defoe could think of many ways in which this could be developed. For example, much more support for in-store merchandising.

However, the core of the new service programme he was considering rested firmly on supplying complete orders, the right mix of products and sizes, at precisely the time requested. The problem was that this kind of service quality depended not on any individual function but on the way in which the whole organization worked together.

In short, Defoe felt that a service-oriented cultural revolution was called for. He needed to focus everyone's energies on getting the right products in the stores at the right time.

Aiming for 90 %

At present, the hit rate was only 70%, particularly with many of the smaller customers; and still Grantley was the market leader. With a new service orientation, this figure could perhaps be pushed to 90%, which would represent enormous gains from lost sales and truly confirm Grantley as the leader in its industry.

It was almost dark when Roger Defoe jogged down the last block in his course – nearly eight miles – to his home. He had plenty of strength left, but that mental "high" was eluding him. He was going to need a few more miles – perhaps a couple of complete marathons – to work out this difficult problem.

The question was, how should he go about creating a service orientation and what approach should he take so as to maximize the pay-off in the coming year?

This Dilemma, though fictionalized by International Management, is similar to a problem once faced by jeans manufacturer Levi Strauss, of San Francisco, and the reply draws upon the successful approach taken by its northern European division president, Robin Dow.

Six principles for making service strategies work

Defoe's dilemma is faced by many firms that find themselves in maturing markets characterized by low growth and fierce price competition. His strategy of achieving differentiation through customer service is a powerful way of also providing value for money, even at premium prices.

Experience from working with some of the world's leading service companies suggests there are six fundamental principles in making service strategies produce good results fast.

First, precise customer targeting. Complexity kills service efficiency. So begin by clearly identifying your ideal customers and what they perceive as value. If what they want fits your own production capabilities, and if they are prepared to pay the price, then streamline your operations to offer precisely the product service package they require.

It is helpful to distinguish between core service elements that absolutely must be present and the attractive extras that increase perceived value but cost relatively little. A high leverage strategy must focus on both but must clearly give priority to the core.

Defoe should concentrate on the major product lines and key accounts. The 80-20 principle is a good guide when developing short-run, high pay-off programmes. But in the longer term, to stay ahead of the competition it is necessary to develop a total, balanced package.

Second, communication of service level expectations. An important prerequisite of success is that top management should set meaningful service goals and be visibly dedicated to their attainment. Pushing hard, and achieving success even on a narrow front, has a tremendous impact.

Once an area for service development has been selected, then it must be communicated and actively involve everyone. The recent introduction of the "Levi's on-time programme" is an excellent example of how this can be done.

Sixty senior managers were brought together, from different functions and geographical locations, for a two-day conference. The overall situation was presented by the president and then small problem-solving groups discussed, both on a functional and inter-functional basis, the issues that had to be tackled. This face-to-face dialogue not only communicated the message but generated an extremely high level of involvement and motivation.

To push the process further down the line, a video film was made of the conference, using a well-known television interviewer. The "Levi's on-time strategy" was translated into an easy-to-read booklet entitled *Service — a strategy for winning*, which was distributed to employees.

Every manager at the conference was responsible for holding a similar event, supported by the video and booklet, with his own people. The president made a personal tour of the country to explain first-hand the background to the programme and why top management was dedicated to its success.

Third, make a service visible. Because of the intangible nature of service, special efforts are needed to make it visible. The art is to select a few indicators that can be fed back weekly, both to top management and to operational staff. As positive improvements are registered, so individuals are motivated to make even greater efforts.

Though simple, the system must allow problem solving to be precisely delegated to those responsible. The "spotlight" of such a system tends to make things happen, particularly when everyone knows that top management is taking service seriously and that career prospects are tied to service success.

Fourth, remove organizational blockages. Very often, core service goals sound obvious. But when a highly professional organization has been unable to achieve them for a number of years, there are very likely major blockages preventing implementation. Typical examples include not having service-minded people in key positions, reward systems that stress volume, not customer satisfaction, and divisional structures that make it impossible to handle small customers effectively.

At the outset, it pays to ask: "If this is so obvious, what has been stopping us so far?" – and then make the necessary changes.

Fifth, image management. Making promises to customers publicly, whether through the media or advertising, is an important way of putting pressure on the organization to perform. This must be used with caution, and top management must feel confident that it is able to deliver.

When positive service results appear, and favourable comments from customers are received, these comments should be fed back to the staff. It is particularly powerful when the business leader himself is interviewed by the media and this interview is then circulated within the organization. The printed word always commands considerable attention. It builds pride and the fighting spirit essential for success.

Sixth, calculation and monitoring of financial benefits. It is important to follow the implementation of the service development programme in financial terms. Without this linkage, people may feel that service simply consists of girls being pleasant on the telephone.

Calculation of the pay-off helps management realize its true significance. A changed customer mix, increasing ideal customers by 10% and losing 10% of those that do not fit, will in most companies produce dramatic improvements in economic performance.

The challenge lies in maintaining service-oriented business development programmes by making them an integral part of corporate life. But, as Defoe realises, the prerequisite is a major visible success in the first year.

This decision was provided by Denis Boyle in his capacity as managing director of London-based Service Management International Ltd., specializing in the business development of service companies.

How can a chain-saw company cope with cut-throat price cutting?

Charles Vance, managing director of Anderson & Co., cut short the pleasantries. "Gentlemen," he said, "we have a crucial decision to make. Just to focus your minds, here is a bit of news I received this morning."

Vance looked round the circle of expectant faces at the boardroom table. "Vanguard, our arch competitors, have cut the trade price of their Supercut chain-saw by a further $10," he announced.

There were groans of dismay.

"This means that a product that sold for $220 as recently as 1979 now is being offered for $100. That is a dramatic reduction by any standard. It undercuts our SpeedEasy saws by a full $28. We are in a price-cutting war and no mistake. So how do we respond?"

"There is only one way that we can respond," growled florid, aggressive Peter Grimes, the marketing director. "We have to undercut them. At the very least we have to offer substantial discounts."

Discount battle?

Philip Agee, the finance director, threw up his hands. "We have been into all that before," he exclaimed. "I thought we agreed a long time ago not to give discounts simply because other people are doing it. We can't afford to get into a discounting battle with Vanguard."

"We can't afford not to," Grimes responded. "Look, I have to sell these saws. There's very little to choose between us and Vanguard on quality. It's just that their company is four times as big as ours. It has a dozen other profitable lines, where we have only two, and frankly they are out to demolish us in this market. They now have an equal share with us."

"We will demolish ourselves if we go mad with discounting," Agee insisted.

"You make it sound as though discounting is an orginal sin," Grimes persisted. "In a mature market you can afford to discount – if it's a matter of survival."

"Let's get back to basics," said the managing director. "Philip, what is the financial position?"

Use the reserves

"As you know, last fiscal year the company made a profit of $500,000 on sales of $23 million," the finance man intoned. "While about half of the sales – $12.9 million to be exact – came from the chain-saws, only about $50,000 of the profits did, due largely to the fact that we had already made very substantial price cuts. That modest profit on the saws compares with $1.8 million profit on sales of $9.5 million in 1979, before this price-cutting madness set in. Since our other lines are just about holding their own, but showing no signs of dramatic improvement in profit terms, we can't rely on them to subsidise a war to the death with Vanguard."

43

"We still have quite substantial reserves," the marketing director observed. "The chain-saws are also contributing about $3 million towards our fixed costs. So it is too important a line to lose. Without it, the company is sunk."

"We have a couple of million, in reserves, if you call that substantial," Agee said.

"Well, let's call Vanguard's bluff," Grimes insisted. "Let's make a really swingeing price cut. Let's lop $30 off our selling price, bringing the price of our SpeedEasy down below the $100 mark."

"The only snag," said Agee, "is that that will mean us paying the dealer about $20 a saw just to move them off the shelves. And will the dealer pass on the price cuts?"

"But we have reserves," Grimes said. "Use them. It won't be for long. Vanguard will be hurt. Later, we can go along to them and get them to agree that there's simply no point in cutting one another's throats."

"But how do we know they *will* respond?" Agee asked. "Only a company with 60% of the market, or more, can be sure of stopping a price war. We have 25%. And anyway, our reserves are needed for other things."

"Do you have a better suggestion?" Grimes asked.

Stewart McGee, the technical director, spoke for the first time.

"In technical terms we are marketing a machine that couldn't be much more basic if we tried," he said.

"It's functional and effective. But have we given sufficient thought to going up market – to producing a Rolls-Royce saw that we can sell at a premium price? There's more than one way to skin a rabbit."

"There's a Swedish company already well established at the upper end," Grimes said.

"But it doesn't have too much competition," McGee remarked. "And the product isn't all that hot. Now if we were to produce a lighter weight saw with a much quieter motor – half as quiet, let us say, as the motor of any other saw on the market – wouldn't that be a selling point?"

"It might," Grimes agreed. "But the age of miracles is past."

"Well, it happens that such a motor is under development by an independent research outfit," McGee said. "I won't bore you now with all the technical details but I think it holds great promise. And it has been offered to us. At a price..."

"Which is?" Vance demanded.

"I reckon that to take out an option, put some money into the development and do some parallel research on the production side, would use up our reserves. It wouldn't leave anything in the kitty to subsidise a $30 price cut on the existing machines," McGee said.

"And how long before the new wonder machine came to market?" Grimes asked.

"I think it could be done in a year," the technical director said. "In fact, I'd stake my reputation on it."

Vance sat back in his chair, conscious that the others were looking in his direction. The immediate dilemma was how to cope with Vanguard's price cutting. On the other hand he ought to be thinking of the longer term future. They could always borrow to finance development of an up market saw. But already he foresaw a current fiscal year in which, thanks to the price cutting, which Grimes now wanted to accelerate, the company would suffer a substantial loss. So what was the best course of action to take?

Chain-saw company should pull out all the stops — and go for differential pricing

This is an ugly problem for the luckless Anderson and Co. Their lack of preparedness is going to cost them dear. Plenty of companies have lost their way in their markets just like this when there is a recession.

Let us sum up the market situation. Here are two competitors, joint brand leaders each with 25% share of the market. Vanguard is clearly making a strong bid for sole brand leadership. Since 1979 the market has been forcibly expanded with heavy advertising and promotion, plus dramatic reductions in the selling prices. These have been made possible by expanded production spreading the overhead cost.

The financial director's gibe about paying the dealer $20 for every machine sold is probably a hoary old remark he has been making for four years, every time the price comes down . As Grimes could easily point out, if he were not so thick, they would be paying the dealer even more per machine if they were selling in declining numbers.

Let us make the assumption that Vanguard is a bright company, making conscious decisions. It probably realizes, along with the Strategic Planning Institute in Massachusetts, that the market leader generally earns a higher profit in terms of return on investment than any other company in the market. Furthermore, the higher the leader's share of the market, the more stable his position is and the higher his return on capital. So Vanguard is planning to buy its way into leadership, probably sacrificing two years' profits to do so.

It will not stop short at cutting the price. And it will not be shaken out of its price cuts easily. It is probably prepared for a counter-attack from Anderson, so it will be putting heavy promotional bonuses into its big accounts in the trade. Beyond that, it will be supporting its price cuts with advertising. It is no good having lower prices in the market if no one knows about them. The penalty of a price-cutting strategy is that it must be backed by advertising.

Rival's weakness

The weakness of Vanguard's strategy is that it has not cut deeply enough. It is just feasible for Anderson to be able to respond.

Anderson's problem divides into short term and medium term. There is no long term for them if they do not solve the first two.

In the medium term, they must look to their product. Here we have a market which can take a wide variety of different products. Product difference is the key to differential pricing.

In this market there will be a low price sector, with products sold cheaply to the ordinary gardener, widely advertised and sold through the hypermarkets, major multiples and do-it-yourself superstores.

There will be another price sector sold to the more serious gardener through gardening shops, hardware stores and the specialist outlets. This will be a much less price-sensitive area for the consumer, although the trade will always squeeze the supplier for better margins.

There will also be a professional market among local authority users, owners of forestry land, and builders. This market will be small in unit sales but very high in quality, reliability and price. Not big enough to interest Anderson, though.

So for the medium term, the solution would be to split the product range. Put a firecracker under Mr. McGee, the technical director. Get him to widen his search for new products. Put him on the next plane to the United States, followed by Korea or Japan. Make him search world markets for a suitable premium quality product and also for a low price alternative.

What the man needs, at this stage, is several alternatives to choose from. Time is not on his side. And if you think it cannot be done quickly, then that is what is wrong with much of industry. Anderson must have something ready for market testing in three months' time.

Anderson is also going to need to find a simple product to suit the mass market. The aim here is to go below the Vanguard price – significantly so. .It must have a product that will sell at around $55. It must be a stripped-out version – designed down to a price. It will take a lower gross profit margin than the rest of the range but would be sold, with limited sales and distribution cost, only to the major outlets. The product cost targets would be very tight, and again the company should aim for a three months' development time. It means development and production managers working 12 hours a day for 13 weeks. But that is part of the fun of competition.

Protect key accounts

Finally, the short term. Protect the key accounts. That must be Anderson's aim. The company must fight a holding fight with bonuses, stocking incentives and special deals to stop Vanguard getting too many of the major customers. The users will not be so sensitive on price as the trade. Vanguard's advertising may force customers into the dealers. But if the dealers can be persuaded to show and display the Anderson product, this will switch a lot of the customers over.

Particular attention needs to be paid to winter stocking finance, so that the trade will continue to stock and buy early, because of favourable financial terms.

For the short term, therefore, Anderson should "buy" its key customers, and use in-store promotions to hold off Vanguard's attack. It will hold them in place for the necessary three to six months.

Finally, the company should hammer its fixed costs. Strip out every bit of cost which is non-essential. Strip out its idle assets, save cash. Put the money into R & D and into sales and marketing effort. The company has a battle on its hands. It must provide itself with arms and ammunition.

This fictionalized Dilemma was developed by "International Management". It is based on ideas to be found in the book, Pricing for Results, *by John Winkler, published by Heinemann on behalf of the U.K.'s Institute of Marketing. The decision was provided by John Winkler.*

Chapter 2

Production, Computers and Finance

Questions of automation, flexible working, exchange rates and making computers pay are tackled by deciders from several countries. Should an insurance company continue to automate its head office? Can flexible work schedules be implemented for only part of the workforce? How can a new computer system be made to pay off? These are contemporary questions that get some expert answers.

Should insurance company continue to automate its head office?

W hen Pierre Lesparre, chief executive of a Paris-based insurance company, convened a meeting early in September to consider plans for automating the head office, he became aware that deep-seated differences among some of his senior managers, which had previously become apparent, had not been resolved.

In August, before the start of the summer vacation, a similar meeting had revealed marked disagreements on how far and fast to automate and, indeed, whether to proceed any further in that direction at all. Lesparre had asked his managers to give some further idle thought to the question while skin-diving or lying on the beach. "I'm a great believer in letting the subconscious mind take over, where thorny problems are involved," he had said. "Maybe you will all come back with your views substantially modified."

Now Lesparre sighed as he realised that the summer sun had not, in fact, worked miracles.

First he asked the finance director, Max Robinet, whether he was still opposed to the company installing a local area network along lines suggested by the data processing manager, Daniel Merten.

"I see no reason to modify my original position," Robinet replied. "As you all know, I am a firm believer in the principle of automation. I certainly agree that we cannot afford to fall too far behind our larger competitors in this respect.

Three differing points of view

"I am fully aware that in his submission in July, Merten favoured a comprehensive local area network of the kind already used by about 20, mainly Anglo-Saxon, companies. But I remain convinced that a more cost-effective solution would be to use our existing PABX, which after all has only recently been installed.

"Incidentally I have since learned that there is a dealer just around the corner who is well qualified to connect our existing equipment to the telephone network. He would provide us with all the support we need."

Lesparre turned to Merten, a younger man who had been hired to manage a small minicomputer the company had purchased three years previously. Since then, many different machines had been purchased and used for different purposes. They included two word processors and several microcomputers all which had been used to handle particular problems at various times.

At an early stage Merten had mentioned to Lesparre the need for some kind of long-range commitment to link up all these machines so that each could communicate with the others. With the approval of Robinet, to whom Merten reported, Lesparre had asked the data processing manager to look at the market and come up with recommendations.

The result had been Merten's July report, in which he had advocated installing a local area network which would, in effect, mean buying or leasing a number of fairly expensive little black boxes to plug into the devices the insurance company already possessed.

It was this expenditure that Robinet now objected to. But Merten made it plain that despite the opposition of his immediate boss, and notwithstanding the mellowing effects of his recent holiday in Corsica, he had not changed his mind on the issue. "I remain as convinced as ever of the need to go the whole hog and choose an industry standard as our system," he said "It will pay off in the long run, even if it means more expenditure now."

Finally Lesparre invited the comments of personnel manager Emile Sergent, who all along had been most opposed to the very idea of what he called "reckless automation".

"I want to put it to you," said Sergent, "that until this whole idea cropped up and became common knowledge, morale in this company was sky high. It is still fairly high. But there is this element of uncertainty, which is not helping things at all. Now the logical conclusion to the process suggested by Merten, by his own admission, is that we shall have to make quite large redundancies. Not only will typists not be needed but many professionals also will have to go. Morale is going to suffer heavily."

"With due respect," said Merten, "that is an argument commonly used by personnel departments looking for an easy life. The fact is that despite increasing turnover we have suffered declining profits in recent years. This has led to lower wage increases which in turn have done more than anything else to cause discontent among the staff. What I am proposing is to end the uncertainty. Of course we will have to work out progressive personnel policies to soften the blow. But that is another problem."

"I resent the suggestion that we just seek an easy life," Sergent replied. "Rather, we are being realistic. Whatever we do to soften the blow, some of the better qualified staff will leave. It can be incredibly boring using computers, or hadn't you noticed?

Morale ought to be kept high
"As a technical man you want the very latest equipment – industry standard, as you put it. But I would suggest that as yet there is no such standard. There is no such thing as a fully functioning management information system and there is no such thing as a fully automated office. So I suggest it would be better to wait and do some research, while watching other companies make the mistakes."

"If we do that we shall fall too far behind," Merten said. "Competitors are making progress now."

"Which is an argument for compromising, and using the PABX we already have," Robinet interposed.

All along, Lesparre had said that the final decision would be his. Now, he realized, the moment of decision was fast approaching. Maybe he should be a bit wary about supporting a data processing manager who had been brought in, originally, just to manage a minicomputer, and whose recommendation was not favoured by his immediate boss.

On the other hand, could the company afford to dither, using as an excuse the question of staff morale? Faced with internal dissension, what should Lesparre do next, and how could staff morale be maintained?

Insurance company should formulate careful development plan

It is reasonably certain that there will be benefits to the French insurance company from the introduction of automation. Therefore Pierre Lesparre should act immediately to construct a development plan based upon the company's requirements over a projected five year period.

There are two basic errors the company has made. The first is to assume that "office automation" will occur "at a stroke". In practice office automation must evolve step by step over a period of time, to allow for adequate testing of systems, proper consultation and staff training.

The second error is that the company is talking about office automation and trying to make technical decisions – for example, PABX versus local area networks – before it has even defined what it means by office automation. What systems are to be automated and when? Why are machines being linked?

It is first of all necessary to develop a plan which should state the objectives and the benefits expected from office automation. The requirements should be defined by analysis of the existing systems, perhaps using such techniques as activity sampling and data analysis.

Scenarios should be devised of how the various functions could be performed using the advanced technology likely to be available. This procedure will indicate the activities which currently use most of the clerical and professional resources and which would therefore benefit by the introduction of automation.

Once the plan is formulated, the insurance company will be able to make a rational choice between the various options open to it. The cost of each approach can then be measured against the benefits that should accrue, and these benefits can be compared with the objectives the organization has set itself.

Lesparre should ensure that a proper cost benefit analysis has been performed for both the various local area network options and the approaches using the PABX, as it is not necessarily true that the PABX approach would be more cost beneficial.

It is important that maximum flexibility with any system is maintained, and as Daniel Merten says, an industry standard local area network can achieve very high flexibility. The need for black boxes, to enable incompatible computers to communicate, can be assessed by examining the tasks needing to be automated and the life of the existing computers. It may be that early replacement of some computers by compatible machines is a better solution than using black boxes.

Convince both management and staff

The company also needs to plan the implementation of the new technology. Management will need to be convinced of the benefits of automation, and both they and their staff will need training. Therefore adequate time for this must be allowed in the development plan. It is important that organizations devise, as part of their plan, a personnel strategy which covers recruitment, training and retraining, redeployment and redundancy, as well as pay policy.

In order to prevent the spread of rumour and hearsay, personnel manager Emile Sergent should communicate the company strategy to the workforce. There is nothing that causes more suspicion and resistance than the fear of change and the introduction of new technology.

Sergent is correct in saying that many professional workers will be affected by the introduction of new technology. Their jobs may not disappear but their roles will change. Many, for example, will be required in the design and implementation of the new systems. Others may find themselves making more decisions and using modelling techniques, rather than merely processing information as before.

It is also true that using a computer can be boring. However, it can also be made interesting, and it is important that systems using new technology are designed carefully so that tasks and decision areas can be widened and jobs enriched. Existing employees are often the best people to help in this type of job design exercise.

When Lesparre considers the detailed plan for office automation, it may be apparent that the company does not possess the requisite skills to design, implement and operate the new technology. It is usually necessary, therefore, to analyse the skills currently available and the skills that will be required, to determine what training or recruitment is needed to match the two.

To sum up, Lesparre must take the initiative and direct the energies of his executives towards the production of a practicable development plan for the company. Until this has been done, no rational decisions can be taken.

This decision was provided by Malcolm Inman in his capacity as senior consultant specializing in office automation with the computer services division of U.K.-based management consultants Binder Hamlyn Fry & Co.

Which of two plants should be closed by a firm in trouble?

Peter Gillie, managing director of Spurling Cycles Ltd., was faced with having to close one of two factories because of declining sales in the current recession. "Well, gentlemen," he said to the four executive directors assembled in his office. "We are all agreed that one of the plants has to go. But which is it to be – the one at Liverpool or the one at Harlow?"

"I don't see how it can be Harlow," said Keith Grant, the personnel director, immediately. "After all, it is a showpiece."

"The fact remains, we are in a financial bind and the Harlow plant is no more productive – in fact is less so, in some respects – than that old barn of a place up at Liverpool," said Keith Fielding, the production director. "On a straightforward cost comparison, we should keep Liverpool going.

Isn't that so, Joe?"

He turned to Joe Greenly the financial director, who nodded. "You have all seen the figures," he said. "Productivity is marginally higher, and production costs are somewhat lower, at Liverpool."

"But Harlow has potential for further productivity improvement and it is a showpiece," Grant protested. "How many parties have we had to look at that plant since it opened, two years ago? At least two a week, I think."

"Which is probably one of the reasons why it hasn't come up to expectations on the production front," Fielding snorted.

"It isn't just the publicity we have had," said the personnel director. "Harlow has been a genuine experiment in greater participation, including the setting up of semi-autonomous work groups. We have had teething troubles, sure. But personally I am convinced that, given another six or nine months, Harlow will more than repay the original investment.

"Tell that to the lads up in Liverpool," Fielding suggested. "Tell them that they are going to be chucked out of a job, in an area of high unemployment, so that we can proceed with an experiment in job enrichment in the rich south-east of the country."

Gillie turned to the fourth director, marketing man John Smedley. "What's your view, John? "

"First of all, let me say there is no immediate sign of an upturn in the market," Smedley said. "If Joe says we can't delay the closure of one of the plants, I accept that. Inventory is already bursting at the seams, and we can't afford to add to it. It seems to me that while Liverpool has marginal advantages in terms of cost and productivity, transport costs from Harlow are less, since most of our market is in Europe. I would also point out that the Harlow plant has been used in a lot of our advertising and has become identified with the product."

Gillie groaned inwardly. For days he had been turning over the arguments and the counter-arguments he had just heard, in his own mind. He had called the executive meeting half hoping for a flash of inspiration or insight from the others that would tip the scales one way or the other so far as he was concerned. He had hoped in vain.

"Let us look again at the figures," he said. "Last year we lost $1 million on a turnover of $15 million. If we close either Liverpool or Harlow, shifting production to the surviving plant, and cut overheads in other ways, we can make a profit of $500,000 on the same turnover, this fiscal year. Right, Joe?"

The financial director nodded.

"Redundancy payments would be about the same at both plants."

"No," said the finance director. "They will be somewhat higher at Liverpool because the workforce is older there, and has been with the company longer."

"Hadn't we better get away from the bare figures, and consider the *social* cost of closing Liverpool?" said the production director. "Okay, so Harlow has been identified with quality products and progressive design in our advertising. I also accept that Harlow has been a well publicised experiment in job enrichment, and that to admit it was all a waste of time sticks in the gullet. It *would* be bad publicity to close down Harlow. But just think of the bad publicity if we close Liverpool."

"I *am* thinking of it," Gillie growled. "But I don't think I ought to be. I think we ought to be making a decision on commercial grounds."

"Where the balance of advantage and disadvantage is not all that clear," the financial director murmured. "The fact is that if we fail as a company, neither Liverpool nor Harlow is going to be a viable proposition any more. We are not, at the moment, in imminent danger of going under, but unless we make the right decision now we could be."

"Let's have a vote on it," Gillie said. "Who favours closing the Liverpool plant?" Grant and Smedley did.

"And Harlow?" Fielding and Greenly both signified assent.

"So it's up to me," said Gillie soberly. What was the correct decision for the managing director to make?

DECISION

Company should try and avoid closing either plant entirely

Gillie, the managing director, should first establish who has failed him, and why. The decision on whether the Liverpool or Harlow plants should be closed will follow automatically; but there may be no need to close either.

Presumably Harlow was built as a joint project between Fielding of production and Grant of personnel. Two years is a long enough time for the new plant to be running efficiently – which, in this case, means with higher productivity than that of the "old men" in the old establishment at Liverpool. While improvements at Harlow may be possible, failure to have reached this target already implies that either the production concept or its implementation has been at fault, or perhaps both.

Gillie's personnel manager, Grant, is progressive and, perhaps, a little bit too ambitious. He has evidently persuaded the firm to introduce a new approach to manufacturing at Harlow. This in itself is to be encouraged. But such methods must be carefully thought out, particularly in relation to advances in available production technology. The new methods must also be carefully monitored during the start-up period.

In fact the manufacture of bicycles is not a particularly complex operation. Nor is it demanding in terms of quality control or product reliability. It is the type of production which lends itself fairly readily to automation. In such a situation the advantages of autonomous work groups are less clear. Furthermore, neither extensive personnel training nor highly skilled operators are key ingredients for success.

However, Grant likes playing to the gallery. Hence the two plant visits a week. This is absurd as, even if Spurling is in the leisure business, the company is definitely not in education or entertainment. Besides, the experiment has not been a success, and is not apparently a thing of which to be proud.

Transport costs are irrelevant

Fielding, on the other hand, seems to relate better to the traditional values and methods of the old plant. He does so even though the new plant gave him the opportunity not only of using better machinery and methods, but also of incorporating design changes into the product itself, which would lead to higher output. At the same time he should have been able to keep in check any excesses of enthusiasm for unproductive

54

changes proposed by Grant, his colleague at personnel.

But perhaps Fielding is too conservative, and has unconsciously, or even consciously, sabotaged the chances of success of the Harlow experiment.

The arguments of Smedley, the marketing manager, are spurious and dangerous. Transport costs from Liverpool to Harlow must be negligible and irrelevant, for a bicycle which is to be sold in Europe. On his own admission, identifying the product with the bright image of the plant at Harlow has failed to sell the product. Perhaps Smedley is not the man for the job. But this is of secondary importance right now.

Peter Gillie must make his own investigation into the failure at Harlow, by spending several days at the plant and discussing the matter at all levels. He should be particularly interested in such topics as absenteeism, and whether or not the existing plant layout leaves room for modification.

For purposes of comparison, Gillie should also spend a few days at Liverpool. And needless to say, all plant visits should be cancelled forthwith. These should be limited to two or three per year, for the benefit of distributors.

The fact that the building at Harlow is easier to sell at a high price, and that both the financial and social costs of closure are less, should not determine the outcome. If Fielding is at fault, Liverpool must close and a new production director be found to rectify the situation at Harlow.

However, I suggest that after Gillie has made his investigation he will, and should, decide to keep Liverpool and sell Harlow as a going concern. This will not involve closing Harlow completely. Machinery which is specifically designed for bicycle manufacture will be transferred to Liverpool, and only certain component manufacture will be left at Harlow – for which a buyer will be found who wants the building, some of the machinery and people.

The buyer would probably be one who wished to manufacture another mechanical product, more sophisticated than a bicycle. A deal should be worked out whereby the component manufacture can be moved out, as the buyer progressively moves his programme into the premises.

Meanwhile, Grant can be given the task of enriching the jobs of the Liverpudlians – but not too much. If he declines to do so and resigns, it might well be to the benefit of Spurling.

In reaching this decision, Gillie will not have lost sight of the fact that, some time in the not-too-distant future, he will probably be faced with the problem of phasing out of bicycle manufacture anyway, and of restricting himself to the business of marketing bicycles made in Korea and China. By that time the men at Liverpool will be even older, and the closure of that plant would be less painful.

This decision was provided by Christopher Hammer in his capacity as a partner of Corporate Development SA, the Brussels subsidiary of international company search consultancy Corporate Development International.

Can flexible work schedules be instituted for only part of the workforce?

As marketing and research director Hans Siegel left for the weekly executive lunch, he passed two of his employees just arriving. One, he knew, had taken a free morning accumulated under the liberal flexible working month system enjoyed by the white-collar workers under his control at Hans Schmidt AG, a company with just under 2,000 employees making electrical appliances. Employees could come in and leave at any time over the month, between 6 a.m. and 6 p.m., as long as they completed their allotted hours.

The other employee, a woman with two small children, worked most of her hours at home, where the company had installed a computer terminal to communicate with headquarters. She came to the office only for meetings with her boss and colleagues in the market research department or to make use of library materials that were not yet on microfilm.

Siegel was proud of his quality of working life programme. Over the past five years he had introduced a range of flexible working patterns including job sharing, study sabbaticals and homeworking. Although some of them had teething problems, the results, he felt, were excellent.

The motivation of the 200-odd people who worked directly for him was immeasurably improved. Labour turnover and absenteeism had plummeted and those hirings he had had to make were of a generally higher calibre because of the increased number of job applicants. The only dissenting notes had been from some of his older managers, who found it difficult to adapt to managing people whom they only saw for part of the day, if that often, and from managers in other divisions who thought the whole programme was a dangerous anomaly.

Siegel had persuaded one of the unenthusiastic older managers, Julius Neckarmann, to move to another part of the company, where flexible working had not been implemented. However, Neckarmann, whose distaste for the free-and-easy working arrangements of the marketing and research division had become an obsession, had now become production director in the main manufacturing plant.

He had complained to managing director Frederik Blohm at a recent management meeting that "those dangerous radicals with their sloppy way are upsetting my plant's routines. Our production people see these characters sauntering in at 11 a.m. and want to know why they should bother to work hard.

Consider flexible hours for the shop floor

"Several of them have sons or daughters working over there. It makes my production workers mad to leave them lazing in bed when they have to get up at 6 a.m. to do a decent day's work. I spent three hours yesterday arguing with the union. They want the same privileges. But we have to keep the assembly line going; we can't just wait till people stroll in at any hour before we begin."

Siegel had to admit that there was a problem in extending flexible working to the shop floor. The plant was a fairly old one, and radical changes in working hours could only be made with an extensive redesign. Even then, it was debatable how much flexibility could be built in. However, he pointed out to Neckarmann, that really wasn't his problem; that was something that had to be dealt with within the plant itself.

As Siegel entered the dining room for the executive lunch, Blohm drew him aside. "Look, Hans," he began, "I don't think you can wash your hands of Neckarmann's problem just because it is a different division. You have bent the rules considerably in introducing your programme – you know you have. That was all right while everything went smoothly, and I agree the results have been good – till now. But this morning the production workers have told the works council they must have the same flexibility as your people have.

"One department has started a go-slow and the union is threatening to strike over the issue if it has to. I don't think things will go that far, but the problem is still serious. They resent your people taking what they see as unfair liberties. I want you to review the freedoms you have been giving your people with a view to pulling back on some of them.

"You have one good excuse: although there have been a lot of positive results, there has not been the increase in productivity that was predicted."

Siegel's reaction was understandably outraged. The programme was tremendous for the corporate image, he pointed out, and had done the company a great deal of good. Productivity might not have risen, but it had not fallen, either. Take away some of the flexibility, however, and people would resent it so much that a drop in productivity was inevitable. If his programme went against the corporate policy handbook, that was simply because the policies had not been revised for too long.

Blohm was in a quandary. The privileges Siegel's subordinates enjoyed were unusual. But they had done no harm and the people who enjoyed them now took them for granted. Taking them away, however, would cause great resentment at a time when the maximum effort was needed for a major product launch.

If this vital launch was to be achieved properly, the utmost co-operation would be needed – between everybody. How could he motivate one set of employees without demotivating the other?

DECISION

Flexible working must cover all employees

F rederick Blohm, the managing director, is committed to a product launch which is vital to the company. Therefore he has to ensure that there is no disruption of production. That must be his overriding priority.

If he allows the marketing and research department to continue operating a wide range of flexible working, he faces a continuing go-slow, and perhaps a strike, among his blue-collar workers. His problem is to prevent this from happening without doing too much damage to the morale of the white-collar people who work for Hans Siegel.

Blohm may well reflect that he himself is to blame for the situation that has arisen. Evidently he gave Siegel his head in the implementation of flexible working arrangements, without too much thought for its impact on other departments.

Siegel pursued his objective with the absolute dedication of an enthusiastic innovator. He took a narrow, rather blinkered view. When Neckarmann, and other older managers, expressed strong reservations, Siegel overrode them. He appears to have made no sustained effort to win them round to his way of thinking. Instead, in the case of Neckarmann, he encouraged him to move to another part of the company.

Consider the interests of the company

Blohm must have known that all this was happening. He must have realized that Siegel was being single-minded, even ruthless, in the pursuit of his ideal of flexible working. Yet apparently he did not, as chief executive, interfere. He did not lead from the top. He cannot have made much effort to get his directors and department heads to agree the level of flexible working compatible with the best interests of the company as a whole, rather than just part of it.

What he has to do first is get more communication between Neckarmann and Siegel. After all, they are now equals and not, as before, superior and subordinate. Neckarmann must be an able manager, or he would not have been appointed director of production. It was not he who introduced flexible working and thereby caused the current friction in the company. Yet it is his department that is being disrupted.

It is clear that communications as a whole, between marketing, research and production, have been poor. Blohm should welcome this opportunity to improve them.

He should call Neckarmann and Siegel together, make it clear to both what he himself thinks about flexible working as a concept and send them away to look jointly at what can be done to ameliorate the discontent in the production department.

Blohm should set them a deadline, by which time they must report back to him with a plan of action. He should in the meantime prepare his own plan should they fail to agree or should their proposals be unacceptable. That plan must be based on the premise that as a last resort there is no choice but to support Neckarmann, even if it means withdrawing some of the flexi-privileges being enjoyed by the white-collar workers.

Blohm should inform the trade union and the works council that by a certain date – say two days after Neckarmann and Siegel are due to report – he will go before them and explain his policy, and the need for compromise in order to avert disaster on the production side. This will serve to concentrate the minds of the two directors in their efforts to find their own solution.

It should not be impossible for Blohm to persuade the white-collar workers to make some sacrifices, on a temporary basis, and also to consult with the blue-collar workers through the works council. The longer-term need, however, is for Blohm to realize that the problem should never have arisen. *Ad hoc* decisions, in matters of this importance, are no substitute for a well-conceived personnel policy, which considers the needs of the whole workforce, rather than just part of it.

This decision was provided by Bob Gattie in his capacity as a partner in the Brussels office of TASA, an executive search organization.

How should European general manager react to demands from the U.S?

Hans Wachter frowned as he made his way to a special meeting with the staff, which was to be followed by an even more critical meeting with the union. As he left the office, his secretary had handed him a copy of the *Frankfurter Allgemeine Zeitung.* "This is publicity we could do without," he said aloud, as he read one of the headlines on the business pages. "TMX reports big jump in earnings," it said.

The president of TMX Corp. had declared in New York that the last year had been the company's best year ever. Normally Wachter, who was general manager of TMX Gears AG in Baden-Württemberg, would have been very keen to have seen the company's name prominently displayed.

Unfortunately, so far as the German subsidiary was concerned, things were far from normal. Demand for the company's standard, off-the-shelf equipment had been slipping in Europe, due to the recession, while the performance of the special equipment business was unspectacular. Wachter had been obliged, under pressure from corporate headquarters, to take some unpleasant decisions. He had put his long-term investment programme on ice. He had laid off about a third of his research and development department.

Now he was on his way to inform the staff, and the union, that further sacrifices were deemed necessary. A few weeks previously, he had got together with key executives to see where additional economies could be made. They had decided to announce restrictions on wage increases, to make staff reductions and operating economies. They planned to consult with worker representatives on how to implement the plans. In this way, they hoped to avoid totally undermining the good relationship they had established with the employees.

Now this! How could he force unpalatable medicine down the throats of people who had worked loyally for the company for a long time, when the company president in New York was proudly announcing a record year? Wachter himself felt that the president was only able to boast increased earnings because of the economies he was demanding abroad, particularly in Europe. Also, Wachter did not have to think very hard to pinpoint in his mind a number of people, both on the staff and the union side, who would make the same point at the meeting he was due to address.

Wachter's problem was compounded by the fact that he was locked in disagreement with corporate headquarters on a major issue of policy. So any representations he made to New York on behalf of the German workforce might not be received with much sympathy.

Wachter believed that the current problem with sales of the standard products was caused by a temporary recession. Headquarters did not see it that way, however. They saw that the standard products had yielded higher profit margins in the past than the special equipment side of the business. They argued that the German subsidiary should dispose of its special equipment business and concentrate resources and effort entirely on the standard lines.

Wachter, who had built up the special equipment side to achieve a sales volume of $20 million and more, pointed out that the division absorbed a substantial amount of overheads that would otherwise put heavy pressure on the profitability of the standard products. Increasing competition from other suppliers would shortly put those lines under even greater pressure. It seemed to him the wrong time altogether to contemplate cutting out the special equipment business and making standard products absorb all the overheads.

The reaction of headquarters to this was that the overheads themselves, by which they meant people, should be cut. If the German company got out of special equipment it could reduce its overheads, headquarters said.

Against this, Wachter had advanced two arguments. One was that re-tooling of the standard product lines would almost certainly be necessary, in the near future, as the car manufacturers who were major customers turned to smaller models to help them out of their own difficulties. Many contracts would have to be renegotiated, with uncertain results. But the special equipment business could be relied upon to go on turning in steady, if small, profits during a period of turmoil.

Secondly, he argued that the good industrial relations the plant had enjoyed were too precious to be placed in jeopardy. Any industrial unrest would hurt a profitability situation that was already fragile.

In reply to these representations, Wachter had been asked to press ahead with the economies already agreed. The question of the product mix, New York had said, was to be decided in the near future.

As Wachter approached the room where he was to speak to the staff, he felt that he was in an impossible position. What should he do?

Should he do exactly as headquarters had asked, announce staff cuts, economies, and the closing down of the special equipment division with all the outrage that would cause, bringing him into conflict with staff and union and facing him with criticism about the U.S. company using the German subsidiary as a milk cow?

Or should he tell the meeting of the seriousness of the impending crisis, but tell them he is going back to headquarters to make one more effort to dissuade them from this disastrous course? This could have the effect of making the US company even more intransigent, perhaps asking for even bigger cuts and even threatening Wachter's own position.

DECISION

General manager should persist in making case to his American bosses

Wachter's problem is common to many multinational companies with operations in the U.S. and in OECD countries. The problem is compounded further when operations extend to the developing countries, although that is not a dilemma that Wachter faces.

The disagreement that appears to remain between Germany and the U.S., even after the discussions they have had, makes it very difficult for Wachter to have an effective and objective meeting with his managers and/or the unions. One suspects that the company does not hold a dominant position with its products in the German market.

But with $20 million worth of special equipment sales, plus a bigger proportion of standard business, the German operation is significant. It would therefore be very much in the interests of the parent company, I think, to take a more active interest in the German company. One would expect direct communication quarterly, with probably alternating visits across the Atlantic by various management levels.

If I were Wachter, my first step would be to go down the corridor and have a very short meeting with the managers, announcing my intention to discuss once again the problems of the German and European market with the president of the corporation. It certainly appears that Wachter's communication with his U.S. masters, and possibly with his own management, leaves a lot to be desired.

My next step would be to set up a market study to consider the life cycle, penetration prospects and pricing levels of the existing "off the shelf" products, and reconsider where the company stands with the special products in terms of margins, price and sales prospects. The market study would include an assessment of the competitors' activities.

With that behind me, it would be easier to judge whether the present problems are temporary or of longer duration. I would then feel more confident about establishing a strategy that I could describe to my American bosses for improved financial performance over the next two to five years. I might also force them to recognize what is not always recognized by either European or American managers, namely that while the German economy grew with the 1950s and 1960s it has subsequently, from the early 1970s, been an increasingly competitive market which has had a declining growth rate.

The measurement of improved financial performance might be return on investment, sales expense ratios, profit per person employed or simple gross margin. The form of measurement will depend on the nature and structure of the organization and the financial arrangements between the American parent company and the German subsidiary.

The importance of this choice cannot be overstressed in these times of volatile parity fluctuations. Otherwise losses or gains in management efficiency and productivity can be eclipsed totally by fickle and varying relationships of the key currencies. Although, in the long run, these may wash out, they make the management control figures very difficult to interpret from afar.

Given that Wachter can generate a strategy acceptable to the parent company, I think the waiting managers would accept unpalatable medicine if it is really necessary. Without that agreement and understanding, sooner or later either some of the managers, or the union representatives, will become convinced that the German company is being exploited by an ill-informed board, president or chief executive, 5,000 kilometres away in America.

As a last resort, and only the last resort, if the parent company is not interested in the German market, perhaps Wachter should consider acquiring the German company. If he has been doing his job properly, he will have been asking himself what he would do if it were *his* company and *his* investment.

This decision was provided by Michael Powell in his capacity as British-based managing director for European, Middle East and African operations of the U.S. instrumentation and process control company Foxboro International.

How can a new computer system be made to pay off?

J ohn Gray was unhappy. He had recently moved from another company to take on the job of chief executive with U.K.-based Superfood Ltd., a national grocery chain owned by Twentieth Century Foods Inc. of the U.S.

One of his most pressing problems concerned the company's data processing, which was only operating on one cylinder yet was costing more than $2 million a year. The EDP people seemed to Gray, who had been trained as an accountant, to be a loss-making law unto themselves. Meanwhile, the company's depots and bakeries were saddled with two computer systems, neither of which was working satisfactorily.

Some years previously, Gray's predecessor as managing director, Charles Wheeler, had backed a scheme suggested by his then systems manager, Harold Thorpe. It was to provide the company with a fully integrated data processing system using the most modern equipment. It would replace equipment which had been doing production scheduling, order processing and internal accounting at the company's bakeries and depots, but which was obsolete. This applied particularly to the peripheral equipment.

Thorpe had proposed a fresh approach, with modern hardware which would add customer accounting and give management instant feedback on every aspect of the business from day to day.

Before agreeing to this, Wheeler had thought it wise to ask the advice of Peter Fairley, the staff vice-president for computer systems, who had no responsibility in the U.K. subsidiary but had the ear of the parent company chairman in New York.

Forcing a resignation

It was fairly common knowledge in the company that Fairley disliked Thorpe, seeing him as a possible threat to his own position. When Fairley advised Wheeler to adopt Thorpe's scheme, there were even some cynics who said "Then he *must* think it is going to fail."

Wheeler too had his differences with Thorpe. One was over a six-figure sum to pay consultants that Thorpe brought in to recommend the most appropriate computer hardware. "I though *you* were the computer expert," Wheeler said plaintively. "Do we really need these people?"

Fairley began dropping hints to Wheeler that he wasn't happy with the way Thorpe objected when Wheeler insisted that a new computer centre be located at Hull, more than 300 kilometres from London, in order to take advantage of investment grants.

The crisis point came when Wheeler told Thorpe that he expected him to move himself to Hull, with his staff. There really was no need, he said, to have the planning done in London.

Thorpe, who had been born in London, was a gourmet and loved the theatre, flatly refused to move. Whereupon Wheeler, after notifying Fairley of his intention and receiving no discouragement, suggested to Thorpe that he should resign. The computer man obliged.

Wheeler had been confident that the development of the new computer system was far enough advanced to dispense with Thorpe's services. Orders for hardware were about to be finalized with the computer manufacturers. The computer centre at Hull was well advanced and Ronald Phillips, a well-respected computer operations manager, was already working at the depot there. He was due for another promotion, so Wheeler appointed him to fill Thorpe's shoes.

Too hasty a decision
That, thought Gray, was where his predecessor had made his biggest mistake. While the new hardware was perfectly good, and Phillips was technically competent to understand it and make it work, he had comparatively little experience on the software side, had done very little work with analysts and programmers and, more seriously, did not have an adequate grasp of the system that Thorpe had been working towards. In fact, the full blueprint for that system existed only inside Thorpe's head.

The situation now facing Gray was this: the expensive new hardware was all in place but the vaunted system was not functioning. Nobody seemed to know how to make it work, and Gray was informed by the EDP people that it would be at least three years before the system could begin to pay off.

Meanwhile the old computer gear was "held together with glue and bits of string," as Gray put it in his gloomier moments. Some of the work was being done on the old computers and some on the new. But there seemed to be no prospect of any short cuts in integrating the two.

Gray had considered selling off the new equipment. But that would have meant writing off a large investment in equipment, plant and the writing of programmes. The old equipment could not take the strain of coping with any additional work.

Gray was under pressure from corporate headquarters in New York to show some positive results for all the time, energy and, especially, money that had been expended on the project. What was his best course of action?

DECISION

Grocery chain grapples with a data processing problem

John Gray, the new managing director of Superfood Ltd., is right to be worried about the EDP situation in his company. His immediate reaction may be to consider replacing Phillips, the computer operations manager promoted by his predecessor when Harold Thorpe, the old systems manager, left.

However, mature reflection should lead him to conclude that the last thing he wants at this stage is any further turnover of senior staff, especially in the EDP area. Already Thorpe has departed, and it is safe to assume that the department is in some disarray.

Even if Phillips is not perfect, as the lack of progress in implementing a new system suggests, the immediate need is to achieve some stability in an organization that clearly does not have a personnel policy worthy of the name, which has increased the problems facing the company.

The first positive step that Gray needs to take is to establish a working group within the company to carry out a systems analysis of the real issues, in terms of the economics of the business and its competitive weaknesses, to see how EDP could improve the situation.

Implement a master plan

The group should be about ten-strong, and should include representatives from the depots, plants, shops, and the distribution fleet, as well as systems analysts and Phillips himself. It should pursue its brief in the presence of the EDP people and involve them fully in deciding what are the real problems facing the company.

What the company needs is a master plan for optimizing its strengths and removing its weaknesses. This needs to be worked out independently from the existing systems and hardware.

In other words, there needs to be a fresh beginning based on the idea that process is more important than the final product. That process must start from actual business issues, and only when those have been identified by the working group should Gray turn to the EDP people for support that will help reduce inventory and do other desirable things.

When a plan takes shape, and the EDP contribution to its achievement is recognized by all, then the company should look urgently at those elements of its existing data processing, including the hardware, that fit in with the plan. Gray should then be quite ruthless in selling off any hardware that the company does not really need, perhaps persuading the suppliers to take some of it back. At worst, he could give it away free, which is preferable to the state of mind that would tinker with equipment that is not really needed to achieve business objectives.

The main questions to which Gray requires an answer are then which software to develop and how long it would take to meet the needs of the users within the company. In order to decide this as speedily and objectively as possible, he should set up project teams, with a systems analyst in charge of each, comprising a number of users in a steering function. The progress of the project teams would be monitored by the working group, which Gray himself would attend so that he could assess for himself the strengths and weaknesses of individuals, not least the EDP people themselves.

Assess the potential objectives

Attending these meetings, Gray would soon detect if anything was missing and then, if necessary, could call in temporary support, either from the company's head office in the U.S. or from outside consultants, to sit in on the working group sessions.

It may be that after he has seen Phillips in action on the working group, and has assessed his ability to mesh with the company's overall objectives, Gray may decide that he is not making the grade and should be replaced. Some other member of the EDP department may emerge as better qualified to do the job.

Utilize skills of others

On the other hand there is quite a good chance that Phillips will make the grade. Usually, under an EDP manager, there are three department heads, one concerned with the operation of the EDP equipment, one with programming and one with systems development. Phillips may be strong in only one of those areas, but if he has able lieutenants, and exhibits some general management skills, that is no problem.

After all, he has been with the company a long time. So he does know it inside and out. His chief disadvantage was that he inherited a system from Thorpe that only Thorpe understood, and tried to make it work – hopelessly as it turned out – under a previous managing director who did not associate the EDP department sufficiently with corporate objectives.

Gray, therefore, should start again, keep an open mind for the time being on the existing hardware and involve the users as well as the specialists in deciding priorities.

This decision was provided by Dr. Tom Sommerlatte in his capacity as Wiesbaden (West Germany)-based director and vice president of Telematics, the European data processing and telecommunications systems arm of the U.S. consultancy firm Arthur D. Little.

DILEMMA

What currency should Canadian firm use to finance new foreign plant?

" "We now come to the question of finance for our new development in France," says Larry Squires, chairman of Canadian firm Excel Air-Conditioning Ltd., which was holding a directors' meeting at its European sales office in London. "Roger..."

"Thank you, Larry," says Roger Parnell, the company's finance director. "We have all been to France and seen the projected site. But I'll just go over the basics again.

"Here we are, a Canadian company with plants in Toronto, the U.S. and Brazil. We are about to launch our riskiest venture in virgin territory, France. We know that Europeans still aren't as sold on air-conditioning as North Americans are. However, we do believe that the energy crisis and increased heating costs are going to lead to better insulated buildings and the need for more cost-effective air-conditioning in Europe. We believe we have a unique product that will take maximum advantage of market growth in air-conditioning within the Common Market. But the price has to be right."

Parnell looked around the table. "*Price*, gentlemen. That is why we propose to build a plant on the Gironde, in western France, within the EEC tariff wall and benefiting fully from the development and fiscal allowances offered by the French government.

"However, we are still going to face substantial costs at a time when our Brazilian plant has yet to settle down and is costing us a great deal of money. If we get our financing of the French venture wrong the accounts are going to look very sick indeed. From a business point of view we might just as well have been less ambitious and continued to ship in products from Toronto."

"Since we have decided to go ahead," said Squires, "what are your recommendations?"

65

"As you know," Parnell continued, "the total capital cost of the project is going to be the equivalent of 50 million French francs. I propose – and I think we may all be agreed on this – that the level of equity capital should be approximately 10% of the total. It will be provided by us, in Canadian dollars, for conversion into French francs:

"I propose that another 40% of the capital cost should be obtained in the form of long-term debt from French banks. We can get that amount at preferential interest rates over a five-year term. Any objections?"

"Sounds very sensible and orthodox to me," said one of the non-executive directors. "But what about the other 25 million French francs or their equivalent?"

Parnell wanted the parent company to borrow the funds outside France and re-lend them to the French company. Such funding would be classified by the French Central Bank as capital for purposes of the debt-equity ratio, allowing further access to short-term local finance if and when required.

But the real question, he said, was determining in which currency the funds should be borrowed.

One alternative would be to go into the Eurocurrency market and borrow in French francs. This would mean that the company would enjoy the advantage of having its debt in the same currency as the revenue and profits of the unit it was financing.

On the other hand, the debt would have to be recorded on the books of the parent company in Canadian dollars. If the Canadian dollar continued to weaken against the French franc, the debt on the books in terms of Canadian dollars would increase and have a negative impact on the balance sheet. Parnell pointed out that a Canadian company that borrowed French francs in 1971 would have incurred such a "translation" loss amounting to 49% of the loan by 1979.

Taking a guess at exchange rates

Another option was to raise the money in Canadian Eurodollars, a market which had existed since 1976. Here the liability for the loan would remain constant on the books of the parent company, and would be easier to repay if the Canadian dollar continued to weaken against the French franc. On the other hand, if the franc weakened, the subsidiary would have to generate extra earnings to buy more expensive Canadian dollars to repay the loan.

The interest rate on the French franc loan would be around 12.5% a year, and the Canadian Eurodollar loan would carry a rate of around 11.5%.

However, the third alternative – borrowing Swiss francs – offered a very advantageous interest rate of around 4.5% a year. If the Canadian dollar and French franc held their value against the Swiss franc over the period of the loan, this would offer the best deal. But, historically, a Canadian company borrowing Swiss francs in 1971 would have incurred a translation loss of 67% by 1979.

"Well, we can't be certain that history will repeat itself," Squires said. "It seems to me we just have to take an educated guess as to what will happen to the exchange rates for these currencies over the next five years, unless someone can think of another solution."

What choice should the board make?

Exchange rate uncertainties raise problems over financing foreign plant

At this stage in its development, Excel Air-Conditioning needs to be rather conservative in arranging the financing of its new French operation. This investment represents a major commitment for the company and clearly is associated with considerable business risk, as indicated by Roger Parnell's description of it as "our riskiest venture in virgin territory".

Substantial extra financial risk is unwarranted. The need for financial conservatism is further reinforced by the financial drain caused by its recently established Brazilian plant.

These considerations suggest the company should finance its French investment with French franc debt. Unfortunately such an approach will require the company to pay a higher interest rate for its finance, at least initially. But it will subject both the French operation and the overall company to the minimum possible exchange risk arising from the changes in the French franc against the Canadian dollar.

Exposure will be limited to the 10% of the capital provided in Canadian dollars by the parent. Should the French franc harden against the Canadian dollar, the Canadian dollar value of the French franc debt will increase. But so too will the value of the French assets in real terms.

It is true that the Canadian parent company may incur a translation loss as a result of Canadian accounting conventions, but this will not represent a real loss to the overall concern. On this point, the company should explore ways of minimizing any translation loss incurred by the Canadian parent. This might be possible by borrowing the funds through a subsidiary company under the guarantee of the Canadian parent. The success of such an approach will depend on the accounting conventions, currently under review, governing consolidation of the company's accounts.

Two alternatives are risky

The two alternatives being considered by Excel Air-Conditioning are fraught with risks. If Canadian dollars were used to finance the deal and the French franc were to drop against the Canadian dollar, then the company would find itself striving to service its debt out of an income stream that was declining in Canadian dollar terms.

Similar problems would arise by financing in Swiss francs. In this case the situation is more complex since three currencies are involved.

In view of these risks, the approach advocated by Squires, the chairman, seems to be cavalier and irresponsible. To take "an educated guess as to what will happen to exchange rates over the next five years" and decide financing arrangements on this basis is tantamount to gambling.

In practice the decision confronting the board of Excel Air-Conditioning would be more complicated than described in the dilemma. First, the costs and revenues of the French company would probably be in a range of currencies. This is particularly so for the revenues which would be generated in several countries across Europe, this being the market for Excel's products.

This situation would materially affect the financing arrangements best suited to the company. For example, if a major portion of sales receipts were in Deutschmarks, the company should consider financing parts of its French operation in Europ Deutschmarks, remembering that part of its costs will be in francs.

Another factor that needs to be considered concerns the tax treatment of losses arising from foreign currency loans. It may be that such losses would be tax deductible in France, and this situation might strengthen the argument for borrowing at least a portion of the finance required in a harder, and therefore lower cost, currency, since any future exchange losses would be softened by the favourable tax treatment.

Although financing in French francs is probably the right decision for Excel, other companies might find another solution appropriate. Many multinational corporations, particularly those headquartered in Canada and the U.S., have preferred to raise a significant part of their long-term capital for financing foreign operations in the currency of their base country. This has been an attempt to minimize the impact of translation losses arising from foreign currency loans.

Other companies might decide to deliberately accept a degree of exchange risk in an attempt to benefit from the lower cost of borrowing in hard currencies. Limited efforts in this direction might be suitable for strong companies that have a good track record in predicting interest and exchange rate movements, and are able to withstand any losses that might occur.

Because the best way of financing an operation will vary from company to company, the question of how to make the most appropriate decision is very relevant. In theory the answer is straightforward, requiring a company to make financial projections of both existing and planned new ventures, with the aim of showing the incremental impact of every new venture.

Though simple in theory, this logical approach is often extremely complicated. Many leading companies have started to deal with this problem by harnessing the power of the computer to make financial projections and highlight explicitly the risks involved.

This decision was provided by Christopher Batt in his capacity as general manager responsible for developing strategies and directing various planning efforts of· the London-headquartered Grindlays Bank Group.

Can a company achieve high targets as well as reliable forecasts?

Reginald Mitchell, managing director of Batt & Glover Ltd., told his secretary he did not want to be disturbed. Mitchell was under pressure from the financial director at group headquarters to give him his sales forecast figures in order to set next year's budget. After many discussions, Mitchell and his colleagues on the board had set themselves sales and budget figures. But now Mitchell had some doubts and hesitated before reporting them to group headquarters.

Batt & Glover, which manufactured sports equipment, was a subsidiary of the Leisuretime Group, based in the north of England. The business recession, inflation and other outside factors were making it hard to forecast sales figures on which to base the company's annual total budget. The group headquarters told Mitchell to cut out all the marketing optimism which had confused the financial forecasts in recent years.

But if the company were to set lower targets, Mitchell felt, it would be difficult to motivate managers and improve sales performance.

At the first budget meeting, Mitchell asked Jack Cowley, his marketing manager, to submit a sales forecast. Cowley gave a forecast figure of $20.3 million in sales at current prices. Joe Wellcome, the production director, expressed surprise. "Much too low," he said. "I do not see where you are planning to make any effort to take care of the additional output from our new equipment. Unless you can sell more our investment in this equipment will be a total waste of time and effort."

"I take your point," replied Cowley. "And I hope to sell more. But I was told to submit a *realistic* budget." He turned to Mitchell for some explanation.

Set reasonable targets

"That is more or less right," said Mitchell. "The group financial director thinks it best to go for maximum profit this year. In order to do this, he suggests the first requirement is a reliable sales forecast. In this way the production department can plan its requirements more carefully and achieve better productivity than before. In the past we have had too much unplanned overtime and other emergency action which has regularly caused unfavourable cost variances."

"But if forecasts are too low," replied Wellcome "I do not see how the sales people can be motivated to achieve more."

"Perhaps we could establish two sets of targets," suggested Cowley, "one for group budget and another with higher figures for our own use. We could then set individual targets accordingly."

Mitchell looked around the table. He could tell that no one else seemed satisfied with the proposal or indeed with the sales target set by Cowley.

"I propose we go for a higher budget, a round $25 million," Mitchell suddenly announced. Wellcome brightened visibly. "We could certainly aim at $25 million."

"And could you meet this in production?" Mitchell asked Wellcome.

"We are a damn sight more likely to meet it if we are given a higher budget," Wellcome assured him.

Clark Kent, the reticent financial manager, spoke up: "I think we have got off the track, gentlemen. You seem to be dreaming up targets from the top of your head."

Cowley referred to his marketing plans with figures from market research. Kent in turn presented figures on the economic situation. He was also unimpressed with the planned exports.

Eventually, the board agreed on a sales target totalling $22.5 million, with a company budget linked to this figure.

But now, the following day, alone in his office, Mitchell was uneasy. Despite all their efforts, he thought they had failed to reach a figure that was anywhere near satisfactory. His financial manager's warning was echoing in his mind: "You seem to be dreaming up targets from the top of your head," the manager had said.

It seemed to Mitchell on reflection that the board had done no more than settle on a compromise figure. Certainly the agreed figure was hardly the realistic figure required by group headquarters. In reality, it seemed no more than last year's figures with a little extra added for good measure.

The fancy internal communication panel on Mitchell's desk buzzed. "I know you did not want to be disturbed," his secretary said. "But it is the group financial director on the telephone. He says he needs your budget figures immediately."

DECISION

Company should estimate maximum and minimum turnover, then compromise

Mitchell, like most managing directors, has to find a correct balance between two contrasting requirements. He has to set internal targets which are realistic while being adventurous enough to motivate his managers. On the other hand, he has to devise plans for wider distribution which are so safe they automatically prevent the full potential of the businesss being realized.

Mitchell should obtain from his colleagues a consensus view of the market demand, forgetting for the moment any limitations of production capacity. The chances of any figures being precisely accurate are virtually nil. But this does not matter, and Mitchell must emphasize this point.

What Mitchell and each of his top managers should do is estimate a minimum figure and a maximum figure between which they feel the demand is certain to fall. They should then estimate the most likely result between the two. In this way, they can each express a view and they do not waste a great deal of time trying to decide on a precise figure.

Consider the bell chart
Mitchell should then draw a bell curve showing the relative probability of each figure.

Suppose for example that they agree a minimum sale of $20 million, a maximum of $26 million and a most likely figure of $22 million. The chart would appear as shown.

At any point on the bell curve the area under the curve to the left represents the probability of the actual demand falling below the value at the point in question. The area under the curve to the right represents the probability of the value being exceeded.

The production director may have estimated that he would be able to produce to a turnover of $23 million. Reference to the bell curve shows that there is about a 70% chance that the $23 million will satisfy demand, and a 30% chance that it will fail. This is a high failure risk and the production director should probably be asked to think of ways of increasing capacity by another $1 million, which represents a 90% chance of fulfilling demand.

There would also be a 5% chance that sales could be less than $21 million. Mitchell should ask the financial director to calculate the effects of this on profits and cash flow. If the result is sufficiently frightening for him not to wish to take even this chance, he should ask each director to draw up a contingency plan to be put into action if the possible lowest sales trend appears. The company could take action on overheads, debtors and stocks, for example.

Set two budgets

For the sales department I suggest a target of $25 million, slightly less than the highest consensus figure to encourage a high level of profitable sales.

Mitchell should then set his basic internal budget for a turnover of $22.5 million, which is slightly higher than the most likely value (the top of the curve), for extra self-discipline.

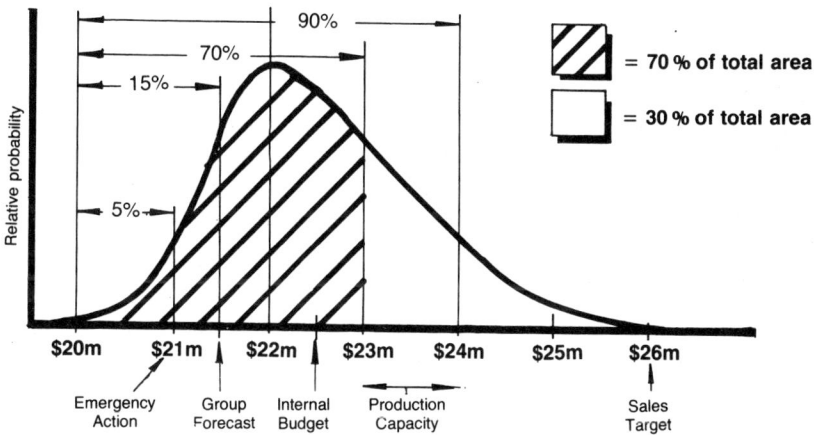

What figure should be given to group headquarters depends very much on Mitchell's relationship with them . They want reliable, and hence low, forecasts. But presumably they are also pressing for high performance. If Mitchell wishes to give them a figure which will have an 85% chance of being achieved, he should drop to the beginning of the curve, about $21.5 million, which is just below the most likely figure of $22 million. But the management team should understand that whereas the internal budget has a 60% chance of success, the one sent to the group must be 85% certain of achievement.

The different target levels, based on agreed demand estimate, are in descending order as follows: sales target, production capacity, internal budget, group forecast and emergency action.

This decision was provided by Nicholas Branch in his capacity as managing director, Binder Hamlyn Fry & Co, London-based management consultants.

How can a company give parity in wages and fringe benefits?

T he Swiss group, Excelsior Optical SA, had begun acquiring small and medium-sized French family firms in the eyewear and optical instrument field during the middle 1960s. In late 1974 Alain Bula had been given the job of administering and rationalizing the six factories.

His first major move was in response to heavy demand for spectacle frames, both from French customers and through a contract with the Swiss parent company.

To increase production he decided to extend the relatively modern plant at Heyrieux, and close the antiquated, multi-storey facility some 20 kilometres away near Trept. Most of the Trept employees had agreed to commute to Heyrieux, where they would enjoy more modern working conditions.

Bula had presented his plan to the board in Switzerland as an integral part of the fiscal 1977 budget review session. The capital expenditure had been approved. A 20% higher provision for wage costs was also included in the budget. Bula felt that he would probably have to grant a general 15% salary rise during the year. The remaining money, he had calculated, would more than cover the limited number of redundancy payments at Trept, plus about a 3% adjustment to put the Trept workers on the same hourly base rate as the workers at Heyrieux.

Bula had also taken pains to call in the union leaders at both plants. The shop steward at the Trept plant had at first wanted a travel allowance built into the new salary for his people. Bula noted that the upward adjustment in hourly pay would offset some of the extra travel costs. And he was adamant in insisting that all employees at the same plant should be treated equally.

Union urges standardization of benefits

This argument backfired on him later when the discussion turned to fringe benefits. The Trept plant gave a straight four weeks' holiday to all employees. Workers at the recently acquired modern plant at Heyrieux were entitled to five weeks and those with over ten years' service received six weeks. The Heyrieux workforce was relatively young and only about 4% qualified for the extra week's holiday. However, approximately 80% of the employees at Trept had been there over ten years. The difference in seniority among the two workforces created an even more severe problem where pensions were concerned, as the Heyrieux plant offered much more generous pensions than had been the case at Trept. On the other hand, the Trept plant had more comprehensive life and medical insurance coverage. The union leaders urged Bula to standardize on the most generous benefit at each plant.

Word of the negotiations soon spread to workers and middle managers at the other four French plants. Bula came under severe pressure from his employees to "treat us all equally and fairly", as an employee in the Roanne microscope plant wrote to him.

Rationalizing salaries and fringe benefits would prove both difficult and expensive Bula realized. Yet he felt that this was going to be necessary if the French group was going to take on a character of its own. He needed to have executives he could transfer from one plant to the other or bring to the new headquarters office he was planning to establish in Lyons. He also realized that from a central administrative point of view, it would be simpler if all plants offered similar fringe benefits and if wages were standardized as much as possible.

When he computed the cost he was stunned to discover that just standardizing fringe benefits at the highest existing level would boost employment costs by 31%. Bula, reacting both to internal pressure and to his own belief in fair play, had gone to group headquarters with a revised proposal on wage costs. If he made the generous adjustments on fringe benefits, he believed he could hold the pay increase to between 5% and 7%. The French operation would probably lose money in fiscal 1977 and possibly break even the following year. However, he argued that efficiencies and improved morale resulting from such a move would enhance its long-term future.

At the end of the day the chairman told him that at the time his budget was approved the directors had felt that a 20% increase in wages was on the high side. They felt now that they must hold him to that commitment.

As Bula studied the half-finished extension to the Heyrieux plant he regretted that it was too late to cancel everything. But with the workers now assuming a threatening stance on achieving parity, and pressure from the parent company to keep the supply of frames flowing, he wondered what he should do.

DECISION

Tell staff their pay and benefits depend on profitability

Bula's own adamant attitude precipitated the dilemma. Bula neglected to find out what the company actually wanted to achieve with its compensation money and apparently what *he* wanted to accomplish was vague.

Moreover, Bula adopted a fixed position – equal treatment for everybody – without having gathered enough facts. He should have thoroughly analysed the workforces at the six French plants to pinpoint differences in age, seniority, wage and salary structures, benefit programmes and union attitudes. He also failed to take into account local labour market conditions and local competitive practices.

Excelsior Optical's apparently haphazard approach to its expansion programme in France is perhaps explained by the distance of the board of directors. After all, the French firms were acquired in the mid-1960s. It took some ten years for the parent company to move toward co-ordinating them. Another two years passed before Bula recognized the need for human resources management as part of his effort to mould the French facilities into a relatively homogeneous group. It was only after the decision had already been made to expand the Heyrieux plant that Bula plunged into compensation matters. He should have identified any wage, salary and benefit problems beforehand, later incorporating proposed solutions in his budget presentation.

Bula's insistence on full harmonization of pay and benefits is unthinkable. Executive mobility can be attained without it. In any case executive transfers often prove too costly to be utilized frequently. Bula could have even administered executives as a separate group.

Ideally, employees filling a given job category at a given plant should be treated identically. But in the absence of a policy directive from Switzerland that he do so, Bula need not strive to be uniform *nationally*. He can offer uniformity as a long-term corporate objective, if that is absolutely necessary, to gain the time he needs to end the unrest.

Draw up a plan

The plant at Heyrieux has top priority. To keep its production line running and win support at the other factories, Bula should immediately take the following steps, working within the 20% increment that has been budgeted for higher labour costs:

● Assure all employees in France that the company will evaluate their compensation programmes; that it will work towards identifying the components of compensation that can be equalized and will lay down guidelines for attaining equalization – including profitability and productivity goals for each plant.

● Develop a pay plan for the employees at the Heyrieux plant that equalizes the pay plan of those who were transferred from Trept. A study of competitive practices in and around Heyrieux could avoid standardizing on the most generous benefits. Instead compromises could be suggested – such as limiting the six-week holiday to those with at least a year's service at Heyrieux.

● Create reserves against the unavoidable redundancy payments at Trept and against the company's increased liability resulting from pay rises under the statutory social security system. The impact of higher wages and salaries on the scope and cost of company-sponsored benefit programmes should also be measured.

Bula should also plan to do the following:

● Undertake an in-depth audit of all existing remuneration programmes and practices at each of the six French factories.

● Review the statutory, union and labour market influences.

● Develop clear-cut philosophies and objectives for total remuneration in France, based on the information assembled. The "umbrella" remuneration objectives must also be adaptable to industries that range from stamping out eyeglass frames at Heyrieux to microscope manufacturing in Roanne.

● Develop specific programmes for each of the plants, taking into account all applicable factors. Probably the changes will have to be implemented on a programmed basis over a period of years. And in all likelihood, the compensation programmes at the various plants should reflect, in part, profitability considerations.

● Communicate to employees that their pay and benefits relate to profit levels and that employees can help profits grow.

This decision was provided by Quentin I. Smith Jr. in his capacity as president of Towers, Perrin, Forster & Crosby, management consultants specializing in employee benefits and executive compensation, headquartered in New York.

Should MD exempt his one profitable division from staff cuts?

Ronald Edgerton, head of Royal Machine Works Ltd.'s valve division, tore open the confidential memorandum.

The memo explained that failure to have expenses in line with declining revenues had caused the company to record a loss in the first half of the year. Therefore, it would be necessary to impose stringent controls on expenditure, especially in the personnel field, during the second half. By the following Friday the division heads were to reduce staff by 10% from the level on June 30. A list of those to be made redundant must be on the managing director's desk by next Friday. A total ban was imposed on new or temporary hiring and salary increases. Even promotions would not carry any rises for the next six months, although the company hoped to make "appropriate adjustments as soon as there is a return to reasonable profitability".

Before he had completed reading the memo Edgerton was on his way to see Stanley Packard, the managing director. "Surely this does not apply to my division," he said as he was ushered into Packard's office.

"I'm afraid it does," Packard replied. "If I exempt you from these economy measures, then everyone will want to be a special case. That was the problem two months ago when we told everybody to bring spending into line with revenues. It simply didn't work.

Exempt the special case

"Everyone had an excuse for why their predicted revenues did not materialize. That is why I decided on prescribing action that is certain to reduce our expenditures."

"My division's sales are 5% ahead of budget and our profits are on target," Edgerton argued. "In addition, we have a very strong order book and the new butterfly valve we have introduced is selling extremely well. We really need to expand both our sales force and our production capacity if we are to be able to capitalize on the strong demand for this new product."

Packard responded: "It is up to you which 10% of the labour force you cut. You can sack secretaries and research people, but you must comply with the directive. As you know we have a major bank loan to re-finance at the end of the year. If we are not in a profit position this may be very difficult. Every division must contribute to that goal, no matter how painful it may be."

"But as long as we can meet our profit and sales forecast, which I assure you we can do, we should be exempt from cutbacks," Edgerton persisted.

Packard replied, "I admit you have a good record behind you. But don't you realize that what you are saying is what every manager will say. Everyone will promise me that he will hit targets if I will spare him from this cutback."

Edgerton stood up. "But you know what I am telling you is the truth," he said. "Ever since I have been with this company I have met or exceeded my targets. My division is the biggest profit contributor in the company. Some of the other divisions have been losing money for two or three years now. I can see the logic of making them adhere to these cutbacks. But surely it is madness to penalize a prosperous division to subsidize money-losing ones. If they are making the loss, let them take the cut, this would seem fair.

Taking a firm stance

"If your division were left untouched even more drastic cuts would have to be made in other divisions," Packard replied. "It is they who most need more money to survive. We're all part of the same group after all. You must realize that although the valve division is profitable now, it required resources from others in the group to set it up. I don't mind saying we deferred a lot of other divisions' proposals in order to establish ourselves in the valve industry."

"Nevertheless, your cutbacks would wreck my division. So don't expect a list from me on your desk. I don't intend to fire anyone. If there are any layoffs in my division they will have to start with me," Edgerton said and strode out.

"That is exactly what I will do," Packard thought. But as he began to consider how he would explain to the board his reasons for sacking the manager of the company's most profitable division, he began to have second thoughts. Perhaps he should simply look the other way if Edgerton did not comply.

DECISION

MD should seek the help of all divisional managers in cutting costs

Stanley Packard's inability, as managing director, to enforce the informal profit improvement measures he proposed two months ago is all too clearly evident. He now finds himself in a desperate situation on three counts. First, the company has made a loss for the half year. Second, it has a major bank loan to re-finance in just six months' time. Third, his ill-conceived memorandum to division heads has led to an open challenge from Ronald Edgerton who is responsible for the company's most profitable unit.

It is easy, of course, to be very critical of Packard. He has adopted an authoritarian, insensitive, edict-issuing style of management. He has been remote, instead of seeking the support of his managers and encouraging them in efforts to cut back costs. He has not involved them in the decision-making processes and policy issues, at a time when involvement, loyalty and teamwork are essential requirements.

Packard must also be criticized for his failure to think through the policy implications of his company's problems. He has not, it seems, examined the nature of his company's financial and operating problems. He has not focused selectively on critical areas, nor on possible opportunities for rationalization within the company. His "solution" of across-the-board staff retrenchments seems certain to create many more problems than it solves.

It is, on the other hand, easy to sympathize with Edgerton. Edgerton is evidently a manager who has obtained good results throughout his time with the company. Moreover, he is immediately prepared to stand up and protect his staff loyally and vigorously.

The unfortunate feature of Edgerton's reaction is that his perspective is parochial rather than company-wide. Unfortunately, difficult times sometimes do require sacrifices, compromises, and some additional economies for the overall good of the company. Yet the reaction is not surprising because evidently Edgerton has not been encouraged to contribute to company-wide policy formulation. This is exactly the sort of experience he needs if his potential for top management is to be developed.

There are more than two choices

There is evidence to suggest that Edgerton's valve division has scope for a better expense budget. Yet the profits are only equalling budget. Normally one would expect any increase in sales to make a proportionally higher contribution to profits. So, even though valve division results are good, there may still be scope for substantial improvement through better expense control.

The most basic question, however, is what should the managing director do now?

Packard seems to believe he is faced with two options. He must either hold fast to his memo and lose Edgerton, or do nothing and let Edgerton have his way. In fact neither of these is desirable and his range of choices is much wider.

The real need is for Packard to make a fresh approach to his company's problems, without being concerned with standing on dignity.

First he must immediately involve the managers in the company's basic policy issues. He must consult with them, and have them genuinely contribute to the decision-making processes. This will enable them to see the issues of short-term financial needs and long-term strategic development in proper perspective. It will encourage them to respond constructively, and to work together as a cohesive team.

Examine each division

Second, the perspective of the cost-reduction exercise must be broadened. The company, after all, has six months before its loan must be renegotiated. Staff cuts might provide short-term though unhappy solutions, but the company has a longer-term management and performance problem. Packard, with his managers, really needs to develop a new strategy so that the company can see the way towards profitable future performance. This is what banks and stockholders are really interested in.

Third, Packard must be prepared to examine each division's situation in depth with the divisional manager. Objectives must be jointly set and a basis agreed for performance evaluation. Different ways of saving costs besides retrenchments need to be considered – for example, inventory savings in finished goods, raw materials or sub-assemblies. Opportunities for product rationalization should also be examined. Packard must obviously abandon his previous policy of treating chronically unprofitable sections of the business in the same way as the most profitable.

This decision was provided by Dr. Brian W. Scott in his capacity as managing director of W.D. Scott & Co. Pty. Ltd., management consultants based in North Sydney, Australia.

Should Flaherty fire his training manager or give him more time to settle down?

Managing director Thomas Flaherty's mind went back to the first time he had heard of the "discovery" courses being put on by his management development manager, Patrick Reilly. The courses were associated with a move to split the company's functions into divisions, which would require rapid development of many managers. "What exactly does this course of yours entail?" Flaherty asked Reilly. Flaherty recalled Reilly's evasive reply followed by an invitation to take part in the course himself.

Flaherty's initial impression of the course had confirmed his doubts. The freedom and lack of structure were at first unnerving. Reilly adopted an extremely non-directive role and for a time nothing seemed to happen. The course was based on the principle of autonomy training. The theory was that by dealing with uncertainty and lack of structure in the course participants would learn to use more initiative in their careers as well.

Once Flaherty and other participants learned how best to use the time and resources available, they found it very exhilarating. Back in his office Flaherty found it much easier to organize his work around the most important tasks. Even his 62-year-old secretary, normally his most ardent critic, commented tartly that he "was not wasting as much time as usual".

It seemed to Flaherty that the managers who had been through it became more responsible, more able to take decisions for themselves.

Varied reactions to the courses

Of course there were problems. Some managers decided that the company did not allow them enough scope for the freedom they had experienced in the course. They left to work in less structured environments. Others went through stages of being very critical of the organization, demanding to be given a greater say in decisions. To counter the ill effects of this, Reilly always tried to make sure that the senior managers at least had a chance to take the course before their subordinates.

Some of the older managers refused to take part in the course. But Flaherty felt all this was a small price to pay for the full expression of other managers' latent capabilities.

Two years later, the divisionalization had been carried out without any serious hitch. Most of the company's managers who had performed best, to help make the new structure work, were those who had reacted favourably to Reilly's discovery courses.

So Flaherty was especially sorry to hear from Reilly that he was leaving to fulfil a long-held ambition to become an independent consultant. However, he accepted Reilly's recommendation to appoint his able young asssistant, Liam Murphy, to succeed him. Reilly did warn Flaherty, however, that Murphy's views were "somewhat more radical" than his own had been.

The first signs that all was not well came just three weeks after Reilly's departure. A new divisional manager who had just been through the course told Flaherty: "Murphy's emphasis seems to be entirely on shaking up the system and destroying the bureaucratic atmosphere. He tends to use terms more in tune with soap-box anarchists than what you would expect in a management course."

Though slightly perturbed, Flaherty said he thought Murphy was referring to the natural tendency towards lethargy in any organization, rather than attacking the company as such.

But within another month, Flaherty learned that three junior managers who had been on the course had resigned. And a number of managers started to complain of the "unsettling" effect the course was having on their subordinates.

Discussing an alarming trend

Flaherty called in Reilly in his new role as external consultant to discuss this alarming new trend. Reilly pointed out that from what he had heard Murphy was doing exactly what he was supposed to. "That is what discovery courses are all about," he asserted. Nevertheless he agreed to talk to the young training manager and try to get him to tone down his behaviour. However, the talks seemed to produce little change in the reactions to the course in the following months.

Now Flaherty wonders whether he should continue to accept Reilly's assessment.

Or should he stop the courses and find Murphy another job, or even fire him. "But it seems such a shame," he tells himself, "when we have benefited so much from this approach in the past. Maybe I should talk to Murphy myself, and give him a deadline by which he must redesign his approach to work *for* the company, not against it."

DECISION

There is a third choice — make sure the training course still benefits the company

The discovery course has obviously been very helpful to the company. Thomas Flaherty was aware in the past that it had an unsettling effect on one or two of the participants who left the company. But he felt it beneficial as it appeared to make them more flexible in their thinking. It made them more open to the suggestions from outside and more willing to accept organizational change than was the case previously.

There are two alternatives which come readily to mind.

Stop the course and get rid of Liam Murphy either by firing him or by giving him another position.

Or keep the course going under Murphy's guidance and ignore all these comments he is getting from line managers.

But neither of these alternatives seems to provide the complete answer.

There is a third, if more radical, alternative, however. That is to retain Patrick Reilly to run the course at normal consultancy fees for a time and to find another job for Murphy if he is felt to be valuable to the company. It is a drastic move, but one that should be taken in these circumstances, despite the extra expense involved.

It is never easy to transfer the skills of one training manger to another.

Certainly each training manager would be different, and this is bound to have some effect on the course.

In this situation the new training manager appears to be extremist, and is even described an an anarchist by a respected manager. There is nothing a company can do to change the personality of the individual, however. The only thing one can do is to modify his behaviour.

Serving the needs of the managers

I believe that Murphy should be given a chance to develop the course with the help of Reilly. This should be possible. Reilly is obviously a very experienced management development manager. He should be able to help in modifying Murphy's behaviour and ensure that the outcome of the course is beneficial to the company. Reilly is the most obvious man to do this. He started the course and he developed it himself.

The course could continue to be run as in the past with both Reilly and Murphy as joint tutors. Reilly can play an important role in helping and guiding Murphy in the right direction. He can indicate, for example, times when Murphy is perhaps bringing his influence to bear on the group too much rather than having the group take care of itself.

If the managing director is really interested in this course, he should personally ensure that it is relevant to the needs of the managers. He should ask what training needs it should satisfy. Then he must determine whether it satisfies these needs.

Bearing in mind that every training course should have a clear intended output that is measurable, an attempt should be made to measure the performance of course participants before and after training to see if it has improved and how.

Bring in outside evaluation

I would suggest that the company call in an academic from a local university who would welcome the opportunity to carry out a study. With questionnaires and personal interviews, the researcher can be asked to determine what benefits and what improvements are being derived directly from this course. The company can then determine whether or not the course is fulfilling its objective.

The survey can be carried out in two parts: before and after participation in the course. This is an easy way of identifying the differences.

This should not be difficult to do where there is sufficient time and with such a well established course as is the situation here.

If, after all this, the course no longer appears to be of any use to the company, either by the line managers or by the managing director, it should be stopped.

This decision was provided by Denis Ryan in his capacity as director of Iford International Institute, a London-based management training consultancy. He was formerly head of managing training services at the British Institute of Management.

How should company restructure its purchasing function?

"I thought I should bring this to your immediate attention," the financial director Lucio Gavello said as he pushed the chart across to Mario Pagano, the managing director.

The graph showed a discrepancy of more than $1,200,000 between the budget figures and the actual expenditure on supplies for the previous three months.

"How did we get into this situation?" Pagano quietly murmured to himself. "It just cannot be a matter of price increases." Then, looking up at Gavello, he demanded: "Why wasn't I told of this before?"

"But you get reports on expenditure from central purchasing and each of the six purchasing departments every month," Gavello replied.

The managing director had to admit that he had noted increases in the monthly reports. At the time the increase had not appeared to be significant. There was no doubt, however, that the total figures in front of him were substantial enough.

"They are obviously not following company policy to keep stocks as low as possible," he exclaimed. Pagano called in his personal assistant and dictated a terse note to all purchasing managers to hold any further purchases until inventories had been reduced by 10%.

Within a few hours the manufacturing director, Giorgio Fabbri, was told by one of the purchasing managers of the managing director's order. Fabbri gasped in disbelief.

"But I deliberately ordered an increase in purchases because of the uncertain materials situation," Fabbri moaned. The purchasing officer nodded his agreement. He had been topping up purchase orders for the same reason.

Cut down on inventory

Fabbri arranged to meet the managing director that afternoon. "We cannot start cutting down on inventory," he told him. "Materials are getting scarce. It is worth investing money in stocks and making sure we have enough to keep the production lines moving. If we start decreasing the stock levels, there is a risk we won't be able to meet delivery dates of customers' orders. We might even lose orders. What is the cost of holding inventory compared to the risk of production stoppage?"

"But what is the benefit of maintaining production if we go bankrupt?" replied the managing director. He called in Gavello to support his view.

"The company simply could not afford to continue to maintain increasing stocks," Gavello carefully explained. "Fabbri's position may have been all right when bank interest was low," he said.

"It isn't just the cost of holding stock or that the money could be better invested," he pointed out. The fact was that the company had already increased its short term borrowing by $1,000,000 to cover inventory and was paying 15.5% interest charges. Further, the added inventory could not be put in existing storage facilities. More space was required and double handling charges of over $100,000 a year were being incurred.

"And have you considered price increases," Fabbri retorted. "If we do not buy materials now we will have to pay more in the future."

The two men started a bitter exchange. Finally Fabbri blurted out: "Lucio, you are just making trouble for me because you want the purchasing departments put back under your control."

Gavello angrily responded: "Well, at least then we would have someone who understands what all this hoarding does to our liquidity."

Later, as he thought the situation through, Pagano felt he was facing two distinct problems. As a short-term measure he had to decide whether to rescind or modify his order to reduce inventories by 10% across the board. Or perhaps he should even give Fabbri an overall objective and leave the mechanics of the cutback to him. But he doubted that Fabbri could actually bring about a reduction, considering his strong feelings about increasing stocks. This brought Pagano to his second line of thought. Perhaps the real long-term solution would be to return the control of purchasing and stocks to the financial director.

He knew that from a purely operational point manufacturing operations had become smoother and more efficient since the purchasing function was put under Fabbri's control. But he felt that with the company facing a critical cash flow position and interest rates at record levels it would be worth some production delays and communications breakdowns to have someone in charge who understood the real costs of inventory accumulation.

DECISION

Company must recognize that logistics are as important as anything else

Manufacturing director Giorgio Fabbri's reasons for buying ahead are valid. So are his comments on the possible impact on production of the managing director's order to hold any further purchases.

However, Fabbri and the purchasing managers evidently did not foresee the results of their decisions accurately. A man in Fabbri's position should have the knowledge, competence and authority to balance the cost of forward buying against the risk of production stoppages and possible price increases. Here the actions of managing director Mario Pagano indicate that this was not the case. When Pagano contemplates the possibility of putting the control of purchasing and inventories back under Lucio Gavello, he is seeking to achieve the right balance between financial and operational considerations by re-emphasizing the financial implications of purchases and stocks.

Raising some questions

There are many questions raised. Why did Fabbri have the authority to exceed the budget by what became an excessive amount? Was this amount an accumulation of excess purchases to all the purchasing managers? The answer is probably yes. Was there some way each could have anticipated that his actions would collectively lead to this discrepancy from budget? Probably not.

What is needed is a better operational reporting and control system for purchasing, reflecting Pagano's objectives. This could have prevented the problem from arising in the first place. Accounting systems are often inadequate for operational control because the financial reports are received too long after decisions are taken.

Given that the problem did arise, however, we question the management style of Pagano. A direct and unilateral order to the purchasing managers, bypassing Fabbri, is certain to produce a negative reaction. Fabbri was the last to know of Pagano's concern when he should have been the first.

At least Pagano's order did flush out these points. Certain decisions to commit his resources were being taken in a manner with which he did not agree. But knowledge of these decisions did not reach him in time to prevent the situation getting out of hand.

To utilize the talents of his executives properly and maintain their full cooperation I suggest that Pagano rescind his order. While this is a hard demand it has many merits.

Pagano should then meet with his manufacturing director and the purchasing managers to set and define their real objective. This could be: to reduce purchased stocks by 10% within, say, 90 days. Pagano should then request a realistic action plan to achieve this reduction, which he can monitor, week by week.

Lacking effective results, he can still reduce purchases gradually, without eliminating them. This allows the manufacturing director to avoid production changes, buying the critical items while reducing the present stock of the less critical items. Discussion of the excess inventory will lead to the consideration of other possible actions, such as the immediate sale of slow-moving or obsolete items.

Develop a planning and reporting system

For the time being Pagano should probably continue with his present organization structure. However, he should plan to appoint a central logistics director reporting directly to him. Pagano seemed to see the growing importance of purchasing and inventory control as an integral part of his physical operations when he placed these functions under manufacturing. But many companies find that even this step is not enough. New departments are being created to handle all the logistical functions of a business: purchasing, inventory control, production planning and distribution. All of these, including the purchasing managers, would report to the logistics director, at least functionally.

Pagano did not go far enough in his first management step. A clearer definition of Fabbri's responsibilities and authorities and better reporting are needed to help the purchasing managers make better decisions and avoid the cash crisis.

In the long term he should solicit the cooperation of Gavello, the financial director, and develop a planning and reporting system tied directly to operations.

The real solution to Pagano's problem, however, is to recognize that the logistical function must take its position alongside marketing and manufacturing as an equal.

Only in this way can he expect to obtain as well as retain the proper quality of staff and effective communications.

This decision was provided by Roger R. Crane in his capacity as managing director, Management Services, Science Management International Europe, a Paris-based management consultancy.

What is the key to open the door to improved production?

Charles Robinson turns impatiently away from his office window. The sight of earth-moving equipment clearing the ground for a new plant extension is an unpleasant reminder that he must soon make the most difficult decision he has faced as managing director of Moorfield Microscopes.

Last year the company decided to expand its only factory by 100% to meet rising demand. As plans to build the extension were proceeding, personnel director Peter Brown decided that before devising a recruiting campaign for new workers he should analyse the present workforce.

Until recently most employees were older married women who had joined the company 25 to 30 years ago. As they retired, their places were being taken by young girls just out of school. The girls learned the semi-skilled assembly work quickly. Each girl would repetitively perform one operation. The assemblies would pile up in an out-bin, to be gathered and carried to the worker who performed the next step.

After a month or two on the job, the young girls' performance began to drop. Nearly half the girls were quitting during their first year.

Brown brought these facts to Robinson's attention. The personnel director maintained productivity was low because the workers lacked proper motivation; they were bored by the limited scope of the repetitive work. Brown suggested using behavioural science consultants to find ways of making the work more satisfying to the firm's employees.

Changing the production methods

Robinson agreed and immediately went to production director Alan Smith to explain the situation. He stressed that the experiment, if successful, would benefit the production department and Smith himself. Smith listened stoically. He then told Robinson that he had grave personal doubts that "a couple of outsiders can come in and solve our problems in a few days".

However, when the consultants arrived Smith was friendly and cooperative. After three weeks' study the consultants suggested breaking up the production line arrangement and assigning teams of seven women to build the complete microscope from the components. Each member of the team would be trained to do a variety of tasks, and the team would be responsible for the finished product, which would then be inspected and packed.

When he heard the proposals, Smith stormed: "You don't really expect to increase productivity by increasing the complexity of the tasks to be performed!" He then produced his own plan. The jobs should be simpler, not more difficult, he contended. The new building should incorporate more automated equipment, such as a conveyor belt on the assembly line. Total employment could be reduced, and the $1-million additional investment required would be recovered within two years.

He said Brown had performed a real service in identifying the change in the workforce. Youngsters lacked the solid responsibility of the older generation. For this reason, more supervision, rather than less, was needed. Two new quality inspectors should be hired and a record kept of the individuals responsible for rejected units.

Robinson decided to experiment with the work team scheme for three months on one of the main product lines. After a drop in the first month, output per employee rose. The incidence of faults dropped. Employees were enthusiastic.

Robinson announced the entire factory would be converted immediately to the new concept and the extension designed to accommodate it. Smith insisted that the girls' performance improved only because everyone was watching the experiment so closely. He asked Robinson to delay construction until further results were in. Robinson replied: "We have to get that plant started. But we don't have to finalize the interior design for another three months. We can change things right up to the time the foundation is laid, if necessary."

Still a drop in output

Now just as the foundations were to be laid the second three months' figures came in. The productivity gains on the original line had been wiped out, although quality remained up. The second product line showed slight improvements in output per employee, with lower fault rate and less labour turnover. But the product line accounting for the biggest-selling microscope showed a worrying 20% drop in output from the previous quarter. There was no change in the percentage of faults.

Smith was urging an emergency session with the contractors to change the plans. The automated production line would cost 50% less if it were put in as the building went up. Brown insists the hitches are temporary and urges Robinson to stick to the original plan.

DECISION

Only a survey will give the answer, but the odds favour teamwork

Managers will easily sympathize with Robinson who finds himself confronted with little time and little data with which to make a decision. He has to choose between an expedient, traditional approach to containing a problem of declining performance and a wholly contradictory approach which offers a real long-term solution, although it involves greater risks of failure.

Increased inspection should limit the number of faults in microscopes received by the customer but probably won't reduce the number of mistakes made during assembly. Increased supervision should halt the decline in productivity. But it alone isn't likely to improve productivity over normal performance. The possibility of few numbers employed, and the advantageous price if automated equipment is installed at the outset, are persuasive arguments.

But what is the cost of "making good" faulty work and what will be the cost of two extra inspectors? What will be the cost of increased supervision? More importantly, what are the real costs of labour turnover, especially when it approaches 50% for those employed less than one year? This normally means that the company will not have had time to get a significant return on its investment in these employees. These are some of the questions Robinson will have to answer before he can judge the long-term viability of Smith's solution to the problem.

On the other hand, Robinson must be wondering if the trials of Brown's solution to the problem were carried on long enough to permit adequate assessment. It is usual for performance to decline for a period after jobs have been restructured until the new methods have settled and people are more certain of management intent. This is even more likely to be true if the changes involve large numbers of people, as is likely to be the case on the line assembling the biggest-selling microscope.

Similarly, he must wonder if Smith's argument that the initial gains in the original pilot area might only be the result of "everyone watching the experiment so closely" is indeed a valid one. The fact that people are likely to behave differently when part of an experiment does provide a plausible explanation.

Robinson must also be asking himself if the changes went far enough for individuals and teams to derive long-term interest and a continuing sense of achievement from what they did. The altered jobs would be more complex and any individual would be likely to do a variety of tasks. But it is not clear whether the teams had the discretion to organize and distribute the work in a way which best suited their own needs and their skills and interests.

The teams might also have realized that they were not really being "held responsible for the finished product", but merely accountable, since final inspection continued to be carried out by someone else. Therein lies the difference between a responsible job and one which is simply more interesting.

Initial gains not sustained

Robinson should also ask if appropriate changes had been made in the company's information and control systems so that the teams had all of the information necessary to do their job most effectively.

In short, did the teams have sufficient authority, discretion, and information with which to manage the task at hand effectively in a responsible and satisfactory way? Also, how much real support did the trials have while being carried out under the auspices of a man with a vested interest in their failure?

Robinson should now attempt to find out from the teams themselves where the trials have fallen short, and why the initial gains have not been sustained. Ideally, he should invite all of the employees involved and their supervisors to fill out a simple opinion survey, covering the main features of the change. He should invite their comments on what else might have been done.

The results of the survey and the performance data could then be discussed with employees and supervisors to determine how employees would feel about carrying on or reverting to traditional methods. This information, coupled with adequate costings of Smith's solution, would at least put Robinson in the position of converting a gamble into a calculated risk.

If my hunch is right, Robinson will find that the long-term advantage lies in building on the team-based approach to assembly inspection.

This decision was provided by Dr. W.J. Paul in his capacity as a director of North Paul & Associates Ltd., a London management consultancy firm.

Should managers follow intuition or heed computer warnings?

With family backing and his own inheritance, Miles Foster formed Meridor in 1951 to make perambulators and folding pushchairs. By 1960 it had acquired a 5% share of the $25-million annual market, dominated by three larger firms. Foster started making nursery tableware and other plastic nursery products.

By 1964, he had been joined on the board by his eldest son, Gordon, an engineer, and his son-in-law Ewart Pascoe, an accountant. His second son, Clifford, was an industrial designer, but not with Meridor. Miles Foster was a happy man, with record pre-tax profits in 1964.

In 1965 the birth rate fell. This fact passed unnoticed by Meridor directors until tableware sales fell in 1968 and pram sales in 1969. Meridor had to face a surplus of production capacity which showed no sign of diminishing. Pascoe tried to calculate the effects on the company of a continued drop in the birth rate. He quickly realized that the clerical work was too lengthy and error-prone, no matter how good his basic assumptions.

Foster was intrigued when Pascoe suggested Meridor should commission a small computer model. This would enable the directors to examine the effects on their business of external trends and of their own policy decisions. The board agreed and consultants started work on the model.

As they discussed the business with the sales directors and the rest of the board, Foster noted that several articles of faith in the company were being seriously questioned. He welcomed this stimulus.

Discovering a useful tool

An arrangement was made to use the model on a "conversational" terminal at the offices of a nearby large company. The model was an undoubted success. It was almost too successful at first in that the directors credited the model with the power to forecast future sales and production costs. It took Pascoe some months to persuade them that it only displayed the consequences of the directors' forecasts about individual aspects of the business. It then became a useful planning tool.

Before the model was completed, the sales decline had eased. The trouble was caused by a change in buying habits more than the declining birth rate. The model confirmed the wisdom of Meridor's switch to putting more emphasis to selling "carrycots," instead of traditional prams. It also helped improve pricing policy.

Meridor was also able to give more weight to the subtleties of the market place, such as the different buying patterns of different social groups and the effect of the small space available for prams in modern houses. Several merely marginally profitable lines were identified and eliminated.

Meridor directors, Foster noted, had become more sophisticated in their whole approach to the future. They now looked at such factors as the trend to early marriage, contraceptive methods, abortion law reforms and fertility drugs. Indeed, Foster felt the model raised as many questions as it answered.

In December 1970 Clifford Foster, still working outside the family company, came up with a revolutionary new design for a pram. It used plastic to solve some stability problems and seemed to offer just the departure from the traditional pram concept that Meridor sought in order to draw ahead of its competitors.

While the directors eagerly awaited the prototype, Pascoe used the model to work out a suitable selling price. To his dismay, the model came up with a profitability forecast which was unacceptable unless Meridor could keep the gross margin low and expand sales to make great inroads into competitors' market shares. An advance in market share was Meridor's aim, but the extent of the production and sales expansion the model indicated brought gasps from Foster and the other directors.

The model's predictions were treated with great scepticism by all except Pascoe, and stalemate ensued for several months. Eventually a new twist came from a surprising quarter.

At a family lunch one Sunday, Clifford's wife Rachel suddenly blurted out that anyone with a grain of sense would have set up a chain of day nurseries on a commercial basis. This would meet an obvious social need and provide a substantial market for all the proven profitable lines in nurseryware, although it would not help prams.

Acting on a whim, Pascoe worked out the figures after he had adapted the model to handle them. He soon found that the model was predicting success for such a move. When Miles Foster heard these, he was thoroughly perplexed. First the model said that the obviously promising new product would need an incredible sales and production volume to succeed. Now it was highlighting profits to be made through this seemingly whimsical scheme to expand markets for the nurseryware products. Which should he back?

DECISION

Business problems cannot be solved by a computer

Faced with Miles Foster's situation, it is clear that he should take a mental step back from his business and decide where he really wants to go.

Meridor has developed a successful share of an important market. But it is still a relatively small firm, and it presumably is at a severe disadvantage to its giant competitors in advertising and distribution. Therefore, it seems likely that either the new pram or the day nurseries could severely strain the resources of the small company. This would mean that failure of the project could mean failure for the firm.

Before assigning such an important decision to a computer model, Foster should consider whether a computer model, or any other technique, can really be applied to resolve all business problems. Second, he should remember that a model is only as good as the input data which management selects for it.

88

So far the model devised for Meridor has made the Fosters think more deeply about the external circumstances which affect their market. This is a proper use of the model. But earlier they allowed the model to lead them into the trap of tying their forecasts too closely to the birth rate. More important, of course, was the change in the buying habits of young parents, which was observed in the marketplace.

This should be a lesson learned. Can Miles Foster really be sure his son-in-law's model is competent to even seriously consider the success of the day nurseries? In fact, it is doubtful a model could ever predict the success of such a novel idea. Most models rely heavily on regression techiques, or a study of the past to predict the future. In this case there is virtually no past.

Cutting costs if possible
Foster has been seduced into believing the model can reduce the required informational input in the decision-making process. Based on this erroneous assumption, he is on the brink of a premature and possibly disastrous decision. More information is needed in both cases.

Certainly Clifford Foster's revolutionary new pram should be studied further. The model can be used on a "what if?" basis to isolate areas in which a modification would have the greatest impact on reducing break-even costs. For example, the model may reveal that the main reason Meridor must obtain such a large market share is to recover the investment costs for expensive dies and moulds needed to make the plastic parts. The firm could possibly seek an outside supplier willing to share the investment risk in return for potential large volume business. Or an attempt could be made to simplify Clifford's design. After all, it was a spare-time effort.

Even if costs can be reduced, a limited number of the new prams should be tested in the market place. Only when as many factors as possible have been collected should a final decision be taken to proceed with mass production. Even then, Meridor should never put all its eggs in one basket. The failure rate of new products, despite all the management aids available, is too high to take such a risk.

Establishing new outlets
On the question of day nurseries, the idea again has merit. Ordinary costing techniques will soon show what is involved in start-up and running costs. The company should then again undertake extensive market tests to see whether people will really pay the fees required. This research should also determine whether the nurseries would really absorb enough output of nursery products.

Meridor should also remember that by establishing its own outlets it may seriously impair its ability to sell through the company's existing retail outlets. This could also adversely affect its pram sales. Again, Meridor should open one or two nurseries to test response before committing itself deeply to this project.

Once a more firmly grounded estimate of the marketability of the two projects is available, then the computer can be used to estimate which will return the greater benefits to the company.

This decision was provided by David Diehl in his capacity as managing director of management consultants Diehl, Golightly & Co., London and New York.

How should CEO rationalize his company's research and development?

"**I**s that the final survey, Hermann?" Rudolf Grossmann asked his marketing director, Hermann Goldring. It was. As soon as Grossmann read it he knew that a decision on the company's future policy could no longer be delayed.

Grossmann had become chairman and chief executive of Swiss transmission manufacturer Johannes Pökel SA a few months previously.

Two years before his appointment Pökel had recognized that as the European car market became saturated the opportunities for growth in its long-established business of car transmission production were becoming limited. Moreover, as competition became more intense, profit margins declined.

Pökel's board had decided to enter another area of technology. Under the guidance of Grossmann's predecessor it had enlarged its research and development (R&D) facilities several times and started developing a transmission unit for electric cars.

The unit was intended to overcome one of the major problems of electric vehicles, the fact that they cannot as yet carry enough power to propel them at high speeds for long periods. It was designed to convert electric current into kinetic energy and recapture some of that energy through a system of magnetic fields.

The company was so pleased with the initial success of its development efforts that, despite the fact that it was dangerously close to going into debt, it began to look for other research projects where it might make a breakthrough.

It toyed with designs for car engine computerization, a radar device for preventing collisions and a method of projecting speed and other essential information on to the windscreen.

The R&D facility grew accordingly, sucking in ever more funds and becoming the major hope for success of the board and senior management. Only Goldring had voiced disquiet at the proportion of funds being diverted from developing the company's basic transmission product into new areas with an uncertain future.

Research survey reveals flaws
Even when the electric car transmission system ran into difficulties under road tests no one was seriously worried. The problem was one of materials technology. It was felt that it could be solved with more research.

Finally, even when some members of the board had begun to be aware that the company was spending heavily in an effort to avoid losses, Grossmann had been given no definite brief to cut back on R&D when he replaced the previous chief executive. He had been invited in to look around and make his recommendations.

First, he had commissioned a survey of the potential markets for all the projects on the R&D drawing boards. The results of the survey had now been placed on his desk.

The report made it obvious that the company's original estimate of the timing of future demand for the electric car was unrealistic. In addition, there was now serious doubt whether electric vehicles would ever make a real impact on the market. Other technologies, such as hydrogen power, showed rather more promise.

Resources spread too thin
Second, Grossmann, in opposition to Pökel's brilliant but often over-optimistic director of research, had instituted an outside technical audit of R&D. This had concluded that Pökel had so many projects on hand that it had spread its resources far too thinly. Quite apart from marketing considerations, the prospect of success in any one of them was doubtful.

Grossmann felt that in one sense he had no choice. He had to rationalize R&D. He had to cut back on the speculative projects and concentrate on one or two. But he had a very difficult choice.

Because it had starved the transmission business of development funds, Pökel had already fallen behind competitors in the constant minor improvements that make one transmission system sell better than its rivals. If Grossmann switched most or all of the development money back into transmissions the company would still find it difficult to catch up. It would also have lost the opportunity of a breakthrough into a more profitable new product line. At best it would be back where it started.

If, however, he invested more money in one of the speculative ventures, which should it be? Should he choose the one with the most obvious market potential, even if it had major technical problems, or the one where the technical problems seemed the easiest and least costly to solve?

DECISION

New products and established markets should take priority

Grossmann must make himself personally responsible for new product strategy. It is surprising how often this particular management function, which is the key to the survival of any manufacturing company, is delegated by chief executives.

Johannes Pökel SA has made the classic mistake of accepting product concepts based on exciting or interesting technology but relying only on intuitive judgments of the size and shape of the potential market. The result has been a cash crisis.

The consequences could be disastrous, however, if Pökel released finance in the medium-term by cutting back the R&D department.

Grossmann must set about developing a new approach to product development and marketing. He can then present this to the shareholders and the appropriate banks as a basis for obtaining both the short-term and long-term financing that Pökel needs.

Establish a product development matrix
The objective should be to capitalize upon the established strengths of the company in the car transmission manufacturing field. And a new product strategy, optimizing those strengths, should be included. With a clear policy, a good new product strategy and an excellent track record,

Grossmann will find that the funds needed at Pökel will be provided.

But the company must also abandon its old hierarchical structure. Modern product development covers a continuous spectrum of various specialities. Products cannot be designed effectively in a "pigeon-hole" called R&D alongside other pigeon-holes with different labels. They reduce communication, raise barriers and can diminish the probability of successful product development.

Grossmann should establish a product development matrix in which departments such as R&D, production engineering, industrial design, manufacturing, engineering and marketing cease to be empires in their own right and become resource banks.

For example, the R&D department could reorganize itself into a matrix oriented towards technology, science or engineering with the specialists in electronics, chemistry, materials and other fields grouped separately.

Each group would have its own manager charged with the responsibility for maintaining the highest possible standards in his particular discipline consistent with a commercial organization. The specialist group manager would also be responsible for allocating optimum resources to the product development team.

This team would be headed by the product manager, the man who must make the hundreds of decisions, compromises and even guesses which characterize new product development in today's industry.

As a project evolves, the team will change in character from being at first dominated by technical specialists to a later domination by manufacturing experts.

Under this system, Pökel would have a flexible product development organization. But it would still have no products. It is a common fallacy to assume that the only action necessary to stimulate innovation is to put a group of people into a room and wait for ideas to come pouring out. They may well do so. But they will be ideas with little chance of paying off.

Grossmann should set up small new product groups, chaired by himself, to meet weekly and review existing projects, assess and decide upon new product developments, and consider new product concepts arising from outside the company's own laboratories.

A programme such as this could have a significant impact on Pökel's existing new product development.

For example, the microcomputer technology developed for the anti-collision radar might be applied to existing automatic transmissions to provide improved fuel efficiency through better gear changing. Almost no modification would be needed to the transmission design and this development could prove a quick short-term solution to preserving Pökel's existing transmission markets.

The energy storage package the company has been developing might be licensed for uses other than electric cars: The unit could be useful in meeting electrical energy storage problems in remote rural areas. Pökel could license its use to a company specializing in the supply of agricultural equipment. The down payment on the licence would also help to improve Pökel's immediate cash problem.

This decision was provided by Dr. Gordon Edge in his capacity as a director of Patscentre International, part of U.K.-based PA management consultancy.

Should family owners get further into debt to save ailing firm?

As a major shareholder as well as managing director of the company, Russi Bilinrosia had to act fast. His production manager, Santosh Mukerjia had just reported to him that the stock room was unable to provide essential components to the sub-assembly lines. Production would come to a complete stop before the end of the day unless further supplies were obtained.

The trouble was that there was little Bilinrosia could do about it. The company just did not have the necessary cash to obtain further supplies.

The medium-sized, family-owned, firm manufactured small domestic electrical appliances. And while sales were not rising, they were stable. Retailers were slow in making payments, however. The company had tried to put pressure on them, but it had to tread cautiously. The company depended heavily on the retailers who were having financial difficulties of their own.

As a consequence Bilinrosia was forced to slow down payments to the firm's own suppliers. The result was that suppliers began to give low priority to the company's orders. Deliveries became erratic, causing immense problems on the assembly lines.

As part of a general reorganization Bilinrosia, about a year before, appointed Raj Gupta, a young, dynamic, administrative assistant, as head of purchasing and stock control, reporting directly to him. Together with the production manager, he established new stock levels and new sources of supply.

Several times Gupta complained to Bilinrosia that key suppliers were complaining of poor payments. He personally brought letters of complaint to the accounts department where he was met with complete indifference, he told Bilinrosia. Suppliers began to insist on cash with orders. Order quantities were reduced, requiring more frequent deliveries. Gupta repeatedly warned Bilinrosia that foremen down the line were complaining that production was being held up because of shortages of supplies.

For this reason, Gupta reacted bitterly when he was called in by Bilinrosia to explain why he had allowed the stock levels to fall so low. "I told you from the beginning," Gupta told his superior, "that I could do nothing unless the invoices from suppliers were paid promptly. I have done all that you can reasonably expect of me. The problem lies with the accounts department. It is their responsibility, not mine."

Consider closing down

Bilinrosia retorted that it was his responsibility to manage within the economic constraints placed on him by the company.

"I do not care who is to blame," Mukerjia interrupted. "As production manager, I am more concerned about keeping the production lines moving. What do you expect me to do? Shall I send everyone home until further notice?"

Bilinrosia hated to send employees home. Everyone in the community would then know the company's plight. It would be the first step towards total closure.

His first instinct was to find a way to borrow more money to keep the plant going. His own bank had refused to advance him a further loan. So he would probably have to go to private lenders who had already assured him the necessary money would be available, though at very high interest rates.

Another alternative was to telephone the suppliers personally to seek further credit. He had failed in the past. But the general market situation was now improving, and there were signs that sales would pick up over the next 12 months. Although suppliers had to be strict about insisting on payments, they surely would not wish to see the company go bankrupt, especially as the company brought a lot of business their way.

The only other alternative, Bilinrosia felt, was to close down the whole enterprise once and for all. This was not the first time Bilinrosia had thought of doing so. The family had already invested more heavily in the business than it had ever intended. The small return on capital, less than 7% last year, hardly seemed worth all the effort and agony involved. The family could earn more by investing elsewhere.

The Bilinrosia family had refrained from taking this course before because it felt a heavy responsibility as the sole major employer in the area. If the company closed, it would mean having to lay off nearly 700 people, which would have disastrous repercussions on the community. On the other hand, Bilinrosia also felt a duty to protect the family's financial interests. If he continued to allow the family's stake in the business to be frittered away, he could not see that anyone would have reason to thank him; the situation was serious.

DECISION

Tell staff and employees the truth — and make an action plan

This company is very close to business failure. It also has little freedom of action, due mainly to the shortage of cash and an obvious lack of good management.

That the company is still able to earn 7% return on capital suggests that the failure of the company is associated with its internal weaknesses, rather than the lack of potential in the external environment.

I do not believe that the problems of this company can really be cured by borrowing more money. This does nothing to solve the real problem. On the other hand, I do not recommend that the plant be closed when there are signs of sales improvements over the next 12 months. I think Bilinrosia should try to eliminate the cause of the organizational ills and only if these actions fail should he then consider shutting down the plant.

The first thing to do is to establish immediately an action plan, both for the short term and the long term.

The short term must be concerned with improving the company's cash levels, while the long term must focus on continuous profitability. I would not recommend borrowing money from private lenders at exorbitant interest rates. I suggest an analysis be conducted of the amounts due to suppliers and the duration of the respective outstanding periods. A similar analysis should be carried out for retailers. These two analyses would enable the company to prepare a realistic cash flow budget, assuming full production.

Bilinrosia should then personally visit the major suppliers and present an honest explanation of the state of the company and explain the newly constructed cash budget. He should then try to arrange for a deferment of present payments and the provision of further supplies.

He should also visit major debtors, particularly those with the greatest potential for making payments, and try to obtain cash. He might offer a cash discount on payments within ten days as a one-time exercise. Special letters should be sent by Bilinrosia to those suppliers and retailers he is unable to visit.

He could consider handing over the debts to an outside debt collecting agency, but this is an expensive exercise.

I think it is also essential for the company to involve employees and commit them to a short-term cost-saving programme. The company could introduce short-term working, for example, to allow stocks to accumulate. Employees might be asked to defer part of their wages and salaries until the crisis is over.

The bank could also be approached with a clear explanation of the company's plans and cash forecasts.

As it is a major employer, the company should try to obtain funds from a government agency which might exist to help rescue such firms in difficulties.

The most likely solution may well be a combination of any of these suggestions.

In the long term, the company will have to formulate a corporate strategy. I recommend that the following actions be taken:

● Acquire more long-term capital as part of an over-all reorganization. This involves a fundamental assessment by the family of their position and their relationship with the company within the community.

● Make more efficient use of existing operations: for example, improve stock and credit control, establish adequate production planning and production control systems, cut down on work in progress and finished goods stocks, install more formalized management control systems and an adequate costing system.

● Ensure a better product mix and market mix in retailing and cut back on marginal activities and product lines. Examine as to whether the company is at present producing too many lines with inadequately financed equipment. Review unit pricing.

● Through the delineation of an organization chart, set out the key areas of management responsibility and then manage the system by balancing the competing resources.

Finally, it is essential that Bilinrosia becomes aware of his ineffective style of managing, particularly as the architect of corporate strategy and coordinator of the enterprise. He must accept a definite commitment to corporate strategy formulation and execution. A high level of organizational leadership will be expected of him as a major shareholder to bring about functional integration. If he cannot manage he should appoint a professional managing director who can.

This decision was provided by Patrick Kehoe in his capacity as director of Irish Pensions Trust Ltd. in Ireland and head of Patrick Kehoe & Associates, a management consultancy based in Singapore.

How should managing director organize new project department?

Graham Hendy, managing director of Queensland Engineering Co., could not believe it. He had just heard that Jack Moss, head of the tube division, had turned down the chance to head the new project assignment. Now, Hendy did not know which way to turn.

The Australian company had just been awarded a $7.6 million contract by an Australian government department for a research and development (R&D) project called "SHEILA" (southern hemisphere electrical impulse locating antenna). The project, the medium-size company's most important assignment yet, required the development of a broad range of electronic equipment with highly advanced performance characteristics.

The question now pressing the firm's managing director was whether to handle it through one of the three technical departments or to organize it as an *ad hoc* project. The question was crucial.

The company stood to earn about $600,000 from the contract. But the contract contained an incentive clause giving the company a share of any saving in the cost. It also imposed heavy financial penalties on the company for exceeding the stated cost, for late delivery or failure to meet specifications. .

The young company was organized along traditional lines, with three technical departments all of which would be involved to some extent in the project. The three departments, which were oriented to various technical disciplines, were each responsible for developing advanced techniques, for engineering, and for giving support to R&D projects in its technical area. In addition, the company had a manufacturing department which did fabrication, assembly and testing of production units.

Workers do not want two bosses

Hendy had automatically thought that Moss should take over the SHEILA project. He had been with the company since the beginning. He had the status and the respect needed to get the cooperation of the other technical departments and their staff.

But now Moss was standing before him shaking his head in disagreement. "I do not want to take over the whole responsibility for this project, and then depend on others over whom I have no control.. I don't believe in project management ..."

"But you would have full authority," interrupted Hendy.

"I would still have to spend my time cajoling various departments to get things done and still be blamed in the end for everything that goes wrong," Moss replied. "We have tried to run these assignments with project managers before, remember. The last time we failed to meet the technical specifications, although the customer did accept them without imposing penalties, I admit. Next time we might not be so lucky."

The last project had been led by Alan Chisholm, head of the circuits department. Hendy considered him to head the new assignment. But he did not want to take him away from his job once again. Anyway, he thought a much more experienced man was needed for this much longer and more complex project. And that was obviously Moss.

"Chisholm had great difficulty in getting the cooperation of the other departments," Moss continued, "even with the authority you gave him. People do not like working for two bosses. He also had trouble in getting the other department heads to give up some of their staff for the project. And this new project will take nine months."

Project management can work

"But we have learned a lot from that experience," replied Hendy. "Chisholm is younger and less experienced than you. That does not mean that project management does not work. This assignment is going to require heavy support and technical advice from all three technical departments, particularly purchasing and data processing. You are the best man to achieve this."

Moss thought for a few moments. "Why not let my department manage SHEILA as a project within the existing organization," he proposed. "We will have to do a large part of the development anyway, and in that way I would still be in charge, but without having to leave my present job."

Hendy had grave reservations. "I do not want this company to be in the awkward position of having one department directing the activities of the others. I am also concerned about giving one department the job of coordinating this project in addition to its regular work. I do not want to upset the stability of any one department by temporarily expanding the size of the workforce," he said.

By this time Hendy was in a dilemma. "Should I really be concerned with how the project is organized?" he thought to himself. "Or is it more important to put the best man for the job in charge, however he wishes to organize it?"

DECISION

MD should set up a project team to operate as a profit centre

Whatever else he may have done wrong, Hendy was right to accept the SHEILA project, and then search for a way to carry it out. This is an attractive assignment. The financial arrangements are quite favourable to the firm, representing a fifth or a quarter of its sales turnover and quite probably more of its annual profits.

But the time to complete the project, nine months, is short and there is a risk of incurring heavy financial penalties. There is also the risk of having to sacrifice other work and of upsetting the existing organizational structure of the company.

It seems inexcusable to me, therefore, that Hendy did not give more thought to the project before calling in Moss. It is surprising that he did not foresee that the project would cause problems or that Moss would react the way he did. Moss has been with the firm for a long time and is very tied to his department. The result is that any solution will still leave the problem of dealing with Moss.

It is also unfortunate that Hendy did not involve his executives in making his decision, to get them to accept any organizational structure that may be necessary.

Expanding on the project

What is more serious, I believe, is Hendy's failure to think of the impact of the project on every aspect of the company – marketing, strategy and organization.

For example, is this project isolated or will there be some other similarly large ones involving intricate systems? The answer could make a difference to the type of structure that should be set up for SHEILA. Will it be possible to look actively for other similar assignments, based on this experience? Is there a new market opening and, if so, how can the company capture it?

If this project is of a different nature to previous work, it may mean an important change for the company. Does Hendy want to expand the company? It may mean engaging more staff and partly changing activities. Does Hendy wish to take this risk? Does he himself feel able to manage a larger and more diversified company?

I agree that the choice of the man to head the SHEILA project is important. But it is also important to adapt the present organizational structure to the project. I believe Hendy should create a specific and dynamic organization, at least temporarily, but permanently if the firm sees a new market opening and wishes to capture it.

I propose that the Queensland Engineering Co. set up a project team with the entire responsibility for completing the SHEILA contract. The team would operate as a profit centre, with financial accounts. It would be in full control of the project, with full responsibility for purchasing, subcontracting, and cooperation between departments for research or implementation of the contract.

Create a new team

The team should be small, made up of an engineer from each department, and one buyer. The head of each department should be sufficiently motivated to release one of their best men full-time for the duration of the contract or permanently should it become necessary. The team should be located separately from all other departments. But Hendy should have direct responsibility for the team, and personally look after the new project as part of his job.

Hendy should appoint as head of the team a young, efficient, aggressive executive, who would be motivated by the possibility of heading a new department.

I believe that this arrangement would be better than giving the entire responsibility, with all the risks involved, to one man such as Moss, even though his competence is unquestioned.

Relations with existing departments must be defined very accurately. I suggest that the team could subcontract work to them under agreement with definite specifications, and with financial penalties for failing to meet specifications or failing to meet delivery dates.

In effect the relationship would be like those between any company and its suppliers and subcontractors. A department could turn down a contract, should it be overloaded or if it could not meet the required deadline. The team should also be able to put any work out to competition, including outside sub-contractors, within the limits of company interests decided by top management.

I believe that the new structure would be radical and significant enough to offset the previous failure of project management and alter the negative attitudes to it which exist.

This decision was provided by Jacques Giroire in his capacity as chairman of GMV Conseil, a French management consultancy based in Paris.

Chapter 3

Industrial Relations

*Should a company president fire a manager to avert a strike?
Should a manager resist cost reductions to maintain
morale? Inevitably managers encounter situations in which
the desirable solution, from a corporate point of view,
conflicts with justice towards individuals and the long-term
interests of industrial relations. There are some
dilemmas like that in this section.*

Should the president fire a manager to avert a strike?

Hassan Al-Kadby, president of Zahara Textiles, a successful weaving and textile firm with a large plant in the Middle East, has to decide how to avoid a damaging strike yet salvage his sense of honour and fair-dealing.

He had been appointed president of the company by the Minister for Industry with instructions to make Zahara a model of progressive management and industrial harmony. "I also want the company to make a substantial contribution to the national economy, which means setting new high standards in productivity," the minister had said.

Fired with enthusiasm, Al-Kadby chose his subordinates carefully. His most controversial move had been the appointment as production manager of Samer Al-Maaloof. The president had personally visited the textile factory in Belgium where he worked and persuaded him to return home.

Al-Maaloof was a young but experienced textile engineer who had studied in the United States and had worked there and in western Europe. His appointment was controversial because he had a reputation as a rather abrasive character, particularly in dealing with the work-force.

Sure enough, almost his first act after his arrival was to make plain that he would not brook any interference, whether from the union or anyone else, in the way he ran production.

Increasing the workload to boost productivity

The president believed in industrial democracy. He sided on several occasions with the three worker representatives on the board, and had implemented improvements in working conditions.

However, he also staunchly backed Al-Maaloof in his drive to improve productivity at the plant. This backing seemed fully justified when innovations introduced by the production manager boosted output by 15%.

Al-Maaloof then approached the president with a more far-reaching proposal. It was that instead of having one worker tend each machine there should be two workers in charge of a group of three machines. This would boost the productivity of the two men while the third could be trained to man new machines under the company's expansion programme.

When this was raised at a board meeting, the three worker representatives and two other directors, who had no particular liking for Al-Maaloof, were distinctly cool towards the proposal.

The production manager pointed out that every time the looms on the machines had to be changed, which happened frequently during the day, the machine operator had to stop production while he attended to the machine. But if two men operated three machines, one of them could keep an eye on two of the machines while the second changed the looms on the third. The two men could alternate the job of changing the looms.

To make the scheme work effectively, Al-Maaloof said, it would be necessary to relocate one machine in every three on the factory floor, so that all three machines were equally accessible to their operatives. Yes, he said in answer to a worried finance director, it would cost quite a lot of money. But he then produced figures to prove that the increase in productivity would more than repay the engineering work involved.

The worker representatives reserved their position, saying that a lot would depend upon the extra payments that would be worked out. Al-Kadby enthusiastically supported the idea and asked Al-Maaloof, in consultation with the personnel director, to implement the plan as fast as resources and union cooperation would permit. He then embarked on a very hectic three-month trip abroad on business.

Al-Maaloof pressed ahead with his usual energy. Although the personnel director was nominally in charge of industrial relations, it was the day-to-day encounters between Al-Maaloof and the shop-floor which carried most significance. And they were increasingly troubled.

When the president returned from his travels, events were reaching crisis point. Although the relocation of some of the machines that Al-Maaloof wanted to change had been accomplished, there was still no agreement about their manning.

Facing up to union displeasure
The union presented the president with an ultimatum. It said that the management was making one man in three redundant. Two men sharing three machines would make work harder for each individual. The regrouping of the machines in a compact unit would increase the noise level for the operators. Also, the union had not been fully consulted.

So, the union said, it could not agree to the job restructuring. Also, unless Al-Maaloof was dismissed as production manager there would be a strike.

The same day Al-Kadby received a call from his minister. He said that Zahara had been so successful that the government was giving it a new "company of the year" award.

Al-Kadby wondered what to do. If there was a strike the government would be embarrassed. The·company's good name would tumble in the dust and he would lose face.

On the other hand, the production manager had done a good job and could justly point out that the president had backed him throughout. Could he be sacrificed now?

DECISION

President chooses between removing manager and work disruption

*Z*ahara Textiles' president, Hassan Al-Kadby, has returned to find a crisis in the plant. Should he take action to avoid a damaging strike or should he accept a strike as the price for supporting Samer Al-Maaloof, his production manager? These are the only two real options open to him.

Since his concern for employee welfare is well known in the company, he should be able to exert considerable influence with the union. However, he may conclude that relationships have deteriorated to such an extent that even that influence would be ineffective.

The production manager, Samer Al-Maaloof, therefore, has to go. The president will handle his departure personally, as sympathetically and generously as possible.

A face-saving announcement will explain an immediate transfer to another post. The president will then devote some of his own time to restoring relationships with the union and ensuring the smooth introduction of the new production plan.

A conflict of loyalties

In making this difficult decision he will have reflected on the reasons why he is faced with such a painful conflict of loyalties. On the one hand, there is his obligation to the production manager, whom he persuaded to take the job and whose efforts to improve productivity he strongly supported. On the other hand, there is his obligation to the Minister for Industry, who relied on him to further the company's performance and reputation. His personal reputation is also, of course, at stake.

The president will recognize that he was himself largely responsible for the crisis. In the first place, he should not have hired Al-Maaloof for the production manager's job. In selecting anyone for a key position it is necessary to establish not only "can he do the job?" but also "will he fit in with us, and with the working environment?"

While Al-Maaloof's technical ability was outstanding, his abrasive management style and his disregard of work-force and union feelings would clearly not fit in with the president's own views on management, nor with the pattern of management/union relationships at the plant.

This should have been clear from Al-Maaloof's reputation. His attitudes should have been explored in depth before deciding to hire him.

The president's second major error was to leave Al-Maaloof too free a hand to introduce the new plan during his own extended absence from the plant on business.

Knowing that it would be essential to get the union's acceptance of the major changes involved, he asked the production manager to proceed only as fast as union cooperation would allow. Events showed that to be inadequate.

In view of the importance of the project, he should have laid down firm guidelines for involving the union at the various stages of the change process. He should have made the personnel director clearly responsible for monitoring progress, and for keeping him informed of developments. Early warning of how things were going wrong could have prevented the crisis.

Al-Maaloof himself is not, of course, free from blame. Inspired by the success of his first innovations, which improved productivity he was determined to drive through his more ambitious plans as quickly as possible, and in his own way.

Lack of communication with the union

He disregarded the president's advice about securing union cooperation, pushed aside employee resistance to the changes and ignored the personnel director. The deterioration in his relationship with the union, and the lack of communication, are reflected in the union's complaint that workers would be made redundant, whereas his intention was to retrain surplus workers for other jobs within the company.

The president is left with a plan which is technically sound and which he still intends to see successfully installed. But such a major change in job structuring requires the involvement of the employees concerned, and their union, if it is to achieve optimum results.

Had he been on site himself, the president might have ensured that this took place, for it was consistent with his own philosophy, and with the work climate he had established in the company.

His analysis of the problem, and what has gone wrong, will confirm the president in his decision to let Al-Maaloof go. He will also have a heightened recognition of the critical importance of selecting the right man for a key job. In future, the man will have to be "right" in all senses of the word.

This decision was provided by Paul Hill in his capacity as director of the human relations division at U.K.-based consultants MSL Group International, and author of the book Towards a New Philosophy of Management, *published by Gower Press in 1971.*

DILEMMA

Should manager resist cost reductions to maintain morale?

The first time that Marcel Dupré set eyes on François Pétain he had a sense of foreboding. Like Cassius in Shakespeare's play *Julius Caesar,* Pétain had a "lean and hungry look", Dupré thought.

This adverse reaction was reinforced when Pétain, at the first executive meeting after his arrival to head the gears division of Duval et Cie, a large manufacturer of industrial machinery, said that he wanted Dupré to implement immediately a comprehensive cost-cutting programme.

His brief from corporate management in Paris, Pétain announced, was to ensure that the division not only met but exceeded its profit targets. Costs had been getting out of hand and there would have to be severe pruning to ensure future growth.

Dupré, who had been plant manager at the division's only factory for five years, and who himself had ambitions to become divisional chief, had heard it all before.

In the recession of 1974, another divisional head provided by headquarters, Michel Leblanc, had wielded an axe fiercely. Managers had been sacked and the plant's administrative, maintenance and quality control departments had been decimated. The plant managers of the day had been prematurely retired and Dupré had been appointed in his place, having previously served as deputy manager.

Profits at the expense of pruned departments
Leblanc had headed the division for exactly 16 months, in which time he had produced impressive-looking profits at the expense of truncated departments and shattered morale. He had returned to Paris, and a seat on the board, like a victorious general.

104

Dupré had learned to steer a precarious course between going along with Leblanc and ameliorating the effects of some of his policies. He strongly believed in positive motivation and a contented workforce. But he had not been brought in and Dupré had found himself serving his third boss within two years.

As plant manager, Dupré had borne the brunt of the havoc caused by Leblanc's purging and cost-cutting. Slowly he had restored to the workforce a sense of harmony and purpose. The economic upturn had also helped the plant to produce results acceptable to headquarters.

Then had come the latest upset. There had been a power struggle in Paris in which Leblanc had been the loser. He had resigned. Within a month, his successor as divisional head also left.

Pétain, who had started life as a management consultant, arrived in the division as the latest chief. It was rumoured that he was the company president's personal nominee.

As Dupré listened to Pétain at the executive meeting, it was like being back in 1974. "I don't want any more hirings ... one secretary for every three managers ... look at your departments and tell me within a week where cuts can be made ... we are now going to produce real profits in this outfit."

Worse was to follow. Pétain made it plain to Dupré that his past performance as plant manager counted for nothing so far as he was concerned. "You have to prove yourself with me, now," he said. "I judge a man on today's performance, not yesterday's."

Cost-cutting exercises increasing
Dupré soon found that Pétain was incapable of real delegation. Not content with weekly reports on inventory, labour turnover, absenteeism, production and sales, he demanded day-by-day verbal updating.

A ceaseless flow of memos emanated from the divisional office, down the corridor from Dupré's own modest room. For example, although the plant's order book was full, Pétain sent a message suggesting that all overtime should be abolished as a cost-cutting exercise. When Dupré pointed out that shipments would then fall behind, Pétain replied: "That is *your* problem."

The most deeply felt blow, however, and the one which convinced Dupré that things could not go on as they were, was when Pétain asked about the dance that Dupré proposed to give to all employees at the grandest ballroom in town.

Dupré explained that the dance had been promised as reward for a special effort in meeting an emergency order. "You must cancel it," Pétain said. "I simply cannot sanction that kind of expense at this time. I couldn't justify it to Paris."

Wanted: A friend in high places
Dupré left the other man's office seething. He unburdened himself to Jacques Gabin, the personnel manager. Gabin had worked with Dupré to restore morale in the plant and was a friend as well as a subordinate.

"Your problem, Marcel," Gabin said, "is that you don't have a friend at headquarters. You're a first-rate production expert and an able administrator. You go about motivating people in the right way. But your record in selling yourself and your ideas to the top is dismal. You deserve to be division manager, yet all these people keep getting appointed over your head."

"I know," Dupré said. "But it's a bit late to start trying to win friends in Paris. Anyway, that's not my style. I don't want to resign. That would really be giving in to Pétain. But if I allow him to cancel the dance and push through all his other measures, this plant will really go downhill. And it won't be Pétain but myself who will get the blame."

Then he said to Gabin: "Tell me, what would you do?"

DECISION

Cost cutting threatens to hit plant manager's morale-building

When a subordinate has differences with his boss there are, I think, three things he can do. He can live with his problem; he can try to change it; or he can resign. The solution to this particular dilemma depends on whether Marcel Dupré decides to take the easy, the difficult or the dramatic way out.

For the majority of people, the first two courses of action are the most common. But those who live with a situation can sometimes become disenchanted. And those who are always trying to make changes can be regarded as troublemakers.

In Dupré's case, the best action he can take would be to try to change François Pétain's ideas. In order to do so, he needs some coaching in the skills of advocacy.

But there are time limitations. Dupré needs to take some positive action before Petain puts into effect the abolition of overtime or the cancelling of the promised dance.

Explore some common ground

It looks, as though Dupré has been, in the past, an excellent buffer between top management and the shop floor. His production schedules have been good and he has managed to build up morale after it was shattered during a previous cost-cutting episode.

Why has he been passed over for promotion? It could be that someone at headquarters recognized the need for continuity at plant manager level. Alternatively, it might be that Dupré has been a little too compliant with his successive "whiz kid" bosses.

Jacques Gabin, the personnel manager, probably hits the nail on the head when he suggests that Dupré's record of selling himself and his ideas to top level people is abysmal. This seems to be a failing among technical men. Many of them just do not know how to present a case effectively. Some of them feel that there is no need to practise the arts of persuasion.

What, then, can Dupré do?

Pétain apparently has a single-minded ambition to cut costs regardless of the consequences. He might refuse to listen to reason. On the other hand, Dupré may well find that he has more common ground with Pétain than he imagines.

He might explore that common ground, first of all, on a personal rather than an official level. Perhaps Pétain has a hobby, or other interests, that coincide with those of Dupré. A common interest in stamp collecting or rose growing can thaw a frozen relationship remarkably.

Beyond that, Dupré may find that Pétain, for all his hard exterior, appreciates some help with his troubles and his inability to delegate. Possibly Dupré can work on these weaknesses.

Keeping up the morale

For example, he can suggest that the time he is forced to spend on the verbal updating of Pétain, on matters such as inventory, decreases efficiency and increases costs. By indicating that he sees himself as there to help Pétain's efficiency drive, and reminding Pétain that he has a lot of experience in that field with Pétain's predecessors, he could win his superior's confidence and work amicably with him.

This would give him the opportunity to restate the problem of the dance. Once he has Pétain's ear it should not be too difficult to prove that the cost of cancelling the dance at this late stage, in terms of the likely blow to morale in the plant, would far outweigh any possible saving.

If Pétain proves unresponsive to any approach from Dupré, the latter could consider using Gabin as an intermediary. Pétain may be more inclined to listen to suggestions delivered by the personnel officer.

Dupré has to accept the fact that since he has reputedly been sent down by the company president himself, Pétain can be assured, at least in the short-term, of support at headquarters for whatever he does. Therefore, despite Dupré's best efforts, traumatic cost-cutting may still be implemented.

Work at re-motivating people

Dupré's problem, if he remains with the company, then becomes one of conveying the new direction and unwelcome policies to the work-force.

So now he has another communications problem in his lap. Can he convey the unpalatable facts of life under Pétain without a drop in morale and productivity?

Probably he can. The fact that he succceeded in raising morale during the tenure of the previous division chief suggests that Dupré does have some communications skills. He is prepared to work at re-motivating people.

However, he still has the problem of learning how to sell himself more effectively. In this respect he may need encouragement, since he feels it is a bit late to start winning friends at head office.

We all need to become better communicators – and better listeners. There are many Duprés and Pétains among us.

More attention needs to be given in industry not only to leadership but also to "followership," by which I mean that subordinates also have responsibilities.

Dupré is Pétain's subordinate. To discharge that role effectively, he needs to put up a good case just as much as Pétain needs to be a receptive leader.

So, in the long-term, anything that Dupré can do to enhance his own powers of self-projection will benefit the company and his colleagues, as well as himself.

This decision was provided by John Read in his capacity as a freelance consultant who was previously a manager with the U.K. arm of the Royal Dutch/Shell Group and assistant director of external affairs at Henley Administrative Staff College in the U.K.

Will change in company's archaic industrial relations disrupt vital order?

Upton Valve & Pump Co. is an old established U.K. engineering company making a range of industrial pumps and valves, which are of high quality and expensive. Sales have grown at 7% a year for the past five years, now totalling $7 million. Profits have been declining slightly, and the company is seeking both to expand sales in Europe and improve efficiency.

For many years the company has been dominated by a forceful chairman who is now in semi-retirement. Since his appointment as managing director 18 months ago, Samuel Wells has been trying to modernize and liberalize all aspects of the company's autocratic management.

Industrial relations were handled by the company secretary who died on the job six months ago. Wells has appointed to succeed him a man in his late thirties, who has been with the company two years as assistant secretary. This man, Alfred Bright, had some limited experience in industrial relations and wage bargaining while employed by another company.

Bright is obviously unhappy with the industrial relations pattern he has inherited. Under the influence of the old chairman, the wages policy was simple and defensive. Most claims put forward by the unions were turned down flat. As the former company secretary used to say, this delayed settlement and saved the company money, even if it did cause some unrest at the time.

Wages kept to the minimum

Every claim in the past had been settled for the least possible amount, and those workers who did not ask for rises, got none. Wages at all levels in the company were thus very low. Until a new industrial estate opened in the same country town approximately a year ago, there had been no competition for labour.

All the production workers, most of them doing semi-skilled machining, are paid on a piece-work system which has changed little in the past 15 years. There are three unions in the factory and an articulate works committee.

Despite the company's autocratic policy and low wages, the labour relations record has been surprisingly good. Two of the unions have only had minor stoppages of a few hours over the past three years. The third union has taken its members on two strikes in that period, one of which last year lasted for ten weeks and lost considerable production.

The reason for the overall good record is that the chairman of the works committee, a union shop steward, had a good working relationship with the late company secretary. They were of the same age and were able to work closely in an atmosphere of trust. After a token stoppage, the unions usually trusted him to secure their best terms.

Bright's attitude was that the company's wages and industrial relations policy was unreasonable. It was also unwise in the long term. He noted the third, more militant union gaining members as a sign of a changing climate, reflecting increased jobs in the neighbourhood.

For too long, he felt, the company had been cushioned from strife by the happy relationship of the convenor and the late company secretary. The convenor would be retiring in 18 months anyway, and Bright was not keen to continue relying on his goodwill.

Bright wanted to overhaul the whole archaic labour relations. He wanted to scrap the old piece rate system and substitute a day-wage system based on work study of all shopfloor jobs. He suspected that two of the unions would oppose this, preferring to press for better rates under the old system. The third union, Bright guessed, was prepared to cooperate, but it would probably demand an initial rise for cooperating.

Attacking the European market

Wells has heard Bright's proposals in outline form in several meetings, but he has reserved judgment on them. The entire product range is being trimmed and altered to prepare for an attack on the European market. An important contract has just been won to supply valves to a giant German company. For the first time, Upton had to sign penalty clauses to insure against late delivery.

Against this background, Wells is wary of initiating any change in the industrial relations. There is no immediate unrest or dispute in sight, and he knows the production director and factory manager would be reluctant to cooperate. Wells also doubts whether Bright has the experience to implement such a radical change.

Yet Bright has his sympathy in his analysis that change is needed in the long run. If he postpones action now, he wonders, will there ever be an ideal time? If he approves a complete revision of industrial relations, how can he be sure everything will be adopted without serious disruption in the meantime?

DECISION

Moving from autocratic paternalism to a more liberal climate must be attempted

The situation of a company struggling to pass from a phase of autocratic paternalism to a more liberal and more constructive climate is fairly familiar to industrial relations practitioners. At least, managing director Wells can be thankful that in Bright he has an industrial relations manager who appears to recognize that some change is needed. Even if there were still the personalities to sustain it, the old pattern would not be adequate to cope with changing attitudes and expectations on the part of workers and trade unions, and new labour market conditions.

This is an enthusiasm which it would be wise not to quench. Indeed one wonders to what extent industrial relations in this company ever were "good," except in the negative sense of a relative absence of strikes; a more relevant test would be to measure the standard of labour efficiency.

In industrial relations, good intentions are not enough, any more than they are in any other function of management. Bright so far has only produced an outline plan based on his desire to completely over-haul the archaic state of industrial relations in the company, and to replace the old piece-work system by a day-wage system founded on work study.

Wells is right to be wary about embarking on such a radical course. In his shoes I would want a more detailed set of proposals, backed by supporting arguments and evidence, before agreeing to proceed. These ought to be based on an audit of strengths and weaknesses in Upton's industrial relations, an assessment of the impact of outside developments in this field, an analysis of alternative courses for the company. Finally, I would need a detailed set of recommendations, complete with plans.

The audit would look at the company's existing policies and procedures. It would examine the arrangements for negotiating or consulting with workers and the part played in industrial relations by each level of management and supervisors.

It should also assess relationships with trade unions, the role of shop stewards and the overall system of representation. The quality of communications should be gauged. Finally, it should look at the scope for raising efficiency by improvement of work practices, the wage structure and other conditions of employment.

Consider the recommendations and plans

The analysis of the alternative courses would attempt to estimate all the costs and benefits involved. For example, something will certainly need to be done about a piecework system which is 15 years old. But what pay-off can be expected from its successor, whether that be a day-wage system or an improved payments by results scheme?

The detailed recommendations and plans will need to spell out who is going to be responsible for doing each part and how managers at each level are to be involved. It would also have to state the extent to which negotiations should take place jointly with all the unions and what the limits of such negotiations would be. It would need to outline how not only shop stewards but employees generally are to be kept informed. Finally, it would have to set a time-table for the whole process.

Detailed proposals along these lines will give the board and senior management something to work on. Ominously, we are told that the production director and the factory manager would be uncooperative; this is certainly a recipe for disaster. To have any real chance of success, such a project needs the support and commitment of top management, at least on the principal objectives and lines of approach.

Wells has some doubts about Bright's knowledge and style. With his limited experience, he is almost certainly going to need some outside advice and guidance in tackling a project on this scale, both in carrying out the initial audit and analysis, and in the process of implementation, which will require a great deal of flexibility and judgment.

There is no dilemma here between action and inaction; the company would be foolish in the circumstances to let its industrial relations drift. The real choice lies between taking action immediately on the basis of half-baked notions of what needs to be done, and pursuing a planned course of action based on thorough assessment of alternatives. The first course offers doubtful gains for high risks; the second presupposes considerable and clearly identifiable gains and, while it cannot eliminate the risks, at least acts to contain and minimize them.

The dilemma was based on material supplied by PA Management consultants Ltd. of the U.K., and the decision was provided by J.G. Smith in his capacity as managing director of MSL Group Ltd., of London, international management consultants.

How much should a company tell its employees?

Bird Sewing Machine Co. was founded in 1912 and became a public company in 1961. Two years later the first personnel manager was appointed. This was followed in 1965 by the first training manager, Robert Badger.

Badger quickly formed the impression that communications were very poor in the company. He thought it would help people do their jobs better and with more enthusiasm if they knew more about the firm.

Badger got his boss's approval to make a presentation to the board on disclosing company information. Among his suggestions was a programme for informing supervisors about new products before they went into production. He also urged that supervisors should be given some outline about the company's profit and marketing objectives, and about how its performance related to competitors'.

Several directors felt that there was little need for such a move, since the company had always prospered without it in the past. Others, however, were clearly impressed by Badger's ideas, particularly as the number of employees was rising. There were signs that the growing size was accompanied by lower productivity per employee and high absenteeism and lateness.

What tipped the scales for the policy of fuller disclosure was Badger's argument that every employee was a representative of the company. The better he was informed of the company's position, the better impression an employee would be able to create of its products and employment practices with a good public relations effect.

A more sophisticated competitor

It was agreed that more information would be passed down to supervisors, concentrating on those aspects of the company's plans which affected them. They were to be fully briefed before new products were launched.

About 80% of Bird's sales of $5 million came from the Eagle sewing machine. When launched five years ago its simple, sturdy design made it an immediate success. It only did simple stitching and sold for $50. Since then Bird had concentrated on production, with little research and development to improve the product.

Six months ago, Bird's major competitor brought out a new and more versatile machine capable of sewing button holes. Catering to a more sophisticated buyer, it sold for $85.

Bird's marketing director, Simon Wolfe, watched this development closely, and quickly judged that Bird needed a product to tap this profitable new market, which was threatening to win customers even from its cheaper, humbler machine. A new product would have to reach the market inside six months, to have stocks on hand for the autumn and early winter rise in sewing machine sales.

The production director, John Fox, insisted that his designers could not bring out a new machine in less than a year, including a testing period.

So a compromise was reached. An improved version of the Eagle would be brought out while work started on a completely new product. Apart from minor changes to the styling and a wider range of colours, the only improvement in the stop-gap version was an ingenious swivelhead for doing button-holing work. This device had not been subjected to the lengthy tests normally made on any product innovation, and there was now no time to do that, before production started.

Concealing some awkward truths

Costings indicated that the revised machine, called the Hawk, could be sold for $55. But two things made the directors decide to price it higher. First, they felt they could not have it too close to the Eagle price, causing dealers to be left with obsolete stock. Secondly, they felt they would be wise to try to tap the higher end of the market,` pioneered by their competitor. So the Hawk was to sell for $72, deliberately over-priced.

The launch of the Hawk was John Badger's first opportunity to put into effect the full disclosure policy to supervisors. It was his task to put together a two-hour presentation, giving all the facts and arguments behind the appearance of the new product.

As he talked this over with production director Fox, Badger realized the difficulty he was in. Fox put it simply. "Look," he said, "when you first suggested that we tell supervisors everything, I thought it was a great idea, but now I am not so sure.

He went on: "Surely we can't take them into our confidence on the Hawk to the extent that we tell them it is untried, that it is over-priced and it's only a stop-gap model. On the other hand, if you gloss over the facts, some awkward questions are going to arise at your presentation. I suggest you tell the personnel director that you want to postpone implementing your employee information policy."

DECISION

Don't start a communications programme unless you intend to follow it through

Badger must go back to the personnel director with some real-life problems and some difficult recommendations.

He ought to ensure that the supervisors understand what happens about the new product. But the awkward circumstances indicate that a dramatic new form of presentation – the two-hour one – should be avoided on this occasion. Normal line management channels should be used to pass down the information, but this must be carried out at each level.

Badger should also suggest a follow-up to see how the supervisors react to the news of the product.

The problems this firm faces include that of communication, but they also go beyond it – they also go beyond the characters in this case study.

Two major principles of business emerge. First, an integral part of any decision is that of communicating the decision. And not just communicating it generally, but using different methods for different people.

Second, even the most effective communication cannot make poor or unethical decisions palatable.

At the heart of this case is the company's decision to bring out a new device without adequate testing. This is the kind of approach that leads Ralph Nader to reach for his press conference – and quite right too.

If a housewife button-holes her finger because the ingenious swivel-head has not been put through its paces, the company is to blame.

The training manager, Robert Badger, emerges fairly well, though there are more arguments for effective communication than are given in the case. Employees have a *right* to know the basic facts about the company, whether or not the knowledge makes them more efficient.

The public relations argument that tipped the scales with the sceptical directors is by no means the strongest one. And it does pre-suppose that the company's policies and products are good.

Workers will expect the facts

But the directors took the right decision to back a communication programme – for the wrong reasons. So often when this happens, a whiff of trouble makes people – in this case, John Fox – want to withdraw.

But it is not so easy to turn off the communication tap once you have started. People then expect to be given the facts and resent it when information they have come to expect is withheld.

It is better not to start a communications programme unless you intend to go along with it. To follow Fox's suggestion would mean starting the information programme immediately after the company had withheld facts on a matter of continuing great importance. This would be a miserable start for the programme.

In addition, Fox's last remark suggests that the supervisors are in blissful ignorance about the failings of the product. Or perhaps more likely he knows that they know, but feels that this kind of thing is better not brought into the open.

Certainly supervisors – and very often workers – know a great deal about situations, even if they have not been told formally.

Find out the firm's objectives

The unfortunate Badger has learnt one precept about company existence: training managers enjoy quieter lives when their training is unrelated to the objectives of the organization.

But the personnel director has an important subject to discuss with his fellow directors, if he hasn't done so already. What are the firm's objectives and responsibilities with regard to the product and the customer?

Do they not include a care for the customer's safety through proper testing? And that he gets an efficient product, and value for his money? It is, of course, possible to test so much that you make the product incredibly expensive but this hardly seems the case here.

There are also practical problems. A highly priced product that may go wrong could do a lot of damage to the company's reputation. Tactical high pricing may not in itself be what this case terms "over-pricing".

But the directors do need to go back to first base and decide why they are in business, and what are their responsibilities to their customers and to their employees.

This dilemma was based on material supplied by the Institute of Works Managers, London, and the decision was provided by Michael Ivens in his capacity as director of the Industrial Educational and Research Foundation.

What action should be taken by union man on the board?

"**W**ell, they've done it. Your crowd has decided to strike at the end of the month." Never one to disguise his feelings, E. Brian Ford, chairman of the National Textile Board, was clearly in the worst of his characteristically bad humours. Striding into the board's committee room, he slammed the heavy oak door behind him.

Phillip Buck winced visibly at the words "your crowd," even though he was used to such barbs from the chairman. As a former union leader he had never been totally sure he had taken the right decision when the government offered him a board post. The textile industry had been nationalized 16 years before and had had a history of bad labour relations ever since. Two years ago, the government decided it would improve labour relations by filling a vacancy on the board with someone whom the textile workers would feel understood their problems. Buck, the head of the powerful food industry union, was an obvious choice. He had a reputation for moderate views, but was not afraid to use the union's strength whenever he considered it necessary. After long consultations with the Trade Union Congress Buck agreed to take the job.

District meetings had failed

From the start, his board colleagues had resented his intrusion into the industry's affairs. Buck had given up his union post and poured all his efforts into creating a better industrial environment in the textile industry. He had set up regular district meetings where members of the board could meet the workers after hours and explain the organization's policies. Far from being the informal get-togethers he had hoped for, however, the meetings had had a tense and strained atmosphere. On one occasion the meeting had degenerated to a slanging match between the managing director and several militant workers. When attendances at the meetings dropped, most of the board members were only too glad to call the whole scheme off.

Buck's company newsletter, to which employees were encouraged to contribute, had suffered a similar fate. He drew on his union experience to make sure the newsletter represented both sides on any topic in a lively way. It had got off to a good start, but line management objected strongly to some contributions, which they labelled as "'blatant" union propaganda. A majority of the board supported the managers' objections. The unions replied that, if the newsletter were to print only the company side of the story, they would advise their members to boycott it. It was now six weeks since the last fortnightly issue had appeared.

Only two of the other 11 board members had lent any real support to Buck, and he reflected ruefully that he had very little to show for his efforts. He tried to see the other board members' point of view, but he often felt that they were basically unsympathetic to workers.

The current troubles began two months ago with a large wage demand by the textile workers' unions. In view of the industry's poor performance over the past two or three years, the board had had little choice but to dismiss the demand as unreasonable. Even so, Buck had pointed out to his colleagues they could at least examine what concessions they *could* make to the unions.

The board voted for a strong line and took Buck's reluctance to agree as a mark of extreme disloyalty. "Your obligation now is to management," declared Ford, a forceful banker, "not to the workers. You must have learned enough about the industry in two years to know that it can't afford to award a wage rise at this time."

Local meetings explain the position

Buck had been sure that, if the workers understood the industry's plight more clearly, they would modify their demands. Then the board members could be persuaded to respond more sympathetically. So he embarked on a round of local meetings to explain the financial reasons for the board's stand. Most of the board dismissed the idea as a waste of his time.

Although the workers had been prepared to listen to him at first, they soon became persuaded he had become a company puppet. Only last week he had been heckled and called a traitor. A meeting arranged for that night had been called off without explanation.

Under attack from both sides, Buck felt near despair at the strike announcement. The easy solution to his problem would be to resign, although this would leave no one to bridge the ever-widening communications gap between the board and the textile workers. Yet could he accomplish anything by staying?

DECISION

The union man has a wrong perception of his role

Phillip Buck should not, of course despair at the news of the strike. If strikes were regarded as indicators of complete failure in industrial relations very few industrial relations directors would be entitled to regard themselves as competent or successful in their jobs at all. Buck's feelings, however, give a clue to the reasons why his overall achievement in his new post has not, so far, been conspicuously successful. He is clearly a romantic and an idealist and needs to adopt a more down to earth and realistic approach to his task. Only a romantic would believe that a history of bad labour relations in the industry over a period of 16 years could be overcome within two years of taking on the job.

In my view Buck has a totally wrong perception of his role. He is not there to provide a one-man conciliation service; nor is he in the job so that he can shield the National Textile Board from its collective responsibility for industrial relations; nor should he see himself as occupying a position halfway between the company and the union.

He is a full board member and as such shares collective responsibility for the overall conduct of the company's affairs. At the same time he has a special responsibility for policy formulation and advice in the field of industrial relations. Instead of organizing face-to-face meetings which were unlikely to be successful in the context of a history of bad labour relations his time would have been more usefully spent creating a better basis for future relationships. He should have four priorities:

He should draft a new industrial relations policy for the company on the basis of consultations with the board and the union. He should then get that policy adopted, get it widely published and known at all levels.

He should overhaul and improve the company's machinery and procedures for handling industrial relations matters.

He should identify the training needs of managers and supervisors in the industrial relations area and institute the appropriate training.

He should advise the board on the handling of specific issues.

One of the first essential steps will be for Buck to win the confidence of his own board. To be seen as a professional member of the board he must show as much interest in, and knowledge of, the company's financial, production and marketing affairs as other board members. At the same time, with regard to his own special responsibility for industrial relations matters, he must obtain the commitment of the board as a whole to his policies and action plans before seeking to implement them. Only by getting fellow board members to identify with the industrial relations policy, and to regard it as *their* policy, will he be able to command the degree of support he will need in this difficult situation.

Adopt a change of tactics

Having established board confidence in himself and his policies he must then help the board as a whole, and the chief executive in particular, to win the confidence and trust of the union and the shop floor. This is much more important than his own personal standing and popularity with which he seems to have been unduly preoccupied so far. There are many ways in which he can promote confidence in the board's good intentions in industrial relations matters. These include, for example, the publication and widespread dissemination within the company of the board's policy for industrial relations matters and its initiatives in improving areas of worker safety, health and welfare. Generally he should seek to change the situation from one in which the board merely responds to union initiatives on the industrial relations front. Progressive personnel and industrial relations policies should be adopted or put forward for discussion by the board in advance of union pressure.

Buck, then, would be wrong to give up and resign at this stage. He must, however, recognize that a change of tactics is necessary. He should set himself a plan of work for the next two or three years and should not look for early results.

One final comment: Whatever Buck's personal suitability for the job he was given, his appointment reflects a common, but, in my view, completely misguided approach to solving industrial relations problems. This is the approach which assumes that the ex-poacher makes the best gamekeeper. In practice an active trade unionist probably faces more problems than most people when taking on a senior management job in industrial relations. He will almost certainly be seen as a turncoat by the union side while having to work very hard to gain acceptance by top management.

This decision was provided by Philip Sadler in his capacity as principal of Ashridge Management College in the U.K.

What action over employee who had a mental breakdown?

Arthur James, personnel director of the Midlands Textiles Co. was angry. His deputy, Valerie Bartlett, had just told him that the name of Frank Southwell had been brought up at the morning's works council meeting. A representative of the white-collar union had announced that his members were no longer prepared to work with Southwell, whose past history had just been discovered.

Southwell, a clerk in the accounts department, had suffered a mental breakdown several years before joining the firm, and had been arrested for an attempted indecent assault on a young woman. After hearing the evidence of a psychiatrist, the court granted Southwell a conditional discharge, subject to treatment at a mental institution.

In the 11 months he had been with the firm, Southwell had given no cause for concern. Unfortunately, a former court clerk, who had just joined the firm, recognized Southwell and expressed her anxiety to Robert Provost, a works council representative.

"We appreciate that Southwell is fulfilling his duties satisfactorily. Nevertheless we cannot take the risk that this man might have a mental lapse and revert to his former behaviour," Provost told the works council.

The breakdown followed the death of his wife

James's deputy thought it wise not to pursue the issue at the works council meeting. She promised to arrange a meeting between James and Provost to discuss the matter in private.

James wasted no time in meeting with Provost. He carefully explained how Southwell had experienced a breakdown following the death of his young wife. He showed Provost the letters of reassurance he had received from the psychiatrist and the head of the mental institution when Southwell was hired. He also offered to arrange for Provost to meet them if he felt it was necessary.

Provost was not be be placated. "I doubt if anything psychiatrists have to say will help to change the attitude of my members," he replied firmly. "They have already voted not to work with Southwell. It is unlikely they can be persuaded to change their minds. Now the truth is out the women are afraid to be in the same building with him. They do not see why they should have to live in fear simply to preserve one man's job, particularly as management did not see fit to inform them of his background in the first place."

The conversation was interrupted by a telephone call. It was Southwell calling from his home. He told James he very much wanted to remain in his job, but that he would understand, if, under the circumstances, the company decided to ask for his resignation. "Absolutely not," James insisted. He told Southwell to return to work whenever he felt up to it.

James replaced the telephone and turned to Provost. He kept his temper with restraint. "I accept that the employees have a right to share in decisions affecting their working conditions," he said. "But I do not feel you have given careful enough consideration to this question. Southwell is a member of a union too. Surely he deserves a little more sympathy and charity. He has been with us nearly a year and has a faultless work record. Our company has a very progressive policy of helping handicapped people. I feel strongly that this policy should embrace mentally handicapped people as well as the physically handicapped. They, too, deserve to be given the chance to be rehabilitated. We hire ex-prisoners, do not forget, and they have always responded by working harder than the average employee."

A company has a right to choose employees

"Well, this is different," replied Provost. "You can never be sure that people with a mental history will not have a relapse. You never know what might trigger it off. Suppose, for example, Southwell drinks too much at an office party and takes advantage of one of our young typists. We simply cannot afford to take the risk."

James was convinced in his own mind that justice was on his side. He had to protect the company's right to hire the people it chose. He was concerned about the bad precedent it would set if he let the white-collar workers force an employee with a good work record out of his job simply out of cold-hearted prejudice. On the other hand, if he stood firm, he felt, the issue would almost certainly escalate. It could easily get out of hand, create hostility within the firm, and conceivably create a major dispute. He was not even sure that Southwell would be strong enough to withstand all the anxiety the issue would provoke. With such a strain placed on him he might indeed suffer another mental breakdown. Nobody would thank James if that happened.

DECISION

The employee deserves to receive every possible support

The most important thing the personnel director can do in an acute situation like this is to give Southwell every possible support.

First of all, I suggest that James should persist with his discussions with the white-collar union representative in the hope of finding a mutually acceptable solution.

If, however, the union representative continues to back those who insist on Southwell's dismissal, James should bring the question up, on an informal basis, at a higher level, probably with the chairman of the local white-collar union.

I am convinced that somewhere in the union hierarchy he should be able to establish contact with responsible union leaders who are prepared to work with the company to solve this problem.

That is not to say it is an easy problem to solve.

I think it is also important to open discussions as soon as possible with those of Southwell's colleagues who want him dismissed. Naturally, all positive facts weighing in his favour should be presented in order to get the employees to realize the absurdity of their attitude. I suggest that

James should also ask a union representative to join in the discussions. Perhaps he should also ask the psychiatrist who treated Southwell to take part as well. If Southwell himself has strength enough for it, he too should be requested to attend the meeting. Both Southwell and the psychiatrist should be asked to state their views.

At best, one, or several, such discussions might result in new and improved relations between Southwell and his colleagues. With greater understanding and support, Southwell could remain in his job. This may sound like wishful thinking, but it is not unreasonable from a psychological point of view. The possibility should in any case be tried before it is rejected.

If, however, all Southwell's colleagues stick to their original attitudes, or even if they formally agree he should remain in the job but continue to adopt a negative attitude towards him, if would be difficult for him to stay in his old work place. I am not referring to his formal rights, but to his own reactions and well-being.

Consider the prejudices and negative attitudes

Perhaps it would then be feasible for him to be transferred to another work group. It is probably very difficult to keep this matter secret. James should, therefore, assume that employees outside Southwell's own work group know the facts. At worst, this might lead employees elsewhere to take a similar negative attitude. On the other hand, they may take his side. In fact, I think it is quite likely that they will do so.

One necessary condition for a successful transfer is Southwell's own conviction that he will now feel comfortable staying with the company. Should he prefer to leave, I think it is reasonable for the company to provide him with any help he needs to secure a job elsewhere.

James should ensure that his department works rapidly to place Southwell in another company. James should get in touch with the employment exchange as soon as possible. He and his colleagues in the personnel department will very likely have good contacts in a number of exchanges, and in the personnel departments of other companies.

James should also obtain the support of psychologists who normally cooperate regularly with employment exchanges, as well as contacting Southwell's own psychiatrist.

In the longer term, I think it is essential that James takes steps to prevent any such problems from arising again. He should sit down with the union representatives and discuss what can be done to change the prejudices and negative attitudes of employees which have come to light as a result of this incident.

In Sweden, all enterprises have a so-called Adjustment Group composed of representatives of management, local unions and the local employment exchange. One of their main tasks is to try to find suitable work for employees who are handicapped – physically, mentally or socially. These adjustment groups consider it their natural obligation to work actively for an improved understanding of people who have problems in securing employment, whatever the reason.

This decision was provided by Lennart Lennerlöf in his capacity as director of PA Rådet, the Swedish Council for Personnel Administration, based in Stockholm.

How should management cope with objections to South African investment?

Jan Pedersen woke to the bump of the landing gear being lowered as the aircraft prepared to land at Johannesburg airport. Since he took over as chairman of Danish metals and engineering group Helsingor Steel AS, six months before, Pedersen had known that the group's South African subsidiary was a thorny problem he would have to tackle. The worker representatives on the group's works council and the worker directors on the board had first taken serious notice of the South African company when its record profits were announced in the last annual report.

"It must be exploitation," said the worker representatives. When the subsidiary shortly afterwards asked the parent company for additional investment capital, there was a fierce and acrimonious row on the advisory board. The worker directors saw the matter as a moral issue. The directors nominated by two of Scandinavia's largest banks admitted that morality played a part, but insisted the most important aspect was the overall financial health of the group. Before long, the worker directors were demanding that the group withdraw from South Africa entirely.

Pedersen had stalled as long as he could. The South African subsidiary had been set up six years ago and was, in many ways, a show-case example of the group's policy of allowing local chief executives maximum autonomy. Certainly with world demand for metal products still well down, it was likely to be one of the few bright stars in the next annual report, too. However, Pedersen had faced up to the fact that he could no longer delay a visit to the South African company.

Conducted tour reveals different attitudes

Pedersen could not complain about the warmth of his welcome, which was effusive and obviously sincere. Henry Maasdijk, the chairman of the local company, was full of charm on the 110-kilometre drive to Bovington, where the subsidiary's two factories, a tube mill and a motor instruments assembly plant, were situated. It did not take him long, however, to get round to the subject of the investment capital he had requested. "This year we'll have fair profits," he said, "but next year I'm none too sure. Our two main competitors in the tube business have teamed up with U.S. and Japanese companies to inject a lot of new technology. Unless we modernize and extend our mill, we shall be in serious trouble."

After lunch, Maasdijk took Pedersen on a conducted tour of the two plants. Pedersen was impressed with the general efficiency of the operation and commented favourably on the company's medical centre, library and weekly literacy and numeracy classes for black employees. "We are the only large employer in this area," explained Maasdijk, "so we spend a lot of money on welfare programmes for our black employees."

On the other hand, there were a number of areas with which Pedersen was far from pleased. Blacks and whites ate in separate dining-rooms. There were also separate washrooms and showers. Most important of all, black workers started on lower scales of pay than white workers.

"You have to accept the South African situation for what it is," said Maasdijk. "Certainly, we could put up the wages for our 2,000 black employees. We'd make only a marginal profit, at best, but we could do it. However, all our local suppliers would have to raise their wages to compete for labour, and that would mean raising their prices to us. We couldn't survive that."

That was not an argument, Pedersen knew, which would cut much ice with the worker directors or the works council in Denmark. Their motivations were not simply political, he said, but arose from a feeling of sympathy with the poor economic conditions of black families.

"Look out of the window," said Maasdijk dramatically, pointing to the cluster of small factories and villages along the Bovington valley. "If our two factories close down it is not only our 2,000 workers who will be unemployed but everyone in the supply industries too. Surely, you don't think that is going to improve their economic conditions?"

Back on the aeroplane, Pedersen tried to draw up a list of the "pros" and "cons" of keeping the subsidiary going. Good relationships with the workforce in Denmark were one of his prime corporate objectives, as it would otherwise be impossible to maintain the growth plans he had instituted when he became chief executive. However, he had already used up much of his credit with the workforce by insisting on over 1,000 redundancies at the main plant in Denmark. All his efforts in restoring their trust would be forfeited if he invested in the South African company.

Maasdijk's last words had been: "You can't play politician and businessman at the same time." But, reflected Pedersen, that was exactly what he *did* have to do.

DECISION

Company should push ahead with its investment plans

At the level of reasoning applied by the people around Pedersen, there seem to be two different answers to the dilemma, depending on whether a business or a political frame of reference is used. In my view Pedersen should push ahead with the investment in South Africa, if it is sound from a business standpoint. But he should not use the business viewpoint as an argument to reject the political viewpoint. The dilemma can be escaped by exploring more deeply the political point of view, which contains a number of challengeable assumptions. It may transpire that the values underlying the stand taken by the worker representatives and the works council rest on false, or at least questionable, assumptions.

There are three higher-level principles, all concerned with both values and efficiency, which Pedersen should claim in support of a decision to go ahead with the investment:

● Obviously it is important what theory one has about how best to help the black South Africans. Presumably the theory of the worker representatives is that some kind of withdrawal from South Africa by everybody would contribute to the fall of the government and a faster re-establishment of the position of the black majority.

This can be contrasted with another (empirically better founded) theory essentially claiming that some short-term improvement is better than very uncertain long-term improvement; that exactly this kind of technologically rather simple industry particularly benefits the development of the type of social and economic infrastructure which is useful to a rather undeveloped economy. Moreover, having a business channel with South Africa is more effective for communicating humanistic and social values in the long run than no channel at all.

● The second principle has to do with the dynamics and logic of a mature industry like steel-tube making. As the technology is becoming more accessible to everyone, it increases the efficiency of the whole industry to move production to places where wages are lower and there is just enough skill to handle the production.

● With the same logic, one should not use skilled resources in the home plant at Helsingor to do things which can be done at lower cost elsewhere.

Less advanced countries need to grow

The last two points are based on the same fundamental principle, namely that resources should always be put to the most efficient use possible. Resources in a more advanced infrastructure such as Helsingor should be used for more difficult tasks than resources functioning in a less advanced one. Otherwise one would not give the less advanced country a chance to grow and one would not put high enough requirements on the more advanced country. Failure to do either of these things would be unethical, in my view.

There are two other aspects to this case. Firstly, I believe that no company can be efficient in the long run without developing, and grappling with, ethical principles and putting them into effect. This particular situation could be an important, critical event for Helsingor Steel. Perhaps a practical idea would be for a group of active people in the company to charter a plane and go to the plant in South Africa This would contribute to a company ethic founded in concrete social reality as well as in business efficiency. It could lead to ideas on how to use the company's influence in South Africa in the future.

Develop a set of company ethics

Secondly, I think this company has a more fundamental problem for which the South African issue has come to serve as a cover-up. Obviously it lacks ideas about what to do with at least 1,000 people employed at home. Rather than letting the black majority in South Africa suffer from the lack of growth in the company, steps must be taken to see how the Scandinavian resources can be used. Perhaps valid investment alternatives could be found. But investment money should not be used to protect Scandinavians doing what South Africans can do more efficiently.

The company's dilemma can be used, if skilfully managed, *not* to reject the "political" point of view but really to develop a higher and more genuine set of ethics in the company, making it possible to face the real problems.

This decision was provided by Richard Normann in his capacity as a director of Scandinavian Institutes for Administrative Research, and head of its Paris office.

How can a car components firm make participation work?

When Charles Hanson became president and chief executive of Weaver Instruments Inc., a US components supplier, he put high on his priorities the introduction into the company of a group incentive plan. All employees would gain from improved productivity and earnings.

However, what had seemed a simple way of obtaining more commitment and production from his work-force ran into problems he had not anticipated.

Weaver supplied small, specialized components for the automobile industry. It had to compete for labour with local industries that offered more congenial working conditions.

Worker discontent in the non-union plant, together with union attempts to achieve recognition, had led to production delays. These in turn had caused the early retirement of the previous president and Hanson's appointment.

His aim was that everybody in the organization should participate in a joint effort to reduce costs, cut down on waste, improve efficiency, increase productivity and share monetary gains in accordance with an agreed formula.

After initial reservations, most workers agreed to try out the idea. Shop-floor production committees were set up.

However, the decision-making powers that were devolved to the committees caused discontent among some middle managers and first-line supervisors. The supervisor in one key production area was not particularly militant. He said he had not given 20 years' service to the company to end up with no authority. He was offered a job in another part of the plant but resigned.

Departmental meetings poorly conducted

In making their productivity suggestions, some of the shop-floor committees abolished the jobs of some of their own members. Hanson had guaranteed that in such cases noone would be fired. However, in one department open warfare developed between the older and the younger men.

The older ones felt that the newcomers to the department should be the ones to transfer to other jobs within the company. The younger men said it was the older ones who should move over, since they were headed for retirement anyway.

At one meeting of this departmental committee, the argument became so heated that men were on their feet shouting at one another. The chairman, who was a worker elected by the committee, was unable to keep order.

Normally under the scheme, management attended the meetings only as an observer. But the manager at this meeting felt compelled to intervene to prevent chaos.

The committee then accused management of ignoring the rules. The department stopped work and within a day all production at the factory came to a sudden halt.

Hanson had set up a steering committee, made up of representatives of all the shop-floor committees, to advise on disagreements within the committees and how they might be resolved. But it had no real authority. When this committee advised the troubled department to return to work and also said that no immediate action should be taken by management to implement the productivity scheme in that department, it was open to question whether the advice would be accepted.

It was accepted. Production restarted. But Hanson now faced a revolt from some of his own managers, including Frank Briggs, the head of production.

"What would you have done if the departmental committee had failed to accept the recommendation of the steering committee?" Briggs asked Hanson one lunch-time.

Pay deals versus incentives

When Hanson made no reply, Briggs continued: "With production schedules so vital, I think you would have waved a big stick and insisted on management's right to manage."

The same day Hanson heard that a unionized competitor in the same town had negotiated a pay deal with the union that was more favourable to its employees, in the short term, than the productivity-related increases at Weaver.

He was left wondering whether he should abandon his incentive plan, with its participation at shop-floor level, accept the union into the plant and negotiate with it. He knew that this course would lose him a lot of respect and credibility.

Alternatively, should he modify the operation of the shop-floor committees to prevent internal disagreements shutting down the plant? But if so, how? It seemed a difficult dilemma.

DECISION

Manager should gain the support of supervisors

Hanson should continue with the establishment of an atmosphere of collaboration and participation at shop-floor level. He should also continue to have as a primary objective the avoidance of unionization of a large proportion of his workers.

Such sentiments, coming from a European, may sound heretical. Indeed in a European setting the issue of whether or not to accept the union into the plant would not be relevant, since legislation as well as normal practice regulates the matter in a different way than in the US.

Hanson's introduction of a group incentive plan and a participation scheme was an excellent move. What could be criticized, however, is the *way* in which the system has been introduced.

A more carefully planned introduction, properly prepared, with adequate information and discussions with other managers and first-line supervisors, would have enhanced the chances of obtaining their consensus and subsequently their cooperation.

The introduction of committees at Weaver Instruments has been quite successful. The problem that emerged in one department was solved in a positive way by the steering committee.

Participation must stay

The real problem confronting Hanson is the negative attitude of some of the first-line supervisors and of Frank Briggs and some middle managers. Hanson should concentrate his efforts on gaining their support, as indeed he should have done more comprehensively at first.

He should convene a meeting of all managers and put it to them that the alternative to continuing with the bonus system, and making participation work, is the unionization of the company. Do they want that?

He should explain that in order to avoid unionization the first thing to be done is to raise the basic wages of employees to match the new wages of workers in other local firms. This must be done before an official request is presented by the workers themselves.

He should say that at the same time it is necessary to keep and revamp the incentive scheme, and its participative character, to make it consistent with the new level of wages.

He should admit frankly that participation has not gone as smoothly as he hoped. He should make it plain, however, that he is as committed as ever to the principle of participation.

There is little doubt that faced with the choice between having to deal with the union in the future or having another go at participation, many of the company's managers will prefer the latter.

Motivating staff reveals management skills

Hanson should then suggest employing a professional mediator to chair a joint working party comprising middle managers, supervisors and chairmen of the shop-floor committees. Its brief would be to amend participation procedures, perhaps giving greater authority to the steering committee, perhaps looking afresh at the rule for selection of chairmen.

It could also lay down an order of priorities for the transfer of personnel, as part of productivity improvements, from one department to another.

Hanson should point out that genuine participation does not detract from the ability of managers to manage and that a criterion of management performance in the company in the future will be how well managers motivate their people and operate successfully in partnership with the shop-floor committees.

This approach will enhance Hanson's credibility, increase the chances of the incentive plan succeeding and minimize the risk of costly interruption of production in the future.

This decision was provided by Salvatore Teresi in his capacity as director general of Centre Européen d'Education Permanente (CEDEP) in Fontainebleau, France. He was previously a professor in marketing and a director at the European Institute of Business Administration (INSEAD) and has acted as a consultant for organization and marketing problems.

How can workers be persuaded to accept a tough boss?

Looking back, Leonid Gorschkov, general manager of three state-owned interrelated factories in an East European state, could see that his troubles became more acute the day he moved Rudolf Zabrodin, a brilliant engineer, from production supervision to financial administration.

The three plants produced components for agricultural machinery. None was fully on target for the current five-year plan, but the transmission factory was well off course.

Six months previously, the government minister responsible for the factories had told Gorschkov that he had to improve the situation in the transmission plant. Gorschkov had made an excuse about teething problems at the plant. Only a year before, it had been converted to transmission manufacture from a much less onerous assembly operation.

Gorschkov had realized that many of the plant's problems stemmed from the workers' resentment of exchanging the quiet environment to which they were accustomed for the increased noise and dirt of an engineering workshop.

He had consulted the works council before putting Zabrodin in charge of production supervision and giving him a virtual free hand to get things right on the production side. The council had been unenthusiastic but had not opposed the idea.

Zabrodin speedily isolated the areas of the production lines that were causing trouble. With tough questioning of the supervisors and workers he cut through the smoke-screen of excuses to the real problem. There had been some dramatic improvements in production.

When man-management abilities are limited

However, Gorschkov had soon become aware of growing discontent with the engineer's lack of tact. Unfortunately, Zabrodin had a tongue as sharp as his mind. His man-management abilities were limited. He found it difficult to command the loyalty of his subordinates. And because he was finding faults on the production line, the negative side of his character and abilities was exposed.

Eventually, the minister summoned Gorschkov to his office again. He said that he had learned, through his own sources, that there were demands from the works council for Zabrodin to be removed. Gorschkov was aware of these demands but had fended them off. "Maybe you ought to heed them," the minister said.

"Will you give me another production engineer of equal calibre?" Gorschkov countered.

"Such men are hard to find," the minister had replied. "Anyway, that is your problem, not mine."

Bowing to combined pressure from the works council, the trade union organizer and, he ruefully admitted, the minister, Gorschkov transferred Zabrodin to a job where he could exercise his mind without spreading ripples of indignation around the shop floor.

126

The move pleased the works council. But almost at once production began to slip badly again. It was clear that Zabrodin's successor, who had a pleasant personality but was relatively inexperienced, was proving to be less than adequate.

At another meeting with the minister, the previous day, Gorschkov was threatened with replacement unless he could get production back on target.

"I need Zabrodin back on the shop floor, preferably with the agreement of the people there," he told the minister. "If I convene a meeting will you come down and address the workers, telling them the importance that the government attaches to fulfilling these production targets?"

Achieving production targets essential

"I am sorry but that is impossible," answered the minister. "Tomorrow I go abroad with a trade delegation. Whatever you do, you will have to do yourself."

Gorschkov realized that he should have fought harder to keep Zabrodin in the job where he could do most good, regardless of democratic and ministerial pressures. He now saw Zabrodin, despite his abrasive nature, as essential to the achievement of production targets in the transmission plant.

There must be a way, he thought, to harness democratic opinion so that he could restore the engineer to his old position with general consent. But how could it be done? Patriotic appeals without the backing of the minister would be useless.

Was there, even at this stage, an alternative he had not thought of?

DECISION

When the right man for the job is the wrong one for the workers

Gorschkov's dilemma exposes a classic management predicament. It can be stated as follows: pushing for production may provoke resentment, which can diminish production even further. If you act to keep people happy, you avoid those actions that are necessary for improved production; therefore, production continues at a low level.

In the case of the abrasive Zabrodin and the urgent need to improve production in the transmission factory, several ways of intervening might be considered. One is more basic than the others. Unfortunately, it is also much longer-term and is not practical under the prevailing circumstances. Therefore, we will formulate the more immediate, though less desirable, alternatives first.

Appeal for loyalty

There are several approaches that might enable Zabrodin to be active on the production side without creating a mini-revolution. One is that Gorschkov might ask the workers for loyalty. Apparently he feels that appeals to patriotism would be useless without the backing of the minister. Even if this were true, there are other forms of loyalty, including, perhaps, loyalty to Gorschkov himself.

He could ask the workers for cooperation because this would not only help production but also ease the tensions that he himself feels from his boss. He could also argue that once the production problem is cleared up the pressures will diminish.

Another possible approach is to use Zabrodin's successor as a buffer. Let Zabrodin make the decisions that would increase productivity but use his successor as the go-between, passing on the message in a manner that would be more acceptable to the works council.

All of these are temporary palliatives. A more enduring, though still inadequate, solution might be for Gorschkov to talk with Zabrodin and make clear to him the nature of the complaints about his method of working.

He might then convene a general session in which the workers who feel the tensions created by Zabrodin have the opportunity to confront him directly with their complaints, spelling out in frank detail the kind of behaviour that causes them to feel antagonistic.

Provide opportunity to clear the air

There are numerous advantages in this kind of approach:

First, it permits existing tensions to be discharged instead of being kept bottled up.

Second, it opens up channels of communication directly with those who feel the tensions.

Third, it means that when, in the future, Zabrodin backslides, as inevitably he will, channels for discussion will have been established. It is easier to communicate once the ice has been broken.

Fourth, it involves the workers themselves in attempting to resolve human problems that are barriers to productivity.

Fifth, it avoids polarizing existing tensions in the plant even further.

Although this alternative is practical, and can be relied upon to relieve the tensions in the situation and permit those involved to refocus on production problems, it is not the ideal long-term solution to the problem Gorschkov faces in the factory.

Teach the theory of man-management

With the best will in the world, and often unwittingly, Zabrodin will provoke new tensions. With each provocation the advantages of better communication and of the new-found frankness will begin to be eroded and become less effective.

Gorschkov needs to have a talk with Zabrodin and needs to let the workers air their grievances in a frank, open session in the hope of solving his immediate problem. But the best long-term solution would be to provide his staff with the theoretical background which will enable them to understand better why people behave as they do.

Only when his managers are aware of the theories of human behaviour, and of people management, will they be able to apply those theories in shop-floor situations.

This decision was provided by U.S. behavioural scientists Dr. Robert Blake and Dr. Jane Mouton who jointly invented Blake's Grid, a method of identifying management styles, in their respective capacities as president and vice president of U.S. consultancy firm Scientific Methods Inc.

Should 'consensus management' be dropped to boost flagging production?

For several months, chief executive William Speight was happy with the new style of management he had introduced at US firm Super-Audio Inc. following a visit to Japan.

Then he began to receive complaints from one or two buyers of Super-Audio's music centre and radiogram components. Some concerned late deliveries. Others were about the delay in confirming whether Super-Audio could modify its products to meet changing customer requirements.

When Speight referred these complaints to his production and marketing managers, they implied that he was to blame. The "Japanese-style consensus management", as they called it, which he had introduced into the plant, was causing them a lot of problems.

"You came back from Japan," said Harold Potts, who was in charge of production, "abolished executive parking spaces, made everyone eat at the same tables in the same canteen, did away with time-clocks and introduced a trust system.

"It went down well with the workers, although personally I don't like the newest recruit to this factory occupying my old parking space next to the front entrance. But I'll go along with that.

"I'll even go along with all this after-hours socializing. But I must draw the line at consensus management, particularly if I am to be blamed for production delays.

Unanimous decisions take longer

"I know that you would like to see an end to demarcation problems. So would I. But all these meetings and all these delays while people experiment with different work routines are playing havoc with my production schedules. Two 20-minute meetings each day between a supervisor and his workers for general discussions about the job are beyond a joke."

Charles Groom, the marketing manager, also complained. "In this plant you have to hold a meeting before you can blow your nose," he grumbled. "I'd like to know where else in the U.S. all work place decisions have to be unanimous. If you want the modifications demanded by customers, and in reasonable time, the engineers must have authority to order them at once, after consulting sales, rather than discussing them with everyone."

Speight pointed out that decisions did not have to be unanimous but depended on a "critical weight of opinion", after which dissenters fell into line. "People said it could never work in a U.S. factory," he said. "Well, it has with us, without too many problems. As for the delays, not all of them are due to the meetings."

He reminded Potts and Groom that absenteeism in the plant was down by 60%, that productivity was up by 8% and that the number of items rejected by quality control had fallen from 5% to 2%.

Even Speight was shaken the following week, however, when the company received a warning from a major music centre manufacturer. Unless there was an end to uncertainty about the supply of a tuning

129

device, the customer said, it would withdraw its business, worth $3 million a year, from Super-Audio.

Groom immediately brought this threat to Speight's attention. He at once summoned Potts to his office. The production manager was blunt. "Delays on the production line," he said, "stem directly from the fact that the work group involved agreed to replace continuously moving belts by ones that could be stopped at will. If someone on the line hasn't fitted a part to his own satisfaction, the line is stopped while he makes the adjustment. This increases the time.

Concensus management favoured over unionization

"More quality control is being done on the job, as you well know. That's the reason rejects are down. But it's also the reason why production is flagging. If you want to catch up on this order, do I have your permission to go down there and instruct them to keep the line going?"

Urged on by Groom, Speight finally agreed. Potts departed, and within an hour the supervisor of that section, a man who had served the company for years, was in the chief executive's office protesting that Potts' directive went against the consensus decision of the work group.

In Potts' presence, Speight explained the situation. The supervisor was not impressed. "I'll tell you something that perhaps you didn't know," he said. "Just before you introduced consensus management here there was a strong move in the work-force to get unionized. We decided, instead, to give your ideas a try. Now we like them. If you try to change back to the old ways of operating you will run into real trouble. After all the things that you have told us about the reasons for Japanese success and how we can emulate them, you can't go back on them now."

"That's all I need," Speight thought. "Now what do I do?"

DECISION

Japanese-style management disrupts U.S. firm

C hief executive William Speight has returned from Japan enthusiastic about an effective style of management. He is learning, however, that while it is important to draw benefits from unfamiliar cultures it is difficult, if not impossible, to duplicate exactly the systems that operate within those cultures.

It appears that Speight's company has gained from "consensus management" in terms of improved productivity and quality control. But now he has encountered problems, he must try to deal with them pragmatically, sorting them out in the culture he knows best, his own.

It is not clear whether Speight's dilemma is a result of trying to adapt Japanese methods or whether it would have arisen in any case, as a result of any attempt to improve employee participation and involvement.

The immediate crisis appears to stem from a simple failure to meet production targets. This suggests unsatisfactory production supervision and control, for which consensus management is an unacceptable excuse.

Perhaps production delays could be reduced by removing an item that

130

needs additional attention to a side bench, so that the flow of other products is not interrupted while the faulty item is attended to.

If this suggestion had been put to the work group concerned, instead of the production manager thundering down, with Speight's agreement, and ordering the line to be kept going, the workers might have agreed to stop the line less often and trouble might have been avoided.

Indeed, in a Japanese factory, with everybody pulling together in a genuine way, the workers themselves probably would have suggested changes. Certainly, delays in production would not have been allowed to proceed to the point where an order was at risk.

Speight, in fact, seems a rather ineffectual, if idealistic, chief executive. The incident should be a warning to him that he needs to rethink his approach to consensus management and what it is realistic to achieve.

Apparently his workers enjoy the management style from Japan. But would they like it if the company went bust and they lost their jobs?

Is Speight really trying to operate a Japanese style of management or does he just think he is?

Decision-making patterns are different

There are many misconceptions concerning Japanese management. Speight abolished differential parking and canteens, for example, evidently feeling he was doing something Japanese. In fact, of course, the Japanese are the prime exponents of hierarchy. If they eat in the same canteen, their behaviour will still be based upon status deriving from age, sex and the university they attended.

Speight also introduced more meetings into his plant so that employees could stop working for 20 minutes for discussions with their supervisor. But in a Japanese plant there is a natural *obayun* (parent) to *kobun* (child) relationship which does not exist, in the normal way, in a Western factory, no matter how paternalistic its management. A Japanese supervisor will refer to a group of about five people as his *kobun*. He might well go to their weddings and be godfather to their children.

So there is a relationship in the Japanese work group, beginning with the morning prayer meeting when the *obayun* announces his targets for the day, that Speight's people cannot hope to emulate.

There is a strong emotional element in the working life of the Japanese. It follows that for a Western company to operate a "Japanese" system, it has to improve the emotional as well as the intellectual climate in a plant.

It also faces the stumbling block that "decision" does not mean the same thing to a Japanese. The Western manager or worker believes that he must think things out, then come to a decision. The Japanese think things out then swing into action. There is no identifiable decision point.

Therefore, any consensus work group in a Western factory is bound to operate differently from a group in a Japanese plant. It will arrive at its consensus as a compromise between widely polarized points of view. This takes longer and is more difficult.

Speight should look at his participation procedures coldly to see if they work and, if not, why not. For this purpose, he should forget Japan entirely.

This decision was provided by Dr. William Barry in his capacity as chairman of the Euro-Japanese Exchange Foundation and of HTS Management Holding Ltd., a U.K.-based finance company involved with about 15 companies, including three management training centres.

Should firm act to stop managers' disclosures to their union?

Lucien Gottfried, the personnel director, sat down heavily. Clearly he was angry. "What's it all about?" asked Bernard Montpelier, who had joined Rambert & Cie., a large confectionery firm in Belgium, as managing director only six months previously.

Gottfried reminded Montpelier that Rambert had recognized a managerial trade union during the term of the previous managing director. Many of the middle managers had joined.

The night before, Gottfried said, he had met a senior official of the union informally, before negotiations began in earnest over the managers' next claim for increased salaries and better working conditions.

One of their main concerns had been to increase the opportunities for promotion and career advancement. These had suffered while Montpelier's predecessor had pursued a policy of consolidation.

"Frankly," the official had said, taking a sheaf of paper from his briefcase, "my members don't consider the first draft of your next five-year plan to be sufficiently expansive. They feel there should be much more emphasis on growth."

He had proceeded to point to several areas where increased investment would provide more career scope for managers and, by implication, for lower levels of employees too.

Essential corporate decisions justify a leak

Gottfried had sat through this stunned, both by the information the man had in his possession and the open way he was discussing it in a crowded restaurant. "Tell me," the union man had concluded, "does the new man at the helm intend to be any more adventurous?"

Not trusting himself to say anything, Gottfried had pleaded a migraine and suggested they meet again the following day.

"Where did this leak come from?" Montpelier demanded.

"Only the corporate planning department has had access to the details of broad investment strategy over the next five years," Gottfried replied. "It didn't take me long to work out who the culprit was. Henri Dulac, the deputy manager there, and one of the most active members of the union.

"I have just had him down in my office, confronted him with it and he agreed he had done it. He was quite unrepentant. He said that union officials had to know essential details of corporate intentions in order to negotiate properly on their members' behalf. I told him it was intolerable and that I was recommending to you that he should be moved to a department where he doesn't have the same access to confidential information."

"As I see it," Gottfried continued, "it's a straight matter of trust. If we don't establish the principle that managers have no right to release confidential information to outsiders, without express permission from a director, then everyone will feel free to reveal company secrets. Now I am due to meet this union official again. Will you come with me?"

They met the official, Pierre Dubois, at a restaurant nearby. After the introductions, and without preliminary discussion, Dubois said: "One of our members, Henri Dulac, has telephoned me to say you intend to dismiss him from his job in the planning department. Any attempt to discipline this man will be regarded by us as victimization."

"We are moving Dulac sideways and not even demoting him," Gottfried retorted. "This is a normal internal management decision that has nothing to do with industrial relations."

"It is intolerable that a company cannot plan and keep its plans confidential," Montpelier said. "I intend to call my managers together and obtain a firm undertaking from them that they will not leak company secrets in future, either to you or to anyone else."

"And at our next union meeting," said Dubois evenly, "we will discuss what action to take. You know it is the policy of the union to keep confidential any information it receives. But that policy can be broken. For example, you have a works council. You are supposed to give it full information but normally you tone it down a lot. You didn't let the council see your initial calculations for manning levels at your projected new factory. We know what those levels will really be, and that didn't come from Dulac, it came from someone else. It would be very easy for us, in a state of open warfare, to leak such information to the manual workers' unions."

It was with this threat ringing in their ears that Montpelier and Gottfried returned to the office. Gottfried argued for a show-down. "We ought to sack him."

Montpelier was undecided. The company could not afford a prolonged confrontation with a managerial union flexing its muscles and determined to establish its power. Yet if he gave in on this issue how could he ever hope to stem the outward flow of confidential information and assert his authority?

DECISION

Disclosures to managerial union threaten firm's confidentiality

When Bernard Montpelier sits down quietly to reflect, he will realize that lack of forethought in the company in the past has landed him with not one, but three, problems.

They are: what to do about Dulac, who has given away confidential information; how to set up an agreed code of practice concerning what information should be passed to the union; and how to counter the union's apparently jaundiced view of the five-year plan.

Undoubtedly Henri Dulac is guilty of an error of judgment in his breach of trust and should be reprimanded for it, at least at the level of an "informal warning." The decision to reprimand, however, should be made and implemented by Dulac's own, immediate manager, and not handed down by Lucien Gottfried or Montpelier, no matter how much they are personally aggrieved or inconvenienced by Dulac's actions.

Indeed, Gottfried should have given to Dulac's manager originally the job of discovering the leak rather than pursuing the matter himself.

Under no circumstances should Montpelier sanction the moving of

Dulac out of the planning department. That would be counter-productive, in that it would transfer Dulac's skills to some place where they would be under-utilized. Moreover, transferring Dulac would not solve the problem of how to regulate confidential information in the future.

It is impossible to prevent information being passed on if there is no agreed code of practice and no common understanding of the ethics involved by the individuals concerned and the union.

The problem, and the question of divided loyalties, should have been faced by Gottfried at the time the managerial trade union was recognized, and included in the procedural agreement. Solving the problem is now a priority and Gottfried has to formulate jointly with the union and the managers a code of practice relating to disclosure of information.

It should not be too difficult to get common agreement that confidentiality is an integral, often explicit, part of certain jobs, and that strict adherence to rules of confidentiality protects not only the company but individuals in it. The union itself would be quick to complain about breaches of confidence in Gottfried's own area, personnel.

The code should attempt to cover not only the current upset but also what information ought to be made available to the union, and by what routes and authorities.

Confidentiality is a complex matter

One thing that is not going to help is escalation of the "them" and "us" attitudes and sabre-rattling that both sides have indulged in so far. Escalation always takes place when people strike attitudes, as both Montpelier and the union official, Pierre Dubois, did at the lunch they convened.

There remains the problem of the union's adverse reaction to the company's five-year plan, as leaked by Dulac. This, in fact, is a golden opportunity for Montpelier, who has been with the company only six months, to make his mark and establish management's right to manage.

He should be prepared to discuss the plan, in confidence, with his managers as a body and perhaps with the blue-collar union as well.

At these meetings he could ram home the business concepts behind the plan and stress that a prime objective of management, in its planning, is the security of employment of all employees.

Montpelier must also discuss the conflicts in business strategy and why it will never at any point be possible to satisfy all the criteria

Finally, Montpelier must ask Gottfried to answer the questions posed by the need to recognize a management union in the first place, including whether, and why, there was insufficient communication with managers.

One thing is certain, Montpelier must rapidly involve the members of the union – the shop stewards or area representatives – without appearing to shut out Dubois, the outside union official.

The whole complex question of confidentiality can only be resolved by a common understanding that there is no real division of loyalties. Business information properly belongs only to the business, and must be recognized as such. Proper facilities must nevertheless be available for managers and union officers to be adequately informed.

This decision was provided by Alan Murton in his capacity as personnel controller at Dexion Ltd., U.K. manufacturer of storage and materials-handling equipment.

Should Brazilian firm fire finance manager to clinch offer of investment cash?

José Carvalho, president of Elétrico do Brasil SA, was interested in the approach made to his company by Worldwide Data Processing Corp. (WDP). It had come at a time when the Brazilian company was approaching a crossroads in its history, and seemed an ideal solution to Elétrico's problems of modernization and diversification. However, there was a condition attached which presented Carvalho with a moral problem.

Established 25 years ago as a small workshop manufacturing electric fires, Elétrico had acquired an expertise in sheet metal working that led it into making filing cabinets and other metal-based items of office furniture. Gradually, office equipment became its main product.

In the past six years, however, technological advances in office equipment had begun to threaten the company's future. Its limited financial and research and development resources meant that it would soon have to decide whether it could continue to offer a complete range.

For example, the company had marketed its own minicomputer, assembled largely from imported components. The board had decided, however, that it could not afford to develop a word processor.

Solving the company's problems

Edward Brassover, chief executive of WDP's Brazilian subsidiary, explained to Carvalho that his company wanted to take large but minority shareholdings in local Brazilian companies and pump in as much modern technology as it could. "In that way we get the best of both worlds – high market penetration and respectability," he said.

Over lunch the two men discussed a proposal which would give WDP 45% of the equity in Elétrico. This would be paid for partly in cash, over a period of three years, and partly in terms of new technology.

Carvalho tried hard to conceal his excitement. He would need to make WDP raise the cash side of its offer, but he sensed that the US company was already expecting to have to do that. The deal would solve most of his corporate problems, it seemed to him, at a stroke.

"There is just one thing, however," Brassover continued. "You know that your finance manager, Antonio Pereira, used to work for us?"

Carvalho nodded.

"Did you check his references?"

"Of course," said Carvalho, "but you know your company never gives any information on employees other than when they joined, when they left and their job title. I am very glad we did hire Pereira, though. It has taken a tremendous amount of financial juggling to provide the investment to keep our products up to date. I doubt there are more than two or three people in Brazil who could have done it."

"Financial juggling is not what WDP wants when large sums of its money are at stake," said Brassover after a pause. "You see, we obliged Pereira to leave after he was found to have misappropriated company money. This deal cannot go through if he remains on your staff."

After thinking over this uncompromising statement for 24 hours, Carvalho tackled the finance manager about it. Was it true, he asked?

"It depends on how you look at it," said Pereira. "Yes, I borrowed some of WDP's money, but I paid it all back and I myself informed the company of what I had done. I simply gave myself an advance to cover some unexpected and heavy family expenses."

When circumstances are desperate

Pereira explained that several members of his family had been in a car crash. Both his daughters had received severe facial injuries, which necessitated expensive plastic surgery. His brother, who had been driving the car, had lost his driving licence and hence his job, so Pereira had had to support two families for several months. When he had asked WDP for a loan he had been curtly told that the company was not a bank. In desperation, he had gathered the money in the only way he could. Such circumstances were never likely to happen again, he stressed.

That evening, Carvalho mulled over the alternatives again. True, Pereira had revealed none of this when he had been appointed to the job five years ago. But then, no one had thought to ask such a question.

It was unlikely that Brassover could be made to change his mind. There was, perhaps, an element of personal animosity between the two men, Carvalho suspected. But Pereira had shown himself to be a hard-working, scrupulously honest employee during his time at Elétrico.

He and Carvalho had become close friends. Was it fair to penalize someone for an apparently harmless misdemeanour in the past?

He had to make a quick decision for Brassover had stressed that WDP's president would be in Brazil next month to begin negotiations.

DECISION

Manager's past misdemeanour threatens his firm's future

José Carvalho's problem is a difficult one. A decision which may meet the needs of his company may well offend the basic tenets of natural justice. On the other hand, if he decides to behave in a decent manner towards a loyal employee, albeit one with a hidden stain on his character, he may put at risk a deal which appears to be of considerable benefit to the firm and all of its employees.

Carvalho should look at all the implications from the point of view of each of the three major parties to the dilemma, including himself.

He may decide that Antonio Pereira behaved in a culpable way when he decided to "borrow" money from Worldwide Data Processing Corp. (WDP) without the company's knowledge and agreement. It was a serious breach of trust. Yet he was never brought to justice. Presumably his employers decided not to submit the matter to the police or to the judicial authorities. We must therefore accept him as innocent in law.

Although his action was an improper one, it must be recognized that the circumstances warranted some compassion. WDP was extremely ruthless in refusing to assist Pereira in dealing with a sad family problem. He was very wrong in "borrowing" the money in a manner which could have landed him in jail. Nevertheless, he repaid it all.

The fact that he had not disclosed this misdemeanour during his subsequent interview should not be held against him. He was never asked questions pertaining to the subject and he did not tell lies. His present loyalty and effectiveness seem to be of the highest, and he deserves some loyalty in return from his employers.

Carvalho may also conclude that Edward Brassover of WDP is a very tough man. He demonstrated his ruthlessness by refusing to help Pereira when he was in a very distressed state. He now demonstrates the same streak by refusing to let bygones be bygones. At the same time his company can be accused of a serious dereliction of propriety in that it refrained from telling Pereira's new employers all that it knew about Pereira. It is doubtful whether this silence stemmed from a desire to be helpful to Pereira, since WDP's general behaviour did not at any stage demonstrate such a wish.

True, there is no legal obligation to disclose improper conduct when one gives a reference to would-be employers. But it is very unkind to complain afterwards, when a man has settled down to a new job in a firm that is unaware of the unsavoury part of his earlier unfortunate history.

Consider a plea for justice and decency
Brassover's present behaviour does not augur well for a happy partnership between the two companies. Indeed, Brassover or his colleagues may have committed an offence by not reporting the matter to the police or the legal authorities. It is curious that while WDP opted not to report the matter to the police, it is taking such an intransigent attitude now. Carvalho should point this out to Brassover.

Carvalho may accuse himself of having been dilatory in his interviewing methods when Pereira did not volunteer to tell his new employers about his earlier problem; it is clear that no searching questions were posed to him. In the light of the poor information given by his previous employers, there was a case for questioning Pereira much more closely.

So Carvalho may feel that he, of all people, is in no position to blame Pereira for non-disclosure of the facts in relation to his "borrowing" episode. He must conclude that Brassover is a hard man who only understands firmness from others. And he must confront Brassover and seek to establish that no other allegations exist against Pereira. If there are none, then Carvalho must stand by Pereira and attempt to convince Brassover of the injustice of his demand.

It is a test of Brassover's sense of natural justice and social decency, which Carvalho can probe gently and diplomatically. If, however, the result is negative, if persuasion is to no avail, then Carvalho would be well advised to look for a new partner, regardless of the short-term problems that it may entail. The appropriate epitaph to the encounter with Brassover would be: "With such friends you do not need enemies."

This decision was provided by Simon Majaro in his capacity as a director of Strategic Management Learning, which organizes training programmes for senior managers, and as managing director of U.K.-based Simon Majaro Ltd., international management consultants.

How can MD find the ideal marketing man?

"All I want is a good marketing man with a bit of drive," mutters Dr. Wolfram Koch, managing director of Brann & Koch AG, as his Mercedes glides up the driveway to his home outside Frankfurt. "That shouldn't be such a difficult job." Yet, he recalls the executive search specialist he engaged has taken five weeks to find three candidates. And none of them seems fully qualified for the duties Koch has in mind.

The man Koch is looking for would be vital to the success of the German cement company's diversification into the booming plasterboard market. When Koch had decided on the new venture, he had realized that his small company would need to obtain financing as well as production expertise from outside. After lengthy discussions the diversified Swiss group Ciments Vulcain SA agreed to support the new venture.

In exchange for providing a sizeable loan and technical help, Vulcain insisted on a majority of the equity and management control of the new firm. Brann & Koch would initially appoint only four of the eleven supervisory board members. However, it would gain majority control and equity when the full amount of the loan had been repaid out of profits. Koch confidently expected that this would take not much more than three years. In the meantime, the joint venture's top executive post would be held by Walther Habbel, a forceful production executive from Vulcain.

Leadership and experience required

Meanwhile, Brann & Koch were to provide the local marketing expertise. Brann & Koch's first responsibility under the agreement was to carry out a much more detailed feasibility and planning study over the next six months. So Koch had approached executive searcher Rudolph Schwarzenbach to find a man who could carry out a study of the potential market and find a suitable plant location. Once the operation was under way, this executive would take over as marketing director seconded from Brann & Koch to the new firm.

The man to be appointed, Koch had explained to Schwarzenbach, would be a person with the medium term potential to take over the top job in the new company, probably in two to three years' time. He would act as the leader of the project for Brann & Koch and should have the stature to take charge of negotiations between the firm and Vulcain. Koch had stated that this man should be at least 35, and should have a wide knowledge of building products, especially plasterboard. To fit into Brann & Koch's salary structure, it would be difficult to pay him more than $28,000. Now, some weeks later, Koch has interviewed Schwarzenbach's three candidates.

The first, an energetic 29-year-old researcher, impressed him as clearly well qualified to take on the market study. But, Koch snorted, he could hardly take on the greater responsibilities he had in mind for later.

The second candidate was a born salesman, and Koch felt certain he would be an ideal sales director. But Koch was concerned about the man's lack of formal education and his overpowering enthusiasm and optimism. He felt that these factors would make it difficult for the candidate to produce an accurate or realistic market survey. And they also worked against his chances of being a hard-headed top manager.

The third candidate was an older man whom Koch had taken to immediately. He had a fine record in general management, with some experience of the plasterboard industry. He had the competence and the even temperament to deal with the Vulcain executives, and Koch could easily visualize him taking over the chief executive role from Habbel in due course. But he was already earning well over the salary limit Koch thought acceptable. And Koch had some doubts about whether he would be prepared to come down to the more prosaic work that would inevitably mark the early days of the new operation.

Decide on the priorities

After the interviews, Koch had turned to the consultant, remarking scornfully: "With 62 million people in Germany, surely you could find someone closer to my requirements."

Schwarzenbach had retorted: "I don't think it is reasonable to expect one man to satisfy all your requirements in every detail, at least not at the salary you are willing to pay.

"I do think any one of these men could do the total job well, and at least one phase of it brilliantly. All you have to do is decide what your priorities are."

Koch, slightly offended by Schwarzenbach's direct answer, dismissed him with a curt: "I will let you know."

Now he pondered the alternatives. Should he hire one of the three candidates? Or should he instruct Schwarzenbach to continue his search? Or maybe he should hire another consultant?

DECISION

Probably only by recruiting from outside and paying the appropriate salary

Dr. Koch's experience is a common one when recruiting: he suddenly has to confront a number of contradictions, which result from poor grasp of a problem.

Let us begin by examining the steps involved in the diversification policy and then the recruitment proposal.

First of all, we learn that a small cement firm, Brann & Koch, plans to diversify by entering the plasterboard market. But then we learn in turn that it will need financial assistance; that it lacks the necessary production expertise; that it must recruit an outside marketing specialist; and that it proposes to make him managing director in the long term.

Now a successful diversification policy always presupposes that the firm has excess resources, such that it has a great advantage over its competitors. This can be strong financial resources, highly-skilled managerial staff, a distribution network, in-depth knowledge of a similar technology or a solid image quality. These resources must naturally be available for the new line of products. This is what some authors have labelled a "diversification base". There is considerable doubt as to whether Koch had such a base for plasterboard. Thus the first question he should have asked himself seriously ought to have been: does my company have the means at its disposal to carry out a diversification policy?

He should then have systematically attempted to find a product which was capable of exploiting the strong points of his firm and for which the weak points were not disastrous. Precise methods for discovering and selecting new activities are available, and are a valuable aid in decision making in this field. There is no evidence that Koch would have adopted the same policy had he used such methods before taking a decision.

But let us look at the recruitment. Koch expects his successful candidate to act in three different capacities: negotiator between Brann & Koch and Vulcain for matters concerning the new firm; marketing director the new firm; and its managing director in about three years.

It is at this point that the contradictions become fully clear. The essential problem boils down to finding a successor to Habbel. Three years is a short time to develop a top manager and there is a long way to go between carrying out a successful marketing study and managing a firm.

Koch is wrongly preoccupied with the study on market potential and location. Brann & Koch should not carry out this study, but must define and supervise it. A specialist firm should be able to provide the study.

Too many jobs for one man
Negotiations with Vulcain must be carried out by *a person who knows Brann & Koch perfectly* and who consequently is already part of the firm's managerial team. But equally it is not a good idea for the role of leader in a negotiation to be held by an individual who will be on the top managerial staff of the joint venture. The negotiation task, then, must be entrusted to a manager of Brann & Koch who will become a non-executive director of the board of the future firm.

As to the eventual managing director, if Brann & Koch cannot develop one of its own managers to succeed Habbel, it must recruit someone from outside. Only the third candidate corresponds approximately to this profile. But he is perhaps too "big" for the position, which is not always desirable. That can be decided by studying the five-year forecast of the firm's turnover, personnel and investments. And he must have enough marketing expertise to oversee the market research.

If all these possible objections are met. Koch then needs to ask himself how the firm will organize its sales function. The second candidate, the "born salesman," would be a poor choice to fill a senior executive position. But if the older man was employed as Habbel's eventual replacement, Koch would do well to consider employing this man too, and putting him in charge of sales.

There is another person who must not be forgotten in this matter: Schwarzenbach. If at the time of the recruitment request he had done his work correctly, he would have defined the job clearly with Koch. He would have pointed out the contradictions in priorities, or between the salary offered and certain priorities. He would have reminded Koch that recruitment depends on the post and the career envisaged, the position and development of the organization and its policy and strategies.

This decision was adapted from a disguised case supplied by the London office of Egon Zehnder International and the decision was provided by Jacques Lesourne in his capacity as managing director of French consulting group Metra International.

Should institute director risk admitting difficulty of recruiting local staff?

Carlos Ruiz stares dejectedly out of the window. The restful Andean valley which stretches beyond contrasts sharply with the turmoil inside his mind.

When the Foreman Foundation decided to establish the Andean Institute of Management, Ruiz, an astute and cool-headed Mexican, was an obvious choice to lead the project. As a member of the foundation's South American advisory team, he had served it well in the past. But this time things were not going well.

Ruiz worked with a team of six other foundation experts, each from a different country. They ran courses in each of their managerial disciplines. They had also trained a number of bright young recruits from university and local industry to take over from them as instructors after three or four years.

The institute was established amid breath-taking mountain scenery within easy reach of a major industrial city, from which most of the course participants were drawn. The Foreman Foundation awarded a grant of $800,000 and this was supplemented by a government donation of $200,000. Further funds would be negotiated when the institute was turned over to local staff at the end of five years.

There had been no difficulty in recruiting local staff of the right calibre. They were strongly motivated by the knowledge that they were helping to build the foundations of a more managerially aware local industry.

Managerial skills earn high wages abroad

Some young understudies learned so rapidly it was decided to send them to the United States to study their fields of interest more deeply. Then the trouble started. Two understudies discovered their managerial skills could earn them high wages in the U.S. and decided to stay there. Another two who returned after studying abroad were quickly snapped up by the local branch of a large multinational firm.

A fifth understudy, Cristóbal Cano, a young marketing specialist, had just that morning told Ruiz that a similar offer had been made to him by a beer firm. Although Cano altruistically felt he should resist the offer, he pointed out that he had a wife and five children to support.

Ruiz suspected that unless he increased Cano's salary he would lose him. But then he would have to do the same for the other local staff, which dwindling institute funds could ill afford.

Ruiz faced yet another crisis with Tomas Vila, a foundation expert from Colombia who taught accountancy. Vila had complained that one of his understudies had returned from an overseas course full of advanced accountancy theories. The understudy, José Torreón, insisted on introducing the theories into the institute's accountancy course. Vila firmly opposed the idea since he felt a developing economy was not ready for such techniques. He warned Ruiz that he would resign if Torreón got his way.

Ruiz agreed with Vila, but he did not want to lose yet another bright young staff member.

All in all, Ruiz found himself in an unenviable position on the eve of the day the Foreman Foundation was sending a top official to review the institute's progress. It seemed to Ruiz he was left with two equally unpalatable alternatives.

He could try to gloss over the current difficulties. While admitting that there had been minor setbacks he could try to assure the foundation official that within the next two years it would be possible to hand the institute over to the local staff as planned. But Ruiz wondered whether he would be able to disguise his misgivings. If he were honest, he could give no guarantee that the institute would meet this target. Even if he managed to halt the high turnover in local staff, he seriously doubted whether they could be persuaded to teach the techniques best suited to local needs. They were easily carried away by the enthusiasm for their own advanced learning.

Alternatively, Ruiz could be candid and tell the foundation official that the concept on which the institute was founded was ill-conceived. He could recommend that the understudy approach be abandoned and request that the foundation provide more money to recruit more professional teachers on a permanent basis. This, however, ran counter to the foundation's avowed policy that its projects should become locally managed. Such an appraisal might cause the foundation to drop the Andean project entirely.

DECISION

Ruíz should seek dedicated teachers and keep them motivated and happy

Carlos Ruiz's dilemma seems to be that he must follow one of two extreme courses of action. On the one hand he will have to convince the donor organization that progress towards the set goals is satisfactory. In this case he would get continued support for the time being, but he would almost certainly be proved wrong in the long run. Or on the other hand he will have to admit the difficulties and press for permanent foreign teachers. In this case he would run the risk of losing the financial support of the foundation, whose policy favours local teachers.

A good decision does not lie in either of the two extremes. The basis for the decision to Ruiz's problem should be what has happened – or, better still, what has gone wrong. The basic consideration should be the recruitment, training and motivation of the institute's teaching staff.

Incorporate a sophisticated selection policy
There appears to be no shortage of suitable local people. So Ruiz should advocate a selection policy that goes beyond academic qualifications. It should seek the dedicated teachers, not those motivated by immediate personal gains, financial and academic, through further training and development. This approach will make it less likely that the local teachers will stay overseas after their training, to enjoy the benefits of the higher living standards of the country in which they have been trained. Nor should they then be attracted away to other jobs soon after their return

home, because for dedicated people money is not everything.

Ruiz's next problem is in developing the type of training system best suited to the young teachers, the state of the economy, and the objectives of the institute. With a developing economy the immediate needs may be in the area of functional training, to develop skills in production, marketing, finance, supervision and personnel administration.

Appraise the teachers of the institute's aims
Assuming this is the case, the training may take the form of short overseas courses lasting no longer than six months in any of the above disciplines, or a combination of them. These could be followed by a supervised teaching period at home with help from foreign experts brought in for short periods of time. This approach will deal with the problem of the "brain drain" to the developed economies as well as the problems associated with foreign staff working on a long-term basis.

Keeping the institute's staff happy and well motivated is Ruiz's next problem. Careful career planning and personal development for each member of the teaching staff should solve most of the difficulties for nearly all the staff. Each member must know where the institute is going, what are its plans for future growth. He should also be made aware that the institute plans to develop and remunerate him to make his financial and status position attractive and competitive with those of industry.

Dedicated teachers tend to get more job satisfaction from the contribution their alumni are making to the economy and society than from pay. Nevertheless, no teacher can remain enthusiastic if his physiological, social and ego needs are not met. This means keeping the rewards under constant review.

Reward the established teaching staff
As the institute grows, it will help the self-esteem of the teachers if they are enabled to do post-graduate work and aim for master's and doctor's degrees. At this stage the established members of the teaching staff will be ready for longer periods of training to gain advanced degrees. But by this time they will have stronger roots in their home country, so the risk of their staying away will be negligible.

Ruiz should therefore face the facts, develop short-term remedial plans as well as long-term plans, and persuade the donor organization to see the worth of his proposals. His first priority must be to keep the institute going. So he must adjust the salary system. Then he must survey and analyse the training needs of the country to solve the problem of over-sophistication and non-localization of management teaching material and styles.

He may need to extend the period for keeping foreign staff. But his long-term plan, based on this approach, must be to have an institute that is staffed by nationals using approaches tailored to meet local needs.

This decision was provided by Chief O.I.A. Akinyemi in his capacity as director-general of the Nigerian Institute of Management.

How far should chairman back woman financial manager under attack?

"Paul, what's the matter with Angela?" asked Michael Denton, chairman of the Torrone Fibre Group. "She seems to have got very touchy in the last few months." He went on to explain to personnel director Paul Garland that Angela Turner, the 35-year-old financial manager, seemed to interpret every request as a criticism of her performance lately. She also no longer showed the capacity for dealing with her fellow executives that had marked her early days on the job.

As the group's financial manager, Turner did not have direct authority over divisional finance matters. But divisional executives were required to provide her with whatever information she requested. Recently, some executives had begun to deal directly with Denton on matters they should have referred to Turner. Though after a mild rebuke from Denton they had reverted to using the proper channels, Denton had taken this as a bad omen. "But when I tried to talk to her about it," he went on, "she just mumbled something about personality conflicts and how she'd sort it out. I didn't want to press her any more, as she seemed a bit upset. Have you any idea of what's gone wrong?"

Garland frowned. "I've been meaning to come and see you about this. It sounds ridiculous, but I'm pretty sure she's being undermined by some of the directors. They resent a woman as financial manager." The role of finance manager to the group was regarded as a stepping stone for bright executive talent. Turner's predecessor had gone on to head one of the group's smaller subsidiaries.

Appointment of a woman at senior level

Before Turner's appointment some ten months before, Denton and Garland had foreseen the possibility of initial resentment from other executives. They had therefore discussed the appointment with the division directors and others who would be dealing with Turner, before her arrival. They had pointed out that her qualifications and experience at a high level in the Civil Service equipped her admirably for the job. In these discussions, all had agreed that there should be no objection in principle to the employment of a woman at a senior level in the company's management.

At first, no one had a bad word to say about Turner. She had proved efficient and friendly. Her charm had disarmed the one or two crusty older executives who had voiced initial scepticism at the appointment.

After a few months in the job, Turner had changed the reporting system. She began to require the divisions to produce more detailed breakdowns of their cost figures. Also, she followed up variances, which enabled her to produce explanations of the figures in the reports. Denton was delighted. He found that management meetings now focused much more sharply on the divisions' critical performance factors.

But, Garland reported, he had lately begun to notice that some managers tended to react slowly, or not at all, to requests for information from Turner. On one occasion, Garland overheard a manager expressing regret that lack of information from his division had delayed a report Turner was to present to the board: "I just didn't receive the memo," he had explained. So Garland had taken Turner aside and asked her whether this was a serious problem. To his dismay, Turner had burst into tears. She told him: "It's always happening." She was convinced that the frequency of such mislaid memorandums and the tardy response to them was no coincidence. And, she added, her face-to-face dealings with certain executives were equally frustrating: "I can never get a straight answer," she complained bitterly. "More authority might help me to get the information, but the real problem is the attitudes of these men."

Senior executives can resent women managers

Garland had tried to encourage Turner, but had only been able to make a vague promise to "see what I can do." He believed that Turner's decline in performance and her currently unstable state were caused by what amounted to a war of attrition waged by resentful senior executives. He suggested that Denton talk quietly to each of the senior men who had to deal with Turner. "It's not necessary to point the finger – just ask them to pay particular attention to cooperating with her in future," he said, "I'm sure that once she starts to get reasonable cooperation again, she will regain her balance."

Denton doubted whether this move in itself would be enough to resolve the situation. It could take some time for Turner to respond to greater cooperation from other executives. In the meantime her erratic behaviour could seriously harm company morale.

So Denton wondered whether a more forceful approach was needed. Perhaps he should give Turner the extra authority she had mentioned to Garland. He could call a meeting of all the executives concerned and confront them with their tactics And he would announce that divisional financial controllers would in future be directly responsible to Turner.

But in Turner's present state, would such a move make or break her?

DECISION

This three-point plan will help the chairman save the situation

Chairman Denton has a classic staff-line management problem. The female executive competing in a man's world is an added element. Denton and Garland have made the mistake of thinking Angela Turner's problem is based purely on divisional executives' resentment at having a woman in such a senior management position.

The fact is that a male executive coming into that position in the organization from the outside would have faced the same problems. A staff position in which success depends on the support and cooperation of line people throughout the organization is particularly failure prone. In addition, the chairman saw Turner's role as that of supplying him with financial data to enable him to probe his divisional managers' performance in critical areas.

I'm sure the divisional directors came away from meetings with the chairman commenting to one another about how they had been "undermined by the chairman and his female numbers wizard". Turner left the same meeting thinking she had done a superb job – after all, hadn't the chairman been pleased? And, of course, Denton came away feeling for the first time that he was really getting a grasp on things!

The new reporting system was evidently imposed from the top down with little or no participation or input from the divisional controllers or directors. So resistance was inevitable when variances began to be followed up directly by Turner with the chairman's blessing. The fact that it was a woman just added to the uncooperativeness of divisional managers.

Turner had fallen into the organizational trap of confusing or crossing staff responsibilities with line responsibilities. So had Denton, but he didn't realize it. Turner's problem was that she had tried to please the chairman rather than help the divisional directors and financial people. Her reporting system and analyses should have been set up to provide them with better information. They themselves should have been enabled to focus on critical problem areas and take steps to improve their own operations. Turner forgot that her role as a staff executive must be to sell ideas to the line executives so that they can benefit from her efforts.

Take a positive, not negative, approach

The question to be asked is not: "Do we give Turner more authority by having the divisional controllers report to her?" It is rather: "What is the responsibility of the group's financial manager?"

If Denton tries to solve his dilemma by giving Turner more authority, he will have a disaster on his hands. The divisional directors will be even more resentful if they lose direct responsibility for their divisions' financial control. The chairman will find himself more involved in detail operating matters, as the divisional directors will tend to pass more of the decisions to head office. And the answer to his question, "Would such a move break her?" will be "yes". The strain of the extra responsibility would almost certainly throw Turner over the brink.

Denton should take three steps. First, he should discuss with Turner the role of group financial manager and the importance of her reporting system in assisting the divisional managers through their controllers. At the same time, he can indicate that her system and performance have been an important step forward for the group.

Second, Denton should review the staff-line concepts with the divisional directors. He should make it clear that the function of the group financial manager is to assist their financial controllers in setting up effective financial control systems that will help them run their operations and take appropriate corrective actions. To confront them about their uncooperative tactics would be a mistake. The situation calls for a positive approach, not a negative one.

And third, both Denton and Garland should, in the future, be more sensitive in analysing the organizational pressures that can occur when a senior executive comes in from the outside. These are especially acute in a staff position, where gaining acceptance is so important.

Denton's dilemma will become more common. As women rise in into senior management the majority necessarily will start in staff positions

This decision was provided by Frederick M. Linton in his capacity as president of U.S. executive selection firm Boyden International Group Inc.

Should Tremblay leave decisions on loans to individual managers?

"Sorry to bother you," apologized Georges Gaudette, manager of the gas boiler plant, as he entered the managing director's office. "Come in, come in," answered René Tremblay, the affable, if paternalistic, head of the medium-sized family firm which produced heating and ventilation equipment. "What's the trouble?"

Gaudette immediately produced a yellow company memorandum and waved it in the air. "This really annoys me," he said. "Why should the personnel department take over administration of personal loans? Plant managers have been taking care of that all these years without any trouble. You know yourself that personal loans have been effective in rewarding our better employees."

Tremblay nodded. It was, in fact, his own idea to allow plant managers to grant "deserving employees" loans up to $2,000 at very attractive interest rates and repayment terms. Over the five years the plan had been in effect there had been only one default by an employee who left the firm. Outstanding loans were less than $250,000.

The memorandum that was troubling Gaudette clearly defined the eligibility requirements and scope of loans available to employees. Under the new scheme any employee with more than two years' service was entitled unconditionally to a company loan for a house mortgage, a car or to buy a season ticket on public transport. Employees with more than five years' service could also apply for an additional loan if they could convince the personnel manager there was a real need.

No system coverd appreciation of loans

"This new system is eroding our authority," Gaudette argued. "Before, we could authorize loans whenever we saw fit. Now anyone can go straight to personnel and get one if they are eligible.

"This isn't the first time we've had a system imposed on us like this," the angry plant manger continued. "Six months ago a new policy was issued giving employees five days' unpaid leave each year. Before, we gave people time off at our discretion. Now the workers no longer ask for time off. They *inform* us they are taking it. It's causing chaos to our planning." Tremblay rang for the company's personnel manager, Thérèse St. Jean, to join them. The managing director repeated Gaudette's complaint to her. St. Jean turned on her charm and smiled at Gaudette.

"I appreciate your view," she began. "But I am sure there's a need for a more rational system."

"I'm not sure I agree," answered Gaudette sharply.

St. Jean's smile disappeared. "In the past, whether or not an employee succeeded in getting a loan depended entirely on his supervisor," she explained. "But the problem was that the loans were not necessarily given to the most deserving employees. Some managers who were sympathetic to personal problems handed out loans freely to almost anyone who

147

asked. Others never approved a loan, and employees ceased asking for them. The result was that employees were not being treated fairly or equally. My argument is that they are all employees of the company, not of individual managers. And they should be treated as such."

"What worries me," Gaudette replied, "is the loss of personal relationship between managers and their subordinates caused by the introduction of these cold, rigid systems of yours. I would have thought that you in personnel more than anyone would want to preserve close relationships between managers and their staff.

"I personally am very concerned about one indivudual in my plant who has repeatedly asked for a loan in the last few months. I have turned him down because I consider him unworthy. His work performance is poor and he is lucky he is still here. He is on the verge of being sacked. The personnel department has no way of knowing this. Now this man is eligible for a loan. I wouldn't be surprised if he is in your office right now waiting to speak to you about it. I think we managers should at least agree these loans first."

"Agree?" echoed St. Jean. "That amounts to the same thing as leaving it to the managers. The whole idea is not to leave it to the discretion of individual managers. Even if your man is fired, that does not mean he won't have to pay the loan back. Anyway, in my view it is better to have a few bad debts than to discriminate among our employees."

Gaudette was astonished. He turned to Tremblay: "The next thing you know the personnel department will be telling me how to weld boilders." Tremblay looked over Gaudette's shoulder and saw another plant manager in the ante-room clutching the yellow memorandum. He realized that he had a minor rebellion on his hands. Should he rescind the new order immediately?

DECISION

The company should consider establishing a uniform system for loans

This situation is a significant example of how the slightest modification in existing rules or procedures can cause conflict between those who make decisions and those who have to implement them. A policy is issued one fine day without any previous discussions. No reasons are given for justifying the change.

Yet it is certain that this sort of problem will be triggered off more and more with the increasing number of social, economic and technological changes which require standardized procedures. Nevertheless, companies in such situations can predict the reactions of different employees and take the necessary precautions to avoid trouble, even if it means departing somewhat from the original intention. In this case nobody seems to have anticipated the objections the change will cause.

The problem of management at all levels is more and more that of getting new measures accepted rather than choosing from among alternative measures. This is particularly so as companies become less autocratic. It is also now well accepted that a decision is implemented much more successfully if it is sufficiently justified and if it has been well discussed with those involved beforehand. A system which is not fully accepted

148

cannot function properly. At the same time it should be realized that employees at different levels see changes from quite different viewpoints. To neglect these aspects is to risk poisoning the whole atmosphere between management and employees and to weaken any system introduced. In this case I would say that these conditions were very badly fulfilled, if they were even considered.

It seems to me that Gaudette and the other managers do not simply want the discretion to hand out loans. They are afraid of losing their authority and the confidence of their staff.

Before a company can determine the best procedures to follow it should first determine its objectives. Are the loans intended to be a form of compensation? Are they to provide personal assistance? Are they intended to provide an advantage over other employers? Or are they a means of integrating the various levels of employees? The company does not appear to have reflected on these questions.

Nevertheless, the idea of standardizing the conditions seems to be a positive measure, in that it attempts to reduce the arbitrariness in providing loans. After all, there is no relationship between performance of merit and satisfying the personal needs of an employee. It would seem unwise for Tremblay to keep a system that is wide open. On the other hand, there is no reason why the department heads should be excluded when it is relatively simple to devise some procedure that would involve them. The company has set up rigid rules governing loans. But these cannot absolve managers from their responsiblity to inform and guide senior management, and to have a formula to offer this.

Create an appeals tribunal to review requests

The company could consider establishing a uniform system, but give some degree of control to individual managers. It could define, for example, when arrangements for loans are acceptable or not, but give each manager the ultimate responsibility for giving the loans.

In addition, the company could institute some sort of appeals tribunal to review request for loans turned down by a manager. This tribunal could comprise representatives of both senior and middle managers, and possibly employee representatives This would depend on the state of maturity which the company has reached in employee participation and on the industrial relations environment which exists.

I am tempted to raise another question which may well lie outside the scope of the issue under discussion. Nevertheless, it is one which I consider important and relevant: What are the views of the employees concerning this matter?

Perhaps they should be consulted. After all, are they not the ones most involved and most affected by any policy which the company may introduce? Would they prefer to apply for a loan to their immediate supervisor, for example? Or would they prefer to deal with a personnel officer they know less well?

The circumstances described in this case study provide a good opportunity for a company to raise this whole subject of employee involvement in decisions affecting them.

This decision was provided by Paul Chaumette in his capacity as director general of L'Entreprise et Personnel, a Paris-based personnel research organization financed by major French companies.

Should firm hire experienced outsiders or maintain control with junior executive?

Henri Sauvage was depressed. A slim, youthful-looking Frenchman in his mid-fifties, he sat alone late on a summer evening, on·the balcony outside his office. Normally, he enjoyed the view of the sunset with the cluster of lights at the distant airport adding a touch of movement and excitement to the-scene.

Tonight it only served as an ironic reminder of the problem he faced. Everyone is now in too much of a greedy rush to move on, he mused, they have no loyalty and no patience. He was contemplating the successive loss of three key managers from his business over the past three years. The third was sales manager Charles Duvalier, who had announced his resignation earlier in the day.

Sauvage was head of the engineering firm Sauvage & Cie, founded by his father before World War II. Sauvage had expanded both the size and scope of the firm. Sales had gone from $1.2 million in 1961 to $10.9 million in 1971. He had led it into new markets. For example, recently the company had begun supplying products to the European aircraft industry which was a completely new venture.

Sauvage remained very much in control of the whole business, as it grew, with three managers acting in key areas – production, technical development and sales. All three joined the company as young men around the same time as Sauvage succeeded his father, 11 years ago.

New young managers are greedy

The technical and production men had both left to work for American companies' French subsidiaries. There were three reasons for their leaving: the American companies paid well; they offered managers freedom to take decisions; and they exposed managers to more modern management techniques.

Both had done well; one became European vice president and the other was general manager of a French subsidiary.

Sauvage's difficulties in recruiting young managers were made more painful by the fact that his son showed no interest in joining the business. He had never been close to his father. And he was now working in the film industry, trying to become a director.

Sauvage had hired replacements for the departed managers after interviewing a large number of respondents to his advertisements. They all seemed to want too much money, in Sauvage's view, and demanded fringe benefits and status titles that he felt they did not deserve. His first choice among the production job candidates turned it down because he would not be a member of the management committee from the start.

The second choice, whom Sauvage eventually hired, proved to be, in his view, a complete disaster. There were continual disagreements about policy in the first month. The production chief resigned after six months, following a major row. Sauvage had reprimanded him about taking decisions to rearrange machine tools without consulting him.

A technical manager had been hired with less trouble and appeared so far to be competent, although not as good as the man he replaced.

Sauvage himself had been doing the production job for the past year, aided by a young engineering graduate. Now he wondered what to do about replacing Duvalier, his capable sales manager.

Earlier in the day, he had had an unpleasant meeting with Duvalier, who was going to take over complete direction of a small, ailing company. Sauvage had reminded Duvalier that he owed his training and experience to the openings that he had been given at Sauvage & Cie. But Duvalier lost his temper: "You older men are behind the times," he exclaimed. "You still expect people to come and work for you for life. My work has repaid whatever I owe you for my training. Now my only obligation is to my family."

Sauvage had cut him short and asked him to leave. But the outburst had struck a nerve. Now he sipped a whisky and reflected on his situation. He saw two courses of action he could follow.

One course was to recruit senior executives by paying them whatever high rates they demanded, and acceding to all their requests for status titles, fringe benefits and involvement in all decision-making. The other course was to promote younger men to do the executive jobs but keep close control over them.

The first course meant handing over the destiny of the business to strangers, trusting in their integrity and competence to preserve what he had worked for all his life.

Yet the second course would increase his own work load. He felt the business was becoming too large and complex for him to run like that, at his age. His work had been his sole interest but now he accepted his wife's view that he ought to relax and enjoy leisure interests.

DECISION

Henri Sauvage should look for a solution that satisfies everybody

This sounds like a very typical case in many European companies today. For 12 years we have been attempting different solutions to this same basic problem. We finally concluded that, except in some rare occasions, the solution is some kind of association with another firm. This ensures that the founder receives financial compensation when he parts with control. If he simply hires a chief executive and retires, he loses control – but gets no benefit.

Henri Sauvage, the chief executive and major shareholder, is about 55. Within ten years, he should have organized the company so that he no longer plays a key role in it. His son will succeed him as the shareholder, but it is highly unlikely that he would become the chief executive.

If he did, there is a risk that his ignorance of business would hurt the company so much that he would eventually have to sell out to another company, from a weak position. Far better that plans are laid for a smooth development in this direction, so that the deal can be made from a position of strength at a better price.

Sauvage's chances of quickly finding a top-class successor as chief executive are slim, since it is unlikely that he could change his working methods so radically as to work closely alongside such a man.

Any firm run by the founder-owner always has problems finding successors. Sauvage sounds rather autocratic, and this is probably the reason why the managers left. Simply because the founder is at the top, managers tend to drift off because of their remote chance of reaching that spot.

In Europe there is a demand for able executives with a good record; simply paying managers more will not be enough to hold them if they are unhappy with other aspects of the job. Sauvage should realize that managers today expect more than a high salary. They seek active participation in the important decision-making of the company. They want clear authority delegated to them in their area. Financially, they are likely to demand some kind of profit-sharing scheme. In a family company like this they would want a chance to become shareholders.

A five-step plan ensures a secure future

Sauvage should realize that the more he can change his way of working, the better it will be for his company. Realizing that this is difficult, the best thing is to move gradually. His aim should be to sell or merge his company in such a way that suits the interests of all concerned.

His plan of action should cover five steps. First, he must hire top-class young managers about 35 years old with ten years' experience. They should be entrepreneurial rather than technical types. To attract them Sauvage will have to explain to them his goals for the company.

He will probably find it necessary to work out a financial arrangement so that when the company is sold they will benefit, in relation to their performance, in the meantime.

Secondly, he will have to make some changes to allow more scope to these men, giving them more authority to take some decisions. An outside adviser whom he trusts would be the best person to guide him in what he could do and how he could do it.

Thirdly, he must survey those companies which might be interested in the technology of his firm. It could be that his big clients, his suppliers or their competitors would be most interested in acquiring the business.

Fourthly, he must contact his selected firms through his banker or solicitor or a management consultant.

Fifthly, he should make a deal along one of two lines. Either he stays as head of his firm with a general manager appointed by the new associate firm or chosen from his young managers. Alternatively, he might choose to become director of the mother company. He will either receive shares in this and/or money.

Such a deal will suit everyone involved. The acquiring company gains the facilities it will find useful. Sauvage will be assured that the firm he has developed in his lifetime will survive after him in a setting which he has chosen as the best. His managers will be held to the firm by the attraction of a larger group in which they will have a financial stake. His son's inheritance has been assured. Finally, his wife will see more of him, as he is freed from the day-to-day control, and less likely to die of a heart attack through worry about his firm's future.

This dilemma was developed in conjunction with MSL Group Ltd., a U.K. management consultancy, and the decision was provided by Jean-Claude Lasanté in his capacity as president of Eurosurvey Groupe, a Paris-based executive search consultancy.

Can a successor be found a bridging job for five years?

Roland Burgess succeeded his father as managing director of the family's Twist Rope Co. when he was 37. His first priority was to boost sales through exports, using many of the contacts he had made while travelling abroad in Europe, the United States and Asia.

Very shortly, his efforts were bearing fruit. Sales were up from $2 million to $3 million, with exports accounting for 15%. Profits were around $120,000.

Burgess ran the company himself. He bought the materials, directed the three salesmen and dealt with major customers. The only other corporate executive was the works manager, 35-year-old George Boddington who had been with the company since leaving school.

Production was difficult, with short runs and awkward individual specifications for customers. Burgess felt that Boddington lacked leadership qualities and had too narrow a view, although he was technically sound. Burgess blamed Boddington's inability to delegate for the mediocre standard of department managers in the company's London factory.

Expanding into Sweden

Burgess had for some years been anxious to move Twist into synthetic rope production. But he could not find the specialist equipment he needed at a price he wanted.

But the New Year brought changes. In January, Burgess' daughter, an only child, Married Henry Ellis, a 33-year-old physics graduate. Burgess offered him a department manager's job, but he said he was happy in his present position as a department manager in a large factory.

The next month Burgess found a small Swedish rope company which made its own machinery for producing synthetic ropes. The owners were thinking of selling. He visited the plant and was so impressed that he offered to buy a controlling interest. His offer was accepted.

His aim in Sweden was to continue some synthetic rope production there, while making the machines needed to start production in London.

While the legal details were being settled, Burgess pondered who should run the Swedish company for him. Ellis turned the offer down because his wife would not move abroad.

Then Burgess had a good idea. He could move Boddington to Sweden and bring Ellis in to replace him. The Swedish task would simply be to maintain operations, looking after Twist's interests. So Boddington would be able to cope.

Boddington, who was a bachelor, cheerfully accepted the chance to move abroad, where he would have greater autonomy. Burgess told him that Ellis would take over as works manager. Boddington's face clouded suddenly. He asked what would happen if the Swedish venture failed and he had to come back. Burgess airily dismissed his fears with a promise to find him an equivalent position in that "unlikely event."

After six months, Boddington had settled into the Swedish job. Burgess noticed a vast change in him when he visited Sweden. Boddington had developed more confidence and authority. The experience seemed to give him the broader outlook he had lacked.

After five years the last of the machines for London was finished and shipped. Within two weeks a disastrous fire wiped out the Swedish plant. The destruction was so great that Burgess decided to abandon the Swedish operation. The plant, it turned out, was under-insured. Also, transferring undelivered orders to the U.K. factory resulted in heavy overtime work. Therefore profits were severely squeezed. On top of his other problems, Burgess had to decide what to do with Boddington.

A moral obligation

He had promised Boddington a good job if things went wrong. But where could he place him now? Ellis was doing well as works manager, with a bright young assistant.

Boddington had developed into a much better executive in Sweden. Burgess was determined to retire at 60, in five years' time. He could see Boddington, now 46, would be a good man to have around then. He hoped that Ellis would be ready to succeed him as managing director, with Boddington as his production chief.

The only place he could offer Boddington in the meantime was running a sisal estate part-owned by Twist in East Africa, producing raw material for the factory. Boddington refused point blank. Instead he pressed Burgess for an answer about where he would be fitted into the company now.

Burgess was now feeling distinctly uncomfortable at having been put on the spot like this. He did not want to lose Boddington and he had a moral obligation to him. But how could he justify his salary in the meantime, when there seemed no suitable executive position for him for another five years. Something would have to be done.

DECISION

The human problem of three executives where only two are needed

The case is full of questions which a consultant would normally want to probe in addition to the basic management succession problem. Was exporting fibre rope a sensible strategy? Was a 15% export share good enough for seven years' work? Who overlooked the fire insurance? Should the Swedish company really be abandoned? But skipping these we get to the central human problem of three main executives where two, it is presumed, will do.

Moralizing about the past will not help Burgess, but in a case study it is worth highlighting one source of trouble – vagueness. "Boddington asked what would happen if the Swedish venture failed and he had to come back. Burgess airily dismissed his fears, with a promise to find him an equivalent position in that unlikely event."

Burgess should have been clearer than that. What did he promise "an equivalent position" to what? Was it put in writing? Did he want to help the loyal Boddington or not? Presumably Boddington trusted him, and now Burgess realizes his moral obligation and there can be no thought of making Boddington redundant.

Ellis sounds a good bet, so a place should be found for both. Ellis seems to be the leader, so if one needs to be superior to the other, it is he. The company's size can be estimated from the fact that the "current" year has to be 1970, the industry is a non-growth one, and a $5-million turnover, say, would be equivalent to 500 people in this industry.

The three main executives would be feasible. The first position is that of chairman and managing director. This could also include direction of finance and administration affairs.

The next position that the company would logically seem to require filling is that of director in charge of sales and company development. Twist's recent history shows clearly that Burgess has not really been able to pursue corporate development wholeheartedly because of the other demands on his time. The sales and development function is particularly important in view of their new synthetic rope expertise and the need to develop the Swedish market, to which they should have access.

The third executive position needing to be filled is head of production. Burgess seems the best man to be chairman, with Ellis for sales head and Boddington in production. However, it is just possible that Boddington and Ellis could exchange these roles.

The three would need to work closely together as a small team, sharing discussion on major decisions in each other's areas. They could be called chairman/managing director, sales director and works director respectively. One trap to be avoided would be a "one-over-one-over-one" relationship. The casualty, would have to be Ellis's assistant.

Burgess may consider getting out five years early, leaving Ellis as the boss, but this would surely be faulty reasoning; the firm needs Burgess's knowledge and since, presumably, he will still live off its fortunes for the five years, little expense will be saved.

Burgess should start a planned programme of action to cope with filling the executive positions properly now, and arranging for a smooth transition to effective management when he retires. The action programme should start with an assessment of Ellis and Boddington.

There must then be individual development programmes to strengthen both in the weak areas revealed by tests. This might involve sending them to short executive courses.

The next element needed is for Burgess to sit down and discuss with each man the role he plays in the firm. This should lead to clearly defined responsibilities and goals for both Boddington and Ellis.

Finally, he must agree with the others on a programme for his withdrawal from the company in five years' time.

As always in a human problem, it all depends on the people. If they are considerate and cooperative as well as dynamic and able, then they should succeed together. But in a small company one difficult executive could cause failure.

This decision was provided by Brian Smith in his capacity as managing director of PA International Management Consultants Ltd., based in London.

Chapter 4

Human Resources

*These include some of the most interesting dilemmas of all —
and carry some of the most original, stimulating and
ingenious solutions. Whether a man should jeopardize his
job to save his marriage is a question to which there can be
no simple answer. What should a chairman do about a
compulsive borrower? Should the chairman's son-in-law
be reported for embezzlement? Fortunately, such awkward
questions don't occur every day.*

Should Forrester jeopardize his job to save his marriage?

Joanna Forrester glared at her husband as he dejectedly entered the front door. "Where on earth have you been, George?" she demanded reproachfully. "I've been waiting for you for two hours, and the meal is burned to a crisp."

George Forrester, who was marketing manager at Smythwell's Engineering Co., looked at his wife meekly. He had been driving around the city for hours before summoning up the courage to break the news to her. He finally forced out the words: "Darling, complications have developed over the Mexican deal I told you about and I have to fly to Mexico City tomorrow to straighten things out. I know I promised I would be home during your operation, but I should only be away a week. If I don't go the company will probably lose the contract and I will probably lose my job into the bargain."

Forrester's wife tried to contain her anger. She had been under severe stress for several weeks waiting for a hysterectomy operation. In two days' time she was due to go into hospital for the operation, which meant that at 36 she would have to give up all hope of having children. Forrester knew the emotional strain she was undergoing and realized that his presence would be important to her recovery.

"How can you possibly even consider going away after all the arguments we had about this last year?" she exclaimed. "You promised then you would stop putting your job before me every time."

Deteriorating relations with his wife

On their wedding anniversary last year they had decided to spend a weekend on the coast. But the day before Forrester was required by the firm to fly to Australia to re-negotiate a vital business deal that had fallen through. After a heated argument with his wife, Forrester suggested to his managing director Alan Baker that the deputy marketing manager go in his place. Baker would not hear of it. Forrester had been the sole negotiator of this contract, which was worth at least $2.4 million to the firm. Forrester went to Australia, and relations with his wife had not been the same since.

Forrester afterwards had a frank talk about his marital problems with Baker. They both agreed that Forrester should endeavour to do less overtime at the office and try to keep to holiday plans. But in fact in the year that followed Forrester found it impossible to carry out his good intentions. Pressure of work often kept Forrester late at the office and he spent many weekends travelling on business. Forrester's wife repeatedly complained of being left alone too much. He suggested she should find herself an undemanding job. "I don't see what that will do for our marriage," she replied curtly. "I want us to spend more time together."

Forrester thought of packing in his job and getting less demanding work himself. But this was not an easy decision for a man of 47. He had been with Smythwell's for nearly 24 years, and could look forward to a good pension. He had worked hard to become marketing manager and was regarded as the most likely prospect for the deputy managing director's job when it became vacant next year. But much depended on his success in expanding the market in Central America. For the past six months he had been negotiating a major contract for three compressors worth $2 million with Fertilizantes Fernández de México SA. The deal looked like going well until Forrester heard the bad news from the managing director that morning.

"We've just received bad news from Mexico," Baker told him irritably. "The fertilizer company is now insisting we provide maintenance engineers to install the equipment and train their own technicians. A U.S. competitor has offered to complete the deal and provide engineers for the same price as our tender. We really need this contract, but we can't afford to spare six engineers for six months to a year."

Forrester was at a loss for words. He muttered something about delaying his departure or being replaced by someone else. He half-heartedly started to explain that his marriage was in jeopardy, that it was a bad time to leave his wife alone, that it could easily lead to his wife demanding a divorce. But he knew he would be wasting his breath. There was only one consideration in Baker's mind. "I don't mean to be hard-hearted," Baker replied predictably. "But this contract is a matter of life or death to us. The responsibility to clinch it is on you."

Forrester's wife was equally unsympathetic about the dilemma her husband faced. She could only see the injustice of her own position. Forrester tried to comfort her, and emphasized that their standard of living and their expensive home depended on his high salary. "To hell with the job," she shouted furiously. "I think you had better decide who you are married to – me or the company. It can't be both!"

DECISION

If he risks his job, he and his wife will get the worst of both worlds

George and Joanna Forrester are both the victims of circumstances and outside pressure. Neither of them has done anything wrong, and neither one can hold the other to blame. No doubt, women are now demanding much more of their marriage than they once did, largely because of their better education and greater freedom. Companies too are asking far more from their managers than before.

The Forresters are faced with this conflict because, like many other couples, they failed to anticipate it. Women married to sailors tend to cope far better precisely because they know this sort of thing will happen, and they accept it. But young businessmen and their wives still do not realize how the demands being made on them tend to build up.

The solution is clear. Forrester must go on his business trip. On the surface it may seem better for him not to go. His wife would be pleased and it might seem his marriage would be made more secure. But this would be short-lived. In the longer term the situation would worsen. He would become very unpopular with his employer. He might lose his chance for promotion and jeopardize his job. He would certainly be humiliated. He would lose his self-confidence. Without good future

158

career prospects he would quickly deteriorate. Nor would he and his wife be any happier.

He would become hostile towards her and she would feel ashamed. She implies that she would be prepared to accept a lower standard of living. But this is rarely true of wives.

Even if he were to promise never to go on a trip again, and delegate responsiblity, the chances are that a similar problem would arise again, aggravating the situation further. It is true that she is in a state of mind that indicates she would leave him if he went abroad. But the chances are that she will remain and they will continue to quarrel over this matter.

Forrester has a responsibility to his employer which he and his wife should well understand.

Moreover, the firm is evidently having difficulties, and is depending heavily on Forrester's success in getting this order. So the future of the organization is involved. The fact that the hysterectomy operation is causing emotional problems is a minor factor. In my experience, even women with children feel unloved and unwanted when their husbands are too involved with work. Even after a hysterectomy a woman can continue her relationship with her husband as before.

Although he must go on his business trip, it is crucial that Forrester ensures that his wife receives attention and that he demonstrates his concern. Joanna Forrester is obviously not very adaptable and is very possessive, probably the result of an insecure background. She needs attention. She needs to be loved.

Before he leaves on his trip, Forrester should make two important telephone calls. He should call Baker and suggest that he send Joanna a bouquet of flowers and a personal letter telling her he knows how distressed she is, and how appreciates her unselfishness. He might even accept some responsibility for Forrester having to go away, and send her flowers at intervals in her husband's absence.

Forrester should then telephone the surgeon who is to perform the operation, explaining that his wife will be alone, and asking him to talk to her about the demands being made on her by her husband's work. A surgeon, who himself may work late hours and have a similar problem with his wife, will normally be happy to cooperate.

While he is away, Forrester should send frequent cables, telling her how worried he is and how he hopes everything is all right, and how much he loves her. He should not telephone her as this could provoke an argument. As a contingency, Forrester should tell his wife he will be away longer than he expects. It is vital that he does not come back later than he says. But he should not surprise her. On his return, he should telephone her from the airport so that she can prepare herself for him

It is vital that Forrester's wife be made to realize the important contribution she is making to her husband's career and feel she is sharing in his success, particularly if he is promoted. Her husband should also take more time to listen to her problems. He should telephone her when he will be late in future.

People want others to appreciate their problems. It is when we have a problem and nobody cares that we are destroyed. This is what is causing Forrester's wife to feel resentful.

This decision was provided by Dr. Doris Odlum in her capacity as president of The Samaritans, a U.K. voluntary organization devoted to helping the distressed and suicidally inclined.

Should production manager accept a risky job offer?

Hannah Koomen was not surprised to see her husband, Jan, sitting at the breakfast table, staring at his cup of black coffee. "You were up early," she remarked, pouring herself a cup. "I heard you tossing and turning all night. Couldn't you sleep?"

"I could not stop thinking about the job offer," Koomen replied.

Koomen's wife did not understand. "I thought it was settled that you would take the job. Have you decided against it now?" she asked.

"I am not sure," replied Koomen. "I had made up my mind to take it. But now everything seems so uncertain. And I have told them I would give them my answer this morning."

Koomen had been quite content with his job as the production manager of one of the main plants of Rembrandt BV. Then he was approached by Piet Wijmer, group production director of Bruegel BV, to join Bruegel as deputy to the plant general manager. Koomen, who had joined Rembrandt as an apprentice, was not a particularly ambitious man. When he was promoted to his present job at the age of 38, he felt that he had achieved as much as he had ever hoped for, and that he would be quite happy in the job for the rest of his life. That was seven years ago.

Now he was being offered a job with the prospect of being appointed general manager, and appointment to the board when the job incumbent retired at 60, in two years' time, "because of failing health," Wijmer had told Koomen. "As deputy, you would serve a training period. And assuming that you succeed in that job," Wijmer explained, "I see no reason why you should not be appointed as general manager after that."

Worrying doubts remain

For Koomen the job offered a unique opportunity. It meant a move from functional to general management which appealed to him. And although Bruegel was a much smaller firm than Rembrandt, Koomen felt he would never be given such an opportunity in his present firm, where academic qualifications seemed to be more important than experience. As general manager, he would also be given more authority, responsibility, status and considerably more money. But doubts still nagged him. From the start Koomen was suspicious of Wijmer, who seemed to him to be rather cold and abrupt in his manner. Koomen had particularly noticed the way Wijmer spoke of pushing aside another man who was the natural successor to the general manager to make room for Koomen to come in as deputy. Koomen's doubts were strengthened the previous afternoon. By chance he met the personnel manager of Bruegel at the local golf club who told him he had no idea that the present general manager was planning to retire at 60, and that he seemed to be quite healthy.

Koomen's wife expressed surprise when Koomen told her this. "I rang Wijmer immediately," Koomen went on. "He assured me that the general manager would be retiring at 60, but that they did not want the employees to know.

"The problem, of course, is that the man could well change his mind," Koomen added. "If so, it would be another seven years until he reached the normal retiring age. And all this time I would be working as his deputy. I would not be any better off than I am now. In fact, as a deputy, I would not have as much autonomy as I do now. And while I do not doubt my abilities to handle the job, it is possible that the company could decide I was not suitable to replace the general manger when he does retire. They could decide to choose a younger man or someone else who might come along with better academic qualifications."

Trading comfort for adventure

"Well as I said yesterday," said Koomen's wife after a long silence, "I leave the decision to you. Your career comes first as far as I am concerned. But I still think it would be a mistake for you to take this job. If you have any doubts then stay where you are, I say. After all, you have got a secure job with a good company. If you left you might be in danger of losing some of your company pension money. We are living comfortably. Why should you gamble all this away?"

Koomen took his glasses off and banged them on the table. His wife knew she had hit a sensitive spot. "And I would go on doing the same dull, routine job for the next 20 years," Koomen snapped. "I am 45 years old, remember. At my age it is very unlikely I would get such a good job offer again. I have got to decide whether to remain content for the rest of my life with my existing job, or be adventurous and grab the opportunity being offered to go to a job where I can make really big decisions."

"Big decisions," echoed Koomen's wife sarcastically. "You cannot even make this decision without a lot of agonizing."

DECISION

Yes, if all his conditions are met. Otherwise he should stay where he is

Koomen has a difficult problem. There are several answers and none is immediately right or wrong. The eventual outcome, and therefore the correct answer, will remain unknown until two years' time.

Koomen certainly has a great deal of thinking to do. He should consider his ability and his present security, and think about Bruegel BV, and the job he is being offered.

Essentially, he faces a fairly common problem. He has a steady, secure job and is adequately compensated. He likes the work, knows every angle, knows all the personalities surrounding him and feels comfortable with his work situation. Mid-way through his career, he is not too ambitious and is prepared to carry on in the same job until his retirement. Then along comes an offer from another company to fill a potentially rewarding position at a higher level in the hierarchy. It sounds fine if everything goes well, but will it? There are always risks involved – not matching the prospective employer's expectations, fitting in with new colleagues, adapting to new systems, and having to change routine standards and procedures.

The main point – and it is a fundamental one – is that Koomen should never have been faced with the uncertainties surrounding the job. It appears from Koomen's confused condition that basic and systematic selection procedures were never employed. Careful selection in itself will not eliminate all the risks of the wrong man taking up the job of deputy to the plant general manager. However, it will considerably reduce them.

Wijmer also has a real problem which he himself has created. He is responsible for finding a capable replacement for the plant general manager. The new man must have the ability eventually to take on an important senior management post and membership of the board. Apparently Koomen does not fit the requirements. Here is a man who is not particularly ambitious by his own admission, and who until this job offer, was content to serve the rest of his career with the same company in the same position, and who has no plans to develop further. He also displays a lack of self-confidence and a psychological blockage about academic qualifications versus experience. It is questionable whether this makes him suitable for general management or the boardroom. It suggests that Koomen is better placed in his present position as production manager at Rembrandt BV where his personality, knowledge of the product and general experience will serve him and his present company better.

Selection by intuition is dangerous
These are the questions that Wijmer should ask himself. But in addition he should be asking questions about the job for which he is recruiting. In order to get the right man Wijmer must have a thorough understanding of the professional and personal requirements demanded by the job. Without this complete awareness, selecting the best candidate will simply be a gamble. In any competitive business environment, selection by intuition is a dangerous technique which may bring disastrous results.

For the post of deputy to the plant general manager and board designate there should be specific requirements embodied in a job description, and backed up by a detailed job specification. A realistic candidate profile can be drawn up from these two basic documents and then a professional and methodical search should be systematically conducted. Wijmer owes it to his company, the employees and himself to carry out this procedure. But this does not help Koomen at the breakfast table.

Koomen should give Bruegel the opportunity to reconsider its offer. He has an uneasy feeling about certain aspects of the recruitment method. It may be mainly concerned with the general manager's plans to retire due to ill health. In view of this doubt, and his present relatively secure and solid position with Rembrandt, he should be in a strong position to test Wijmer's intentions towards future promotion and question the firm's inadequate recruiting methods. He should ask for a written job description and job specification and be prepared to discuss how he measures up. In addition, he should agree an overall planned training programme during his two years as deputy. In this way Koomen is showing that he has the foresight to anticipate problems and protect the company's interests as well as his own.

If Wijmer produces these and agrees to such discussions and still offers the job, Koomen should take it. If he does not then he should remain in his present position and prepare himself for 20 comfortable and less demanding years with his present firm.

This decision was provided by Hasan J. Hadeed in his capacity as director of Hadeed Management Service Counsellors in Kuwait.

Should the personnel man probe finance officer's changed lifestyle?

" "N ow there's a man who likes the good life," sales manager Ian MacArthur told his colleagues in the company canteen. "I always thought Angus Stewart was a bit of a wet blanket, but I've had to revise my opinion since one of my customers told me about his antics last week. Not the sort of thing you expect from a finance officer."

Malcolm Frazer, personnel director of Whippets of Scotland Ltd., a savoury spread manufacturer, was intrigued as the sales manager unfolded his tale with ill-concealed relish. Apparently Stewart had arrived at a party without his wife in the company of a group of girls. At the end of the party he had ended up dancing fully clothed in the fountain with one of his young companions.

It certainly didn't fit the image of Stewart that he was familiar with, mused Frazer as he made his way back to the executive floor. He tried to think if there had been any sign of change in Stewart's behaviour at work. Stewart was accepted by most of the executives as a dull, colourless and unenterprising man, although a good and conscientious worker. His rejection for a board post only three months previously almost certainly stemmed from this assessment of his character.

Had the 40-year-old finance officer taken the message and decided to get out of his rut? A telephone call to one of Frazer's *protégés* in Stewart's department seemed to confirm that he had. Over the past six weeks or so the finance officer had invested in much more stylish clothes, no longer came into the office an hour ahead of everyone else and had bought a smart new red Ferrari. The car alone must have cost nearly a year's salary.

Keep social life private

Frazer decided that, on the whole, the change in life style was probably a good thing. But Frazer was worried by Stewart's behaviour. The incident at the party, Frazer grumbled to his wife that night, had been witnessed by several important customers. Stewart should make sure his social life did not affect the reputation of the company he worked for.

His wife persuaded him that it would probably be sensible to let the matter drop, especially as the incident was only hearsay. "After all," she added, "it's up to him what he does in his free time. You wouldn't like it if the managing director told you that you are too involved in local politics."

However, a week later MacArthur brought the subject up again. He had happened to be entertaining a customer in a local pub the evening before. Stewart had come in, looking slightly worse for wear and talking loudly, in the company of a group of young stockbrokers. "He seemed quite embarrassed to see me," remarked the garrulous sales manager. "I was quite relieved because I didn't like the idea of him joining us in that state. He was noisy and would have spoilt the evening."

Frazer knew that the sales manager often embellished his stories. But the incident triggered a number of dormant suspicions in his mind. What, he asked himself, if Stewart's behaviour was due to more than just a new lease of life? The finance officer had taken hard the lost opportunity to sit on the board. Suppose he was getting his revenge by tapping the company for the money to pay for his new life style, which must be close to, if not above, his means. Maybe there was something more than just friendship with this crowd of stockbrokers. It was not unknown for dishonest executives to buy shares for the company's investment portfolio, in the hopes that this would raise the price. If the price rose, a cooperative broker friend would credit the deal to the executive's personal account, selling off the shares at a profit. If there was no quick profit the deal would go to the company account.

Frazer found it hard to believe that Stewart was the type of person who would be dishonest. But then, he would scarcely have believed that the Stewart he had thought he knew would behave in the extrovert fashion of the past six weeks.

With some reluctance, Frazer's *protégé* in Stewart's department ran a brief and surreptitious check of the department's work. He reported that he could find nothing amiss. Although there was a minor increase in share dealings over the past two months, this was not unusual, as the level of activity varied from season to season.

Frazer knew that if he went straight to the managing director with his suspicions, he would be expected to have proof. If Stewart proved to be totally innocent Frazer's own position in the firm would become untenable. If he simply brought up Stewart's uncharacteristic behaviour, the managing director would probably accuse him of being a busy-body. Should he let sleeping dogs lie? Or should he take some action?

DECISION

A private meeting with the finance officer must come first

This is a delicate situation. In matters of human relations it is essential to avoid making mistakes and making bad judgments. And it is difficult to establish the truth.

Malcolm Frazer, director of personnel at Whippets of Scotland Ltd., must make a real effort to re-examine the situation objectively and establish the facts. As he has already contacted one of his *protégés* in Angus Stewart's department, he should start his investigation here. He should discreetly seek information about his work performance and ensure that no irregularity has been committed, in order to ensure Stewart's integrity and competence.

If Frazer can find no cause for complaint regarding Stewart's work, he should arrange a private meeting to speak candidly with him about his problems. Frazer should bring up the subject of his behaviour outside the firm, stressing at the very start that his personal life and freedom is respected by the company. He should then advise him to be more discreet in his behaviour in places frequented by influential people, which could reflect adversely on the company's reputation. Frazer should ensure, however, that any specific examples given are factual. In the course of the discussion it would be natural for Frazer to ask Stewart to explain certain incidents reported to him so Frazer may hear his story.

164

Frazer should then proceed to speak frankly to Stewart about any problems which may have caused his change in behaviour and in his living style, his change of appearance and his new Ferrari, for example. He should try to discover whether these changes arise from Stewart's frustration that he was not appointed to the board, or from other personal difficulties. Again it is essential Frazer stress the company's respect for his individual freedom. Frazer can also try to advise Stewart, assuming that sufficient confidence exists between the two men.

In the course of this first interview with Stewart, Frazer should try to stop the situation from going any further. Frazer should make clear to Stewart that he has no intention of speaking to the managing director about the matter at this point, and that he would like to end the situation then and there. He should recommend that Stewart make a conscious effort for the next six months to be more discreet and avoid new incidents arising which would give rise to further complaints and gossip among his colleagues at work.

Company advancement based on good reputation

At the same time Frazer should inform Stewart that if there are new incidents reported to him, which are found to be true, then he would have no alternative but to speak to the managing director.

If at the end of the interview it appears to Frazer that Stewart is either frustrated or disappointed because he has not been offered a board position, Frazer should indicate that such an appointment is still possible if he considers him capable of such a position. Stewart must understand however, any advancement within the company depends on his concern for his own reputation, and that of the firm.

After the interview with Stewart, Frazer should arrange an interview with Ian MacArthur in an effort to calm the situation. He should try to determine whether MacArthur is hostile to or jealous of Stewart for any reason, whether they have quarrelled in the past.

Frazer should obtain from MacArthur an assurance that he will try to avoid any further tensions between himself and Stewart and make a conscientious effort to understand and show consideration to his colleague, particularly at this time.

Frazer himself should make an effort to improve the personal relationship betwen the two men by fostering better personal contacts and communication. If after all this there does not appear to be any improvement in the situation, Frazer must then face the need to speak to the managing director and ask him to arbitrate and reach a final decision.

The managing director should then call in Stewart and remind him of his responsibilities to his colleagues and the company. He should make it quite clear to Stewart that any further irresponsible behaviour on his part invites the risk of his being sacked. Stewart should then be given three months to prove himself.

If, despite this warning, the managing director is convinced that Stewart is guilty of further indiscretions, he should dismiss him immediatley. Obviously, such a decision must be based on good evidence, and not on hearsay.

This decision was provided by Christian Le Clercq in his capacity as president of L'Entreprise de Demain, a professional association of Belgian executives, based in Brussels.

Is there any hope for marketing manager Rosemary Broom?

Rosemary Broom had given up a lot to climb the management tree and she felt she had had to fight male prejudice all the way. After all these years – she was nearly 44 – she still resented the automatic assumption by male telephone callers that she must be the marketing manager's secretary. In fact, Broom had been North American marketing manager for Canadian detergent manufacturers Lee & Brun Ltd. for six years.

Since Georges Marnier took over as managing director three years ago, however, she felt that she had not progressed at all. Marnier had recognized immediately that the home market had little growth potential and had concentrated the company's resources on expansion overseas. He had brought with him the bright young sales director of his previous company, Jim Tattershall. After a brief period as Broom's assistant Tattershall was promoted to international sales director, reporting directly to Marnier. Tattershall had more than justified his promise, and the European and Japanese divisions had shown rapid and profitable growth.

Broom, whose responsibilities were still tied to Canada and the United States, had little opportunity to let her light shine. Yet she had done well in consolidating the company's home sales during the past few years while competitors' sales fell in a declining market. Part of her success was the ease with which she formed good relationships with the wholesalers and chain stores that were the company's main customers. Her strong feminist views had made her a "character" and customers genuinely looked forward to her visits.

Feminism can create barriers

At the office, however, it was not the same. Marnier always felt ill at ease with her, and had somehow never managed to tell her that he appreciated the job she was doing. This strained relationsip could probably be traced back to the first board meeting over which he presided. He had asked Broom to take the minutes and was taken aback when she quietly but firmly refused. It was, she informed him, pure male chauvinism that prompted him to choose her for the task.

Most of her executive colleagues were well used to her feminism and took care, for example, not to hold doors open for her. On the whole, she got on cordially with them, but she was generally considered a little aloof, and had made no close friendships. As one executive put it: "It's as if she felt she might have to fight us, sometimes."

So it was hardly surprising that Quebec-born Marnier was not looking forward to telling Broom about his plans for reorganizing the company structure. A grey-haired man of correct and impeccable manners, he rose to meet Broom as she entered his office. "Sit down, Rosemary," he said, remembering just in time not to pull out her chair.

"I wanted to talk to you about the board changes I intend to make. You've been home marketing manager for six years now and I think its about time you had a change."

Before Broom could speak up, Marnier hurriedly pressed on. He explained that in view of the increasing amount of pressure on companies from government and consumers, he had decided it was time to appoint an executive to deal solely with that area. "We need a representative," he enthused, "someone to represent us before government committees and to consumer groups. You fit the bill admirably, not just because of your marketing experience, but because, as a woman, you will attract the sympathy of our housewife customers."

"I'm sorry, but I'm happy enough in marketing," interrupted Broom.

In obvious embarrassment, Marnier dropped his bombshell. "That will not be possible unless you want to be Jim Tattershall's second-in-command. We need to bring both marketing organizations under one central control. I've already promised to appoint Jim overall marketing director for our global operation."

"So that's it," shouted Broom losing her temper. "You're pushing me aside. In six months' time you'll decide you don't need a consumer representative after all. Then you won't have to put up with *any* women on the board, will you?"

Marnier started to explain that he genuinely did attach great importance to the job, which he had previously dealt with entirely himself. Far from a demotion ... But Broom was on her way out of the door, slamming it behind her.

Marnier had to admit that he had been remiss in not asking for her opinions beforehand.

Now he found himself in a quandary that only deepened as Broom stayed away from work for the next two days, with the telephone off the hook. He had honestly considered the job a prestige post, but now he began to wonder if someone who could take such offence was really a suitable public representative of the company. Should he encourage her to give the new job a try he wondered? She was unlikely to stay on in her present job, under a former subordinate. Perhaps the easiest solution would be to ask for her resignation?

DECISION

Managing director should restore Broom's self-confidence and give support

The implication of this dilemma is that it is a women's liberation problem. In fact, the distinction as to whether Rosemary Broom is male or female is largely irrelevant.

At the beginning, when Georges Marnier took over as managing director, he did what many people do. He brought in Jim Tattershall from his previous company, in this case a "bright young sales director". This was a perfectly natural thing to do but the way in which it was done had rather unfortunate results.

From the start Marnier failed to convey to Broom any recognition that she had acted well to consolidate the company's home sales while competitors' sales fell in a declining market. The fault may also have been partly hers not to have "sold" to Marnier what a good job she had done. This would indicate a lack of self-confidence and a withdrawal from competition to head the company's entire sales effort.

What Marnier should have done was to acknowledge Broom's achievement and persuade her to maintain the level of home sales volume over say the next nine to 12 months. During this time he could have prepared a new marketing structure and policy objectives. This period would have given Marnier breathing space and time to sell Broom on the new job that he had in mind for her; representing the company with government committees and consumer groups.

Initially he should have persuaded Broom that the main scope for expansion was overseas and that new skills would be required in the company to exploit these opportunities.

The nine to 12 months would have given Marnier time to establish good relationships with the sales team, and to formulate and communicate his ideas and intentions.

Recognize a job well done

Alternatively Marnier could have understood more clearly what a good job Broom had done for home sales and offered her a trial as overseas marketing manger. This would have been more creative but also more risky. This is because doubts would probably arise in Marnier's (chauvinistic) mind about Broom's ability, stature and self-confidence in negotiations with overseas buyers.

Furthermore, Marnier's old associate, Tattershall, was a known quantity whereas Marnier lacked familiarity with Broom's work.

Either course of action would have probably enabled Marnier to avoid his present dilemma.

Let us now consider how to solve Marnier's problem. The trouble arises mainly from the lack of communication between Marnier and Broom. Marnier should allow time for Broom to regain her composure. Then he should communicate with her directly, or through an intermediary, requesting a meeting.

Offer a worthwhile new job

At this meeting Marnier should acknowledge that the lack of liaison was at least partly his fault and explain the reasoning,behind the creation of the new job. The explanation should be in depth, giving the objectives, resources and the time needed to achieve results.

Marnier should build up Broom's shattered self-confidence by emphasizing that he and his colleagues respected her for her past record. He should offer her his own strong personal support in the proposed new job, and follow her progress with interest.

It is then up to Broom to accept or reject the offer. Her decision will depend upon whether she thinks Marnier is committed to the new job.

He must therefore persuade her that the job is really necessary. Otherwise Broom's skills will be lost to the company and she will go elsewhere.

This decision was provided by Colette Gilbert in her capacity as director of Knight Wegenstein Ltd., the British subsidiary of a Swiss-headquartered management consultancy.

Should Roca get the presidency of La Refrescante?

Jorge Roca was deep in thought when Alto Cobo, the chairman of La Refrescante SA, one of the biggest soft drinks firms in the Andean Pact nations, walked into his office.

"Roca, I have good news for you," Cobo said ebulliently. "Our board will meet tomorrow to confirm the appointment of Alberto Morante y Castro, who is joining the company as successor to Don Jorge Blanco. You will be promoted to the new position of executive vice president. I am sure that both you and Morante will get along perfectly. He is a nice man and is well aware of your excellent performance in the company."

Blanco, a member of the family that founded the firm in 1893, was to retire after 25 years as president of La Refrescante. Blanco was a pragmatic man who followed a policy of rewarding talent. This explained the brilliant career of Roca, who joined the company after finishing his engineering studies. He started in the production department and after 12 years was appointed vice-president in charge of production, a position never held before by anyone outside the powerful Blanco family.

Family ties are the strongest

Roca was a very able man. After 11 years of outstanding leadership as vice-president of production, he had felt he was the "heir apparent" to Blanco. But he was not the "natural heir" in a firm still ruled by a powerful few who traditionally had rotated among themselves the memberships of the boards and the highest executive positions. La Refrescante was a public company but the Blanco family still controlled the majority of the shares.

Morante y Castro was married to a member of the Blanco family. A rich and educated man, he had spent several years in foreign universities, had great personal charm and for the past five years he had concentrated on managing the family's financial investments. He did not have any previous experience in the beverage industry, but was an intelligent man who could handle La Refrescante's top post providing he had strong administrative support. Rumours had been spread in circles connected with the board that Morante y Castro had expressed his wish to become the president, and would probably get the job.

These rumours were so widespread that Roca had been approached by at least three other firms within the last few days. The offer that he was contemplating when Cobo entered his office was from El Vergel. This was a fast growing real estate firm. Its founder was interested in giving up the day-to-day management and taking the ceremonial post of chairman. Although the firm was much smaller and less prestigious than La Refrescante, the salary it offered was in excess of what Roca now earned. In addition, it offered him generous share options that would give him a chance to become a part-owner. At 48, Roca felt he had reached a crucial point in his career. Cobo's message indicated to him that he would never be given the presidency of La Refrescante.

He turned slowly to face the chairman, and said, "I am very sorry, Mr. Cobo, I do not have any intention of accepting the offer to be executive vice-president. I have had several offers in recent days from firms that value talent over family connections. If I am not given the presidency I intend to take one of these." Cobo was stunned. The board had never considered the possibility of Roca leaving.

The next day at the board meeting Cobo explained the situation. "Surely he is ungrateful," said one of the family directors. "After all, he has been offered great opportunities and given an important post in the nation's third largest company. But it should be obvious even to him that he does not have the social connections, nor the personal wealth, to maintain the position as the head of this company."

However, some outside directors expressed concern for the fate of the company if its most able executive departed just as a complete newcomer was taking over. "We are living in a new era," said one. "Perhaps it is best to give in to the times and let Roca have the top job."

Eduardo Blanco, the father-in-law of Morante interrupted: "Impossible! My daughter has already planned a huge celebration party for this evening. We have already made the choice, and we have a moral commitment to give Alberto the job." The outside director retorted: "Well, nothing is official yet, why don't we see if we can work out a solution that is in the company's best interest?"

DECISION

Roca should resign, to his own and the company's benefit

As I see it there are three alternatives facing the directors. The first is the one that the board is in fact considering; the appointment of Alberto Morante y Castro as president and Jorge Roca as vice-president. The second alternative is to appoint Roca as president.

The third alternative is to appoint Morante as president and accept Roca's resignation. This is the solution I favour.

If we consider and accept what are historical facts, in this case tradition and family prestige, the appointment of Morante seems inevitable and logical. To many this decision may seem retrogressive and unfair. But, paradoxically, it is also the best solution under the circumstances.

A working relationship should not be discordant

Because of his background, Morante is the person who seems most likely to introduce changes in the company and to initiate the structural and managerial changes which are desirable. But the "duo" of Morante and Roca would be a discordant one. It would not succeed as a working relationship. It would generate conflict. Given the existing situation in the company, Roca would fail to contribute to the modernization of the company which Morante would probably initiate.

But the continued presence of Roca in the company, if Morante were appointed, would be more negative than that. Roca's seniority and his many years of service to the company, added to the fact that he has a host of loyal followers, would create a negative force acting against the new president. Roca's supporters would close ranks and would engage all means to oppose the change and resist the sweep of a new broom.

The other alternative, to appoint Roca as president, is on the face of it an attractive solution because it involves a certain sense of fairness.

It should not be forgotten, however, that the company has acquired over the years a managerial structure both rigid and pragmatic, shaped by men who have built up a network of informal communications among themselves.

In every company resistance to change is strong; stronger than the desire to accept change. The appointment of Roca as president would be taken to indicate a willingness by the board to start a change in both the company structure and the company image, making it a more open and democratic company.

Power can be concentrated in a few people

It would seem more likely, however, that Roca would continue to be a loyal and faithful follower of the former president, Don Jorge Blanco. Roca's gratitude, admiration and indebtedness to the Blanco family suggest that if he were appointed he would not only continue the former policies of management but would apply them in the same way. Roca was created and shaped in the Blanco mould. If he were to be appointed, any changes would be conditioned by the family influence.

Under these circumstances it seems likely that he would be less interested in making changes than in maintaining the existing situation.

One fact that confirms my point, I think, is that the board is not willing to select a third candidate. The concentration of power in a few people has been a clear obstacle to modernization and change. It has also prevented the development of a spirit of teamwork which is so important in management today.

The company needs, above all, change agents. In the circumstances and considering the situation in which the company finds itself, the least advisable solution would be to appoint Roca, who is inclined to continuity and complacency.

There are several other reasons why I favour the appointment of Morante as president, but only if Roca's resignation is accepted.

Morante shows qualities which the company badly needs at this time. He appears to be dynamic, forward-looking and adaptable. His academic background appears to be excellent. He has financial expertise and experience equal to and perhaps even greater than that required by the company. He has been in charge of the Blanco family's financial affairs for five years. He is young and well-informed. It is certainly likely that he would recruit a capable management team to support him in making the changes the company so badly needs to make.

Roca's resignation would favour the process of change in two ways. A potential threat to the new president's success would be eliminated. Furthermore, the new president could use this vacancy and the need for replacements as an excuse for making the desired changes.

By resigning, Roca would also benefit. He would be taking advantage of an opportunity to take on new challenges, with increased personal fulfilment and better remuneration, at a crucial stage in his life.

This decision was provided by Saul Duque Gómez in his capacity as executive director of the Instituto Colombiano de Administración (INCOLDA), based in Bogotá, Colombia.

What should a chairman do about a compulsive borrower?

It was an embarrassing moment for Frederick Pressett, the chairman of Pressett & Green Ltd., a small U.K. manufacturer of household and commercial scales. A chauffeur who worked for the much larger company from which Pressett & Green leased space had wandered into his office looking for Wilbur Wolff, the sales manager Pressett had hired eight months before.

Pressett & Green had an arrangement with its landlord to use its limousine on a stand-by basis. Five weeks ago, Wolff had taken the limousine to the railway station. In something of a state, he told the chauffeur he had left his wallet in his office. He had asked the chauffeur for a loan to tide him over the two-day trip.

The chauffeur, who had just been paid, somewhat hesitantly lent the money. But he was not particularly concerned, since Wolff was an executive of a tenant company.

The chauffeur explained that, on four or five occasions since, he had seen Wolff in passing and had reminded him of the loan. Wolff had always been in a hurry, but had promised to send his secretary down with the money. However, it had not been delivered. Now the chauffeur had some pressing bills of his own to pay and needed the money rather urgently. Wolff, as it happened, was on a week-long selling trip.

Pressett had called in George Crenshaw, the firm's accountant. Crenshaw drew the sum from petty cash to pay the chauffeur, who was obviously deeply relieved to get his money back.

Financial obligations must be met

"This is serious," Pressett said when the chauffeur had left. "I should have expected something like this would happen."

The accountant nodded, recalling silently the day the first court attachment to Wolff's pay was delivered. He had reported the fact to Pressett. When the second and third attachments came, shortly thereafter Pressett had called Wolff into his office.

Wolff had been very contrite. He explained that in his previous sales position he had been promised a very large, long-term order which meant very sizeable commissions. On this basis he had, unwisely, he now admitted, moved to a much more elegant rented flat and purchased an expensive new car and a boat. The sale had fallen through, and left him heavily overcommitted. That, he explained, was why he had been prompted to find a better job to meet the obligations. With the money he was now earning, he hoped to get out of debt within 18 months.

A few weeks later Pressett was surprised to hear someone praising Wolff's generosity in buying several rounds of drinks at a local bar. This was followed by an angry letter from a local garage complaining that Wolff's account was four months overdue. When a process server showed up one day looking for Wolff, Pressett decided it was time for a second talk on the matter.

"How you handle your personal finances is your affair," Pressett began. "But I want to warn you that it must not interefere with your work.

Also, I must insist that you draw only the money you can account for in entertaining expenses at the end of the month."

Pressett went on to give Wolff the praise that was due him as a sales manager. He was an extremely likeable person, with an ability to work well and effectively with the firm's eight salesmen. Within three months of his arrival there had been a marked increase in sales. But Wolff also appeared to be a spendthrift who was constantly and deeply in debt.

"Has Wolff been overdrawing on expenses?" asked Pressett.

"No," Crenshaw replied. "I have been watching carefully. He does occasionally seem to go overboard entertaining a client, but nothing that appears fraudulent or excessive.

Then, after a pause, Crenshaw added: "You do know that this business with the chauffeur is not an isolated case. He borrowed a small sum from my secretary and was a very long time in paying it back. And I have heard that he does owe one or two of the salesmen rather larger sums which he has not repaid."

Pressett was now deeply concerned. He wanted to be fair to Wolff. He was doing a good job and, so far at least, had not tried to use company money to alleviate his personal financial problems.

On the other hand, he felt an obligation to protect his workers, and indeed others in the community, against the profligate ways of his sales manager before they become worse.

He would certainly confront Wolff, when he returned, abut the money the company had paid the chauffeur on his behalf. But what more should he, or could he, do?

DECISION

Firm's chairman must deal with debt-ridden sales manager

Frederick Pressett, the chairman of Pressett & Green, evidently feels that he must confront his sales manager, Wolff, when the latter returns to the office, about the money he borrowed from the chauffeur.

It will not be the first confrontation between the two. Pressett has already warned Wolff that his personal financial affairs must not interfere with his work. But that warning appears to have had little effect. So now Pressett should ask himself whether further confrontation is either necessary or desirable. Perhaps a more constructive approach, involving counselling Wolff rather than upbraiding him, would be more effective.

Personally, I have yet to come across a sales manager, who after all occupies a senior position and is in a high income bracket, who would find it necessary to borrow from a chauffeur. However, Wolff has done so, and it is clear that he is unable to cope with his financial affairs without some help of a practical nature.

Unbridled borrowing by an individual, around the office, inevitably causes gossip, discontent, lowers the esteem of the individual in the eyes of his colleagues and can be bad for morale. On the other hand. Wolff appears to be cooperative and well liked. More to the point from Pressett's point of view, he is a good salesman and manager who delivers the goods. So Pressett will conclude that things will have to get a lot worse before he considers sacking Wolff.

There are only two alternatives, which could be acted upon singly or in combination. One is to take the public step of saying to members of the staff: "Don't on any account lend Wolff any money." The other is to extend a helping hand to Wolff, in private, and get him to see that it is in the interests of himself and the company that he solve his problems.

I do not recommend the first alternative because it does not get to the root of the problem. It puts the onus on others to make it difficult for Wolff to borrow without exerting influence on him to mend his ways.

Pressett should again summon Wolff to his office for a heart-to-heart talk. At the meeting he should take the line that he has realized Wolff *does* have real financial problems and that with his own experience of financial affairs, which has taken him to the top of the company, he may be able to help.

"As I said on a previous occasion," Pressett could tell Wolff, "I don't want to meddle in your personal affairs. But now (and here he should mention the chauffeur episode) it is a business matter and I'd like you to view it as such. Just as I accept my responsibility to help, you will perhaps accept your responsibility towards the business, in this matter."

Pressett should ask Wolff directly whether he has, in fact, been borrowing money from his own salesmen, as the firm's accountant, Crenshaw, has heard. If he admits that he has, Pressett can quickly get Wolff to agree that it is indeed a serious matter with business implications. Only if Wolff hedges on this point, and is clearly being less than frank, should Pressett check the facts out with the salesmen individually.

Pressett should then ask Wolff to enlighten him, as factually as if they were discussing sales turnover or the company's accounts, what his current situation is.

"Previously you told me you had bought an expensive boat. Do you still have it or have you now sold it?

"Previously, also, you told me you hoped to be out of debt within 18 months. Was that over-optimistic? What progress are you making towards that goal?"

If Pressett conducts the discussion in a businesslike rather than an emotional manner, Wolff will respond in like fashion. Clearly he is not a stupid man, or he would not have got where he is.

Pressett should establish once and for all whether Wolff gets into financial difficulties through excessive personal extravagance, poor money management or a combination of the two.

Does his extravagance have any connection with his job? Does he have the idea that ownership of a boat is essential to entertaining clients? If so, it shouldn't be difficult for Pressett to disabuse him of the notion.

Finally, Pressett can offer Wolff practical assistance to solve his monetary problems. If Wolff is really deeply in debt, the offer by the company of financial support loans, with fixed repayments, might be appropriate in return for Wolff's acceptance of regular monitoring of his return to solvency.

If, however, Wolff is beset essentially by cash flow problems, Pressett might well instruct the company's accountant, and persuade Wolff, that his expenses should be settled twice a month, instead of monthly.

This decision was provided by Erling Vindeby in his capacity as a Brussels-based European personnel manager with Intel International, a subsidiary of the U.S. electronics company Intel Corp.

Should a manager be allowed to make a martyr of himself?

Pierre Duval, chief executive of a Paris-based firm that makes electric motors, wished he could delegate to someone else his annual encounter with the company doctor.

"I don't think there is much wrong with you," the doctor said as he pushed and prodded Duval. "I wish I could say the same about Marcel Lautrec."

Duval frowned. "I didn't know you had examined Marcel," he said. "I thought he had declared his aversion to company medicals."

"That's what worries me," the doctor said. "But I do see him around the place and he hasn't been looking too good lately. I also hear through the grapevine that he practically collapsed at an executive meeting last week."

"He went very white, sweated a little and had to have a large brandy before he could resume his part in the discussion," Duval said. "I must admit I was worried. But Marcel laughed it off. He said it must have been something he had eaten." .

"Did you believe him?" the doctor said.

"He's a grown man, doctor, not a child. It's not my job to nurse-maid my executives. He has been working very hard, you know, leading the research team dealing with this new lightweight motor of ours. Research is at a crucial stage."

"His own 'engine' may be at a crucial stage," the doctor observed. "I mean his heart. That's what I am worried about. Will you try and get him to come along and see me?"

Health checks for the employee or the company?

"I'll try," said Duval, buttoning up his shirt. "If he does have a heart problem, you'll advise him to take it easy?"

"Unless you want a corpse as head of research, yes," the doctor replied.

Immediately after this encounter, Duval called on Lautrec. "How are things going?" he asked.

"As well as can be expected," said Lautrec, looking up from a pile of papers. "As I said at the executive meeting, we do have a vibration problem and one or two other bugs to iron out. But I think we can deal with them if we apply our minds to it."

"The doctor is worried about you. He wants you to go and see him."

"Not a chance," Lautrec shook his head.

"Why not, Marcel?"

"Because we have a job to do, don't we? Two months to get this device ready for evaluation by the client. I am not going to let the Germans steal a march on us this time. It is going to be our electric motor that goes into the Eurocar."

"But seeing the company doctor doesn't commit you to anything," Duval pointed out. "If you are perfectly fit you have nothing to worry about."

"I believe that my health is my own affair," Lautrec said. "It has nothing to do with the company."

175

"Then what does you own doctor say? You can't convince me that performance you gave at the executive meeting was due to over-eating."

Lautrec looked at him silently. Then he said: "What would *you* put it down to?"

"Well, the doctor says he thinks your heart might be a bit troublesome. If it is, and you are still putting in a 16-hour day, that is crazy, Marcel."

"Do you want this project finished or don't you?"

"You could delegate more work."

Companies care for their employees

"Not on the problems we are facing. I do not claim to be indispensable all the time. But I do have a knack for getting to the heart of problems. That is something I can't delegate. I have bright boys on my team but I can't trust them to get these bugs sorted out. Not on the kind of deadline we are up against. And I don't intend to see the company doctor."

The following day Duval mentioned the conversation to Jacques Leclerc, the personnel director. "I'm pretty certain all is not well with him physically," he said. "But he won't see the doctor and if I'm honest with myself I'm not too displeased. If the doctor did tell him to take it easy, this project could be in real trouble."

"On the other hand," said Leclerc quietly, "this company does have a slogan which says 'we care about you'. That means caring about employees as well as clients. It also applies to board members, as much as to junior apprentices, presumably."

"If we don't have this engine ready for evaluation," Duval continued, as though he had not heard Leclerc, "the Eurocar consortium is not going to wait. They will choose the German engine, which our sources tell us is perfectly good."

"What if Lautrec dies in harness?" Leclerc asked. "Then you are not going to get the engine finished in time. And do you relish having Madame Lautrec in your office accusing you of conniving in the death of her husband?"

"Do *you* want 4,000 employees in *your* office asking why they have been made redundant when they thought we had a new engine that would keep them in work for the next decade?"

The conversation was inconclusive. The company needed that contract. It needed it badly. If Lautrec continued to work and had a heart attack, Duval could always say that the man had brought it on himself. But could he live with the thought that he, Duval, had done nothing to prevent it? Indeed, in view of Lautrec's refusal to see the company doctor, what *could* he do?

DECISION

How to deal with a manager who may be seriously ill

Chief executive Pierre Duval is torn between his sense of duty towards the well-being of a colleague and his wish not to delay the research and development of the new electric motor. At first sight it seems a terrible predicament. However, no doubt the right course of action will occur to him. He will decide that he has to take a tough line immediately with research director Marcel Lautrec.

There are no certainties in the situation. But what are the alternatives as far as Lautrec is concerned?

First, he may stay at work, triumphantly deliver a motor that meets the client's needs and still be alive and well at the end of it all.

Second, he may stay on the job and die in harness because his heart gives out. That would not help himself, the project or the company in the short or long term.

Irresponsibility should be checked

Third, he may remain at his post and, whether or not his health suffers, not solve the technical problems besetting the new product. In that case he will have taken an unwarrantable risk to no purpose.

Neither Duval nor Lautrec is in a position to guarantee any of these three outcomes. Everything is left to chance. The project which is said to be so vital to the company's future becomes a lottery. Rational management has flown out of the office window.

Duval, therefore, should take the only alternative left. He should assert himself as chief executive of the enterprise. He should seek out Lautrec and lay it on the line.

"Marcel," he should say, "I have been thinking about our conversation the other day. I have come to the conclusion that you are behaving irresponsibly, and on reflection I think you will agree with that. I appreciate your loyalty to the company and your desire to see this device, which is your brainchild, through to completion.

"However, we are grown men, not children. We can't just leave things to chance. Therefore I must insist that you see the company doctor.

"Only then, when we know the state of your health, can we reach a rational decision what to do, not only in your best interests but in the interests of the smooth completion of the project which ought to be a serious consideration."

If Lautrec still insisits that he is not going to see the doctor, Duval should get even tougher. He should tell the research director that he is being silly, obstructive, and that if necessary he will be suspended from his post entirely, regardless of the project.

The fact is, there comes a time when hesitation and procrastination will solve nothing and hard decisions have to be taken. For example, it is not uncommon for the wives of executives about to be posted abroad to get an aversion to the idea and pressure their husbands not to go. Then it may be necessary to tell the husband: 'Sorry, but you have to choose between your job and your wife."

In Lautrec's case, he is either being heroic, in his own eyes, because his own doctor has told him of the risk he is running, and yet he continues at work, or he is being stupidly stubborn because he will not go to see the company doctor for fear of hearing the worst.

He has to be forced to make a choice between the heroics, which in the end will help nobody, and planning his immediate future in the light of the medical facts.

If, after a physical examination, the company doctor decrees that Lautrec is in imminent danger of a serious heart attack, then Duval has no choice but to suspend him, or to insist that he works shorter hours under medical supervision.

It may not be as bad as that. The doctor may decide that Lautrec's heart is perhaps not all that it should be but that he may continue at his post for the time being. Overwork of the kind in which Lautrec is involved – doing something that he enjoys – is not usually, in itself, a lethal activity. It is possible that if he dies at his laboratory bench he would have died anyway, and that it has nothing to do with overwork.

Of more concern to Duval should be the episode at the executive meeting, when Lautrec was taken ill and had to have a brandy to recover. Usually there are more stresses in committee meetings, with their internal politics, than in research laboratories. So the question must arise in Duval's mind whether Lautrec is equipped to continue in the business as a senior executive or whether he should not be persuaded to retire.

Duval's immediate task, though, is to tell Lautrec in no uncertain terms that all pretence must end and that he must see the company doctor immediately. That's an order.

This decision was provided by David Moreau in his capacity as a director and former chief executive of Elga Products Ltd., a U.K. company specializing in water treatment.

DILEMMA

How much of a manager's private life is of concern to his company?

Just as Karl Schmidt thought that his monthly talk with the chairman of the supervisory board was at an end, the old man said: "Karl, how is Hans Raab getting on?"

Schmidt, who was chairman of the management board at West German office equipment manufacturer Johan Kraus AG, looked puzzled. "He is doing well," he said. "As you know, he has been promoted to the job of general manager, personnel. Why do you ask?"

"You preferred him over a lot of others, didn't you?" the chairman said, rising to his feet. "Well, all I would say is: 'When did he last mention his wife to you?' Ask him how his home life is getting along some day, Karl."

Following up on chance remarks

Schmidt stared after the departing figure of the chairman. He rememberd that Raab, like the old man, lived in Heidelberg. Maybe the chairman had heard some gossip or had some information that had eluded Schmidt. But what then? He, as chief executive, was quite satisfied with the performance of his personnel manager. Nevertheless, he mentally filed the chairman's remark for future attention.

Later that week he had an appointment with Raab to discuss two important matters. One was the need to slim down the work-force at one of the company's typewriter plants. He also wanted to discuss what the company's attitude should be if a young machinist with left-wing politics, Dieter Mueller, was elected chairman of the works council.

In Schmidt's office, Raab submitted a plan for retiring some of the typewriter workers early, moving others to a calculator plant in a nearby town and ensuring that both the works council and the union saw the moves in a positive light.

"That's fine," Schmidt said. "Now about this other matter."

"Mueller is quite a firebrand," Raab said. Then he grinned unexpectedly. "But I can handle him."

Schmidt frowned. "You think he will be elected?"

"Yes, but he won't be any trouble."

"Why?"

"We see eye to eye on many things."

When gossip cannot be ignored

Schmidt let the matter drop. But there had been something in Raab's voice and expresion that was vaguely worrying. It hinted, Schmidt thought, at a relationship with Mueller that went beyond the friendly formality that Schmidt expected from his managers in their dealings with worker representatives.

In the following weeks various references to Raab, some of them malicious, came to Schmidt's ears. One concerned a party which Raab was supposed to have given at his home. It had been attended, Schmidt was informed, by several of the company's employees and had ended with nude bathing in a open-air swimming pool.

Schmidt felt that the gossip coming on top of what the chairman had said, could not be ignored. He obtained Raab's home address and wrote it in his diary.

The first week-end in June he suggested that his wife might like to visit an old friend in Heidelberg. She readily agreed and while the women talked Schmidt drove into the hills overlooking the picturesque town, determined to pay Raab a social visit. He had some misgivings about arriving at his subordinate's house unannounced. But he decided it was natural to call in for a drink while passing an idle hour on a glorious summer's day.

He had some difficulty finding the road, which turned into an unmade track heading towards some trees. Schmidt parked his car and walked until he found a small gate hidden in the trees. Beyond the trees he could see a lawn and a chalet-style house.

He was just going to walk from the shadow of the trees into the bright sunlight of the lawn when the house door opened and Raab appeared.

He was dressed in shorts and a caftan shirt and had a cigarette or possibly a reefer, Schmidt thought, hanging at the end of a long holder. With his cadaverous face, Raab reminded Schmidt of some of the hippies he had encountered on a business trip to southern California.

On his arm was a blonde woman – definitely not his wife, for Schmidt recalled having met Raab's wife at a cocktail party long ago. The woman was dragging a poodle at the end of a lead.

The couple were followed by several men and women, including a man whom Schmidt recognized. It was Mueller, whose election to the chair in the works council was now only days away. He too had a woman with him, whose reputation, Schmidt felt, he would have been loath to defend in a court of law.

As the procession disappeared round a corner of the house, Schmidt retreated. He returned to his car and sat in it thoughtfully, making no attempt to drive away.

What should he do? Should he join the party? Should he call Raab to his office on the Monday and ask him to explain himself? But what had the man done wrong? So far, professionally speaking, he had done a first-class job.

There was also the familiarity between Raab and Mueller. It was totally against Schmidt's own instinct. But what if it worked? What if Raab was initiating a period of real industrial harmony at the company? Whatever the relationship between Raab and Mueller, should the chief executive interfere?

DECISION

Manager's life-style provokes worries about its effect on his company

Karl Schmidt has made the right first decision. He did not go into the party at Hans Raab's house. He should now go home and analyse the situation calmly.

He will find that he has only rumour and circumstantial evidence to go on. Can he be certain that the blonde woman is not Raab's wife? When he met her "long ago," she was younger, slimmer, dressed up for a cocktail party to meet the boss. Is she now a different type of woman, relaxing with friends? Cigarettes and poodles do not always mean drugs and adultery. And can he be sure that the lady with Dieter Mueller, the prospective chairman of the works council, isn't his wife?

But even if his insticts are right, what conclusions can he draw? He may conclude that Raab has a "swinging" social life. That may mean that his marriage is on the rocks or that he and his wife have an unconventional arrangement or that she is ignorant of his philandering. None of this is any concern to Schmidt or to the company, unless it affects Raab's job.

Establishing definite facts
The factors affecting performance are whether damage to the company can arise from an undesirable relationship with Mueller. Can Raab's behaviour damage the company or expose him to blackmail? Can his conduct result in a loss of confidence in his objectivity or judgment or in his dealings with the unions and his management colleagues?

There are also considerations relating to the social culture of the community and the company. The way in which Raab's conduct is perceived is bound to be influenced by such considerations. The attitude and influence of the chairman may also be something that cannot be ignored, particularly if it undermines Raab's influence in the boardroom.

If Schmidt is to solve the problem responsibly and professionally, he must put aside gossip and speculation and establish some facts. To do this he has to talk to Raab.

He should do it in the right environment. The formal setting of an appraisal interview may be right, especially in view of Raab's recent promotion. Or it may be better in the informality of a meal or on an aeroplane journey.

Schmidt should draw out Raab about his job satisfactions and difficulties and his ideas for problem solving and performance improvement.

180

He should ask him about his family life and leisure interests. He should ask him to explain his confidence in handling Mueller. In this setting, he must ask a direct question about his personal relationship with Mueller.

This discussion needs to be planned carefully. Schmidt must retain the initiative. He must ask the questions he needs to have answered, but there must be a business justification for each question. Schmidt's task will be easier if he has made a practice of thorough conversations with his subordinates.

The outcome of this meeting may be that Schmidt is reassured about Raab's integrity and competence. He may need to do no more than to keep in close touch with Raab's work in the future. In these circumstances, Schmidt needs to tell his chairman in a suitable way that he continues to back Raab.

There may be a simple explanation
But the interview may go differently. Raab is in real trouble if he denies any social contact with Mueller or if he says anything which contradicts facts in Schmidt's possession. Schmidt must pursue any contradiction to a conclusion even if he has to reveal his visit to Raab's home. If Raab's integrity is destroyed he may have to go. But it should be noted that the lack of integrity would be the reason for his going, not his private life.

But perhaps it will all end happily. There may be a simple and perfectly acceptable explanation.

For example, it may be that Raab and Mueller are married to sisters and that the sisters came out of the house, when Schmidt was watching, on the arms of their respective brothers-in-law.

It may be that Mueller, who has been a "firebrand" to get himself elected, intends to work constructively with his sister-in-law's husband in the interests of all concerned.

Maybe all that Schmidt needs to do is to realize that his eyesight is deteriorating and make an appointment with an optician.

This decision was provided by Parry Rogers in his capacity as director of personnel and Europe for the Plessey Co. He was president of the U.K.'s Institute of Personnel Management from 1975 to 1977.

DILEMMA

Should chairman's son-in-law be reported for embezzlement?

Ahmed Marzouk remembered very well picking up the internal phone, at a Cairo branch of Egypt's Al-Kinanah bank, and asking to see the office manager. The voice at the other end, which Marzouk identified as that of a junior assistant, said that the manager was not available, and he offered to take a message.

Marzouk, who was managing director of the branch, looked at his watch and frowned. This was the bank's busiest hour and the manager ought to have been at his desk. "Where is he?" Marzouk demanded. Finally he was informed that the manager was taking two days off.

Marzouk put down the phone and looked at the weekly list of staff on leave, ill or transferred. The office manager's name was not on the list.

The managing director then asked Aly Sadiq, the personnel manager, to come to his office.

When Sadiq arrived, Marzouk looked at him with distaste. The man was distinctly shifty, he decided. He recalled the day, some months ago, when Sadiq had been transferred to Cairo from Luxor following a scandal involving some missing money.

Marzouk had not wanted to take him but Sadiq had one great advantage: he was the son-in-law of the chairman of the board of directors of the bank, Ibrahim Kamal. The chairman had called Marzouk on the phone and personally asked him to take on the young man.

Marzouk knew that Sadiq had married the favourite daughter of the chairman. He knew that to refuse to have him would have done his own career no good. And although he was aged 61, Marzouk was looking forward to many more years of service at the bank.

Sadiq explained that the office manager's name was not on the absence list because of an oversight. Marzouk, however, was not reassured.

When Sadiq had left the office, the managing director arranged to see all the applications for leave received during the past six months. He checked them against attendance lists and also made enquiries around the building concerning who had been absent and when.

Disturbing discrepancies come to light

There were many discrepancies. Not only had some employees had leave to which they were not entitled, or leave which had not been registered, but something even more disturbing came to light.

Within a few days Marzouk was aware that applications for leave from the staff had not, in many cases, been stamped with the duty stamp required by the government's internal revenue service. Yet money for these stamps had been drawn by someone in the personnel department, namely Sadiq.

Marzouk was forced to the unwelcome conclusion that Sadiq had been sending a messenger out to buy only a small proportion of the stamps, while pocketing the rest of the cash. He was repeating the dishonesty that had resulted in his being transferred from Luxor.

At board meetings, which were held twice a month, the chairman would say to Marzouk: "How is Sadiq getting on?" Marzouk would take the easy way out and reply "all right" or "very well." But at the next board meeting, after he had discovered what Sadiq was up to, he could only grunt.

When he confronted Sadiq with his suspicions, the young man did not even bother to deny them. "What if I am making some money on the side?" he said. "Who isn't, these days?"

"You are training to be a banker," Marzouk reminded him, his voice rising. "Bankers are men of honour, who have to be trusted."

"There is no need to lose your temper," Sadiq said, looking at him coldly. "Afer all, you are the one who employed me. It wouldn't say much for your judgment if you had to admit I was fiddling the petty cash."

"Your father-in-law would not approve," Marzouk said.

"If you report me to him," Sadiq replied, "you will be finished. You

182

will be out of the bank within a year. Even if the chairman disciplines me, which I do not for one moment think he will, he would not forget who told him of the disgraceful conduct of one of his family."

Marzouk made an angry retort. But privately he half agreed with what Sadiq had said. Family loyalty was strong, and even if Kamal transferred his son-in-law again he might still hold a grudge against Marzouk.

What made the situation more humiliating was the knowledge that everyone in the office, except himself, must have known about the fraud for some time. The employees had either benefited from it, by taking unrecorded leave, or turned a blind eye towards Sadiq's activities because of his family connections.

Not only were the employees waiting and watching to see what Marzouk would do, but so were other executives of the bank who had seats on the board.

Marzouk found himself dreading the next board meeting. The chairman would ask him again how his son-in-law was getting on. Should Marzouk say: "Sir, you son-in-law is a thief," despite the dire consequences he suspected? Or should he keep quiet once again?

If he kept quiet, what would happen if Sadiq's actions – and his own silence on the matter – came to the chairman's attention from other sources?

Marzouk was too proud a man to discuss his problems with friends. He had to decide for himself. What should he do?

DECISION

Managing director must tell chairman of son-in-law's dishonesty

The problem facing Ahmed Marzouk is typical of many such problems posed not only in Egypt but throughout the Middle East, where sectarian, family or class favouritism can occur.

Given the prevailing conditions in the society in which Marzouk lives, there is no single ideal solution to the problem. However, there are two possible solutions, both of which require caution, skill and shrewdness if they are to be applied successfully.

Certainly Marzouk needs to do something constructive to make up for his past mistakes. The situation is serious because, apart from anything else, it involves the embezzlement of money which the state would have received from stamp duties. This is a matter which properly concerns the state and the Ministry of Finance, the auditing department and the Treasury. It is a crime which incurs a heavy penalty.

Marzouk's first, and crucial, mistake was that it was he who accepted Aly Sadiq in the first place, although at the chairman's personal request, and assigned him to a key job in the bank despite his transfer because of a financial scandal.

Having made the appointment, he failed to keep an eye on the younger man, despite the knowledge of his previous misdeeds, until the accidental discovery of his latest transgressions.

Now, although he fears the possible reaction of the chairman, Ibrahim Kamal, to the news that his son-in-law has been dishonest, Marzouk must overcome his fears. He should ask for a personal interview with the chairman and agree with him on the transfer of Sadiq to any other job.

He must tell the chairman that Sadiq has been exposed and that all his colleagues know about his embezzlements. As a result, it is no longer possible to keep quiet and avoid taking disciplinary action.

Marzouk may find that the chairman Kamal will realize that it is neither in his interest nor in that of his son-in-law that matters should reach the stage of collision with an experienced director such as Marzouk. Deep in his heart, the chairman may feel gratitude towards Marzouk for tackling the matter with him privately, and thus caring for the interests and future of Sadiq and protecting the family name.

By virtue of his long relations with the chairman, Marzouk should be able to persuade him that the exposure of Sadiq will cause a scandal for the chairman too, particularly in a society where a good reputation is held in high esteem. It is possible that Kamal himself will censure his son-in-law because of his repeated problems and that this might be a lesson for Sadiq which he will not forget.

The other, or additional, action which Marzouk could take would be to form a committee comprising two or more divisional heads to investigate absenteeism and the multiplicity and frequency of leave taken by each employee in the branch in the course of a year.

Marzouk could put a number of written questions on absenteeism to Sadiq and ask him to answer them on the same day. Or he could ask him the questions in the presence of other staff; then write the minutes of such a meeting, together with the answers; let the staff sign them and ask Sadiq to sign them too.

Marzouk could also ask the financial control department to examine the bank's records and carry out surprise inspection raids to ensure that revenue has been collected in respect of all leaves taken.

Marzouk should not fear expulsion. He will be expelled anyway if he keeps quiet about Sadiq's actions or takes no action himself. This is because all Sadiq's colleagues are now familiar with, and aware of, the problem.

If Marzouk takes no action, the other employees might follow Sadiq's example. Then the bank would have other untrustworthy employees on its hands. Alternatively, the other employees may feel conscientious enough to expose Sadiq and Marzouk, perhaps accusing them both of jointly committing the contravention.

Also, Marzouk is bound to find supporters among the members of the board of directors, who expect him to do something to save the bank from such people as Sadiq.

I believe that the first solution, that of Marzouk speaking personally with the chairman, would be enough to get rid of Sadiq peacefully, particularly in the social and environmental conditions and traditions that govern employee relations in a bank.

Following Sadiq's transfer, Marzouk himself should begin a campaign of reform within the bank. He should appoint assistants to help him. He should also reduce the degree of decentralization, which seems to be excessive and which allowed Sadiq to operate as he did without being challenged earlier.

This decision was provided by Nazek Khalid Damreh in his capacity as the Jordanian managing director of Al-Manee Trading & Contracting Corp. in Saudi Arabia.

Have retiring chief executive's succession plans gone awry?

Harry Thompson's mind drifted back over nearly 30 years to when he had founded Auckland Chemical Co. The fledgling company was less than two years old when the young George Bolton had joined it. In those precarious years, when the company was in danger of failing, Bolton had chipped in his meagre savings to keep it afloat. Bolton's tireless energy in scouting out sales prospects for the firm's products had been a critical factor in Auckland's survival. But with the development of a new enzyme the company suddenly began to prosper. Today, after large-scale diversification, Thompson was chairman and president of a group with annual sales of $250 million. The company was a success.

Now, as Thompson faced his 65th birthday in two months, he was increasingly concerned over his successor as chief executive officer. It had long been the unspoken assumption that the job would go to Bolton, who was five years Thompson's junior. But Thompson had begun to have serious reservations about Bolton's judgment. More and more he tended to delay taking decisions. And he seemed unwilling to change with the times. At a recent management meeting Bolton had fought fiercely against installing anti-pollution equipment in the firm's new riverside plant. Michael Summers, vice-president for industrial products, had carried the day, arguing that he felt that such pollution control equipment would become a legal necessity. Indeed, six months later such a law was passed.

Choice of two bright managers

Thompson also feared that the bright young managers in the firm might grow restive under Bolton's indecisive leadership in today's uncertain circumstances. He was particularly worried about the possibility of losing either Summers or John Kemp, vice-president for pharmaceuticals. Both men were in their early forties. Thompson had privately earmarked them both as chief executive material. At this point, it was almost impossible to choose between the two.

Summers was the more visibly brilliant of the two. His division had grown faster than any of the others. He had a sharp, analytical mind that struck immediately to the heart of a problem. And he was never afraid to make changes, and adjust to new conditions. But Thompson suspected that sometimes Summers changed things just for the sake of it. The industrial products division was noted throughout the group for the frequency of its executives' vertical and lateral job moves. In Thompson's view the booming sales of industrial products had been achieved in spite of, not because of, job rotation that occurred as often as three times a year for some executives.

Kemp, on the other hand, was a far less flamboyant manager. Of unimpressive appearance, he had a knack of getting people to work effectively together. He was content to let others get the credit. For instance, Bolton was Auckland's official representative in negotiations over a joint operation last year. But a director of the other firm involved later told Thompson: "We didn't think Auckland would be able to handle this. After all, you had little experience in this field. It was Kemp who finally persuaded us." The operation had since proved profitable.

However, Kemp sometimes seemed to lack decisiveness. He still occasionally referred decisions on whether to go ahead with a new product to Thompson, who had started his career in the pharmaceuticals division. And he had retained some managers, admittedly in relatively unimportant posts, long after they were not performing satisfactorily.

Before his retirement had become so imminent, Thompson had coasted along, avoiding the soul-wrenching experience he felt now faced him. For five years he had seen the managerial transition as merely a matter of handing the reins over to Bolton. Thus he would fulfil the unspoken promise, and Bolton would realize his dream of running the company he had helped to build. In the meantime, Thompson pictured either Kemp or Summers coming to the fore as Bolton's obvious successor. And the company would have another five years' hard work from both these brilliant executives.

In fact, Thompson now admitted to himself, the choice between the two men would be just as difficult five years hence. The only difference was that he would be spared the unpleasant task of making the choice.

But now, as his departure was imminent Thompson felt that perhaps he owed it to the company and to its thousands of employees to act decisively, to ruin a life-long friendship and to trigger the departure of one valuable executive in order to continue the firm under strong leadership. If he was right, was Summers or Kemp the man for the top job?

DECISION

CEO must evaluate in-house candidates and possibly look outside as well

Harry Thompson, chairman and president of Auckland Chemical Co., two months away from retirement, has an immediate decision to make. To wit, he must stay on for another year to clear up the situation he has created.

Almost at the last moment, with very little information, with much necessary homework not done, he is considering appointing his successor to head a $250 million, highly diversified chemicals company. He is prepared to choose between two of his division vice-presidents, about both of whom he has serious reservations. He believes that he owes it "to the company and to its thousands of employees to act decisively". He is confusing decisiveness with correctness. He does not recognize that a decisive, actively implemented wrong decision is the worst possible legacy he can leave behind.

What is wrong with his proposed decision? First, the decision as to who will replace him is being made in the absence of any clear long-range plans for the organization. Where is Auckland Chemical going? What kind of an organization will it be ten years from now? Will it be stressing the development of new products or the broadening of sales and market penetration with the existing ones? How will the organization be structured? The best choice for president will be that person who is best able to promote the company's continued growth. And until Auckland

Chemical's long-range objectives have been stated in specific terms, it will be difficult to say who might best accomplish them.

In addition, he is thinking only about the one top man. He needs to be considering his entire top operating group.

Once the long-range objectives of the company have been stated in specific terms, it will be possible for Thompson to list the performance criteria and characteristics of the *ideal* candidate for the position. Not that the ideal president will ever be found. But the best real-life candidate will be that person who most nearly resembles the ideal. And without a profile of the ideal president against which to compare, it would be nearly impossible to recognize the best candidate.

Draw up a list of required qualities

Let us make some assumptions about the long-range objectives of the company. It will direct itself toward increased market penetration with its existing products. It will not attempt to achieve wider diversification through technological proliferation. It will continue to be organized on the basis of semi-autonomous divisions. Thompson will have to go much further than this in spelling out the shape, form and nature of Auckland for the future. When this is done, he can think though his list of criteria and characteristics of the ideal candidate. This man should have demonstrated his ability to make a profit. He should have a strong marketing and sales background, and ability to manage diverse activities. The ideal man should also have a strong sense of systems and priorities, should be a self-starter and initiator and should be young. He needs to be adept at working with people, at leading and motivating. Thompson will have to decide the weight that each of these criteria will exercise in the final selection.

Now that he has his measuring stick, he can concern himself with the available alternatives. Are Summers and Kemp the only possible candidates for the position? Or does he not owe it to the company to look to the outside for someone closer to the ideal? Of course, an outsider would raise some problems of disruption amongst the insiders. In no case, however, would the disruption approach the havoc created by promoting the wrong man.

At this point Thompson can begin to evaluate the candidates and tentatively determine who has proven himself the better man for the job.

But only tentatively, Before he can make his selection, he must examine the specific consequences of giving the job to that particular individual. What will happen as a result of the move? What kind of a final top operating team will this make? Will this selection create other problems and if so, what can be done to lessen their impact?

Thompson's task is not yet over. Once the decision is made, he will have to work in parallel with the new president for some months. This is particularly important, as Thompson has built the company from its inception. If he is like most entrepreneurs, he is carrying a major amount of history, know-how and procedures in his head.

Only when all of these foregoing steps have been completed can Thompson feel that he has indeed discharged his obligation to Auckland Chemical and its employees.

This decision was provided by Benjamin B. Tregoe in his capacity as chairman of U.S. organization development consultants Kepner-Tregoe Inc.

Should board accept chief executive's choice of successor?

Peter Heflin was energetic and successful. He was four years short of his company's retirement age of 65, but had decided to retire early in order to devote himself full-time to non-executive directorships and a new career in politics.

He knew that his decision would surprise the board of Precision Components Inc., a U.S. manufacturing company that had grown into a highly profitable enterprise during his 12 years as president and chief executive officer.

Heflin had been identified in the business press as a prime factor behind the company's success. His premature departure would be bound to cause a stir and could be misconstrued in some quarters.

Before announcing his decision to the board, therefore, Heflin related his intentions to board associate Christopher Taylor, who represented an influential group of shareholders.

Taylor was surprised but not dismayed. "If that's what you want, Peter, I am sure that the board will wish you well," he said. "It goes without saying you will be a great loss to the company. Who do you have in mind as your successor?"

Heflin named financial vice president Malcolm Sharpe, and frowned when he saw Taylor grimace. "You have nothing against him, have you?" he asked. "You know he has done a first-class job."

Sharpe had been in charge first of long-range planning and then of finance. He had provided much of the often brilliant strategic thinking that had contributed to the company's growth. "He is a good incisive thinker and has courage," Heflin added.

Protégés are not always popular

"He is a man in your image," Taylor said. "Like you, he can be a prickly customer. Maybe that's why the company needs a change.

"I am sorry to say this, Peter, but I think I'll have to go against you on this. Malcolm has done a good job but always in a staff role. He has no direct operating experience. I think that what the company needs now is a real production genius at the helm. That can only mean one man: Richard Pym."

But Richard doesn't have Malcolm's brain or the same fire in his belly," Helfin objected.

"That's just it," Taylor replied. "Malcolm in my view can be too overpowering. He is your protégé, Peter, and always has been. There are some on the board, certainly among the non-executive directors, who think that perhaps you haven't always been totally dispassionate in your assessment of the relative abilities of some of your executives who would consider resigning if Malcolm were appointed."

Heflin could hardly believe his ears. He had heard no whispers, no hints, of board dissatisfaction with his judgment or his sponsorship of Sharpe. "This is a pretty late hour to question my judgment," he said angrily as he paced round the room.

"Maybe it is, and maybe that's the trouble," Taylor replied. "While you are boss, people accept your decisions. It is difficult to argue with success. But now we are talking about your successor. The board owes no allegiance to you over that, except to take your views into account. We must do what is best for the company.

"Don't take it so personally, Peter," he added. "If it comes to a showdown over this, you can always decide to stay on yourself. Or we could consider bringing in an outsider."

As Heflin drove home he wondered what Sharpe could have done to earn Taylor's displeasure. There must be more to this than meets the eye, he thought.

As for Taylor's alternative that he, Heflin, might decide to stay on, that was out of the question. He was committed to running for political office. As for bringing in an outsider, that was a laughable idea. It would demotivate a successful management team in which there were no failures, put its members in disarray.

As he calmed down, Heflin admitted to himself that he had erred in his assessment of boardroom thinking. He also recalled with dismay that in an unguarded moment he had intimated to Sharpe that he was his chosen successor for the job.

If he now failed to back Sharpe to the hilt, and the financial vice president did not get the job, that spikey individual would almost certainly offer his services to a competitor.

If he did fight tooth and nail for Sharpe, however, and won through, there was a strong chance he would irretrievably split and ruin a successful team. That would be a disaster for the company and a most inauspicious entry into politics.

DECISION

Succession choice threatens to split top management

P eter Heflin has been so preoccupied with his own career that he has underestimated the difficulty of appointing a successor. Now he has realized that the problem is greater than he thought, and he has to make a decision.

Although the unexpected reaction of board member Christopher Taylor has upset him, Heflin should be glad that he had the conversation with him. Otherwise, he might have had a more embarrassing confrontation later with the entire board.

Now he has the chance of looking at the situation coolly and thinking it through properly.

He should appreciate that his situation is completely changed. Previously, in his capacity as the company's chief decision maker, it was he who lived with the consequences of his decisions. Now he needs to see himself as an adviser. It is the board and his successor who will inherit the consequences of the decisions.

The succession problem stems directly from his failure to have continuous discussions with the board about personnel planning for key people and the future manning of the company's vital functions.

His lack of planning has caused a situation in which it could be very costly, in human terms, to find a solution to the problem. He has to find the answer that will do least harm to the company.

It is very important that any board discussion about his successor should be conducted rationally, and be based upon facts rather than upon emotions and personalities.

Although Heflin has decided to retire early, he has the advantge that he can, no doubt, postpone his departure long enough to analyse the total situation of the company, its problems and opportunities.

He should start this process without delay, so that he can present the board with a thorough overview of the company's future markets, production, capital requirements, product development, strengths and weaknesses.

However, although he can make extra time for himself he will not want to delay his meeting with the board The longer he fails to present the board with all the relevant facts, the more likely it is that the grapevine, that informal channel of communication that exists in all companies, will swing into action with unpredictable results.

At the first board meeting, therefore, Heflin should formally announce that he intends to retire and give a date beyond which he will not continue as chief executive.

He should say that he has his own ideas about his successor, that he wants full participation from everyone in reaching the best solution, and intends to present, at the next board meeting, a full review of the company's situation.

He will undoubtedly gain, at the first board meeting, a sound idea of individual members' views, which will either confirm or deny Taylor's assessment of the likely reaction to Malcolm Sharpe's appointment.

If Sharpe, as financial vice president, has a seat on the board, Heflin should take him aside before the meeting, tell him the line he has decided to take and try to get him to agree that if, eventually, the board decision goes against him, he will abide by it loyally.

If Sharpe is not on the board, Heflin should inform him, immediately after the board meeting, about the decision to consider all aspects and persons.

He should also talk privately with each member of the top management team, partly to get a better idea of their attitudes and partly to take the heat out of the situation in case some of them are being unrealistic in their expectations.

If he takes this course the risk of splitting up the management team will still exist. But it will be less of a risk than if he simply handed down his decision without explanation.

It should be clear to Heflin by now that his successor, whoever he may be, has to work more consciously in the area of career planning. He has to work out guidelines for management development. This will make the company less vulnerable should any other experienced individual decide to leave earlier than was expected.

Undoubtedly, the realization that this aspect of the company has been neglected in the past will influence the choice of Heflin's successor. And it should be made by the whole board on rational, rather than emotional, grounds.

This decision was provided by Laurids Hedaa in his capacity as director of the Danish Institute of Personnel Management.

190

Can firm allow 'high-flyer' to flout rule on overseas posting?

The executive board meeting at the London headquarters of Prepacked Foods Group was almost over. "There's just one other thing," said chairman John Dempster. "I take it we all agree that Philip Knight has done an exceptional job and should be groomed as managing director of our Birmingham chocolate company, Cocoa Products Ltd., when the post falls vacant next year?"

"Leading to a seat on the board, eh, John?" said another board member affably putting together his papers.

It was well known that Knight was one of Dempster's protégés. It was also generally recognized that Knight, who had trained as an accountant and had tackled a variety of trouble-shooting assignments in and out of corporate headquarters, had real talent and deserved to be identified as a "high-flyer".

Charles Goodwin, the personnel director, produced Knight's file and turned towards Dempster. "In line with company policy we now have to post him overseas to widen his horizons and give him operating management experience," Goodwin said.

Dempster nodded.

Overseas postings provide experience

"I suggest Ghana," Goodwin continued. "He can take over from Spencer, who has been our co-ordinator in Accra for five years and is due for retirement anyway. In a year's time, if all goes well, he can then come back and step into the chief executive slot in Birmingham."

"I'll tell him myself," Dempster said.

The following day he called Knight into his office. "How do you like the tropics?"

Knight looked at him suspiciously and Dempster grinned. "You're posted to Accra," he said. "Twelve months of steamy heat will do you good. And when you've made that operation really hum, you can come back and stick 'managing director' on your door."

Knight's response was not too enthusiastic, Dempster thought. But he dismissed the matter from his mind.

Personal problems affect foreign travel

A few days later, Knight asked to see him. "About Accra," the young man said. "I don't want to go."

Dempster stared at him. "You can't be serious," he growled.

"I'm very serious," Knight replied. "I've talked it over with my wife, Mary, and we have decided that, for a variety of personal reasons, we don't want to leave the U.K. just now. For one thing, we have a backward child, as you know. We feel that in Ghana he couldn't get the specialist medical attention he needs."

"Leave him with relations," Dempster suggested.

"He's only five," said Knight. "We wouldn't do that."

"Philip," said Dempster, frowning, "you really have got it in you to head this company some day. But to get that far you have to have overseas experience. You know that as well as I do. So don't make any hasty decisions. Go away and think very carefully about this. Meanwhile, so far as the company is concerned, your posting is confirmed."

"I have already thought carefully about it," Knight said. "It all boils down to how much you think I'm an asset to this company and how much you really want me."

When Knight had left, Dempster sat thinking. He decided that the company could ill afford to lose a man of Knight's calibre.

He walked down the corridor to Goodwin's office. "What do you want me to do?" Goodwin asked, after Dempster had explained the situation.

"He is worried about this backward child of his." Dempster said. "Does it *have* to be Ghana?"

High-flyers must be tested

"Ghana is the only place where he can get the right kind of experience," Goodwin said. "They do have medical experts over there, you know."

"How about delaying posting him abroad until next year?" Dempster said.

"He'll still have a backward child," Goodwin observed. "Also, he may go off the boil if he hangs around head office for another year. You know as well as I do, John, that once we identify high-flyers we push them through, make them or break them, within a very tight schedule. It's a cornerstone of our personnel policy and it's not one that I want to change.

"I know all about Philip's potential," Goodwin added. "In formal test after formal test, as well as in his performance on the job, he is the most promising boardroom material we have had around for some time."

"Exactly," Dempster butted in. "That's why I don't want to lose him. He's the best of the bunch."

"But he does have competition," Goodwin pointed out. "Look, if we make an exception in Philip's case, what about the other high-flyers who don't want to leave their homes and go to West Africa? And what about all those people, like myself, who have done their stint in far-away places?

Personnel policy in jeopardy

"Philip would have to serve on the board with these same people. And everyone else climbing the hierarchy in this company would use his case as an argument for similar preferential treatment. What am I to say to them? Where does that put the personnel development policy?"

As he returned to his office Dempster admitted that if he insisted that Goodwin keep Knight at home, and still promoted him, it would be unfair to others and put the personnel department's policy in jeopardy. If, however, he ordered Knight to go to Ghana, this high-flyer, instead of benefiting the company, would at best be disgruntled and demotivated or at worst hand in his resignation and possibly join the opposition. What should he do?

Overseas service rule means firm could lose 'high-flyer'

It is clear from the dilemma that John Dempster values the services of Philip Knight very highly. It is also clear that Charles Goodwin, the personnel director, firmly and rightly, intends to defend the company's personnel policy which, as everyone agrees, has served Prepacked Foods Group so well in the past.

As Dempster ponders over Knight's possible careeer development paths, he realizes that a decision cannot be delayed. But he may conclude that the decision need not be such a stark one as appears at first sight. It need not be one that offends Goodwin or, alternatively, results in Knight's premature departure from the company.

With a little bit of cunning and diplomacy, in other words, Dempster should be able to arrange things so that everyone involved remains fairly well satisfied and no one loses face.

The immediate stumbling block in the path of Dempster giving in to Knight's desire not to go to Ghana is the inflexible attitude of Goodwin, who stands on principle and refuses to make an exception in Knight's case. Goodwin will resent any attempt by Dempster to override him in this matter.

It is perfectly within Dempster's rights as chairman, however, to say to Goodwin that he wants to think afresh about the company's personnel situation as a whole. He can then request Goodwin to provide him, within a few days, with the following information:

- A list of all key positions in each overseas company
- Prerequisites to fill these key positions
- The names of those who currently fill them
- Background data on each incumbent – age, marital status and the number and age of any children
- The date since when each position has been held by the present incumbent
- The approximate date when each key position needs to be filled again, and/or the date when the next promotion of the present incumbent is due
- Possible future assignments of all the personnel involved
- A list of the possible candidates for each position if and when it falls vacant

While Goodwin is preparing this report, Dempster should take steps to find out details of the medical treatment required by Knight's child, and in which countries it can best be provided.

If he can acquire this information without the direct help of Knight, so much the better. It needs to be held in reserve and put to Knight at the right psychological moment, so that he appreciates the fact that the company really is interested in him and has gone to great lengths to meet his needs and his child's requirements.

The key to solving the problem in a satisfactory way, however, lies in the overall personnel postings review provided by Goodwin.

193

It is very likely that after studying it, analysing the key overseas positions, their requirements and their present and potential incumbents, Dempster will discern some loophole. He might find some executive who is very near retirement from his present post, or some other possibility. He can then put these to Goodwin as a positive argument for creating a post for Knight somewhere other than Ghana.

Goodwin, after all, is interested in the overall effectiveness of the company's personnel policy world-wide. If making an exception in Knight's case can be shown not to conflict with the overall objective of sound personnel management, it is unlikely he will object to any positive suggestion, made on rational grounds, which emanates from Dempster.

As a result of a review of overseas postings, which can be done with Goodwin's cooperation, rather than behind his back, it should be possible to recommend a generally acceptable action programme which includes the next step in Knight's career development.

In other words, "special treatment" for Knight can be transmuted into a general promotion review that will help solve not only the immediate dilemma but also correct other possible organizational weaknesses on the personnel side.

If Knight is a man of goodwill towards the company, he will appreciate the efforts that have been made on his behalf and accept an alternative arrangement to going to Ghana, even if it does mean that he cannot remain in the U.K.

If, however, he still does not agree to leave, he can always be retained in his present position. In that case, however, both he and Dempster will have to accept that there will be diminished likelihood of him ever achieving high office in the company.

This decision was provided by Dr. Manfred Brede in his capacity as managing partner of Assocon Management Consultants, a West German company involved in developing and implementing corporate strategies for companies in Europe, Africa and the United States.

DILEMMA

Should overworked manager resign from community activities?

Jacques Villiers, director of finance for Albert Frères, a large French regional contracting firm, startled his secretary as he rushed in the door at 3.30 p.m. He was returning from a hospital fund-raising committee luncheon.

"Here," he said to his secretary. "I have checked the names of the directors who are at the top table and would like to send them a short note thanking them for their support.

"Also," he continued, barely drawing breath, "I have to write my friend Philippe Gris and thank him for his help in lining up Dominique Bouchette to speak. Thanks to him, we got her at a fraction of what a top class author can command on the speaking circuit. I'll write to her personally to thank her for her witty speech."

Finally his secretary was able to interrupt. "Mr. Maisonblanche has

194

called three times since 2 p.m. and wants you to come to his office as soon as you return," she said.

"Well, I guess these letters will have to wait," Villiers said as he headed down the hall.

Jean-Paul Maisonblanche, the managing director, seemed a bit formal, asking Villiers to sit in the chair facing his large walnut desk. "What has happened to the counter-proposal on the joint venture deal you were supposed to prepare?" he asked.

"I'll get that out this afternoon," Villiers responded, edging forward in his chair as if he were preparing to leave. "I simply haven't had time to get to it, until now."

"There are a lot of things you haven't had time for lately," Maisonblanche responded. "When I tried to locate you, earlier today, I discovered a bit of discontent among your subordinates. They were complaining about sitting around twiddling their thumbs, waiting for you to make decisions. Really, Jacques, this is strange behaviour for you. You used to be so well organized that you always came up with the required work, well ahead of deadline."

Community work produces good developments

"The trouble is," Villiers replied, "these charities you asked me to serve on are taking up about 90% of my time."

A year earlier Maisonblanche had asked Villiers to sit on a committee that was raising funds for holidays and playgrounds for disadvantaged children. When the chairman of the committee suffered a heart attack, the committee had asked Villiers to take over the job.

He had embarked on that task with characteristic vigour. What had been a moribund committee suddenly came to life and began staging fairs, benefits and fund-raising lunches. It had raised enough money to buy a hectare of land in a poorer section of town and build a football field and playground on it.

Villiers' efforts had not gone unnoticed in the community. Maisonblanche recalled how the mayor had asked him whether Villiers could also be spared to head up the hospital fund-raising committee. Indeed, the managing director had volunteered Villiers' services, and the finance director had added that to his duties without complaint. The company began to receive favourable mentions in the local press for its civic activities. More important, a long dormant request for planning permission to expand the company's premises was suddenly approved.

Reflecting on these developments, the managing director's attitude changed. "Well, Jacques," he said, walking around the desk, "you have been doing a superb job with those charities." Then, as if a brainwave had struck him, Maisonblanche suggested that he make Villiers director in charge of public and corporate affairs. Pierre Duval – he named an ambitious young deputy in Villiers' department – could take over the finance job.

Villiers stiffened. He suspected that Duval had been the one to complain most vociferously about his preoccupation with charitable work. And now Maisonblanche wanted to promote Duval and appoint Villiers to a post where he would be taken out of the firm's mainstream of business.

Villiers enjoyed the prominence that civic duties had offered him. However, his eye was firmly fixed on eventually landing a top financial job with a large Paris-based company. He didn't want to move away entirely from the field of finance. Also, his home life had been suffering due to the long hours he spent on charitable work.

As he expressed some of these thoughts to Maisonblanche, the managing director suddenly realized he might lose Villiers' services altogether. "I guess perhaps I over-reacted to the slight delay in getting the counterproposal out," he said. "Let us just leave things as they are for a while. I'll try to think of some way of lightening your work load."

But Villiers was reluctant to let things rest there. "I think that you have touched on a very important point," he said. "I am doing too much on the outside to function effectively as the finance director, which after all is my prime job and expertise. I simply think I'm going to have to resign from the committees."

Maisonblanche was now thoroughly alarmed. Albert Frères had an excellent opportunity to win a very large contract from the city. It was being awarded partly on the basis of competitive bidding but also partly on the basis of "contribution to the community". If Villiers gave up that work, it could have incalculable consequences.

Both men faced a dilemma. Having stirred up a hornet's nest, how should Maisonblanche proceed? And from the viewpoint of his own career, as well as his home life, what action should Villiers take?

DECISION

Career aspirations should take precedence over charitable deeds

The decision for Jacques Villiers is relatively simple. He wants a future as a finance director. He wants to be in the mainstream of the business as he sees it. While public relations and public affairs is increasingly becoming a mainstream activity of many major companies, it is not a primary role for the financial director.

So, while his public service work helps provide him with important contacts, and is an outlet for his civic-mindedness, it cannot usurp the major thrust of his activities.

If I were Villiers, I would start looking for a job with a Paris-based company. Certainly I would do so if Jean-Paul Maisonblanche is likely to remain in the post of managing director well into the future.

Maisonblanche should have been working closely with Villiers on a continuing basis, because a finance director is an important position in a contracting company. He should also have known that the number of charities that he has asked Villiers to serve, and the results Villiers has obtained, must be taking up a disproportionate amount, even if not 90%, of his time.

For him to state that Villiers' being behind is "strange behaviour for you" makes me question Maisonblanche's competence. To compound that, the suggestion that the deputy, Pierre Duval, should take over the job of finance manager, while Villiers becomes director of public and corporate affairs, is a strange one.

It is made without even ascertaining what Villiers would prefer. It shows little understanding of the public affairs role and even less of employee relations. Instead of calling Villiers in to criticize him, Maisonblanche should have called him in to thank him for the personal sacrifice he has been making, virtually running two jobs for the good of the company.

But let us say that all of that is past, and that Maisonblanche has been struck with a degree of wisdom comparable to St. Paul's on the road to Damascus. What should he do?

First, he should make it clear to Villiers that he understands the importance of the role of the financial director and agrees that is where his future lies. He should add that at this stage he thinks it is important for Villiers to retain his charitable activities, but with a declining involvement. With that in mind, he will provide him with adequate support staff.

New appointment to cover expanding public affairs

Villiers, understanding that a major contract is at stake, will certainly not want to jeopardize it. Therefore he should be willing to put in more time on his public affairs work than he might desire at this particular period realising it is for a short time.

Equally important, Maisonblanche should now realize the value to his company of a public affairs programme, though engaging in charitable works is only a small part of such a corporate programme.

The company should add to its table of organization a director of corporate and public affairs. But it is vital that Maisonblanche understands that the company, and not the individual, must obtain the reputation for discerning the needs of, and contributing to, the local community. Villiers could have left at any time – and so can any future public affairs director.

While public and corporate affairs can be headed by a director, it must be the role of the whole company. Even or especially, Maisonblanche, as the chief executive officer, should become more involved. Villiers, because of his skill in this area, should allocate a certain part of his time (possibly 10% or 15%) to it. His financial department should be staffed accordingly.

This decision was provided by Robert S. Leaf in his capacity as president of Burson-Marsteller International, the London-headquartered overseas operation of the U.S. public relations agency Burson-Marsteller.

How should firm handle manager with 're-entry' problems?

Derek Carr, managing director of Newsome and Hobbs, an international trading company that acts as a selling agent for several fast-moving lines of consumer goods, did not enjoy having his own words thrown back in his face. However, that is what was happening in his office.

"You said yourself that we can no longer afford to carry passengers," said Charles LeRoy, the finance director. "That is a statement with which I concur. But Neville Shlllington *is* a passenger. By my book, he isn't

197

doing his job. I recommend we take action."

"I wouldn't say he isn't doing his job," said Harry Foster the personnel director . "He is handling the day-to-day running of his department quite effectively. Certainly, fewer salesmen are leaving."

"Exactly," said LeRoy. "Because he is too soft with them. Naturally they don't want to leave. Look, we asked him for a plan to reorganize sales in the U.K. and what does he come up with? Hardly a salesman less. No recognition that what we need is highly centralized, computerized selling and quick response to the needs of supermarkets. He's still mentally in Africa."

"True, he is taking some time to readjust," said Foster. "However, it wasn't his fault that he had to stay in Nigeria twice as long as usual, and got out of touch with developments here."

"Wherever the fault lies," LeRoy said, "the hard fact is that the haemorrhaging of our profits is occurring in the U.K. It is here and now that we need to take action."

Overseas service must be recognized

"There are no senior vacancies for Shillington elsewhere in the group, Carr said. "He is hardly old enough to retire. To give him some sinecure job would be a transparent ploy to encourage him to resign."

"I agree with that," said Foster. "If we rewarded Shillington by shunting him into a siding, it would run directly counter to our long-term policy of posting good people abroad to gain experience, before bringing them back to head office. Very soon, an overseas posting would be seen as a repository for dead wood. That is precisely the attitude of mind we wish to avoid, as you know."

"The fact remains," Le Roy persisted "that the U.K. selling operation needs to be shaken up. The man who does the job has to start with the right attitude. Does Shillington have it?"

"He did a very good job in Nigeria," Carr said, thinking aloud.

"He went out there in 1974 for what was going to be a three-year stint," Foster said. "He took over a lazy demoralized sales force. He got them on the road. He boosted their morale with personal incentive schemes and really turned things round. He only agreed to stay on because the man we had picked to replace him died of a heart attack – literally on his way to London airport."

"So Shillington stayed and practically went native," LeRoy said, brusquely. "But what qualification did that give him for his present job?"

"You know as well as I do we have always gone for generalists," Foster said. "His experiences in Nigeria enhanced his appreciation of the business as a whole."

"His attitude seems to me to be casual and lacking in urgency." LeRoy continued as though Foster had not spoken. "Maybe that is the way things are in Nigeria . But not here. Also, from what I hear he's patronizing towards his people Again, maybe that worked in Africa. But...."

"He's a good 'people' man," Foster interrupted.

"Is that relevant to what essentially is now a reorganization task?"

"There is still no substitute for sound judgment and overall knowledge of our worldwide business," Foster insisted. "Keeping Shillington on in Nigeria for six years instead of three probably was a mistake. But the principle of overseas service is a good one. Remeber this" – he wagged a finger in LeRoy's direction – "despite the contribution, or the lack of it, of the U.K. to our profits, more than half of our business still is overseas. We don't want to discourage good people from going abroad. And we can't afford to have two totally distinct career paths."

"Why not promote his deputy on a temporary basis?" LeRoy asked. "Send Shillington on an extended training course."

"We thought of that," said Carr, interrupting the dialogue between the other two. "We suggested privately to the deputy manager in Shillington's department that he take the job on a temporary basis. He argued, reasonably, that a temporary stand-in couldn't do much, by way of reorganization, even if he wanted to."

"Also," said Foster, "if we promote his deputy, other people now overseas are going to feel bypassed."

"Sometimes you have to wield a knife even if people get hurt," said LeRoy. "I still think we ought to let Shillington go. Give him a golden handshake, if you want. What better way to persuade the sales force to accept redundancies than to say we started at the top?"

Carr weighed the conflicting arguments. What should he decide?

DECISION

Managing director should persist with poorly performing sales manager

Derek Carr, the managing director of Newsome & Hobbs, should not take the advice of his finance director and fire sales manager Neville Shillington. Instead, he should tell the sales manager that he is in trouble, build on his strengths and help him to overcome his weaknesses.

It seldom pays to react to personnel problems by immediately using that ultimate means at a company's disposal, separation. This is particularly true of employees who can demonstrate, as Shillington can, a good performance record.

There is another reason why Carr should not fire Shillington immediately. Newsome & Hobbs seems to be going through a phase of fundamental change. Due to new developments in the market place, it has to face both external and internal instability.

Terms such as reoganization, computerization and centralization are not ones that are well liked by any staff – certainly not by jaded salesmen. Using them too often, and in connection with the sacking of a well-respected sales manager, might cause other employees to decide to leave.

Develop and train potential leaders

At a time of organizational change a manager should avoid any panic in the organization. Otherwise he might lose the very people he wants to keep; people who normally have the most options so far as alternative employment is concerned.

He should also carefully select those people who have enough potential to succeed under the changing circumstances, and develop them to fulfil their function.

So far as Shillington is concerned, at present it is not clear whether his inefficiency is due to lack of management potential or, as seems more likely, to a lack of training, or proper experience, in appropriate areas.

The decision to keep Shillington on should not be allowed to disguise the fact that he is in trouble. The basis for any career development is a clear understanding of one's strengths and weaknesses.

Shillington has to be made aware of the fact that the function of the sales manager in the U.K. requires not only good "people" skills but also analytical skills. He has to know that he fulfils only one of these two specifications.

Selling fast-moving consumer goods in Nigeria is different from doing the same thing in the U.K. Shillington, through no fault of his own, has had an extended assignment abroad that has caused him to over-adapt to the foreign environment. There is nothing strange in that. Many of W. Somerset Maugham's short stories show how extended living in a different culture can change a person.

Shillington has to understand that in the view of the board members he "went native". After that it is his decision whether he wants to make the effort to change his style of working.

Optimization rather than maximization
So far in his career, with his "sound judgment," he has fared very well. He seems to be a competent people manager. But in his new job this is obviously not enough.

It is now Carr's task to make him aware of that shortcoming, and help him overcome it. Carr has to be flexible and creative in finding ways to help by external training, training on the job or job rotation. The perfect fit between function and employee seldom occurs. One has to operate under the principle of optimization, rather than maximization, of the talents available.

If, however, after about six months it turns out that despite all Carr's efforts Shillington shows no development, no sign of being able to adapt sufficiently to the new demands of his job, then Carr *will* have to resort to "the golden handshake".

This decision was provided by Jürgen B. Mülder in his capacity as vice president of AMROP, an international executive search federation, and managing partner of Jürgen B. Mülder & Partner, West Germany.

DILEMMA

Should a boss be dissuaded from promoting his son?

"Good of you to drop in, John," said Kenneth McMaster, chairman of the family-owned electrical appliance company of the same name. "How is the search going for someone to head the new subsidiary?"

"I should be able to produce a short-list by the end of the week," said John Carey, who had been McMaster's personnel director for the past year.

"I assume Colin is on the list," said McMaster, referring to his only son.

Carey lit a cigarette. "No," he said. "He isn't. Probably there will be three people on it. Not Colin, on this occasion. I don't think he is quite ready for that level of responsibility."

McMaster glared. He was a ruddy-faced man at the best of times, suffering, Carey suspected, from high blood pressure. He had also had a heart attack.

Now he was beet-red as he roared: "So you don't think he's ready for that level of responsibility. But he's been with us for five years, man! He has had experience in sales, in finance and in administration. He didn't do badly in any of those positions. John, are you being fair to Colin?"

"Mr. McMaster," Carey said, a note of exasperation in his voice. "You hired me to bring some order and discipline into personnel affairs in this company. I am not being unfair to anybody. I try to be objective. I just don't think Colin is ready. That is my professional judgment."

"But why don't you think he is ready?" McMaster persisted. "He's creative. He's an abstract thinker. He has a fine intellect. He's good at planning."

Include an honest assessment

"The word 'abstract' is the key one," Carey replied. "Whoever takes this job is going to need a practical approach, particularly when it comes to solving the problems that are bound to arise with a new subsidiary. He is going to need drive and enthusiasm in selling new ideas. He is also going to need a bucketful of sound experience, especially in handling people."

"What it boils down to," said McMaster, "is that you don't believe my son *has* the experience. Well, neither had I, when I started this firm. I learned as I went along.

"So I'd like you to put Colin's name on the list," McMaster added. "It's no skin off your nose, John. He is there to be considered, like the others. That's all. Remember, I have the final say anyway, when appointments at this level are made."

That was true, Carey told himself afterwards. All that he could do was to put Colin's name on the short-list, with his own honest assessment attached, and let McMaster do the deciding.

"If his mind is already made up, I'd need a very persuasive argument to change it," Carey told his wife. "You know, the old man dotes on the boy."

"Perhaps there *is* such an argument," his wife replied. "Do you want to hear it?"

"If you put it like that," said Carey carefully, "have I any choice?"

"I am told that young Colin McMaster is on drugs."

Carey stared at her. "Told by whom?"

"By our daughter. Fiona was at a party the other night. Rather a posh affair, which is why she bought that dress. She says Colin was there, very bright-eyed. She actually saw him injecting himself."

"Injecting himself! In the middle of the dance floor?"

"No. Since the bathroom was occupied, Fiona barged into one of the bedrooms looking for a mirror to powder her nose. Colin was sitting on the bed with a girl. His sleeve was rolled up and he had a needle in his hand."

"She is sure it was Colin McMaster?"

"Absolutely sure. She has seen his photograph. He arrived in his red sports car, with the MCM number plate. Why not check with Fiona?"

Carey did check. Fiona made a good witness and gave her father a clear description of the party and what had been going on there. There was absolutely no doubt that it was McMaster's son she had seen in the bedroom with the girl. However Fiona had not seen Colin injecting himself, but only with the needle poised. There was also the possibility that the injection, whatever it was, was prescribed for some medical condition, and was therefore necessary.

Carey decided he had no choice but to do a little detective work around the company. "Have you noticed anything strange about Colin recently?" he asked a manager who worked alongside Colin, the following day. At first the manager said that he hadn't. But then he mentioned that Colin had seemed unusually elated. "It's unusual because he's inclined to be a bit introspective," the manager said. "I asked him why he was so happy and he virtually told me to mind my own business."

Carey called for Colin's medical records. There was nothing that hinted at a chronic condition requiring injections. He would have checked further with the company doctor, but the medic was attending a conference abroad and Carey felt it was something that could not be handled on the telephone.

On the Friday he received a telephone call from McMaster. "I'm waiting for the short-list you promised, John," McMaster said. "But I might as well tell you now. I've virtually decided to give Colin a chance to prove himself in this job. You'll have to put up a damned good alternative candidate to make me change my mind."

When he put down the phone, Carey looked unseeingly at the neatly typed assessments of three potential candidates, two of them from outside the company, which he had prepared. They lay on the desk top along with the assessment of Colin, which was still only half prepared.

He could complete that assessment in neutral terms and leave it to the old man.

He could tell McMaster about his suspicions. But Carey thought with dismay that the shock might even bring on another heart attack.

He could insist on one of the others being appointed – and press that insistence to the point of resignation.

Or was there something else he could do?

DECISION

Chairman must be encouraged to see son's prospects objectively

There are two possible solutions to Carey's dilemma. But only one can be recommended. I do not think that this is a matter over which Carey should consider resigning. Only if he finds he is continually blocked or overruled by McMaster would he have no alternative but to seek another job.

The first possible solution assumes that there are other non-family directors in the company, in addition to the personnel director. If this is correct, then Carey could discuss the matter with the other directors and, if they agreed, they could all go and see McMaster and oppose Colin's appointment. This, however, would sour the atmosphere.

The better solution is for Carey to play his cards cunningly with McMaster, enlisting his help in viewing the problem objectively. This will not be easy. But it is the only way.

Carey should begin by writing down the objectives of the subsidiary in the context of the entire company, and draw up a job description for the top position. This should list, in order of importance, the various attributes required from whoever is chosen for the job.

Carey should match this list against his own three candidates and against Colin, who I assume is in his late twenties, has no previous industrial experience, having joined the family firm at the end of full-time education, and has not held a managerial position so far. It is therefore highly unlikely, quite apart from any other failings he may have, that Colin would head an objective list of candidates.

Carey should then present his case to McMaster, beginning by asking questions that will draw the latter into a constructive discussion – questions with which he knows McMaster can agree. For example: "Am I right in assuming that you want Colin to succeed you, in due course, and carry on the company? Can I assume that, if you were hit by a bus tomorrow, Colin would not be ready to step straight into your shoes and take full responsibility for the entire company? Do you agree that the success of the new subsidiary is vital to our continued growth?"

Experience must match job vacancy

These questions may sound naïve, but I would expect most people to answer them sensibly. I would expect McMaster to answer "yes" to each one of them.

Carey should then produce his summary of what is expected from the head of the new subsidiary, and ask for McMaster's help in finalizing the list. This will get the chairman thinking constructively about the future of the company, and help Carey check his own conclusions before he takes the final plunge.

That "plunge" is to get McMaster to face the fact that Colin, for the moment, does not match up to the job vacancy. Suppose the boy falls flat on his face, Carey should ask McMaster. What happens then?

If the chairman fails to answer that question, Carey should answer it for him. Most likely the subsidiary would fail to perform, Colin would lose the respect of his father's employees and the family would be hurt.

"I believe we can avoid all this and give Colin the chance you want," Carey should say. "I recommend that we appoint Mr 'X', who fits the job description best, and that we appoint Colin as his personal assistant or as his deputy. Thus, he gains virtually all the experience he would have had, but with a guiding hand to look after his interests, your interests and the company's interests.

"We can monitor his performance and help his learning. Then you can move him up, to succeed you, when you wish, knowing that he can do the job and that he has already won the respect of the employees. If things don't work out, the company is safeguarded while you have the time to decide what to do with Colin."

So far as the drugs question is concerned, Carey should handle that directly with Colin. It may be true; but there is insufficient evidence. If it is true, it may be only a passing phase or an "experiment".

Assuming that the family does not know about any drug taking, Colin may even welcome Carey's help and advice. Of course, Colin may be taking drugs because he dislikes the firm and his father, which opens up a whole new scene. But Carey should go to McMaster with this topic only if the situation gets worse.

Speaking as the sixth generation chairman of the family firm that appointed the first non-family man to its board in 1950 I would add the following points:

First, McMaster and Carey clearly don't communicate very well. They should have discussed the job's requirements, and Colin's position, long before any short lists were produced. The other directors should have been involved too.

Second, there is absolutely no sense in appointing a professional to any job in the company if you are not prepared to give him all the information he needs to do it, and also stand back and let him get on with it. It is a hard thing to do, because it means giving up daily control of some aspect of the business. But it must be done.

Third, family companies of any size need professional management if they are to survive in today's environment. I would go further, and say that family employees need proper training before they are allowed to take on any responsibility. It is one thing to start from nothing, as McMaster did. It is quite another to take over a thriving business, which has a responsibility to its employees, its customers and suppliers, possibly shareholders and the bank.

Fourth, I believe that a professional personnel adviser is essential today, as the law is now so complicated, and frequently changes. I am not convinced that a director is necessary. But probably a man to fill the personnel job at senior manager level is.

If a family employee has the interest and relevant training for a job, fine. If not, bring in a professional and let him have his head.

This decision was provided by Martin J. Kenrick in his capacity as chairman and managing director of Archibald Kenrick & Sons Ltd., manufacturer of castors, door and window furniture and other quality hardware in the U.K.

DILEMMA

Should a chief executive have insisted that a manager take some tests?

"I am sorry, but I have no intention of taking these tests," David Black said. "A man with my experience and track record doesn't need to sit down and play damnfool games devised by a bunch of eggheads."

Black was in charge of production at one of the bigger plants of Benson Metal Products, a diversified manufacturing company which had sustained a heavy trading loss in each of the past three years. He addressed his remarks to Eric Vindeby, the newly appointed group chief executive, whose task was to pull the company round.

"You don't *have* to take the tests," Vindeby said, soothingly. "I don't want to force upon you, or anyone else, anything that goes completely against the grain. But I would ask you to reconsider. I ought to point out that I think such tests are extremely useful in deciding whether people are in the wrong jobs. My instinct is that an awful lot of managers in this company are."

Vindeby had been appointed chief executive in order to breathe new life into a company whose performance had slipped badly, in relation to that of its chief competitors. He soon reached the conclusion that there was a general slackness in many strata of management, and that a number of key individuals were not performing effectively as line managers.

The solution, he believed, was to institute written tests, starting with senior management personnel. These would give a much clearer indication than he already had of the intellectual and management resources available to him.

The tests lasted several hours, were extremely thorough and searching, and Vindeby had expected a lot of resistance from the managers, many of whom were at a mid-point in their careers.

Surprisingly, most of the managers had gone along with the idea. But not Black. He was production executive at a key components plant that had suffered a lot of labour troubles in the past. These had had a disruptive effect upon the rest of the company, and after his appointment Vindeby had given his personal attention to the plant as a matter of priority.

Judgment ought to be based on similar assessment

Management consultants had been engaged to help him diagnose the company's ills. They had reported back to him at an early stage that Black was "an able engineer, a practical man of considerable energy, but somewhat lacking in human skills".

Vindeby had noted this, but had reserved his own judgment, for he knew that many times in the past corporate top management had failed to back plant management when it had tried to exert greater discipline on the shopfloor. He was loath to declare any manager unsuited to his job until the psychological and other tests were completed.

It was therefore doubly annoying that Black, whom the consultants had disparaged but whom Vindeby personally liked and to whom he wanted to give the benefit of the doubt, should be the one to stubbornly refuse to take part in the tests.

When the results of all the tests were in, Vindeby sat down with his personnel director, Philip Small, who had joined the company recently from a major U.S. firm. It was clear that 30% of the company's managers were in the wrong job, while between 15% and 20% would have to be asked to resign.

"How about David Black?" Small asked. "We are judging all the others on set criteria and he is escaping the net. It is well known in the company that he has refused to take the tests. Now we intend to terminate several managers who failed, and who are certain to complain of unfair treatment if Black is not subjected to some kind of investigation or assessment."

"I have looked closely at Black's record," Vindeby countered. "I know that you have, too. What's your opinion?"

"Whatever my *opinion* is," said Small, "is irrelevant because it is subjective, while the results of these tests are objective. We would have been able to come to an objective view of Black's qualities and failings if only he had agreed to take the tests."

Not infallible

"As I told Black," Vindeby remarked, "I think such tests are very useful in deciding whether people are in the wrong jobs. I did not say I thought they were infalliable."

"Well, if you want my personal opinion," said Small, "I think you should have insisted that all managers. including Black, take the tests."

"I did ask him to reconsider," Vindeby replied, "But he countered by saying that while he agreed tests might be useful when applied to new entrants, they were an insult to men of his own standing and experience. He also saw them as a gross invasion of privacy. In those circumstances, I don't see how, in a democracy, a man can be forced to take such tests. And if he refuses, is it fair to hold it against him?"

Unfair to others

"By not insisting that he take the tests, others are going to see it as unfair to *them*," Small persisted. "Whatever your views about the right to privacy, aren't you being intellectually dishonest, having all the other managers take the tests and making an exception for one man?"

Vindeby frowned. Although he had asked Small to join him at the company, he didn't like being taken to task by him. "It's a bit late now," he said, "to raise such objections."

But, he asked himself, *had* he blundered in his handling of Black and the implementation of the tests? It went directly against his principles to compel a man of 43, in a free society, to put his job on the line doing something with which he profoundly disagreed. But what should he do when every other manager had agreed to be tested?

Should he insist that Black take the tests, even at this late stage? Should he leave him where he was, and risk charges of inconsistency from other managers he hoped to weld into a winning team? Or should he make a token gesture, and move Black to another job within the company?

DECISION

Chief executive should not insist on tests or penalize manager

Whatever else Eric Vindeby does or does not do, he cannot now penalize David Black for not taking the tests, since he has already told him that he did not have to do so. He cannot make statements like that and then say he did not mean them, without losing credibility.

Similarly, if other managers are now complaining of unfairness, because they took the tests and Black did not, Vindeby has only himself to blame. Such complaints can only have arisen because the chief executive did not explain clearly enough in the first place *why* he did not insist on the tests being taken. If he had said "no manager will be compromised if he refuses to take the tests on conscientious grounds, or on grounds of invasion of privacy", any complaints would have been stillborn.

All that Vindeby can do now is use his own judgment about Black's management qualities and the post best suited to him within Benson Metal Products. Since he has examined the test results of all the other managers very thoroughly, along with the personnel director, he will have a clear idea what the criteria are for judging competence to do a particular job in the company now.

He can therefore augment his "subjective judgment" of Black, applying similar criteria to that individual without using the tests themselves. He should say to Black verbally: "I have to evaluate you on certain parameters. You don't write anything but I'd like to talk to you."

Unfortunately, Vindeby's approach to the tests has not been a happy one. It is not the approach of a man seeking the truth, but of one who knows all about his people already and just wants an instrument to lean on when making some unpleasant decisions. He himself says that he doesn't think the tests are totally objective – a healthy attitude for which he is to be applauded. On the other hand, if he does not think that the tests have any validity at all, why is he using them?

Vindeby should have appreciated at a much earlier stage that nobody objects to taking tests of practical ability, whether it be tests of language competence or of typing speeds. But tests that involve personal analysis, judgments of people's ability to cooperate, and their degree of initiative and drive are taken much more seriously. It is natural for people to try to avoid exposing their weak spots.

Highlight the positive aspect

That being so, it is important to explain very clearly to participants in tests what the goals and aims of the exercise are, so that people can decide for themselves the degree of risk they run.

The positive aspect of testing should also be pointed out to testees. Test results that assesss personal and social competence can be to the great advantage of the testee, as well as his organization, helping him to pursue the planning of his career on a more rational basis.

Many companies today consider testing not as an end in itself but as a very useful tool in augmenting other data about individuals. However, most practitioners would agree with Vindeby that tests are not objective. You end up with a score, in figures. But the final assessment still depends on judgment.

Incidentally, if I were Vindeby, I would have grave doubts about the personnel director, Small, who seems to think that tests are objective.

I believe that testing has in fact lost much of the stigma that attached to it 10 years ago, when many companies, as well as individuals, considered that the use of tests was inappropriate. Fears about confidentiality can be calmed by assuring the testee that the results of the test will not be used for any other purpose, without his permission.

So far as personal freedom is concerned, fears on that score are so complex that it is difficult to analyse them and assess their validity. This should be pointed out to the testee, who should be told that if he refuses a test on those grounds, while his attitude will be respected and not questioned, he must be prepared for any consequences.

This advice is too late to help Vindeby now, though he could usefully bear it in mind for the future. Meanwhile, he is fortunate that his dilemma involves only one man. Most of his managers did the tests, and if one man slips through the net it is not going to make much difference.

To sum up, he should leave Black where he is, at least for the time being, call him to his office, invite him to express himself at length, form a judgment about his ability to shine in his present job, or whether to move him, and act upon that decision.

This decision was provided by Oluf Aagaard in his capacity as a former military psychologist, consultant and professor at the Copenhagen Business School, and managing director of the Danish Institute of Personnel Management.

Ought business development manager to oppose ambitious young executive?

Gaston Caubet, business development manager at the family-owned company Bottin et Fils, half knew what to expect when he went into the office of managing director Michel Bottin, eldest son of the founder of the Paris-based firm.

The previous week, Caubet had presented Bottin with details of a device for raking lawns and applying fertilizer directly to the roots of the grass. However, the managing director was not in the mood to authorize further expenditure on new products. "We are under pressure financially," he said. "Until next year, we don't have any money to spend on additional development and promotion. The priority now must be to make a profit on our last new product."

He pushed across his desk a single sheet of paper containing statistics, half of them printed in red. "Will you let me have, by Friday, your views on why the sales of *Shootup* have not met expectations."

Can do no wrong

Shootup was a new feed for indoor plants that combined standard fertilizers with micro organisms. The cost of the launch, six months ago, had been much higher than expected; the launch had also been badly timed, a rival having come on the market at the same time; and Caubet felt the product had been over-priced.

He blamed these failings on the chief executive of the subsidiary that had marketed *Shootup*. It had been Caubet's baby for 20 months of development. But then Laurence Venet, the subsidiary chief, had insisted on handling most of the details of the launch himself.

Bottin had started in 1934 by making simple garden tools such as spades, forks and hoes. Recently the profit on these had been much reduced by price cuts that were considered necessary to counter cheap imports. Lately the company had also developed a line of gardening sundries – everything from plant feeds to concrete gnomes – which promised a greater profit potential.

Caubet had favoured the creation of a separate subsidiary to handle this potentially lucrative part of the business. He had felt that he was in line to head such a subsidiary. But Bottin had said that he valued his services as a business developer too much to let him go. He had then appointed Venet, a younger man who was the scion of a family that had long been close to the Bottins.

Venet's first act had been to make himself directly responsible for sales. He had appointed his own sales force, which functioned alongside the existing garden tools sales force, visiting many of the same outlets. Bottin, who normally watched the expenditure of company francs carefully, had gone along with this, saying that it would be interesting to see how the younger men recruited by Venet compared with the old brigade.

It seemed to Caubet that Venet could do no wrong in Bottin's eyes. He even half suspected that Bottin had turned down his lawn rake not because of a genuine shortage of funds – after all, the family was rich – but because it would have been an addition to the garden tools product range, and would not have benefited Venet's operation directly.

Although Caubet had been closely concerned with the development of *Shootup*, it was Venet who had the final say in its launch. Caubet would have preferred to launch through well-chosen advertising and his personal contacts in the gardening and women's journal press. Venet had insisted on employing a very expensive public relations company and had, Caubet thought, been wrong in both the timing and the pricing of the product. Now Bottin was asking *him* to explain why sales to date had not come up to expectations. That question, he felt, should have been directed at the subsidiary chief.

Cut-price sales

Also, Venet had insisted on selling certain product lines through cut-price supermarkets that had gardening departments, against Caubet's advice. Venet argued that the greater volume would compensate for the price reductions that had to be made in order to stay competitive. Caubet had opposed this, saying that it was mortgaging the company's future. It was undercutting traditional, long-established retail outlets whose goodwill Bottin could not afford to lose. But again Caubet had been overruled.

Meanwhile the garden tools sales force had jogged along comfortably, reporting to a sales manager who had been with the family company for 30 years. While 30% of Venet's salesmen left the company each year in search of greener pastures, it was unusual for one of the garden tools people to leave. When Caubet used this is an argument against Venet's management of his sales force, the latter produced figures that seemed to prove that his men were considerably more productive than the garden tools men. "You have to have a fast turnover of personnel in selling," Venet said, "to keep them on their toes."

Venet then told Caubet that he agreed with him – running two parallel sales forces *was* too expensive. "Since sundries accounts for most of our sales, these days," he said, "I am going to suggest to Bottin that we incorporate the garden tools in what was my subsidiary, and have one company."

"With you as managing director?" Caubet enquired.

"No, as his deputy. But Bottin wants to travel, he wants to enjoy his money. I would be effectively in charge, and I hope that you, Gaston, would continue to give me your support. I do value your new product ideas and valuable help."

That was something, at least, Caubet thought. But as he sat down to write the report on *Shootup*, he realised that his own career was in jeopardy. All along he had been ineffectual in countering Venet's influence with Bottin. Now he was being asked to explain a failure that he felt was really not his fault.

So should he now present Bottin not with a report solely on *Shootup*, but with a closely reasoned, wide-ranging analysis of what was going wrong in the company in terms of people management, division of responsibility and forward planning? Such a report, inevitably, would imply strong criticism of Bottin himself.

On the other hand, was it better now to back Venet, and use what influence he had to guide the latter into better paths?

Manager should produce a factual report – and register with a recruitment agency

Decisions at Bottin et Fils seem to rely more on personal influence and judgment than rational analysis. This has led to haphazard development and personal conflict. Caubet seems poorly placed to influence Venet and Bottin in a wide-ranging debate on company strategy, and should therefore initially present a clear, factual report on the *Shootup* project, as requested.

The report should identify the assumptions that were made during the development of the project on external variables, and on the strategies to be adopted by the company justifying these assumptions where possible. The areas covered should include economic and social background, competitors, target customers, pricing, distribution channels, advertising and promotion support. It should explain how and why the environment and strategies at the time of the launch differed from expectation, separating clearly fact from opinion.

Venet, who was responsible for the launch, may possess information that Caubet does not. Caubet must avoid the possibility of an incomplete report being used by Venet against him and he should thus enlist Venet's support in undertaking the analysis, although without relinquishing any responsibility for it. Venet will probably be willing to contribute both facts and opinions, so as to avoid being seen as uncooperative.

Some indisputable facts would be identified, but inevitably a number of differences of opinion would remain. If these differences could not be resolved, and were crucial to the analysis, consultants might be used to provide an objective analysis of the time situation.

Caubet should not cover wider issues in this report and should avoid direct criticism of individuals. He should draw concise conclusions on the implications of the *Shootup* launch for company strategy, based only on the data he presents. This approach would illustrate Caubet's ability to analyse problems and work alongside Venet.

It is unlikely that Caubet could work under Venet, given his aspirations to Venet's job and his low opinion of him. It is also unlikely that he could influence him significantly, given his past failure to do so. Caubet could become a scapegoat for any failure. So his position would be insecure. He should not therefore openly support Venet.

No need for pessimism
Caubet takes a pessimistic view of his position in the company; but this may not be justified. Bottin requested his analysis of the *Shootup* project and Venet wanted to enlist Caubet's support for his proposals to Bottin. Both may indicate that he is a well respected employee who could influence events.

It appears that the traditional sales force lacks the aggression that is required in highly competitive markets. The staff turnover in Venet's force is too high, and the latter's assertion that it is good for morale unreasonable. There appears to be scope for improving the productivity of each sales force, but the comparison between the original sales force and Venet's men should be questioned. The higher margin brands that

Venet's sales force sells, and the costs of recruitment and training of new representatives, need to be considered.

The merging of the sales forces is a possibility. But an objective analysis of the extent to which outlets, buyers and selling skills for the two product ranges are common, and of the financial benefits of the merger, is required before any decision is made.

The company has been successful in introducing new products in the past but appears to lack structured plans. The management team lacks unity, and Venet seems to have been given too much freedom. He has manipulated both Bottin and Caubet but appears to have taken some poor business decisions.

Caubet, whilst being a good "ideas man", seems to lack the financial awareness necessary for a business development manager.

What the right decisions for the company are is not clear. But prevarication is clearly wrong.

Bottin used to watch expenditure closely and must therefore be interested in the success of his company. He seems to have recently lost control through over-reliance on family ties with Venet. But his request for Caubet's report may indicate that he wishes to regain control.

If Caubet can establish his credibility through his analysis of the launch of *Shootup* and its implications, he will be in a much stronger position to offer a wider analysis of the company, and to influence its future.

Whatever his analysis of *Shootup* reveals, Caubet will have to fight for influence against strong opposition, and therefore would be wise to register himself with a good recruitment agency, and to read the relevant trade press for situations vacant.

This decision was provided by Frank Milton in his capacity as senior marketing manager with London-based management consultancy Deloitte Haskins & Sells.

DILEMMA

How can a family company ensure smooth executive succession?

"You are not looking very well, dear," said Emily, the wife of the company's owner, Harry Greenbaum.

"I'm okay," he replied. "Just tired."

"You ought to retire and let Peter take over," his wife added, referring to their eldest son. "After all, you are 62. Remember what the doctor said about your blood pressure. There's absolutely no need to work yourself into an early grave."

Greenbaum grunted. What could he say? It wasn't as though the same thought hadn't occurred to him. He *wanted* to relinquish day-to-day executive control of the family food manufacturing company he had started 40 years ago, and become non-executive chairman.

The question was, who should take over as chief executive? In Emily's eyes, that was no problem. Their son Peter, now 38, had done a competent job as production manager at one of the plants, and was now a vice president with special responsibility for marketing.

Doubts about son

Although Greenbaum had always wanted Peter to succeed him, recently he had developed doubts about his son's ability to cope with the challenging, fast-moving situations that were cropping up increasingly in the food business and elsewhere.

Greenbaum believed that his number two, executive vice president Stanley Lawson, who was not related to the family, was well suited by training and temperament to be chief executive. He told himself that if this was a non-family firm, and he was recommending the appointment of a chief executive purely on merit, he would have appointed Lawson with very little hesitation.

Greenbaum, however, was a logical man and considered it would be very illogical to bar his own son from the top job just at the time when he had taken steps, in consultation with his legal advisers, to ensure that the company remained in family ownership. When he died, 60% of the shares would go to his wife and 10% to each of their children – to Peter, to second son George, who was a lawyer, and daughters Hilda and Clara.

Then, on the death of his wife, her shares would be divided equally among the children, so that each would own a quarter of the company. And none could sell his shares except to one of the others. Only a unanimous vote of all the family members could dispose of the business to an outsider.

Barely had Greenbaum concluded this legal arrangement, however, when he became disturbingly aware of friction in the top echelons of the company. Friction of a disturbing nature.

Lawson was a forceful character, aged 41, who had worked for Greenbaum for 15 years. An able all-round manager, he had also exhibited an entrepreneurial flair that appealed to Greenbaum. He had started a successful fast-food division and played a significant role in the company's growth from $300 million sales, two years ago, to the present $400 million. A creditable increase.

Although Greenbaum had never promised Lawson that he might be his successor, he knew that the latter had turned down offers from other companies, and must entertain hopes that he would in fact succeed. Greenbaum reflected that had he been in Lawson's shoes he probably would have left the company years ago.

Son Peter, meanwhile, had successfully managed a meat packing plant and held a variety of staff jobs. Now he was chafing at the prospect of many more years of living in his father's shadow. Indeed, since becoming vice president, marketing, he had begun to behave, at executive meetings, almost as though he was already in his father's shoes.

Personal offence

But was he fit for supreme command? Greenbaum noted that when a rival company had introduced a line of prepacked cheese and pickle snacks, in a segment of the market where the family firm had long been dominant, Peter had blamed the marketing people at divisional level – when in fact, as Lawson pointed out at an executive meeting, it was the failure of market planning at corporate level that was chiefly to blame.

Peter had taken personal offence, retorting that since Lawson had never himself been a marketing man he was not in a position to pass judgment. He had also complained to his father, privately, that he found Lawson increasingly difficult to get along with.

Another complication had arisen, on the family side, when daughter Clara, whose husband has been acting as a financial adviser to the company, asked her father to give his son-in-law a permanent executive role. "When Peter becomes chief executive he is going to need a finance man at his elbow," his daughter had said: "You must know how bad he is with figures."

The day after his wife had remarked how tired he looked, Greenbaum shut himself in his office, told his secretary to intercept all calls and tried to think things through. It was clear to him now that if he semi-retired, to the role of non-executive chairman, and appointed Peter as chief executive, there would be trouble with Lawson, who might even quit. If he appointed Lawson, he would have to contend not only with his son's reaction but also that of his wife and the rest of his family, who would question whether he was in his right senses keeping ownership in the family while only postponing an eventual showdown on management control. This did not seem to be the answer.

An alternative would be to appoint his son and Lawson as joint managing directors. But the more that Greenbaum thought about their respective strengths, weaknesses and their different personalities, the more he decided that that wouldn't work either.

Gaining time

He thought briefly that maybe his son-in-law could come in as acting chief executive until another solution could be sorted out. At least he had a level head and some of his financial advice had proved eminently sound. On the other hand, he had no direct management experience and only knew the business at second hand; such a move would be seen by all the other executives as a transparent ploy to gain time.

As he considered these, and other, alternatives, Greenbaum cursed himself for being too insensitive in the past – for taking Lawson's loyalty for granted and not designing, with his cooperation, a coherent executive succession plan; and not appreciating his elder son's resentment at the challenge from a successful outsider.

But what should he do now, with his own health failing and time running out?

DECISION

Family chief should distinguish clearly the issues of ownership and management

Harry Greenbaum should separate very clearly in his mind two different issues, those of ownership and management. He has already ensured that the family will keep control of the company; now he has to make the management secure. If he fails to do so, it will, in the end, be the family's interests that suffer.

Greenbaum should override the expectations of his wife, and the objections of other members of the family, and appoint Lawson as chief executive. Despite son Peter's accusations, it is clear that Lawson does have some sound marketing experience.

He has a good track record in the company. He is a loyal servant of the family. He has proved himself as an entrepreneur, having started a profitable fast-foods division. And this company is in a business in which marketing flair really counts. So it cannot afford the luxury of having an amateur, or a man who lacks drive and ideas, at the top.

Clearly Lawson is better qualified for the top job than Peter, whose only success to date appears to have been in running a plant. Greenbaum should therefore appoint Lawson as chief executive and make Peter deputy chairman with some executive responsibility. This responsibility, however, should preferably be of an operational, rather than a marketing or strategic, nature.

Wives and in-laws can complicate issues

Later, when he retires, Greenbaum can move Lawson up to executive chairman and appoint Peter chief executive. This will provide a period in which the two men can work together in a kind of office of the chairman. This will help Peter to imbibe more of the marketing experience and strategic thinking of the older man.

Although the two men appear not to get along, it is in their own interests that they should. Lawson knows that ultimately the family is in control, that he can do nothing about it, and that at least while the old man is alive he can enjoy a period of real power and influence. Peter, meanwhile, will realize that he has no choice but to fall in with his father's wishes and that an able outsider at the helm cannot be against the family's interests in a pecuniary sense.

Having said that, the fact remains that, in real life, problems do arise because too many companies fail to separate family from business issues. And often it is the wives and in-laws, rather than the principals in the firm, who stir things up.

Strengths and failings

There is the problem of families accepting outsiders in any senior capacity. I know of several outside managing directors who are accepted for their skill and experience in the office but, around the family dinner table, come across as second-class citizens.

It is unfortunately true that many family firms are still prone to appointing less than able executives from within. That is perhaps their biggest failing. But they have built-in advantages, too. The family firm is good at taking a long-term business view, partly because it does not have a horde of dividend-hungry shareholders to worry about. Also it is much more quickly responsive, especially in cash-related issues, than a lot of public companies. The family simply makes money available.

The great need, of course, is for coherent succession planning in the family firm, with the company identifying its future chief executive early – say five or 10 years before the contingency is likely to arise.

Non-family professionals, if they are to function effectively, need to know very clearly what their position is. And family members earmarked to succeed their father, or uncle, will benefit from three things: a good education, including attendance at the summer courses of a management school; an enormous breadth of training in a functional sense; and an element of executive responsibility at an early age. Preferably this experience should be in marketing or technology. Finance provides too limited an experience of the problems that have to be tackled by a chief executive who has to have breadth of vision.

214

In Greenbaum's case it might be wise not only to clarify the management succession but also to outline a suitable role for each of the family interest groups, each of which will own 25% of the company on Greenbaum's death.

In the context of the chief executive job, consideration of daughter Clara's husband for the post is a red herring. It would only complicate the issue that arises between Lawson and the eldest son. But because Clara will ultimately own a quarter of the company, the son-in-law cannot be ignored. It might be sensible to bring him on as full-time financial director, especially as Peter will have need of a financial adviser.

Unfortunate skills mix

The skills mix between Lawson and Peter is unfortunate, because it is usually better for the family man to end up doing the strategic work. But here it is the other way round.

I repeat, however, that Greenbaum's predicament is not unique. Only some very clear thinking can bring a satisfactory conclusion.

This decision was provided by Brian Scanlon in his capacity as director of marketing and strategic studies at A.T. Kearney Ltd., the British subsidiary of the U.S.-owned consultancy A.T. Kearney Inc.

DILEMMA

How can staff development manager maintain his credibility?

Philip Randall felt trapped. Nine months previously his ego, as well as his bank balance, had been considerably boosted when he was headhunted for the job of staff development manager at Pettigrew Oil Services Ltd., which supplied drilling services to the oil industry.

He had no previous experience in oil. But the salary offered had been good. So he had given up a staff development job in a division of an international foods company, Excel Foods, in the south of England, to move to Aberdeen, where his wife had been born and raised.

"The easy days, when oil companies were queueing up for our services, have gone," the chief executive of Pettigrew, a rugged Scottish-American, Iain McDougall, told him, "Now we have to sell ourselves hard, to win any of the contracts that are going. It means developing the selling skills of our engineers, and I'll tell you frankly that in the past I've never been a believer in non-technical training. Good salesmen are born, not made. But right now, we do need more sales, and I'm prepared to try anything which will help get orders."

Lukewarm comments on training

If Randall, aged 34, had felt any qualms at McDougall's blunt but somewhat lukewarm comments on training, he had not allowed them to surface. Pettigrew, after all, was a company with sales of around $100 million. It had been formed to cash in on the North Sea oil strike and, if cooks and bottle washers were included, had a payroll of about 2,000.

Asking around about the company before he accepted the job, Randall had been warned that Pettigrew, like all subcontractors to the oil industry, was facing leaner times. It was clear to him, however, that oil companies and oil services would always be needed. As he believed strongly that training needs and techniques are universal, and totally transferable, the idea of switching from a food to an engineering service company intrigued him. Besides, his wife was strongly in favour of Aberdeen... she knew it well.

Disconcerting view of the company

It didn't take Randall long to realize how different things were at Pettigrew. The company was much less formalized in its operating procedures than Excel Foods had been. Personnel came and left to join other companies in the same business with disconcerting frequency. And the engineers closely in contact with the oil company customers were proud of their technical bent and set in their attitudes.

As one field engineer told Randall, the day after he arrived: "So you're the wallah that's going to send us all back to school, are you? Staff development manager, is it? Well I, for one, have no ambitions to train as a salesperson. What's the *point*, when I'm already on pint-drinking terms with everyone I need to know in the client companies?"

Randall had laughed this off. He had seen it before – the initial, professed reluctance to get involved in training to the detriment of getting on with the main job. But he believed that once a course was organized and properly conducted, everyone would fall into line. Peer pressure would see to that.

Only this time it didn't work. As part of his programme, Randall organized a series of three-day training sessions which the field engineers attended. It would have helped if he had been able to get McDougall to come in and make an introductory speech at these sessions, stressing how much importance he attached to sales training and why it was not beneath the dignity of an engineer to participate. Still better, if McDougall had said that in future sales ability would be taken fully into account in salary reviews, the reaction might have been more positive.

Unfortunately the chief executive was abroad, looking for business in the Gulf of Mexico and offshore California. The engineers attended the sessions because they had been ordered to, and although Randall was a capable trainer it was clear, from their attitude, that the participants in the courses resented their three days in the lecture room at head office.

Opposition from staff

Randall also found considerable opposition from his own staff, who seemed to resent an outsider being brought in, from a food company, at a time when five of the headquarters staff had been dismissed in a cost-cutting exercise.

Randall, however, followed up with additional training, designed to sharpen negotiating skills, and teach the engineers how to repond to clients who offered stiff resistance to reasoned arguments.

But his troubles increased. At the first session, three of those who should have attended failed to turn up, and later pleaded they were too busy writing out tenders. After the second session, one senior engineer actually claimed that a contract had been lost because he was sitting in a classroom instead of taking a potential client out to lunch.

In all his classes, participation was half-hearted. The engineers had a camaraderie among themselves that excluded Randall and left him feeling ineffectual. At times, in private, he began to wonder whether they were right in their view.

"Maybe this is a counter-productive exercise. What am I doing here?" he mused to himself. But his own sense of professionalism helped him to overcome his doubts.

He had been told time and again, by training people he respected, that no such thing as an untrainable person or body of people existed. So surely all he had to do was persevere, and all would be well.

An unexpected complication was that the supervisors, to whom the field engineers reported, had no enthusiasm for the training. On one occasion, in the gentleman's cloakroom, Randall overheard a supervisor say: "Well, Harry, what did they teach you this time? Surely you are not going to use that load of old rubbish."

Randall realised, in that instant, that he had made a tactical mistake in not beginning with the supervisors and gaining their commitment to what he had in mind.

But now it was painfully clear that the supervisors felt no commitment at all to the training programme. What is more, they felt their subordinates were wasting their time attending courses.

The same evening, he sat down and gave the matter serious thought. What should he do? He didn't want to go cap in hand to the chief executive, and ask him to exert his authority – he knew that McDougall was extremely busy, and that the business side of things was not going well. Yet clearly, to let things continue as they were would be a confession of failure.

DECISION

Manager must secure commitment from the chief executive

Randall's strategy must be to face up to the problem and lay his cards on the table to the chief executive, McDougall. He has to convince the latter of the need to follow through, and get his personal commitment to the success of the programme.

True, a meeting with the chief executive is likely to be difficult. With the company's recent poor showing, budgets may need further trimming – and the training budget is always the most vulnerable. Costs will have risen disproportionately, and in all probability the worsening currency situation will make the bottom line look even leaner. McDougall will be unhappy, and the news of the failure of the sales training programme could not come at a worse time.

Randall is in a very unenviable, though by no means uncommon, position. His own personal credibility is at stake, not to mention his job. He could well be forgiven for being human and ignoring the situation, hoping it will go away. But this one won't.

Look at Randall's predicament. First, he has already spent considerable time and money in the training already undertaken. Second, the investment will be squandered if there are no results.

McDougall needs results, and Randall must convince him that these will only come about if he lends his full support to a management training programme. This will provide the supervisors with the necessary impetus,

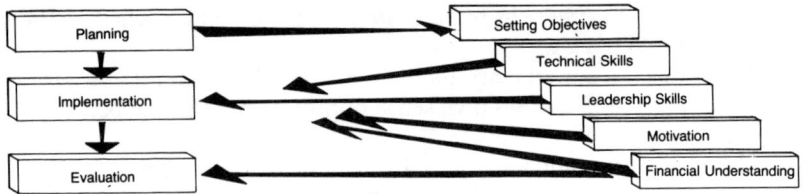

Planning → Setting Objectives → Technical Skills → Leadership Skills → Motivation → Financial Understanding → Implementation → Evaluation

and Randall will get some protection if it goes wrong – plus a lot of support if it goes right.

Results from training, incidentally, are notoriously difficult to measure. The results of management training are the most obscure of all. But lack of proof of what the results are does not equate with lack of effect. The returns, in fact, need only be very modest to make them cost-effective. It would be a rare manager indeed that could not improve his productivity by at least 5%.

The cost of such a person in the oil services industry is frequently in excess of $100,000 a year, including attributable overheads. So the savings, say, over the cost of a short course are almost certainly cost-effective, even in the first year, possibly in the first month and certainly for as long as the manager remains with the company.

Even if the improvement in such a person's skills and attitudes was only 1% it would still pay off. It is the lack of "visibility" of training returns that makes it hard to justify.

Randall has himself to blame for some of his troubles. He has clearly not stimulated a personal commitment from the sales force. Undoubtedly his efforts are being sabotaged by the attitude of the supervisors. This is where he has already made his most fundamental error. "Start at the top and work downwards" is the way.

In training terms, the supervisors need firstly to be convinced that training is necessary. Every manager is paid to get things done through people. The problem is, he doesn't always know what he is trying to do, how he is trying to do it and why he is doing it. A good starting place would be to look at the skills necessary for effective leadership.

Taking out technical skills, all of the others mentioned in the illustration are people-related. Motivation and leadership are the most challenging and difficult aspects of management, but they *can* be taught.

The only question is whether Randall, with his background and at the age of 34, has the ability to bring it off.

In this particular case, the introduction of an outside training body could be the answer. So long as Randall selects the outsiders carefully, and gets McDougall to make the final sanction, all could be well.

Naturally the trainers, will need to be well-briefed, preferably spending some time with the client to get to know the business. Randall should also keep them fully informed about his own training programme. No matter how cruel the taunt that "an expert is anyone more than 100 miles from home", it is a fact that many a controversial message is put across more effectively by an outsider.

Of *course* this is going to hurt the budget. But if success costs money, how much more will failure?

This decision was provided by Mrs. Deirdre Spencer in her capacity as an associate director of Tack Training International. Previously she had sales and field management experience with international operations.

What is the answer to a sex harassment complaint?

Two weeks earlier Peeter Nieswand, personnel director of Argelco NV, had had a complaint from a female laboratory assistant that her boss had threatened to fire her if she refused to go to bed with him. Visibly upset, she demanded that her boss be fired. She said she intended to remain at home and not return to work in the laboratory while he was still there.

The manager in question was a long-serving and virtually irreplaceable employee. The woman had only been with the company a matter of months.

In the speciality world of biotechnology, there were probably no more than 25 people who could fill Hans Sommerlein's job. Even if the accusation were true, firing him was out of the question, Nieswand reasoned.

Sommerlein, knowing his value to the company, had played for a variety of privileges which had been readily granted. But had he gone too far this time? Nieswand's first priority was to find out exactly what had happened.

According to the laboratory assistant, Maria Rosenboom, Sommerlein had been pursuing her since she arrived in the firm. At first she had been flattered by the extra attention he had paid her and the compliments he had passed about her work. But gradually she had noticed that he seemed to find more and more excuses to touch her as he checked on her work. She also found that her relationships with some of the the other women in the department had deteriorated, a situation she ascribed to jealousy on their part.

Suggestive remarks are unwelcome

Then Sommerlein had asked her to come to lunch with him, to celebrate the successful completion of one of the experiments she had been working on. Sommerlein had drunk heavily over the meal, she claimed, and became increasingly suggestive. After the meal, he had put his arm around her and suggested they should not return to the laboratory but should go back to his apartment. When she refused, he became abusive, and threatened to "make your job hell – while you still have it".

Following a lead from Rosenboom, Nieswand contacted another female employee who claimed to have suffered a similar experience at the hands of Sommerlein.

"There have been two or three others," she said, "but he has made life so uncomfortable for them that they have left."

Nieswand decided he had to hear Sommerlein's story, too. Sommerlein freely admitted he had paid extra attention to Rosenboom during her first few months. She was inexperienced and needed the supervision. And, of course, he had been encouraging about her work – that was all part of the process of motivation. Sommerlein even admitted he had had a lot to drink that lunchtime but strenuously denied making any sexual advances.

When Nieswand said that another female employee claimed to have had a similar experience, Sommerlein immediately guessed who it was.

219

"That's just spite," he declared. "She is an old flame. But I keep everything on an entirely business relationship."

As they talked, however, it became clear that Sommerlein considered flirtations with female subordinates a natural result of men and women working together. But, he added, he wouldn't be upset by a rejection and would certainly not let it affect the working relationship. As evidence, he cited the fact that his "old flame" was still "happily employed".

Redress through the courts

Nieswand became increasingly convinced, however, that Sommerlein had harassed Rosenboom sexually. He called her in for another meeting and offered her a transfer to another job within the research library where her skills would also be of value. She refused point blank, on the grounds that she considered it a demotion. "If anyone should have to move, it should be him," she sobbed.

The next day Nieswand received a telephone call from a lawyer acting for Rosenboom. "Either appropriate disciplinary action is taken against this man," said the lawyer, "or my client will seek redress through the courts."

Nieswand decided to tell Sommerlein of this development, and was met with the angry retort: "If you cannot accept my version of what happened, and the consequences of accepting my version, then I might as well resign. You know as well as I do that there are several competitors that have made me offers recently. I don't have to stay."

Nieswand felt he had reached an impasse, with both parties engaged in brinkmanship. He did not want to risk being blamed for causing Sommerlein to leave the firm or for having Argelco's name dragged through the newspapers as a lecher's paradise. He knew it was time to bring the matter to the managing director's attention. The trouble was that the managing director would expect a recommendation on a course of action.

DECISION

Harassment should be treated as any other management problem

For some reason people seem to think that sexual harassment is different from any other management problem. In part this may be because it was thought to be a woman's issue. Recent data suggests that it is not limited to women but includes men as well. As such, it impacts the organization processes and becomes a management problem. Sexual harassment is no different from embezzlement, white- or blue-collar crime, proprietary information theft or blackmail. It attacks the work environment, affecting productivity, performance and morale directly.

Peeter Nieswand assumed that Hans Sommerlein was irreplaceable and then compounded the problem by suggesting a demotion to the victim. What would Nieswand have done if Sommerlein had embezzled company funds; suggest that it be ignored? At this point, Nieswand is rewarding the inappropriate behaviour and thereby setting an example for all other potential wrongdoers. Further, Nieswand's short-term vision blinded him to the organization impact of such a decision.

220

It is estimated that preparations of legal briefs in the United States for such cases cost approximately $50,000 apiece. Cases that are settled in court are carrying awards of not less than $150,000, not to mention the additional actions that the organization must take in restitution. The adverse publicity has the potential of diminishing profits, particularly if the company produces for the general public where feelings on this subject run high. These are only some of the external implications of Nieswand's indecisiveness.

The internal ones are even more costly over time. The fact that others are already involved brings an added dimension to the problem. Other employees have taken sides, as we saw when Maria Rosenboom indicated that her relationships with some members of the department had deteriorated.

Personal values are involved

This raises the question of what other people are experiencing in terms of punishment, false accusations and ostracism. While this classic dilemma did not discuss the psychological or physical implications of harassment, research clearly indicates that illnesses in either area escalate when it occurs directly or is witnessed by a spectator. Therefore an increase in health care demands and absenteeism can also be expected.

Because the subject is one which impinges on personal values, passivity is not to be expected from the victim or from bystanders. As we know, two or three other employees have terminated their employment for similar reasons. This is another cost which the company is incurring when it fails to view this problem in broad perspective.

Further, the subject is "exciting" and therefore will probably be the topic of many idle conversations where work should be done. Hence, productivity and performance are affected.

Sommerlein's response is not unusual. We have heard the same defensive responses on numerous occasions when a person has run out of other excuses for inexcusable behaviour. We also know that much of sexual harassment is developmental in the same way that other human factors problems are developmental. Nieswand's resolution addresses the effect of the behaviour and not the cause.

It should also be understood that Rosenboom took a risk in bringing the situation to the attention of Nieswand. Historically, persons who did bring charges were dismissed from their respective companies as being "unable to get along with fellow employees". This should have provided a clue to the serious intent of Rosenboom.

Encourage personal responsibility

She too could have addressed the situation earlier and perhaps prevented its escalation. Given that sexual harassment is developmental, when she noticed that Sommerlein was moving from admiration to touching behaviour it appears that she gave no clearly defined feedback that this behaviour was distressing to her.

While this does not vindicate Sommerlein's action, it does suggest that organizations can empower employees with methods for direct confrontation. This not only addresses the situation at hand but has the long term benefit of having employees that are capable of addressing organization problems effectively. Too often we are guilty of parenting the employee at the expense of encouraging personal responsibility and therefore liability for actions.

Nieswand should recommend to the managing director appropriate disciplinary action for Sommerlein according to the current policy in force. He should explain the company liability for failing to take disciplinary action. He should contact Rosenboom's lawyer and advise him that disciplinary action is being taken.

Then, with a look to the future, Nieswand should take the preventative action of reviewing all policies and procedures with respect to business practices and make sure that they are appropriately disseminated to the organization. This reinforces the company posture as well as giving direction to employees.

This decision was provided by Mary Coeli Meyer in her capacity as president of Cheshire Ltd., a U.S.-based management consulting firm specializing in the integration of technology and human factors. She is co-author of Sexual Harassment, *published by Van Nostrand Reinhold.*

How can boss control unorthodox salesman?

When Pierre Savoyard was named marketing manager of Babylon International SA, he had been warned that he would have to use "a great deal of diplomacy and tact" in dealing with Jean-Claude Mouchard. Mouchard was the long-serving salesman who covered Italy, Spain and Portugal for the toy manufacturer.

Mouchard had begun his career with Babylon only two years after it was founded. As a salesman he had enjoyed remarkable success, and the business coming in from his territories amounted to 18% of Babylon's total sales. He was regarded as a "character" by both his customers and the two Papillon brothers who had founded the company.

Georges Papillon, the brother who had been responsible for marketing and sales, had on many occasions threatened to fire Mouchard for his lavish entertainment and his extravagances on presents for customers, only to have his star salesman turn up with a major new order a few days later.

As a boy Louis Papillon had often heard his father regale friends with the latest Mouchard story. He remembered particularly the one about the time Mouchard had gone out for an evening of heavy entertainment and "lost" the company car. When he couldn't find it the following morning he reported it as stolen to the police.

Three weeks later the buyer for a major Italian department store returned the car, which Mouchard had apparently lent him for his holiday at the end of a very convivial evening on the town. He not only got the car back but he also got a very large order from the customer.

Hence it was not surprising that when Louis, now a 32-year-old Harvard Business School graduate, succeeded his father and uncle and

222

became chief executive of the company, he did not feel confident in making Mouchard sales director. Louis soon learned from his father, however, that Mouchard had expected the job as a reward for his long and successful service in the field. He later told Savoyard of this incident. He said he had told his father that he was now in charge of the family business, and if he was expected to run it then he would have to do it his own way.

"I even told him that I felt Mouchard should be brought a little more under management's control than had been the case in the past," Louis Papillon said. His father, who was still on the board, but no longer played an active role in management, grumbled: "Better let well enough alone."

Savoyard set out on his new job to learn the territories. He had initially called Mouchard and told him that he would like to travel around Italy with him and meet the company's most important customers there. Mouchard had put him off. First he was taking his own holiday. Later it was because key customers would not be in. Savoyard had let the situation drift while he made calls with salesmen in other territories.

After Savoyard had covered all the other territories, Mouchard was still making excuses as to why a visit would not be appropriate. Rather brusquely Savoyard said: "I will give you three dates. You pick the best one and I am coming to make calls with you for that week." Savoyard confirmed the conversation on a telex and asked for a reply by the following Monday.

He was now sitting in the double-bedroomed Milan hotel suite that he was sharing with Mouchard, reflecting on the unsatisfactory progress to date. Mouchard had met him at the airport and they had spent most of the day driving to visit store owners in two medium-sized towns.

The second day they had driven into Bologna for a very lavish lunch with a person who turned out to be the second assistant buyer for a discount group, but who had no real influence, as far as Savoyard could ascertain.

Tracking down the main contacts

After a slow start the following morning they had arrived back in Milan late for an appointment with another small customer, who could then only spare them a few minutes. Savoyard had suggested that the two of them have dinner sent up to the room and use the evening to work out ways in which Mouchard could better organize his time, and furnish more documentation on his sales efforts.

Indeed, Savoyard was a bit alarmed in that he had very little idea who Mouchard's actual contacts were.

Mouchard apologized that he had made an appointment with some old personal friends in Milan for that evening. Savoyard couldn't help feeling slighted. Yet he also recognized that Mouchard was entitled to his own private life, and that as a boss he should respect this. After all, he was much more interested in Mouchard's performance than his companionship, he told himself.

Mouchard had just left the suite to go downstairs when the phone rang. It was the concierge saying that Carlo Boldoni was in the lobby waiting for Mr. Mouchard.

One of the things that Savoyard did know about the Italian territory was that Carlo Boldoni was probably Babylon's most important customer, as the head of a large mail order company. He had specifically asked Mouchard to arrange a sales call on Boldoni. Mouchard had responded a few days later that Boldoni's secretary said that he was "too busy" to see them on this trip.

The annoyance at being abandoned by his subordinate now flared into anger at being deceived by him. Savoyard had a long evening to himself to plan his strategy. It was obvious to him that Mouchard was being purposely obstructive, and making every effort to keep Savoyard away from his important sales contacts. What approach should he take with his recalcitrant salesman the following morning, recognizing that they still had sales calls to make in Florence, Sienna and Rome?

DECISION

Sales manager should prepare for a developmental talk the following morning

In any sales territory the future business expected is based on three "platforms". The first is the buying platform, which consists of customers who have been making purchases more or less regularly. There is a probability, depending on the strength of their links with the company, that they will continue to do business with it.

The second is the working platform, which consists of prospects that have been approached, but are not yet buying. The higher and better the effort put in, the more likely that the prospect can be converted into a customer. The third is the market platform, which comprises prospects that have been identified, but not yet approached.

Even on the limited information that obviously has to be given in a case like this, and on assumptions that have to be made, it is quite obvious that Jean-Claude Mouchard has a buying platform. That is why he can pull a big order out of his pocket whenever it is urgently required.

Promotion dependent on training a successor

As Mouchard seems to be the only one within Babylon International SA who has a real picture of the buying platform and working platform – if the latter exists at all – within his territory, Pierre Savoyard must have cooperation from Mouchard. If not, there is a risk that this market, which provides approximately 18% of the turnover – we don't know about the profit – will disappear.

For this reason, Savoyard needs to act fast and firmly. The following morning he should have a developmental talk with Mouchard; a talk that is calm, factual and unemotional. During this talk it is of the utmost importance for Savoyard to get Mouchard *to tell him* how he sees his own situation.

Savoyard must draw Mouchard out on how he feels about the territory and the importance of his own efforts in the territory. They should discuss Mouchard's ability to establish and develop contacts with prospects and customers. Then Savoyard can lead him subtly into a discussion of his disillusionment at not being made sales director. This would then lead to a talk about his desire to receive a promotion.

At this point Savoyard can introduce the key element of the discussion: how can Mouchard be promoted unless there is someone else there to take over his territory?

Once this subject is broached, he should lead Mouchard into talking about the possibility of recruiting and developing a replacement and how long it would take to get him ready. Mouchard should also discuss his degree of commitment, motivation and cooperation if an acceptable promotion is forthcoming.

Savoyard must have the ability to get all this from Mouchard in the developmental talk. Otherwise it will all fail. Having obtained this information, Savoyard should reveal that he would honestly like to promote Mouchard to director of public relations in order to use, in other territories, the strong social skills he has. He should arrange in the very near future to bring Mouchard to headquarters to finalize the plans together on how they should find and develop his successor.

In this way, Savoyard will accomplish his short-term goal of getting control of the buying platform as well as the working platform, if that exists at all. He will also, with a new man in place, have a chance to achieve his longer-term goal of fully developing all three platforms.

As Savoyard should regard this task as very high priority, he has no reason to join Mouchard on any more visits to customers. Having obtained a firm commitment from Mouchard on the date by which they should finalize future plans, he should fly back to headquarters. He should then immediately confirm everything to Mouchard and start the operation.

This decision was provided by Lars Sjögren in his capacity as managing director of Mercuri Goldmann Ltd., the U.K. subsidiary of Mercuri Goldmann International which specializes in the development of people in marketing and selling, worldwide.

DILEMMA

Should directors refuse to promote the president's protégée?

Charles Veal was chairman of the nominations committee of Rodell Inc., a diversified company with sales of $3 billion. Its main business was in aerospace, but it also had important offshoots in consumer electronics.

"Gentlemen," he said to his four colleagues, who were also non-executive directors, "we are asked to approve promoting this young woman, Valerie Stewart, to vice president in charge of planning. Any views on that?"

There was an uneasy silence. Everyone knew that Samuel Grant, the firm's young, innovative chief executive, had promoted Stewart at a meteoric pace, from his personal assistant to head of public affairs, and now the proposed move to vice presidential rank. Stewart constantly accompanied Grant on out-of-town business trips and was often seen with him at public, and even social, functions.

The first to speak was Steven Hewitt, a banker. "In the past," he said "this committee has tended to rubber-stamp appointments. However, my own view is that this is one we should refuse."

"Or defer a decision pending further investigation," said David Williams, chairman of a retail chain.

"What *kind* of investigation?" snorted millionaire Philip Small, who had retired from his own company after making a fortune in real estate. "What do we discover? Whether Sam is having an affair with Valerie? If so, is that relevant? After all, I do understand he is separated from his wife."

"Living apart, maybe. But I don't think they are divorced," said Peter Broom, a lawyer who was on the board as a consumer representative. "The fact is he is pushing this girl forward at an indecent rate. Leaders of large businesses ought to set a high moral tone. They certainly should not show favouritism."

Introducing aggressive and open methods

"The fact is he has pushed a number of young people along at what might ordinarily be called an 'indecent' rate," interjected Williams. "After all, he has come along pretty fast himself. He had been running a $300 million company for five years when we hired him at the age of 32. That decision was taken on the basis that he would bring a fresh, innovative approach to this company."

Indeed, Grant had shaken things up considerably at the company, and in the process had increased sales and earnings sharply. He had brought along some fast-track MBA graduates from his former employer and had hired many more. He had succeeded in changing the culture of the company from being secretive and conservative to one which was aggressive and open. He even did recruiting at some of the country's leading business schools, offering virtually unlimited opportunity to attract the top graduates. "An ounce of talent is worth 20 years' seniority," he was fond of saying.

"Surely the only two points at issue here," Small said, "are, first, is Valerie Stewart competent to do the planning job and, second, are all the rumours in the company about their supposed relationship having an adverse effect on corporate performance?"

"I admit I have mixed feelings about her ability to do the job," Williams said. "Certainly she has the educational qualifications and brain power. She finished among the top 10% at one of the country's most prestigious business schools. You will remember it wasn't easy for Sam to recruit her as his personal assistant. He was up against some $40,000 to $50,000 a year offers from consultants and merchant banks.

"Undoubtedly she has done a good job here," Williams continued. "She introduced the Rodell story to security analysts across the country. She was so closely in tune with Sam's thinking that the presentations were real works of art. She probably added $2 or $3 to our share price.

"On the other hand, I sincerely question whether anyone that young, who has picked up most of her knowledge from books, has the insight born of actual experience to do any effective long-range planning."

"That is really the chief executive's job, isn't it?" retorted Small. "If Valerie is acting as a sounding board for Sam, I would say that she is the ideal person for the job. In fact, doesn't Rodell benefit from their intimacy?"

"That brings us to the other point," Broom said. "It is common gossip in the company that Valerie Stewart is sleeping her way to the top. If we endorse this promotion, we will be adding fuel to the fire. It will wreck morale. A number of other people in line for that post may quit in disgust, feeling they have not been considered."

"Doesn't Sam realize the kind of position he is putting himself, and us, in by proposing this promotion?" Hewitt asked. "Has anybody discussed this with him?"

"Of course I have," Veal answered. "He says he is well aware of the rumours, but won't dignify them by a response."

The members of the committee looked silently at each other. If they vetoed Stewart's appointment, the woman, and perhaps Grant too, might feel it necessary to resign. Even if Grant accepted the committee's decision, he would probably bear it resentment at having singled out his protégée as the first appointment it had ever refused to ratify. If presidents and prime ministers were entitled to confidants, off whom they could bounce ideas, why not chief executives?

There was the question of fairness to Stewart herself. Should she be, in effect, victimized on the basis of rumour and gossip?

On the other hand, if things were allowed to continue as they were, there seemed to be a danger of events getting out of control. Other executives might leave. The firm's image might suffer.

DECISION

Stewart's promotion should be approved on the basis of merit

The compensation committee should endorse Grant's recommendation for the promotion of Stewart to vice president for planning.

Grant, the chief executive, is acknowledged to have made excellent progress in the task for which he was hired by the committee, namely to bring a fresh and innovative approach to Rodell Inc. He has established credibility with the committee, which has shown its approval of his judgment by rubber stamping in the past his appointment recommendations.

Stewart is recognized by the committee as having the right sort of educational qualifications for the job, good brain power, a proven ability to work as a member of the chief executive's operating team and to have done a good job to date. The confidence placed in this manager so far has been fully justified.

High flyers trained by top executives

Grant recruited the manager, who finished among the top 10% at one of the country's most prestigious business schools, as his personal assistant. PA to a top executive is a post frequently used by companies as a specific development step in the training of bright, intelligent business graduates who are regarded as potential high-flyers.

Working alongside the chief executive as his right hand will, for example, have enabled Stewart to study how Grant manages his team, how and when he delegates and how he utilizes the professional expertise, technical know-how and the experience of other managers.

It will have enabled the PA to note how Grant gathers, sifts and processes the information emanating from the various functions reporting to him. It will also have enabled Stewart to observe the way Grant thinks and makes decisions, while at the same time displaying versatility in handling a variety of people and situations.

In other words, Stewart's grounding here will have covered some of the key ingredients in the art of managing-delegation, decision making and risk taking, objectivity, logical and creative thinking, intereacting with people, accepting and handling responsibility, stamina for hard work, the organizing of other people and information and willingness to put the job first.

Gossip and rumour feed on discontent

Whilst experience is a most welcome and valuable commodity, lack of it through tender years need not be an insurmountable stumbling block, particularly if good managing ability is evident. Having shown both ability and willingness to take young talent under his wing, and then guide and develop it, Grant is not going to see lack of experience in Stewart as a hazard.

As for the gossip and rumours, in both the PA role and as head of public affairs this manager would have been seen to work closely with the chief executive, might well have travelled with him in the former role and most certainly will have attended many of the same meetings and functions. It is now quite common for members of the business community to be expected to take some part in local affairs, which inevitably will mean attending gatherings of a more social nature. So, based on some fact, gossip and rumour have embroidered the picture with interpretations.

Gossip and rumour, of course, have a tendency to feed on discontent. Additionally, what is being said often masks the real reason for the discontent.

Find the real reason for discontent

What discontent could there be in Rodell? A very likely source will be the change in climate from a conservative way of doing things to the now fast-moving, dynamic approach. The managers Rodell attracted in the past will have been comfortable with the old ways of working. Otherwise they would not have stayed. Grant's promotion of young people to posts of responsibiity, his progressive ways, his innovative approach, will all be foreign to the entrenched Rodell manager.

In confirming Stewart's promotion, the chairman of the committee should suggest to Grant, who is after all interested in establishing an open culture in the company, that questions in the right places could reveal the real reason for the discontent on which the rumours are feeding. With help, such as counselling and coaching, some managers might be able and willing to change to the new set of values, and they should be offered such an opportunity.

One fact I have not mentioned in this reply. Stewart is a woman.

This decision was provided by Dorothy M. Monks in her capacity as chairman and managing director of Westfield Management Associates (Oxford) Ltd., a consultancy in the U.K.

228

How should manager tackle Middle East 'culture shock'?

When George Barry signed a contract to work as a site manager for Zahra Construction Co., he regarded it as a challenge as great as any in his 10 years of supervising construction sites.

He had a public reputation, of which he was proud, of never having failed to complete a job on time. Privately, he took equal pride in the fact that he had never encountered any difficulties which he could not overcome by open, rather than underhand, methods. Indeed, he had once hit a man who had offered him a bribe so hard that the offender had ended up in hospital.

Barry's previous jobs had been in the United States, Brazil and Korea. He had never worked in Arabia and was intrigued at the prospect, particularly since the managing director of Zahra, Mohammed Hussein, had come to him with an offer he felt he couldn't refuse.

More than incompetence is involved

"Already we have got through two site managers. The project is five months behind schedule," Hussein had said. "If you take this job you can go, or be fired, at any time during the contract. But if you do succeed in finishing the job on schedule, 15 months from now, I will double your pay, and that's a promise."

So Barry had signed – and afterwards a friend had bet him $1,000 that this time, since he was new to Arabia, he would not complete on time. Barry had accepted the bet, and stood to earn enough to retire for a year or set up in business on his own.

Within days of arriving at the site where Zahra was building a complex that included shops, a sports centre and a 400-bed hospital, as well as living quarters for doctors and nurses, Barry realized that he was going to have to earn his money.

The site was in chaos. It was clear there was no system for storing incoming material, which was dumped anywhere. The size of the labour force varied unpredictably, from day to day, as labourers wandered in from another site, in which the same company was a contractor, or left with equal ease. Skilled craftsmen stood around with nothing to do, and when Barry walked into the site office he found it quite sumptuously furnished but bereft of any kind of progress chart, to help him get a grip on the situation.

He was not unused to such situations, however. Speedily, the site assumed a more ordered and businesslike appearance. But the more he delved, the more he realized that not just incompetence was involved.

The payroll clerk, for example, very clearly was lining his own pocket, both by taking kickbacks from some of the men he signed on, and by employing non-existent "ghost" workers, whose wages he appropriated. Barry sacked the man, as he did several others who were either dishonest or who resisted implementing routines which he considered essential if lost time was ever to be made up.

Gradually, work took on a new tempo. But after Barry had solved the immediate problems, and taken stock, he realized that he had only just scratched the surface.

For one thing, many of the Indians who had been recruited to do skilled jobs had no qualifications. Simply sacking them was no answer, because of the well-nigh insuperable problem of finding replacements quickly, in a tight labour market. On the other hand, training them to the required standard would take a long time and would be no guarantee of success.

There was a chronic shortage of structural drawings, and of detailed specifications. An architect hundreds of miles away, in Beirut, kept coming up with endless excuses for delays in producing such specifications, driving Barry to distraction.

To cap it all, Barry discovered that 2,000 tons of steel rods had been delivered to the site, when only 1,200 tons was needed. Thousands of bags of cement, grossly over-supplied, were rotting unreachable at the bottom of a growing pile.

When Barry tried to replace the purchasing manager, whom he suspected of being hand-in-glove with the suppliers and of taking a rake-off from the over-ordering, he learned that the man was a nephew of the managing director, Hussein, and therefore untouchable.

Hussein travelled widely and was in the Middle East, on average, only two or three days each month. When Barry tracked him down to insist that the purchasing manager was corrupt and had to be fired, Hussein replied: "He is my sister's son and we are a big happy family in Zahra. That is our tradition. But why should financial affairs concern you?"

When Barry had asked Hussein to put a bomb, metaphorically speaking, under the architect whose dilatory methods were holding up the specifications, Hussein replied: "Yes, he is a dear friend of mine. Why don't you join us for a drink tonight?" But the drink never materialized. Hussein flew off to Jordan on urgent business.

Back at the site, Barry took stock of his situation. The corruption by the purchasing agent could be discouraged, but he was sure would continue so long as the man remained. The job, thanks to his efforts, was now only three months behind schedule. But with the architect sitting complacently at home, and replacements for the Indians still not found, he wished that he had not accepted that $1,000 bet.

What could he do now, in this Arabian environment, to get the job finished and maintain both his public reputation and his own self-esteem?

DECISION

Compromise and a positive approach can save situation

George Barry's past success and established reputation suggest that he is a competent and knowledgeable site manager. However, he also appears to be proud and somewhat hasty. If he is willing to review his uncompromising approach, he is very likely to be successful in his new job.

Barry must try to stand back from the detail of the job for a moment and recognize three essential points. First, he must put out of his mind worries about his reputation and the $1,000 bet. Second, he will have to adopt problem-solving techniques that he may not have tried before. Third, his haste in challenging the position of the purchasing manager must teach him to collect his facts and know enough to act with a good chance of success.

Faced with the problems he has encountered, Barry could take the view that he is unwilling to work surrounded by corrupt practices, nepotism and a general lack of the attitudes to which he is accustomed. But he does not appear from his record to be a man who accepts defeat that easily.

His first task is to work out with his key site staff a detailed and achievable plan. This should be based on the outstanding work to be done on the contract and the labour that he already has or could possibly recruit. The plan should yield income and expenditure data. If he is to get the managing director's support, he must be able to show that his plan will turn the site round from being a cash sink to a cash source.

He must also get the full support of his key staff, or at least of those who show any sign of energy, determination and skill. By sacking the site clerk he has shown that he is determined to take control and run an honest site. This will have been appreciated by the good people working with him and will have gingered up the not so good.

The target may have been unrealistic

If the plan does not show the project finishing on time and cannot be redrawn reasonably to do so, Barry must accept that the target was unrealistic by the time he took over. He should not allow his ego and a bet to cloud the real issue, which is to do the best possible job.

From the plan he should derive a material requirements schedule and appoint one of his most able people to ensure that the orders get placed on time for on-schedule deliveries. He cannot yet concern himself about what he believes are corrupt practices but must first ensure that his own project is well run.

As far as drawings are concerned, Barry should recognize that in the Middle East, as in many other parts of the world, nothing succeeds like personal contact. If the architect will not come to the site, then Barry must go to the architect. It is unlikely that the principal architect is doing much design work himself so Barry must make contacts at an appropriate level, obtain authority from the top and harass until he gets what he wants.

The site labour problems are not unique and are unlikely to be solved quickly by further recruitment of expatriate workers. Again this is a problem that starts with planning. Within the overall site production plan, Barry must spread out work requiring higher levels of skill and, instead of assigning a team of, say, carpenters to do a job from start to finish, he will have to move his best team on when the most skilled work is completed.

Overstocking of materials may be annoying but Barry should realize that it is not a crucial problem. Indeed, he should be grateful for the overstocks at this stage as they will help him obtain operating flexibility.

Barry has become accustomed to what may broadly be described as the Western business approach based on an organization structure, systems and planning. He is now confronted with the Middle Eastern style, much more oriented towards personality and contracts where simply issuing a purchase requisition does not guarantee delivery of materials. He must become adept at running his project efficiently even where many of those about him are not as aware of plans and time-scales as he would wish.

He must be conscious of the need to motivate his first-line managers and to identify their strengths and weaknesses. Once he has delegated much of the work in accordance with his judgment, he can concentrate on dealing with certain key issues himself and on supporting and monitoring his subordinates.

If he sees clear shortcomings in the capabilities of his staff, or a larger number of key tasks than can be handled by the people available, he must use short-term support from outside the company until his own staff have learned the skills or until a need for longer term recruitment is proven.

With this type of positive approach, Barry need not worry about his reputation, his bet or his double salary. He will not lose his reputation, he may lose his bet, but his managing director will not be eager to lose a man who has shown how things can be done and who has turned a potential disaster into a success.

This decision was provided by Dr. Colin Robinson in his capacity as manager of the international construction division of U.K.-based management consultants Peat, Marwick, Mitchell & Co.

DILEMMA

What to do when a job offer sparks a marriage crisis?

John Harbinger puts the phone down and clenches his fists with excitement. They've offered him the job. At the relatively tender age of 32 he has been invited to join Honeydew International, one of the world's largest soft drinks companies, as vice president, marketing, for Europe and the Middle East. For Harbinger this is a quantum leap from being marketing director of a regional brewery in south-east England.

But a split second later his mood becomes sombre. How is his wife, Anne, going to take the news? She has recently been named personnel director of a furniture manufacturing firm close to their home in Cambridge. Accepting Honeydew's offer would mean going to live in Brussels, not commuting to London.

Unfortunately, Anne Harbinger knows nothing about her husband's talks with Honeydew. Harbinger curses himself for not having told her three months before when he was first approached by an executive recruiting firm or at least when things started to look serious. The day of reckoning is now at hand, as he has promised to give Honeydew an answer in a week's time.

A democratic partnership

Five years ago, when John and Anne Harbinger enthusiastically embarked on their dual-career marriage, they thought of themselves as a "liberated" couple. In those heady days theirs was to be a democratic partnership. Not for them the traditional roles of breadwinner and homemaker.

John had said solemnly: "Anne, your career is just as important to me as my own." He was proud of her independence and her flair for industrial relations. He appreciated having a wife who could help him with his office problems. Anne was grateful to have such a supportive husband, one who could understand the difficulties she faced as a female manager in a predominantly male environment. They both enjoyed the high standard of living which two salaries provided.

Of course, the Harbingers expected to have to make compromises. John had already passed up an offer from a larger brewery in the north of England to do much the same kind of work for slightly more money. Anne had traded an opportunity to attend a 10-month programme at INSEAD, the Business Administration Institute at Fontainebleau outside Paris, for a ten-week course at London Business School. No great sacrifices for either of them.

Testing a working marriage

But John and Anne Harbinger recognized that sooner or later they would be faced with a serious dilemma which would test their working marriage. What if one of them were to be offered a significant career challenge outside commuting range of their home? Rather than discuss a hypothetical case, they resolved to face this eventuality when it arose. They were secure in their relationship and confident, at least in the early days, that they could "talk through" any such conflict between career and marriage.

The Harbingers had agreed they wanted to have a family one day. But Anne had persuaded her husband to wait until she felt "more secure and established" in her job. John Harbinger willingly went along with this. But he had recently begun to caution her that it was dangerous to delay having a first child past her early 30s.

Harbinger admitted to himself that this was partly a rationalization for growing resentment of his wife's success. Within the last year, her career had really taken off. Her latest promotion meant she was earning more than he was. Anne was working late and travelling a lot. Harbinger had to spend more time with domestic chores. Intellectually he accepted this. But still he felt frustrated and resentful.

Presenting a *fait accompli*

At home there was growing tension and often animosity. Small things caused irritation. Anne would come home unexpectedly late from the office when he had a meal prepared. John would forget a telephone message. There was less open discussion between them; a subtle drawing apart, as working pressures increased.

Perhaps this was why he had delayed telling his wife about the Honeydew discussions. He wanted to avoid any conflict until he had a firm offer. Belatedly he realized that he was now presenting his wife with a virtual *fait accompli*.

Harbinger wants the job badly. He needs it, he tells himself, for his career and his self-esteem. What approach should he take in breaking the news to his wife? What should he do if she refuses to give up her job to go to Brussels?

Man and Wife:
'Let no (job) put asunder..'

How easy it would have been to have dealt with this dilemma against even fairly recent moral concepts of marriage, parenthood and career! Yet today such situations are cropping up and will no doubt become commonplace. Does the answer lie in the advice of a priest, a marriage counsellor, a psychologist or a search consultant?

The initial responsibility, at least, lies with the search consultant. He should prevent such a situation arising.

Both the search consultant and his client, the employer, should have realized that a problem existed long before this stage. If their questions failed to reveal it because John Harbinger was being less than honest in his replies, then it must have emerged at the next stage. John should have been invited to take his wife over to Brussels in order to try to ensure that the proposed move would be successful. No employer should sanction an offer of employment without this safeguard. It is possible that this would have resulted in John not getting his big chance.

Too late for preventive medicine

But at least the employer would not have been saddled with the effects of John's marital problems. We all know the devastating result domestic circumstances can have on work performance. John's work task will be difficult enough in itself – a new company, a new role, a new country – without the persistent nagging worry of an unhappy or broken marriage.

It is, however, too late for preventive medicine. At issue now is the marriage, not the career of one or both of the "happy couple".

It appears at first that John has behaved in an unthinking, selfish and even foolish way. On reflection this seems rather inconsistent with the impression gained of him from the earlier history of the marriage. He does not appear to have been fundamentally a selfish or unthinking person. It may well be therefore that, consciously or unconsciously, John was seeking to bring about a confrontation with Anne.

Anne is intelligent, successful, determined and wrapped up in her job. It is fair to add that she is also a woman who wanted to get married. There seems to be little doubt that if John had discussed things openly with her from the beginning, discussion would have turned into argument and worry. If the employer did not in the end offer him the job, no useful purpose would have been served. In fact the marriage would have been further weakened.

Most worthwhile people show up best in a sudden crisis. When the chips are down, reality takes over and fundamental considerations rule. In this sense, John may so far have done the right thing. What should he do next?

It would be wrong for him to provoke an open crisis with Anne on a take-it-or-leave it basis. He should first apologize and ask her to discuss it as a common problem.

The text may go something like this:

"Darling, I'm afraid I've created a problem for us. I'm sorry — I should have told you about it at the start, but I didn't want to worry you when nothing might have come of it. You see, I got a call from one of those wretched head-hunters — I was flattered and intrigued — and now I've been offered a fabulous job, but it's in Brussels. I know it's ridiculous to have reached this point without consulting you — but there we are. What can we do about it?"

Anne's reaction and the subsequent discussion may take one of two opposite courses. John should weigh the consequences of both and realize where either course will lead him.

Open conflict may result

In an ideal world, Anne, who is clearly adventurous, would eventually react favourably and seek happiness and satisfaction through the new environment and, if possible, a new job in Brussels. Her skills are rare and she ought to be able to find a suitable opportunity which will enhance her own experience. And if she happens to become pregnant on the second honeymoon, well, it's roses round the door. She could resume her career later when the children start school.

Life is rarely ideal, however, and Anne's attitudes, representing, as they seem to, today's women, may well bring irreconcilable open conflict in place of the previous discontent. If that happens then they had better continue to be thoroughly modern and accept divorce as inevitable and desirable.

There appears at first to be attractions in the middle ground of a continuing marriage but mainly separate life.

Since – perhaps sadly – marriage needs to be rather more than a succession of "dirty week-ends," this does not represent a long-term solution.

Jobs arise where they exist

So John and Anne inevitably must find their own answer, make their own terms, and live the consequences. One wonders if they can begin to understand the long-term consequences of their brave new marriage.

It seems doubtful that two ambitious, able young people can simultaneously pursue a first marriage and fulfil separate careers. Jobs arise where they exist, not always where they are wanted. Sooner or later either the man or the woman must in all probability accept frustration in his or her own career and become in growing measure a "merry peasant".

This decision was provided by George Harris in his capacity as co-founder and joint managing director of Canny Bowen and Associates Ltd., a London-based executive recruitment consultancy. He is past chairman of AMROP International, an executive search partnership in which Canny Bowen has joined with other companies in Belgium, Brazil, the Netherlands, France, Germany, Italy, Scandinavia and the United States.

Should manager accept an attractive job offer from a rival?

" " I hope I have given you all a clear picture of where we stand," the chairman concluded. "Frankly, things could hardly have been worse for us last year. But now I think we are well placed to pick up, with the new line of products which development manager Tom Smith and his team are working on."

Smith's face was serious as he listened to this speech. "If only I shared the boss' confidence," he thought. He slipped out of the meeting as the chairman was detained answering questions.

As he drove home he thought of the events of the past year that bred these doubts. Omega Inc.'s military electronics contracts had dried up with the cut-back in such military spending; the volume of general electronic systems work had also declined, as customers trimmed their requirements. Orders had slumped 40%, and there had been a 30% cut in staff. Profits were down by 50%.

Now, thought Smith, too much hope is being placed on this one big contract to supply hardware units for one major computer company. He had sat through all the meetings on the negotiations. He knew how tough the terms were on prices, quality and delivery. Everything will have to go smoothly in developing the prototype equipment for volume production, he reflected. And that is asking a lot.

The next few days were a hectic round of meetings with colleagues, suppliers and the Omega marketing staff. The chairman explained to the salesmen how important the computer contract was. "If we have something to show in this field, next year we can really go out and chase more business, first as suppliers, and later bringing this equipment right to the computer user who wants to add it to his installation. That's why we're relying so much on Tom Smith and his team."

Enthusiasm for a new project

Throughout the whole week, Smith radiated confidence and determination at all the meetings. Colleagues and suppliers responded with enthusiasm to make the project work.

But Smith still worried that it might be too late for the U.K. company to expect instant recovery through one big contract. There doesn't seem to be enough overall planning and direction at the top, he mused.

On Thursday he received a call from George Thomson, an old colleague at Omega, who was now vice president of Delta Systems. Could he meet him for lunch on Friday, to discuss something important? Smith agreed, happy at a brief escape from the hectic meetings.

Thomson came straight to the point. He wanted Smith to join him at Delta as research and development manager in the growing hardware manufacturing division. The company had been growing at 15% a year for five years and now it wanted to invest some of the profits in a hardware manufacturing facility, to supply its booming systems contracts side. Thomson was the corporate man overseeing manufacturing development, and thought Smith would be an asset.

Smith asked for time to think it over, and it was agreed he should contact Thomson by the next Friday with his verdict. That night Smith discussed the offer with his wife. "He says the salary will be $5,000 over the $25,000 I'm making today," he explained. "When the operation gets off the ground with a range of products, there will be a chance for me to step up to manage the whole show as a separate unit of the company."

He checked with an investment analyst friend who confirmed the rosy view of Delta's future given by Thomson. Its systems contracts covered a range of military, industrial and government applications, so there was a secure base for growth.

He also took stock of his career with Omega. He was now 44 and had joined the company eight years ago as an applications engineer. Inside five years, he became project manager and then was promoted to development manager. In three years, he had been allowed to expand the scope of the job, linking research and design work to planning and marketing, and he had done well.

He enjoyed the work and felt the salary was generous. But this very fact reminded him of his key role in the company at this moment. He had no illusions about being indispensable, but in the short run his departure would hurt Omega. The work would suffer a delay until a new man worked himself in, and this could be critical in Omega's weak position.

There would also be the psychological effect. His leaving would be interpreted as an ominous indication that the recovery was impossible.

Yet he must protect himself. If Omega went under, he would have to take his wife and two teenage daughters with him to another town. Delta offered the only alternative employment in the town, at his level in that field, and this was a major consideration.

DECISION

A new job without uprooting the family appears attractive

A number of factors can influence a successful executive to change jobs. Surprisingly, greater financial reward alone is not usually a compelling reason.

By far the most common motivation is the desire to have wider scope, greater challenge and the intangible benefits which accompany recognized success. Next come a host of lesser reasons. These include a more attractive geographical location, further promotion blocked by the age of the next more senior executive, the risk of redundancy in the executive's present firm – to mention a few.

In Tom Smith's case, and in the absence of a personal interview, it is difficult to assess the real reason for his dilemma. He appears to be weighing such things as lack of confidence in his chairman and the possible failure of the company; an attractive but not overwhelming salary increase and possibly greater scope for personal growth with Delta; the desire not to move from his present location; and, finally, an apparent lack of confidence in his own ability to push through the crash programme at Omega successfully and on schedule.

Ethically, there can be no criticism of an executive who accepts a better job, with demonstrably bigger responsibility and opportunity, than his present company affords. It is a natural progression.

Practically, he should explore carefully the new opportunity in terms of immediate and future rewards and security. He must consider that, if he leaves and Omega does not succeed with the new product launch, he will be blamed. If the new product is successful, he will not receive the credit, since he will no longer be there.

He should ask himself: "What am I able to do for Delta?" We are told that Delta has a secure base for growth and presumably this means it has no great product problems. Hence it must have enjoyed good research and development (R&D) planning and execution. Being a strong competitor, Delta must surely know something of the plight of Omega: how will Omega's head of R&D have any credibility with the staff at Delta?

It is also possible that Smith has taken Thomson's motives too much on trust. Has Thomson really looked for the best R&D man – and found Smith – or is Smith being hauled in as an ally for Thomson's company politics? The R&D position in a company can be crucial, but it can be a cipher, and Smith must satisfy himself that this last is not the case.

What if the project fails?

It appears that the chairman has a sense of euphoria which must have come from somewhere. Smith seems to be the one person who has the responsibility and duty to keep the chairman advised of the true status of the project. If he has not done so, he should do it now. Then, before making his decision, Smith should have a frank discussion with his chairman to ascertain what his future would likely be, from both the standpoint of position and monetary reward, if the new project succeeds. He should have the chairman spell out his potential salary and promotion in definite terms. He should ask for a contract covering several years to protect himself. He should also ask the chairman what the alternatives would be for the company if the project fails or is delayed beyond the deadline.

Smith should realize that at Delta his new job would be to accomplish what he is doubtful of achieving at Omega – the development of new products in a growing hardware manufacturing division. Thus Delta will not offer any escape from the uncomfortable obligation to complete difficult tasks, with limited resources and time. This should prompt Smith to analyse his own abilities; if he has serious doubts, perhaps he should seek a less arduous position, in a company where R&D is not so demanding or critical to the company's future.

Little to be gained from a move

On balance, the picture I draw from the description given of Smith is that of an executive who is not sure of himself, critical of his chairman's management capacity, and beset with doubts as to his own team's ability to make a success of his own project.

Smith's dilemma exists only because he has not really analysed the situation – or himself. If the grass looks greener at Delta, if his chances of success there appear to be greater, it could be merely "confidence born of ignorance". I can see little to be gained by the move and would counsel Smith to remain at Omega and strive for a successful product launch.

This decision was provided by Reece Hatchitt in his capacity as managing director of the London operation of Boyden Associates, international management consultants.

Should chief executive accept the sales director's resignation?

Managing director George Saunders' secretary had just said "goodnight," when sales director Frank Wallace brushed past her into his office. "For the past three years, I've been trying to do a good job here," Wallace exploded. "I think my record shows that I've been quite successful. But I just don't have to put up with the stupidity and obstruction from within our own company."

Saunders stopped stuffing papers in his brief-case. "What do you mean, Frank?" he asked.

Wallace continued in a hard, even voice. "One of our salesmen finally cracked the Atlas account. They are having trouble getting deliveries from one of their regular suppliers. They told us that if we can fill the order by next Wednesday, they'll become regular customers."

"That's great news, Frank," Saunders said. "What's the problem?"

"The problem is that the salesman phoned in the order to our production department. They couldn't possibly get around to it for three weeks. The salesman called me, and I went to see our stalwart production director, Elroy Travers.

Overtime costs can wipe out profits

"I kept as calm as I could and explained the importance of the Atlas order. His first response was that this was great for my bonus, but it would wreck his budget to interrupt a long production run to process a rush order. Then he tells me he thinks maybe Atlas is in a tight spot now and even if we do get the order, they'll go back to their old suppliers as soon as the emergency is over. Yet he knows nothing of the Atlas situation. I reminded him that the last time we went through this battle, he worked a weekend shift and we got the Consolidated business.

"Then he tells me the overtime costs on such a rush job would wipe out any profit – before he even sat down to look at the order specification. Five minutes later he's telling me they couldn't possibly deliver it by next Wednesday even if they wanted to. Damn it, I'm not a production man, but I know I could get that order out."

Saunders had listened thoughtfully, and at last he interrupted. "Look, I agree with you. I'm late for a party right now, but Elroy usually works late. I'll see if he's around."

Saunders scooped up the telephone and after a number of rings Travers answered. A short conversation ensued. Finally Saunders said: "Elroy, I know you can do it. This order means a lot to the company and we're counting on you." He hung up the telephone and turned to Wallace. You'll have the work out on Wednesday. You just have to humour Elroy a little – make him feel important."

Wallace's reaction surprised him: "Maybe *you* have to humour him; I don't. I knew he could get that order out. What if you'd been out of town? Besides, why should I have to put up with a lot of obstruction from an incompetent like him?"

Saunders' tone hardened. "Look, Frank, you've got your order coming. Why not let it go at that? As I've said before, you aren't really in a position to judge Elroy's abilities.

"Maybe not," Wallace replied "But I decided this afternoon that no matter what happened to this Atlas order, I'm not going to work in the same company with Travers any longer."

Saunders was angry about the ultimatum as he drove home. He felt that to capitulate to Wallace would undermine his authority. Yet, he felt, Wallace was partly right. Of the two men, he would much prefer to keep Wallace. Saunders had risen through the marketing department, and he recognized that Wallace was definitely the best sales director the company had ever had. In the three years since Saunders had hired him from a competitor, Wallace had boosted sales by 20% a year.

Travers was in his early fifties and had been with the company for 23 years. He had a reputation for being uncooperative, but Saunders relied on his technical expertise, since he knew or cared little about production details himself. Also he owed Travers something for his years of loyalty to both him and the firm.

Saunders recalled a similar confrontation two years earlier. He had intervened on Wallace's behalf then too. But when Wallace continued to complain about every production delay, Saunders showed his annoyance. Wallace had stopped complaining, ending a tense situation. Saunders resolved to say nothing more and hope the storm would blow out again.

Three days later, however, Wallace came into his office, asking whether a decision had been made. "I'm going to talk firmly to Travers," Saunders assured him. But Wallace pulled two envelopes from his pocket and handed one to Saunders. It was his resignation, outlining all his complaints against Travers. The other was a carbon copy for the chairman. "I'm sorry I have to do this," Wallace said. What should Saunders do?

DECISION

Saunders should build up his managers' trust

The question, "What to do?" about an organizational problem has two dimensions: what to do in the immediate crisis facing the manager, and what to do about the larger organizational problem which caused the crisis. In this case, the larger organization problem is the more important and I shall deal with it first.

Marketing and production should be closely linked in purpose since a company's success depends upon their mutual cooperation. All too frequently, however, the formal systems of evaluation for the two functions put them at odds with each other. In this case, for example, marketing is rewarded with a bonus on sales; production, by contrast, seems to be evaluated on the basis of cost minimization. Marketing is rewarded for additional sales at almost any cost, while production is rewarded for resisting the increased costs of fulfilling the rush sales order.

Inevitably, these conflicting evaluation systems produce conflicts between the two departments. The behaviour of both Travers and Wallace is quite rational, given the systems. When a quick decision is needed (such as in the Atlas order in this case), the evaluation systems serve to reduce organizational flexibility.

240

George Saunders' personal relationship with department heads only exacerbates the difficulties. As a marketing man he admits little interest in production and has left such decisions to Travers in the past, left them, that is, until the sales manager needs help. Then, Saunders identifies with sales, intervenes and "wins" the conflict for marketing. Such problems often occur because the managing director has risen through one functional speciality in the organization and continues to define all problems in terms of his own speciality, rather than the total organization.

From the organization's point of view, a case like this can be extremely delicate since there usually is no one to tell the managing director about the effects of his own behaviour. Travers, for example, must feel that Saunders only trusts him with production decisions when there are no difficulties. When conflicts arise, Saunders countermands him. What else can Tavers do in the relationship but complain and resist in order to defend his own needs?

What has occurred is that Saunders has "taught" the organization to respond as it does. Both his personal responses and the evaluation systems have reinforced the behaviour that led to this problem. Saunders, furthermore, provides no leadership outside of crises. Then he undermines the relationship between the two department heads, a relationship which he should have been helping to develop. Travers and Wallace have learned that they do not need to resolve their conflicts, Saunders will do it for them.

The organization will continue to respond in the same way unless Saunders changes his behaviour. He must start a system of evaluation which allows marketing and production to see their interests as mutual and which gives them a framework for settling their differences without having to refer to him. Then Saunders must support both production and sales directors. After all, if sales increased 20% each year, production must have increased too. Travers deserves some credit for this increase just as Wallace does and he, too, needs some incentive for rush orders.

Now what about the immediate situation? Saunders is confronted by his enraged sales manager who has just tossed his written resignation on the desk. Since the relationship with Wallace has deteriorated to the point that ultimatums and written attacks are the mode of communication, so little trust seems to be left that there is not much point in preventing his departure. Saunders should accept the resignation on the spot.

At the same time, however, recognizing his own contribution to the crisis, Saunders should see if a new relationship with Wallace is possible. He can attempt to provide the psychological climate necessary for them to cancel the resignation and attempt to work together. This may not be possible but, given Wallace's success as sales manager, it is worth a try. More likely, however, a new sales manager will have to be the starting point from which a more aware Saunders begins a new approach to the organization. Saunders must attempt to develop trust by opening up organization communication. At the outset he should propose three-way discussions about marketing and production problems.

The important point is this: when the immediate crisis situation has been decided, the basic problem still remains. Whether or not Wallace leaves, the fundamental problem is the underlying organizational one. It is this one that Saunders must attack head on.

This decision was provided by Prof. Alvar Elbing from IMEDE Management Development Institute, Lausanne, Switzerland.

Should a manager succumb to pressure to hire a friend of the boss?

About nine months after Nels Smid had been named European sales manager for Braun's Business Forms NV's international division, there was a big top management shake-up.

The managing director had resigned in the face of strong criticism by the supervisory board of his money-losing foray into computer software. His replacement, Frans van den Dyk, had quickly moved to close the software division down and sell off as much of the assets as possible. He had also made a far-reaching management reshuffle. As a result Jan Kraar was given responsibility for international operations and Smid's former boss, with whom he had developed a reasonable rapport, was transferred to a planning function.

For Kraar the move to director level represented a major promotion. He was formerly manager of the company's second largest plant, and had established a good record there, mainly for labour relations and improving productivity. However, he was not an expert on international marketing. It was a new field for him.

The international operation was in some difficulty. In the recession, sales had fallen to a point that Smid was planning to combine some territories, and try to persuade some of the sales force to take voluntary redundancy or early retirement. Although he could have used some help from his new boss in this area, what he got was a problem.

At his first meeting with Kraar, his new boss had asked him whether, as a favour, he could possibly find a suitable place in the organization for Hendrik Skyver, who had been put out of a job by the closure of the software division.

Smid had explained that he was already in a position of having to rationalize his sales force to keep the percentage costs of selling within target. "Well, see what you can do," was Kraar's response.

Smid dutifully interviewed Skyver and was somewhat alarmed to discover that he had held the title of marketing and new product development manager in the now defunct division. "It was mostly a PR operation," Skyver explained. "That's what I really like to do, although I once did some selling when we were in the cheque-book printing business."

No selling qualifications

Smid called one of his friends, who was deputy director of public relations, to see if he might have an opening for Skyver. When the public relations man heard that Skyver was involved he emitted a long laugh. "Don't you know the story about him?" he asked.

Smid replied: "Well, I guess he's some sort of friend of Kraar's."

"As far as I know," came the reply, "he only has one friend in the company. Unfortunately, that is Frans van den Dyk. They are old hunting and fishing friends from the days when they were both in the Eindhoven office. Skyver is a walking disaster and it's a mystery to me why van den Dyk protects him. He has obviously put the arm on your boss to find him a place in the company where he can do little harm."

"Little harm!" Smid exploded. "If he's not good enough for public relations he's certainly not good enough to take on a tough selling job."

Smid arranged a meeting with Kraar and explained in detail the problems he had had trying to trim his sales force to help meet the division's profit targets. He explained, tactfully, that he did not think Skyver had the right type of qualifications and that if he forced one of his sales staff out, only to give a similar job to a less qualified person, it would create immense morale problems. It would also mean putting a new, inexperienced man into a recently expanded sales territory.

At the end of the interview Kraar said: "Well, Mr. van den Dyk seems to feel that he is a very talented man and I would certainly urge you to try to find something for him, so the company doesn't lose his talents."

In vain did Smid plead that such an assessment of Skyver's capabilities did not accord with his own information. Kraar replied that perhaps Smid was taking too narrow a view, and that the managing director, after all, was better placed to relate the potential of individuals to the future needs of the organization. "I hope you are not suggesting that Mr. van den Dyk is not being objective in his judgement," he added.

Relationships in jeopardy

Finally Smid said exasperatedly: "Look, I don't mind giving Skyver a sinecure job in my operation as long as his wages don't have to come out of my sales salary budget."

"I couldn't possibly agree to giving somebody a job where they did nothing," Kraar retorted. "And you'll have to pay him out of your budget just like you would another good employee. I'm not ordering you to put him on your payroll. I just think he would make an excellent addition to our team. The fact that van den Dyk thinks highly of him can't help but be in our favour."

Smid is in a rage as he drives home that evening. He feels certain that if he does not employ Skyver in some capacity it will sour his relationship with the new boss, on whom he relies for putting his department's case at senior level. On the other hand, he sincerely believes Skyver to be incompetent and certainly a weak link in an already over-extended sales operation. The effect on morale could be disastrous.

What should he do?

DECISION

Manager should do an analysis to circumvent pressure

It is obvious that Smid, in the position he finds himself in, should rapidly produce a "strategic" analysis of his market – Europe – in order to establish his needs in personnel, with profiles adapted to the company's actual requirements.

Simultaneously he should make a structured evaluation, in a systematic, objective manner, of available staff, and draft *real* profiles of its individual members.

As he is under pressure from van den Dyk, via Kraar, he should of course include Skyver's profile. This must take into account both the past experience and the potentialities of each person.

He must do this in cooperation with the head of the personnel department, insisting on the importance of the human factor for his planned "reshuffle". The personnel department head should ensure, among other items, that information is obtained from Skyver's former superiors regarding his abilities, knowledge and potential, this being completed or confirmed by interviews, in cases of doubt or ambiguity.

Request specialized personnel help

If, against any expectation, the firm does not have its own fully competent personnel manager, Smid should propose to ask help from outside, calling upon a consultant specialized in staff recruiting and selection. He could even request help from the personnel manager of another firm where the Braun company has good friends.

At any rate, considering that Kraar has dealt in the past with personnel matters, Smid should ascertain that the chosen "expert" is known and accepted by Kraar as being acceptable and trustworthy for this audit. Kraar would find it very difficult to refuse such a request from Smid. He might even find it to his own advantage, for unless he is totally incompetent and used to toadying to van den Dyk, he cannot wholly relish the role he has be called upon to play.

Armed with the information about personnel requirements and the qualities of those available, Smid and the expert should make a joint presentation of their work, and its conclusions, to Kraar or preferably – if suitable in view of the diplomatic atmosphere prevailing in the company – to van den Dyk and Kraar together. They should start with a detailed discussion of the company's needs before ending with the names of individuals and their credentials.

In this "objectivization", if Skyver emerges as being of value for a given job, and being better than others, he should be retained in the proposals. If not, the report by Smid and his expert must include explanations of the reasons why each candidate has been discarded, describing them preferably in alphabetical order, without putting Skyver's name in the forefront in any way.

This evidently means that Smid will have committed himself on the proposed choices of persons and must, in view of this, have given extremely careful consideration to all the contents of his report. If the report is seen to be objective, van den Dyk will find it hard to continue supporting Skyver, should that individual prove unworthy of the post, no matter how close the two have been on the golf course.

Finally, should Kraar refuse to let Smid follow this course of action, or should van den Dyk persist in supporting Skyver despite an unfavourable report, then Smid has only one course of action left: he must resign. No conscientious manager would have a future in such a company.

This decision was provided by Jean-Pierre Balle in his capacity as general manager of nv Helping SA, a Brussels-based team of management consultants.

Chapter 5

Corporate Strategy

*Whether to decentralize, where and when to relocate — these are
the kinds of dilemmas which, in real life situations,
probably would be solved by boards in full possession of
the pros and cons over weeks and months of deliberations. But
what happens if time is at a premium? What happens if the board
of directors is split down the middle? How should a company
committed to the wrong objectives change its investment plans?*

How should a Chinese firm reorganize to stop losing money?

L ee Boon Eng had not wanted to bring the British-based firm of management consultants into his toy business in Singapore. His eldest son, Chow Fung, had badgered him so much, however, that he had given in.

The reason for his reluctance, he had to admit to himself, had been only partly his distaste of opening the family business to outsiders. More than anything else he had been afraid of what the consultants might tell him. He did not want to encounter unnecessary complications at a time when his own retirement lay not so far ahead.

Lee Boon Eng (Pte) was losing money fast. Its main market, plastic toys, was not expanding. What is more, as competitors showed they were able to deliver more quickly, and in some cases more cheaply, the company was losing its market share.

Lee had tried to keep his costs down by avoiding wage increases over the past year. But that had resulted in an extra rapid turnover of his skilled workers. "There is no loyalty any more," he would frequently complain as people left the firm.

Managers must adapt to new ways

Now the management consultants' report lay open on his desk. Apart from suggesting the purchase of several items of new machinery, and the introduction of a more efficient stock control and general management information system, the consultants made it clear the company should lower its horizons.

A smaller force of higher paid workers, making products of higher value, was the only recipe for survival, the consultants concluded. Several managers would have to go, because they did not have the flexibility to adapt to new ways.

Lee was not sure that he personally had the flexibility to adapt. Most of the managers were his friends, and had been with the company for 20 years or more. Two of them were related to his wife. He knew that he did not have the courage to fire them himself. Yet he could not accept the loss of face involved in getting someone else to do the firing.

His son was a bright and inventive 22-year-old who had started to acquire a basic knowledge of the business and was far more open than his father was to Western ideas of management.

However, at the moment, Chow Fung was too young and headstrong to be given the reins of the company. His brash approach, by Chinese standards, had already offended some of the older managers.

Lee glanced through the pages of the report again. One of the reasons, it said, that the company finances had reached their serious state was that senior managers had not brought problems to the head of the company soon enough. Unwilling to admit they were not in control of the situation, they had tried to bury problems such as over-large stocks of slow-moving products. They had also been affected by the traditional Chinese reluctance to bring bad news.

The consultants confirmed that Chow Fung needed a thorough grounding in business methods before he could take over the firm. Perhaps he should work for a year in a local multinational company to gain experience, the report suggested. The experience would also mellow him, they believed, showing him that management problems do not often have obvious solutions.

From the figures in the report, the company could not wait a year or more before taking some kind of drastic action. The consultants suggested that they should lend the company an acting chief executive.

But Lee knew that this was not a practical solution. Getting the company back on its feet depended on cooperation, if only from those managers who were left after the axe had fallen.

Lee felt that for all their careful analysis of the company's production and marketing problems, the consultants had little grasp of the complex relationships on which life in a Chinese business depends.

Lee knew that he had to make up his mind and that time was short. He could ignore the report provided by the consultants whom his son had recommended, and appoint the young man as his successor. Or he could take other steps to save the company. But what steps?

DECISION

Lee Boon Eng must consider the advice of the management consultants

The dilemma confronting Lee Boon Eng is typical of a small, indigenous organization caught in a conflict of tradition versus modernity. This conflict is probably most sharply defined in a traditional Chinese family business having to come to grips with rapid modernization and the increasing international competitiveness of Singapore.

In such a transitional society it would be an acceptable and appropriate solution for Lee Boon Eng to continue running his business, but with his son Chow Fung increasingly accepting more and more responsibilities in the immediate future.

Lee Boon Eng's greatest fault was not to have planned sufficiently early enough for his own succession and retirement, and allowing the firm to deteriorate to the extent it did.

Father and son to work together

A solution would be for father and son to work together on a plan that will have Chow Fung as chief executive officer within the next two years. This would reconcile the traditional elements of face-saving and family control against the urgent requirements for survival.

Lee's own admission that he personally was not sufficiently flexible to adapt is courageous. But he failed to recognize that the complication that would be caused by his sudden retirement from the business would be far

248

worse than the complication of what the consultants might disclose to him in their plan.

Bringing in a British-based firm of management consultants symbolizes the first breach in the typical Chinese-operated family business. Presumably, the whole organization is now expecting some action to follow.

In the circumstances it is probably advisable to retain the services of the consultants in an advisory capacity until the son is sufficiently able to run the business on his own. It would also be useful to assign to the son responsibility for supervising stocks, checking on sales and distribution and looking after finances, and other areas critical to the firm's rehabilitation to widen his attitudes.

Older managers to be eased out

The father, meanwhile, can concentrate on phasing out the firm's network of loyal friends and relatives. Once it is recognized that Lee will be phasing himself out of the business, it will be far easier to ease out the older managers.

Lee Boon Eng's earlier decision to halt wage increases over the past year, in a competitive and inflationary economy, only compounded the present problem by retaining unskilled workers who were not productive.

As these workers are eased out, it is necessary for the company to revise its compensation policy to attract skilled talent in order to compete effectively. Once the transition is made, future recruitment could be based on a more rational basis, which is productivity oriented rather than loyalty based.

Chow Fung could derive sufficient business education, training and development from the company itself, from the association with the management consultants and through carefully selected management development programmes offered in Singapore.

Assigning him to work for a year in a local multinational company to gain experience will only delay, and further aggravate the already difficult situation in the company.

Try to keep traditional Chinese values

The suggestion of appointing an acting chief executive officer from outside, while probably useful in a Western setting, very often is not in harmony with the running of a traditional Chinese family business. For Lee, it would represent a measure of his personal failure as a manager, which could lead to a greater loss of face for himself and, in the long run, for his son.

The other alternative, of resigning immediately and leaving the management of the company to his son, is also not in harmony with traditional Chinese values.

This decision was provided by Dr. Tarcisius Chin in his capacity as general manager of the Malaysian Institute of Management in Kuala Lumpur.

The company's board wonders: Should it decentralize?

Marcel Dubois knew that next day's board meeting could decide the company's structure and future competitiveness. He was president of Decoration SA, formerly Louis Legrande et Frères, a Paris-based firm that had moved from wallpaper into paints and all kinds of do-it-yourself products.

The company was organized into three manufacturing divisions, each of which was a profit centre with its own production, marketing and selling operations.

The divisions competed against one another, as well as against external competitors. The only real coordinating body was the board, on which the divisional chiefs sat together with Dubois, Pierre Legrande, who was a grandson of the founder of the company, and the finance director.

After the company had gone public, some 20 years previously, the Legrande family in effect had continued to run it. Then in 1970 one of the two grandsons of the founder had sold out, leaving the other grandson with a sizeable minority holding.

Two large institutions were now the dominant owners. They had invited Dubois, a successful professional manager, to be president. Legrande had become vice-president.

More centralization advocated

Dubois had set up the three-division structure, which had worked well. In the five years to 1975, sales had doubled and profits had more than tripled. In the last three years, however, there had been several cases where divisional autonomy had been at cross-purposes with the best interests of the corporation as a whole. The growth in sales had slowed.

Legrande advocated much more centralization. The company should have a master strategy for attacking the total home decorations market, he argued. If this meant coordinating planning, product development, advertising and promotion, among all the other things, so be it. What was the sense, he asked, in delivery vans from the wall-coverings divisions following vans from the paints division down the same street, to the same wholesalers, when they could be centrally coordinated?

As Legrande plugged away at this theme, the three divisional chiefs, united only in preserving their autonomy, cited results as their chief justification. Unfettered competition, they pointed out, had served the company well. Of the three, only one had been with the company when it was a family concern. The other two had been brought in from outside by Dubois and had worked well for the company.

One of them suggested to Dubois that perhaps Legrande's enthusiasm for centralization was just an attempt by the family to take back the reins of power and authority.

Twelve months previously, Dubois had compromised by setting up a coordinating function that was supervised by Legrande. It had limited powers to iron out some of the divisional anomalies in purchasing, distribution and marketing.

Some coordination did take place, mainly in the purchasing area. But it was at the expense of board meetings that became more and more acrimonious and argumentative.

Events seemed to be heading for a showdown between the three divisional board members on the one hand and Legrande – backed, Dubois suspected, by the finance director – on the other.

Legrande was outvoted on the board. But then Dubois learned that Legrande had the backing of one of the two major shareholders in believing that he, Dubois, had been too half-hearted in centralizing the company with his compromise plan.

Dubois could see a scenario in his mind's eye in which he was replaced as president by Legrande.

He honestly felt that there was still much to be said for divisional autonomy. He felt that the gesture he had made towards centralization was just about right, given the present situation both in the company and among the competition.

But what should he do? If he sided with the divisional chiefs in an open fight with Legrande, he would invite intervention from at least one of the principal shareholders and perhaps his own removal.

If he pushed through much greater centralization against the wishes of half the board, two of whose members he himself had appointed, at best he would lose credibility and at worst there might be resignations by men the company could ill afford to lose.

DECISION

Dubois should concentrate on the best interests of the firm

The board of Decoration SA is divided. Personal axes are being ground over an issue which has been raised on a matter of principle. Dubois' first job must be to re-establish a common purpose for everyone to consider.

Presumably, things have not yet gone so far that the board members would rather see the company fail altogether than yield. Dubois should therefore seek to concentrate their minds on a more important issue. This must be the faltering in the company's rate of growth.

It is most unlikely that decentralization actually caused that faltering. Centralization could at best reduce costs and thereby increase profitability at a time of shrinking margins. However, continued decentralization could provide the best chance of speedy reaction to changes in the market place.

Consider other options

But no great amount of thought appears to have been given to the costs and benefits of the options facing the company. The issue has quickly become a matter of principle unrelated to facts. Members of the board are shadow-boxing while the company sinks into the mire.

The narrow issue of centralization versus decentralization must be moved from the boardroom agenda and transferred to the consultants' or corporate planners' office, to get the facts sorted out objectively. The main issue of the company's future must be brought back to the boardroom, where it properly belongs.

It is not clear whether Decoration SA means to operate as an industrial holding company or as an integrated enterprise. In either case, it is doubtful whether it should weight its main board so heavily with representatives of the operating subsidiaries.

Dubois must make the point to the operating divisional directors that their continued presence on the main board, to a large extent, depends on their acceptance that the group is the directing force of the enterprise.

This question of divisional chief executives on the main board is often a tricky one.

It is good that the men who are responsible for a large proportion of a firm's profits should be recognized and in a position to influence corporate policy.

On the other hand, the first responsibility of the board of directors is the business as a whole and, therefore, to measure the group's existing resources against any possible future developments.

Divisional chief executives are not always able to do this objectively when their primary job is to meet divisional targets.

If the company is large enough, it is probably better to have divisional chiefs below board level and directors with overall responsibility for parts of the business, including individual divisions or groups of divisions.

In small to medium-sized companies, of course, this may not be possible. However, in the case of Decoration SA, the divisional directors seem to be numerically too strong. The addition of one or two good non-executive directors should be considered.

I do not envy Dubois. A great deal will depend upon his diplomacy in getting his colleagues to sink their differences. I am sure his best hope lies in getting them to work on the strategic issues of the future of the company as a whole. This would both enable them to put the centralization issue in perspective and open the way to their acceptance of non-executive directors.

This decision was provided by Jan Hildreth in his capacity as director-general of the Institute of Directors in the U.K.

DILEMMA

Where should German firm locate new plant?

Hans Hundig, chairman of Schwartzwald AG, a medium-sized but fast-expanding German electronics company, was uncertain what to recommend at a board meeting next day.
He had returned from his holiday hoping that the problem of where to locate a new manufacturing plant would be settled. However, he now had news from Brazil which complicated the issue.

The major Brazilian supplier of components to the Schwartzwald subsidiary there had been taken over by a U.S. multinational, which indicated that the Schwartzwald contract would not be renewed.

Schwartzwald already had marketing companies in ten countries outside Germany. It also had manufacturing facilities in the U.K. and Brazil.

It wanted to expand an existing consumer product in a country where labour costs would enable it to compete more effectively with electronics produced in the Far East. One possibility had been to expand in Brazil. But Hundig had also commissioned studies which explored siting a plant in Ireland, Portugal, Africa and the Far East. Two of these studies had favoured Ireland, since that country was also well situated geographically for the intended markets.

Just to complicate matters, Schwartzwald also wanted to produce a new sophisticated electronic gadget overseas. This was a departure for the company since, in the past, the more highly "value added" products had been manufactured in Germany.

However, most members of the management board felt that if Schwartzwald were ever to break into the big league, internationally, it had to be prepared to manufacture overseas not only its relatively simple products but also some of its more advanced products. They had recommended this to the supervisory board although they knew that the worker representatives on that board would have preferred to keep the production in Germany.

Facing up to three long-term alternatives

On holiday, Hundig had decided on Ireland rather than Brazil for the low-cost product, since the surveys made a convincing case in its favour. The main contender for the new sophisticated product was the U.K., where the product idea had originated and the managing director was keen to expand. Hundig, however, had decided to throw his weight behind those who favoured a more costly incursion into the U.S.

Then came the Brazilian bombshell. The takeover of a supplier meant that the company had lost a major independent source of supply – and gained a formidable competitor.

Now, Hundig mused, there were just three long-term alternatives in Brazil. One was to find an alternative supplier within the country, an almost impossible task. Another was to set up an entirely new Brazilian plant to make components. The third was to close down manufacturing there altogether, and treat Brazil purely as a marketing operation.

Hundig knew that both the production and marketing directors were against terminating production in Brazil. He was faced, however, with a memo from the finance director which pointed out that building a components plant in Brazil was hardly justified by current turnover.

It would be possible to build the projected low labour-cost plant in Brazil, however, under the same roof as a new components plant, and thereby minimize construction costs. But that would mean abandoning his objective first choice, Ireland.

To make matters worse, the finance director pointed out that whatever happened in Brazil the extra costs would mean that the company had not the financial resources to place the new sophisticated product in the U.S., as planned. It would have to be deferred, sited in the U.K., where a subsidiary already existed, or manufactured in Germany.

Hundig sighed. Putting it in the U.K. would mean taking a gamble on industrial peace. Manufacturing it in Germany would be something of a climb-down after the arguments that he personally had advanced, on behalf of the management board, to the supervisory board.

"What," he said to himself, "*should* I recommend tomorrow?"

Delaying the decision may be the best answer

Hundig is facing the pressure to make a recommendation to his board, when it is painfully obvious that he and his management team have done an inadequate job in defining either their product strategies or the external factors affecting their strategic decisions.

I believe the unexpected events in Brazil, which should have been foreseen, provide Hundig with ample justification to ask the supervisory board for a delay in the decision-making. At first sight this may seem a negative solution. But sometimes it is necessary to backtrack in order to move forward again.

The loss of the Brazilian manufacturing facility would take at least a year to replace, with a new plant supplying the necessary components. Unless these components can be supplied from the U.K. or Germany, the Brazilian company to all intents and purposes, is out of business.

The loss of this, one of the three or four major growth markets in the world, must necessitate a reassessment of the company's strategy. This would be the justification for asking the supervisory board to ignore prior recommendations and wait a few months for the presentation of a revised strategic plan.

The Schwartzwald case is not unusual. Many companies find themselves today in a dilemma regarding both their basic product strategies and their ability to define, and evaluate, the external forces which could affect their strategies.

Consider changing the manufacturing strategy

Each product strategy must define the relative strength of the product in regional and global markets. Schwartzwald management appears to be making the classic mistake of defining basic product strategy in terms of prior commitments. A strategy reassessment must take place within a mental framework of starting out from the beginning, with no entanglements, or commitments

Hopefully they will find at the end of the process that they have strengths in their present sourcing locations. If that turns out to be wrong, they must begin the long and painful process of changing their manufacturing strategy to fit the realities of the overall product strategy.

Hundig has two product strategies to define. He must solve the dilemma of the present product line before he can intelligently tackle the questions relating to the newer, more sophisticated product line.

If strategic studies indicate that the present products have business strengths and growth potential in both Europe and Brazil, the location of a new production facility would depend primarily on the present and future logistics issues. The history of labour costs is that they eventually catch up wherever you start out. The major emphasis in the electronics industry, therefore, should be on relative rates of productivity. This, assumes that all marketing issues are equal – which they rarely are.

Hundig should reassess his strategy on the existing product line. I am inclined to think such a study will lean towards filling the void in Brazil, because of its much greater growth potential and lower labour costs.

The decisions reached on existing product line strategy clearly will greatly affect the definition of business strengths of the new product line. If definition of business strengths indicates technological leadership, but a lack of cash, Hundig may want to seek a joint venture partner in the U.S.

He must step back, reassess the company's business strengths and define precise business strategies for both product lines. He also needs to identify and evaluate the external non-market forces which could affect each alternative strategy.

If he carries out this process he should be able to convince the worker representatives on the supervisory board, his fellow managers and the local works council that his recommendations are soundly thought out and make the most sense for the long-term best interests of the company, its shareholders and employees.

This decision was provided by John Alan James in his capacity as head of the Brussels-based consultancy Management Counsellors International SA.

Should family firm take financial risk and fight U.S. competitor?

For as long as anyone could remember, Abonos Ceres SA had been one of Latin America's principal manufacturers of fertilizers. The family-owned company had built up a strong reputation over two generations and was very well-known for dependability of supplies. The company had never found it necessary to go in for much advertising or marketing. It was known to everyone in agriculture. Farmers asked for its products by brand name.

But now the commanding position the company had so carefully built up over the years was in jeopardy. A U.S. chemicals conglomerate, Agro-Makers Inc., was suddenly threatening to become a direct competitor to Abonos Ceres.

"The Americans are not interested in fair competition," Román Tique, president of Abonos Ceres, told his brother. "They want to dominate the market. They leave only the less profitable customers to their competitors, I fear."

Tique and his brother were the grandsons of the founder of the company. They managed the group together and held equal shares with their sister. They all lived comfortably off the dividends.

Leon Rampa, president of Veta Fina, the firm's main supplier of phosphate, had informed the two brothers that the American multinational had made a bid to take over his company for $10 million. It was Rampa's understanding that the U.S. group was planning to buy the company as part of its strategy to expand throughout the Andean Pact countries which Abonos Ceres now served.

Rampa informed the Tique brothers that he had virtually decided to accept the Americans' offer. He considered it only right, however, to offer them the first option to buy his company.

On the face of it, Rampa's offer was an attractive one. It would enable Abonos Ceres to control its main source of supply. It would safeguard the company against potential shortages and help ensure dependable deliveries. It would also give the company greater strength with which to compete against the American conglomerate.

The price was high, however. Tique calculated that the company would have to use almost its entire financial reserves, and would have to tighten its credit terms with the farmers, most of whom were small and barely making a living. Moreover, the three shareholders would have to forfeit receiving any dividends for the next year or two. There was also a real possibility they would receive less than half the normal dividends for some years to come.

The company would have to borrow heavily from the bank and would be faced with an acute cash flow problem.

In addition, the company would have to adopt much more aggressive management methods to run the greatly expanded business. This would certainly be the case if it had to compete against the American group.

It was highly probable that even if Abonos Ceres succeeded in taking over Veta Fina, the American group would still be able to establish itself in the market. "There is no question about it," Tique told his brother. "If the American group does manage to establish itself here it will do everything to drive us out of business."

He recalled how the same American company had set up in Mexico a few years previously. It had undercut by about 40% the prices of an old-established Mexican firm, which was eventually forced out of business. The U.S. firm then raised its prices to normal levels.

In the past the Tique brothers had always followed the advice of their father, who had constantly warned about getting too big and losing personal contact with the farmers. Certainly the two brothers had never intended to manage a mammoth enterprise.

It now seemed, however, that they had little choice. They either had to expand dramatically or face the prospect of going out of business.

DECISION

Small firm must be prepared to defend its market

In this case, two different business environments are in opposition. On the one side there is a well established, highly reputable family company, well-known for its goods.

This respectable, profit-oriented company is about to be challenged by a highly efficient and determined multinational organization.

Certainly, the present organizational structure of Abonos Ceres does not give rise to optimism. The family owners are also operating directors, which is not unusual for such a company. But a business which is run by owners who have inherited it is not necessarily an efficient business.

To know customers personally is very cosy. But it usually does not pay to be on too friendly terms with them.

Abonos Ceres has probably always made a reasonable profit, but has probably never tried to expand beyond what was strictly necessary.

It is possible that as Abonos Ceres has never tried to develop its market fully there is room for competitors as well. What is important is that Abonos Ceres should not lose its present share of the market.

In my opinion, Abonos Ceres must be prepared to defend its market. It is, at present, the market leader, so Agro-Makers will have to take up the offensive, if it wants to break into the market.

Abonos Ceres should realize that it does not have the organizational structure to allow it to manage a company that expands greatly overnight. However, the American company has probably assumed that Abonos Ceres has sufficient financial resources to put up a fight for some time. In this event, Agro-Makers' strategy may well have been to give the impression that it is about to buy Veta Fina in the hope that this will stampede Abonos Ceres itself into rushing to buy Veta Fina. This would commit the local firm to investing all its financial resources.

Having said this, it should not be overlooked that Agro-Makers is a large multinational organization, with vast financial resources of its own. But it is probably looking for a far higher percentage return on its investments than Abonos Ceres is content with.

Accept every challenge

It has probably decided to invest part of its financial resources in Latin America because it has seen the possibility of a better return there than somewhere else. Certainly it will be counting on a handsome return on investment. The pay-back period it is prepared to consider may be two, three or four years. We do not know. But undoubtedly this will have all been worked out in great detail.

For one reason or another it may become apparent to the U.S. firm that either the pay-back period is likely to be longer than anticipated or that the return on investment is going to be less than expected. In this event someone back at headquarters will soon be having second thoughts.

So, in my opinion, Abonos Ceres only has one way to survive. It must defend its market vigorously by accepting every challenge that Agro-Makers throws at it. This will of course mean employing Abonos Ceres' financial resources in the fight for survival. It will probably mean doing without profits for some time to come but the company should hold on to its market doggedly. If Agro-Makers reduces its prices by 40%, Abonos Ceres should do the same. Customers will then have no special reason to buy Agro-Makers' products. Again, if Agro-Makers appoints a set of specialists to demonstrate to farmers how to use fertilizers more effectively, Abonos Ceres must do something similar. If Agro-Makers buys Veta Fina, Abonos Ceres must find an alternative supplier.

It very much depends on how much money the two firms are able to commit to the contest. Undoubtedly, Agro-Makers will not employ a disproportionate amount of its available worldwide resources to this one market. And it may be it has far less money to play with than Abonos Ceres imagines. However, Abonos Ceres should not shrink from the battle. The most likely outcome is that the market will expand and there will be room for both firms.

This decision was provided by Mario Fantechi in his capacity as director of Coopers & Lybrand SpA, management consultants, in Milan, Italy.

Can firm manage without government support?

A nton Rosenkrantz was furious. Yet another policy document from the government had ruined his company's forward planning. Although a public firm quoted on the stock exchange, chemicals company Rumbolt & Cie. was 40% owned by the government, which was the main shareholder and appointed four of the ten directors. As such, the government put pressure on Rosenkrantz and his board colleagues to set an example in conforming to government economic policies.

At the beginning of the year it had issued a request for companies not to invest in an African country. This country had begun to interfere in the affairs of a neighbouring state in which Rosenkrantz's government had considerable interests. Rosenkrantz had only been out to the African country a few weeks before to iron out some minor problems in a promised contract to supply a fertilizer plant. When Rumbolt attempted to stall the contract until the political situation eased up, the African minister responsible abruptly cancelled it.

Continual controversial directives

An unexpected directive from the interior ministry had also put back a new product launch by several weeks, at a cost of more than $200,000. Rumbolt had spent considerable time and effort discussing with the industry ministry how to pack the mildly toxic chemicals produced by a new plant. The minister had given the company an outline of the packaging regulations he was about to introduce and had advised Rosenkrantz to plan his packaging and transporting arrangements in accordance with them. Only days before the product launch, however, the minister had suddenly changed his mind, under unexpected pressure from an environmental group. He introduced far more stringent standards than originally planned and refused to give the chemical products official clearance. Rumbolt was left with several hundred thousand bags of chemicals all of which had to be opened and repacked.

Another directive from the industry ministry put pressure on Rumbolt to phase out some of its road transport fleet in order to send some of its chemicals by the loss-making rail service. Having spent an extra $1 million to site the new plant near a motorway rather than near the railway, the company was understandably annoyed.

Facing the frustration of losing company control

Now the ministry wanted the company to halt a planned programme of redundancies. The new plant had taken up capacity from two old and inefficient sites, which could now be run down. The savings from the redundancies and from selling the sites would more than cover an $18 million loan which the government had made the company just under a year ago.

"I will not do it," Rosenkrantz declared to his deputy, white-haired Bernt Schirm. "Do you realize that if I put every one of these petty government interferences into the wastepaper-basket, we should be one of the most profitable firms in Europe? As things are, though, we could be in trouble within 18 months.

"It is not just the nuisance of having to liaise with civil servants who know nothing about the chemicals industry and the cost and time to prepare detailed reports for government departments. It is the sheer frustration of no longer being in control of the company."

Two days later he told the minister: "From now on this company is putting profit first and social obligations second. If the government wants to freeze our redundancy programme it will have to pass a law to do it. This company is responsible to all its shareholders – not just the government."

"You are not in much of a position to argue," retorted the minister. "You know I have the authority to revoke investment grants and cut tax credits. I certainly will not hesitate to use it if you do not cooperate with us. If I really wanted to put pressure on the firm, I could call in the loan that the government made you last year, or insist on exchanging it for a majority shareholding. If you cannot keep a healthy company and meet your social obligations, then maybe a new chairman is needed."

Rumbolt was left in a quandary. The redundancy programme had to start within the next two weeks if it was going to effect the necessary savings. He was confident that, even if the minister carried out his ultimate threat to call in the loan, he could raise the money via a recent large customer in the Middle East, pending the sale of the old plant sites. But it was a highly risky venture deliberately to confront the government. Was he justified in gambling with the shareholders' interests in such a way?

DECISION

Rosenkrantz should consider his strengths

Anton Rosenkrantz's chances of operating effectively depend very largely on how important he regards the government interest in his group. If he believes he has enough strength in the rest of the company to ignore the government directives, both now and especially in the long term, he should by all means do what he thinks best for the company. By this I am referring to the government not as a shareholder but as a legislator and supporter of industry. The fact that the government is a minority shareholder in this case does not seem to be all that relevant.

Rosenkrantz's real problem is his attitude which resembles that of a manager used to making decisions in circumstances that prevailed decades ago. The economic system of the Western industrialized countries has gone through a fundamental structural change during the past ten or 20 years. Decision making has become considerably polarized by trade unions and other pressure groups on the one side and by the strengthening role of the public sector on the other. The public authorities have some powerful tools at their disposal.

Government now deals with legislation concerning many industrial policies. For example, it is involved in the regulation of work safety, environmental protection, the use of the company's labour force and the location of industry.

The public authorities also now provide direct support to private companies, such as professional training, research allowances, special loans, financial support to industry in developing areas and in matters of foreign trade policy.

Social objectives may have to be considered

Anton Rosenkrantz states that "this company is putting profit first and social obligations second". We are here approaching one of the basic principles in our economic system. What are the main criteria in a socially-oriented society which should be used to appraise the operations of an industrial enterprise? In a market economy it was simply the maximization of profit. But it is questionable whether we are still living in a market economy.

It has been suggested that the so-called social objectives should be incorporated in a company's main policy objectives in the same way that the maximization of profit is. To some extent I agree with those who maintain that the pursuit of profit, of maximum profit in the long term, should remain as the main criterion of appraising a company's achievements. But what has changed is indicated by Rosenkrantz's angry remark to Bernt Schrim: "It is the sheer frustration of no longer being in control of the company."

The pursuit of profit cannot any longer be carried out by freely chosen means, but under the constraints created by the expectations of various interest groups, including the public sector. These interest groups also have the power to have their expectations carried out. Decision making in industry is now profit maximization under severe constraint.

These are the circumstances under which Rosenkrantz must operate and on which his chances rest.

In my opinion, Rosenkrantz should adapt himself to the times and accept the change in the decision-making conditions.

This means he should proceed as follows:

● Try to foresee the expectations of the public sector concerning his company in good time.

● Find out which of the expectations of the public sector he can influence and which of them he must merely accept as a fact of life.

● Try to influence government authorities, no matter how frustrating it is to deal with "civil servants who know nothing about the chemicals industry", as he puts it. Perhaps a formalized system for passing on information to politicians and civil servants would gradually decrease their ignorance. Moreover, it is only through continuous personal contact that one learns how to deal well with both partners and opponents. Don Quixote lost his fight against the windmills because of his ignorance.

● Try to adapt himself to facts he cannot influence. An old prayer says: "My Lord, give me strength to accept things which cannot be changed. Give me courage to change things which can and ought to be changed. And give me the wisdom to distinguish one from the other."

This decision was provided Antero Kallio in his capacity as managing director of management consultants Oy Mec-Rastor AB based in Helsinki, Finland.

How can the top man push an agreement through managers who are stalling?

Sixteen months ago Jan van der Pijl, president of a Dutch surgical equipment firm, attended a management seminar staged on a yacht cruising the Greek Islands. During the session he struck an immediate friendship with a British manufacturer of hotel and restaurant uniforms who had a few weeks earlier diversified into disposable babies' napkins. Stimulated by the daily lectures and the evening rounds of ouzo, the two men came up with the idea of merging their companies.

It had started as a joke. Andrew Evans had suggested that through van der Pijl's operations in Holland, Germany, Belgium and France, and his own outlets in the U.K., Ireland and France, they could capture the European disposable nappy market. Van der Pijl had laughingly rejoined: "Yes, and I could diversify into safety pins to fasten the nappies." Then van der Pijl suggested that if Evans would produce uniforms and bandages, his salesmen could sell them to the hospitals. Evans retorted that perhaps van der Pijl could produce table cutlery as well as scalpels, which his salesmen could sell to hotels. As the seminar went on, the men continued exploring these ideas, becoming progressively more serious. By the end of the course they had agreed in principle to merge.

New firm to be split into thirds

As soon as the value of the two firms had been established by an independent auditor, van der Pijl announced the merger to his employees. He said that he and Evans would each hold a one-third interest in the firm. Shares in the remaining third would be offered to employees. This would put the deciding vote in the hands of the employees should he and Evans reach an impasse. And the employees would get a direct participation in the fortunes of the group.

As no one showed any visible reaction, he asked for questions. The managing director of the Belgian operations spoke up: "Presumably they will be in charge of the British and Irish operations, but what about France, where we both have companies?"

Van der Pijl answered: "Rather than deciding anything rigid and inflexible at the top, we plan to have the negotiating and bargaining done by the very people involved in making the merger work. When everything is worked out, then we will sign the papers, and you will have a chance to buy stock."

A day later he flew to London to be on hand while Evans made a similar announcement. Here, too, reaction was muted.

As the months passed, negotiations at the second and third levels of management were fraught with delays and petty squabbles. One day van der Pijl even had to speak sharply to some third level managers who were stubbornly insisting on speaking Dutch, though they were all quite fluent in English.

Now, three days later, Johannes Grijs, vice-president in charge of the Dutch operation entered van der Pijl's office.

He had just come from an impromptu meeting of the national managing directors. "We're all unhappy about this merger," he said. When he paused, van der Pijl urged him: "Please speak frankly about this trouble." Grijs went on: "As you know, their top managers are organized on product lines, and we are organized by countries. We fought this out for six months, and finally agreed on a matrix, where the sales and product people report to two bosses. But there is no resolution of final authority, and we don't really feel the system is workable.

"And then our sales people are balking at having to sell uniforms. They claim it would destroy our quality image in surgical equipment. And production don't want paper nappy salesmen selling their instruments.

"I think we've learned a lot from these discussions. We all agree we should extend our operations throughout the Common Market. But we feel that as the larger company, we should maintain control. Or we should drop the merger idea and set up national subsidiaries in England, Ireland, Denmark and Italy on our own, selling our quality product."

Van der Pijl pondered the situation. The expanded Common Market was a reality. He needed to make some positive move to capitalize on this. Yet despite his own enthusiasm and efforts, his employees had failed to take advantage of this obvious opportunity. Should he telephone Evans, and suggest the two of them hammer out a detailed agreement, and hand it to their employees on a"take it or leave it" basis? Or should he terminate merger talks, and try to expand in his own limited line?

DECISION

Companies ought to develop their own growth strategies

An Aegean cruise is a wonderful way to form a friendship, but it is a hell of a way to decide on a merger. Unfortunately, this situation isn't too unusual. It usually happens when you put together a couple of highly imaginative super salesmen, dazzled by their own romanticism.

But this is an impossible merger. There is a whole series of incompatibilities. The product lines are incompatible. The first thing van der Pijl and Evans do is to begin talking about the *new* products they will make! Manufacturing technologies of the two companies are incompatible. Channels of distribution and customers are incompatible.

Even assuming there were some basis for cooperation, Evans and van der Pijl seem to have abdicated all management responsibility as soon as the ouzo supply dried up. They cannot simply assign vague responsibility to everyone in the companies to put together something as unpredicatable as a merger. They must offer top-level leadership, set the guide-lines for the merger and make final decisions.

The two principals need not sit in on the day-to-day negotiations. These can be handled by a joint committee of high-ranking executives from the two companies. Ideally, the representatives of the major functions or divisions should be represented on this committee. Or they can assign an outside consultancy to the task of drawing up recommendations. This might bring more objectivity into solving conflicts between the two companies.

262

In any event van der Pijl and Evans have made a mistake by bringing so many people into the negotiations and decision-making process. They have correctly recognized that it is important for all individuals who will be affected by the merger to get a chance to speak their piece. However, this can be accomplished by having the group charged with drawing up recommendations conduct interviews throughout the company. If this group establishes itself as being impartial, it raises the whole level of thinking about the merger. They begin talking to people about the merger. They begin talking to people about "what are the opportunities for synergism?" They seek advice from individuals, not only about their own domain, but also about how the individual's expertise can help the broader organization. When this approach is taken, there is a very good chance of coming up with a "best answer" for organizing the merger.

Aim for company-wide acceptance

On the basic issues, such as whether to organize along geographical or product lines, there is almost always one solution which is rationally superior. My experience suggests that on technical or organizational issues you can find a best answer to something like 98% of the questions.

Based on this information, the committee can work out recommendations on how the merger should be organized. However, before submitting these recommendations, it would be a good idea to review them with everyone who will be affected. This will give the employees a final opportunity to challenge any recommendation they have misgivings about. It also gives the committee an ideal opportunity to explain the rationale behind its moves in order to win company-wide acceptance.

However, even proper implementation would not have saved this merger. It would have simply flushed out the problems much sooner.

At this point, Evans and van der Pijl should stop the merger talks and go back to square one. Each of these companies has got to set its own growth objectives in sales, in earnings and in return on investment. The companies must then decide whether they can attain these objectives in their present business. They should first identify their own internal resources such as management, specialist know-how, technological know-how and capital. They must also identify which of these areas represent constraints on growth.

Then the companies must develop their own growth strategies. The initial growth effort should be through existing products, services and markets. If, after examining these areas, they find they must diversify to attain growth objectives, then the companies should establish such diversification criteria as kinds of businesses, kinds of markets, types of technologies, size of operations and location of markets. Only after these factors are determined should the companies begin a search for possible partners. Various modes of business cooperation must be considered, including acquisition, merger, joint venture or even licensing.

Only then can top management really expect the full cooperation of their subordinates in the difficult task of welding two companies together. If either Evans or van der Pijl discovers a compatible merger partner, then he must put more than a few sun-soaked days on the Aegean into guiding it through to completion.

This decision was provided by Georges Petitpas in his capacity as European director for U.S. consultancy Cresap, McCormick & Paget Inc. Brussels.

Should new plant be built abroad to emphasize an international image?

Flochem is a U.K. chemical firm with yearly sales of $60 million. That makes it a small competitor in an industry dominated by global giants. Its three manufacturing divisions produce fertilizers, crop protection products and pharmaceuticals. Flochem is well established in its chosen sectors of each of these markets.

It has an international division, which markets all its products outside the U.K. The problem managing director Jonathan Priestley faces is a dispute between the pharmaceutical and international divisions over the site of a new $5-million plant to make animal foodstuff additives.

Pharmaceutical division manager John Lock thinks that it should be built in the north-east of England. This would place it near the division's main plants. Henri Lussac, the Belgian hired from outside to head the international division on its formation two years ago, argues for the plant to be built in the Netherlands.

So far the international division activities have been restricted to marketing and distribution of U.K.-made products. By the time the dispute reaches Priestley, a lot of work has gone into sifting the facts. Priestley's young business graduate assistant, who coordinates group planning, has summarized the case on both sides.

New plant should be home-based

Lock argues that the plant must be near his base, because the production technology is new and difficult. His technical staff and research scientists ought to be able to be on hand to help if any crisis arises in the early days of running the plant.

Anyway, Lock continues, a move to Europe would mark the first direct overseas investment by the company. Surely it would only be adding to the predictable difficulties of the technically innovative venture to have the plant built in a foreign country. The overseas move should await an easier plant, in the technical sense.

The English site is well placed for exporting to the Continent. A nearby container port on the English North Sea coast is well equipped to handle the plant's product and deliver it to major Continental ports.

Finally, Lock concludes, his division shows the highest return-on-capital and output-per-employee figures in the company. He is worried that he might not be able to maintain strict managerial control if the plant were in the Netherlands or Belgium.

Lock's fears on this score are fed by the suspicion that his Belgian colleague, Lussac, wants the international division to have a large say in managing the plant, even though it should belong in the pharmaceutical division.

Lussac is impatient with the arguments put forward by Lock. He regards Lock as an insular Englishman in an international business world. Lussac has repeatedly turned up in Priestley's London office, often at short notice, on some pretext to press his case.

First, argues Lussac, the marketing people predict that at least 60% of the plant's product will sell in Europe rather than the U.K. They foresee a continued drive to improve agricultural efficiency in European Economic Community countries as the group enlarges.

With this practical argument to back up his claim that it is time for Flochem to become more involved in Europe, Lussac has an apparently powerful case. No longer is it enough just to export one's products, he says. Where it makes business sense, he would like to see the company build several plants in Europe.

Apart from these long-term points, Lussac points to the labour troubles in England and to the higher output per man achieved in European chemical plants. Also, construction would be quicker, with fewer planning hurdles for the project to overcome.

The technical expertise problem does not matter, he continues. The men can be flown in from the U.K. when any problem arises. Suitable men to operate and supervise the plant could be hired in either the Netherlands or Belgium.

Looking through the well-documented arguments of both sides, Priestley notes that they both have effective points. The difficulties of setting up and running a new process plant are a major cause of concern with him. The company had troubles with its last new plant in the U.K. five years earlier. Production was late and more expensive in the first three years than planned. So Lock's cautious approach has appeal.

On the other hand, he is struck by the far-sighted view of Lussac. Of the two men, he has to admit that Lock appears from his record to be the more effective manager, with a ruthless eye for detail and a passion for keeping costs and objectives right on the target line.

With the arguments so finely balanced, he wonders about the long-term effects of a decision to invest in Europe at this point. What would it mean for the company, and is it properly organized to cope with a more international spread? Who should manage the plant, and how would Lock and Lussac work together, if the plant goes to the Netherlands?

DECISION

Company should treat Europe as an extension of the U.K. market

Priestley could not take a decision on this dilemma without considering further information. All the arguments put forth are important, but they are purely qualitative. Quantitative arguments are needed to bring the issue more clearly into focus.

Nonetheless, many decisions must be taken with limited facts. Or the quantitative factors are sometimes evenly balanced. So, based on the arguments given in the case, I would favour the Netherlands. But I would have the plant managed by the U.K. pharmaceutical division.

Before going on to give my reasons for that decision, I would like to identify the additional data needed for a thoroughly researched decision. Essentially what Priestley needs is a comparison of operating costs, capital costs, profitability and return on investment.

To arrive at this, he needs: volume forecasts by market over a five-year period; investment forecasts for each site in terms of land, building and equipment; any investment grants or tax concessions at the respective sites; source and cost of raw materials for both sites; destination and cost of distribution to respective markets for both sites; estimates of labour and overhead costs; working capital requirements.

Based on these he could get a comparison of return on investment. This could also be done with a discounted cash flow calculation.

But these figures might show little significant differences between the sites, and the decision must still be made. This brings me to my reasons for favouring the Netherlands.

In the first place, the company is rather small. Assuming it has the financial resources, it should probably seize the growth opportunities of a broader Europe or be threatened by a takeover. The firm is in three product areas (fertilizer, crop protection and pharmaceuticals) that are characterized by major competitors that operate on a European scale.

Flochem must also be prepared to operate on this scale in the future. A European facility would be the first step in this direction.

Pharmaceutical division to retain control

I would not share the pharmaceutical manager's concern about Holland as an initial overseas location for an English company. It is, of course, the most English sector of continental Europe, in the sense that it already has the Anglo-Dutch companies, Shell and Unilever. Moreover, it is only a short distance from the north-east of England where the pharmaceutical division manager wants to build.

Another factor is not only the cost of building but also the time factor. The U.K. chemical industry has been plagued with plant completion and start-up costs over the past few years. I know of three major catastrophes that immediately come to mind.

Flochem itself admits to similar problems in the past. These delays have a terrific adverse effect on any return on investment calculation.

Accordingly, I would be more confident of getting the plant on stream according to plan in Holland – though I would certainly second technicians and engineers to the project from England to help in getting the plant built and working.

As to operating costs, although we do not have the basis for a true comparison, I would suspect they favour Holland. The ruling factor would probably be the distribution advantage.

The European market is admittedly 60% of the total – although the opportunities should be higher than this figure. I would not expect the plant to be labour intensive for the type of product, so labour costs should not be a compelling issue.

Finally, there is the organization question. I would be inclined to keep the plant under the U.K. pharmaceutical manager to maintain that division as a profit centre. I am assuming that the new products will complement the existing line. Following through on this, I would no longer treat the continent of Europe as an export market, but rather as an extension of the U.K. market.

Ironically, then, the European manager would see the decision go in his favour, but lose his organizational role – at least for pharmaceutical sales. At the same time if the Englishman is insular at present, he should soon lose that characteristic. He might even learn Dutch.

This decision was provided by F. Newton Parks in his capacity as managing director, Europe, of consultants Booz, Allen & Hamilton.

Should funds be allocated for a new acquisiton or for consolidation?

Heetman Maatschappij NV is a Dutch corporation making heating systems for industrial, construction and domestic markets. Johan Heethoofd, the managing director, has built it up since 1964, when sales were $18 million from a range of factory space heaters. He added two divisions. One sells electric ducted-air heating to house-building contractors, the other makes household fans and fume extractors. Total sales are now $40 million, and profits are a healthy $8 million.

Heethoofd has taken the company into all the West European markets, using both travelling salesmen and local agents. The industrial division, headed by Bernard Brand, remains the backbone, selling $18 million, with profits of $4 million.

Ger Straal is head of the domestic heating division, which has annual sales of $14 million and profits of $3 million. The newest and smallest division makes household fans and extractors. It is led by Rijn Zonneschijn, and it has sales of $8 million and profits of $1 million.

Like the chief executive, Heethoofd, these divisional directors are all entrepreneurial types. But in 1967 Heethoofd appointed a young business graduate, Jan Ijsman, to corporate planning. Ijsman had excelled in his contribution to the development of the industrial and domestic heating divisions. His surveys and predictions had guided their planning so that they are able to bring in new products and regain their 14% annual growth rate, which had dipped in 1966 to only 5%.

Division must widen its range

But now Heethoofd was faced with a conflict between Ijsman and Zonneschijn of the household fans division. Ijsman was recommending a course of action which ran entirely counter to Zonneschijn's entrepreneurial instincts. It was the first time there had been any serious conflict between the planner and the line managers.

Until now, Heethoofd had been pleased with the way they had accepted the bright young planner who was only 32, eight years younger than Zonneschijn, the youngest of the line managers.

The background to this dispute concerned a new product, already launched, and the need to quickly launch more new products. As usual Ijsman had discussed the short and long-term future with Zonneschijn before either put anything on paper for the annual update of the five-year plan which would be the next step.

Both agreed on the need for the division to widen its product range. They agreed the best way to do this was through acquisition within the next two years. Ijsman was to investigate likely small companies which had the products, the expertise and the plant for making more elaborate air-conditioning products for the home.

In the meantime, Zonneschijn was busy with the promotion of a new luxury, copper-covered oven hood. This product extracted all the cooking smells while adding a pleasing touch to the appearance of a kitchen. It was sold mainly in expensive department stores in Europe's capital cities.

267

After several favourable mentions in consumer magazines, the oven hood sales boomed until they were ahead of stocks. Soon Zonneschijn faced a crisis: so many agents and customers were demanding stocks that he was having to quote six months' delivery of replenishments to them. Already several important stores had delivered ultimatums. They threatened to stop orders for not only this product but Zonneschijn's other lines, unless he could improve deliveries.

Zonneschijn's response was to draft proposals for spending $1 million on a factory extension, which could come into production over the next year, since the site had previously been cleared. However, his request for the capital came to Heethoofd at the same time as Ijsman delivered his proposal to acquire a company that met all the requirements outlined in the plan. And the time to buy the company was now, to take advantage of its low price, depressed by poor results. The bad results, said Ijsman, were solely due to bad management, and Heetman NV would be able to use the resources of the company much more efficiently. The price of $3 million would use all Heetman's disposable profit if it were financed that way.

Realizing that he could not spend money on both, Heethoofd called the managers to a meeting. Zonneschijn said the new acquisition would have to wait. His whole marketing posture was affected by the sudden success of the oven hood. Surely it would be good business sense to take advantage of this success. Anyway, he remarked pointedly, if Ijsman's planning was so good, why had he not been able to foresee the 150% increase in demand for the oven hood?

Ijsman dismissed this attack. The oven hood sales were a short-term boom, which would soon fade. There was no need for extra capacity; instead they should proceed with the acquisition which was in the plan.

DECISION

Managing director should try to have his cake and eat it

The case appears to be a classic example of stalemate between an operations manager and a staff planner. But is there any reason for conflict at all? The managing director should regard the problem as a challenge to select the best methods of achieving growth rather than as a choice between two alternative courses of action.

Thus he should, as objectively as possible, scrutinize both projects in the light of the plan. He should also take account of changes in the market and the firm's resources.

A major observation about Heetman is that the personal relationships are as important as the business decisions. The managing director has developed a successful top management team that backs creative and aggressive management with sound staff work. The future of the company depends on the continuing motivation of both groups of men and on their working together.

The managing director needs to recognize that he must at all costs carry his team with him. To do this he must be objective. One of the key factors in this type of situation is that there will be very little reliable information on which to base a decision, and no time to carry out further detailed market research.

Nevertheless, it is still possible to appraise both projects independently as business opportunities, and to reach a decision based on such information and know-how as may be available within the company. The scarcity of resources and consequent possible need to proceed with only one of the projects should not be taken into account until it is confirmed that both are commercially viable.

Find resources to finance both projects

The viability of the $1 million factory extension will depend on the management team being reasonably convinced that there is a worthwhile continuing market for copper-covered oven hoods or similar products. Another factor will clearly be the effect on future growth of continued poor deliveries. However, there may well be other ways of satisfying a short-term sales demand – for example, by subcontracting much of the work on this particular product.

If the appraisal suggests both projects offer an attractive return on investment and if both appear to fit into the company plan, the problem then comes down to means of implementation.

If both projects are compelling in their own right, then means should be sought to find the resources to implement both. Here the most important relevant fact stated in the case is that disposable profits are insufficient to finance both projects. This is a self-imposed constraint that, if both projects justify investment, can surely be removed. After all, both projects are long-term in nature and could quite reasonably be financed by medium-term and long-term debt.

The total required is only $4 million. For a company making pretax profits of $8 million, the financing of either project by a medium-term loan should not be difficult. An alternative is to use paper or some form of deferred consideration for $1 million of the price of the company to be acquired at its present reasonable price.

Hold together the management team

However, Heethoofd should realize that management talent probably will be even harder to find than money. This is a critical factor that should not be overlooked. Zonneschijn will find it difficult to deal with booming sales, delivery problems and new construction at the same time as planning and negotiating a fairly major acquisition.

Ijsman could be given responsibility for the latter, working closely with Zonneschijn, or it may be possible to recruit a manager for the company to be acquired either within Heetman Maatschappij or from outside. Unless the management problem can be resolved, a choice will clearly have to be made in favour of the internal investment as against the acquisition, the former being less demanding in management terms.

To sum up: the means of implementing the projects are less important than the way in which the managing director handles the problem. He must be flexible in his use of physical and financial resources, and above all he must work hard to hold together a first-rate and well-balanced management team.

This decision was provided by Anthony Frodsham in his capacity as managing director of P-E Consulting Group Ltd., a U.K. management consultancy.

Ought an executive to quit over losing line responsibility?

D avid Keller, 52-year-old deputy managing director for consumer goods at Hy-tex Enterprises Ltd., was leafing through his post on a bleak Friday morning. He was puzzled when he came across an official memo announcing a major corporate reorganization that he had not heard about.

Warren Green, his counterpart for industrial applications, the memo said, was taking early retirement at the age of 63. Keller knew that Green had been under considerable pressure from group managing director David Grimsby and the board because of falling profit margins. Green had complained to Keller about what he considered unwarranted criticism and interference in his operations.

Keller was even more surprised as he read on. The reorganization involved all three industrial division heads who had reported to Green. They would now report directly to Grimsby. In addition, the three unit heads who reported to Keller were also named divisional managing directors reporting directly to the group managing director. Keller, the announcement said, would retain his title of deputy group managing director with a new responsibility for planning and future development.

Keller went storming to Grimsby's office, only to find that he had left for the week-end. Green, he discovered, had cleared his desk and left the previous evening after a prolonged meeting with the board.

Rage and bewilderment

Once he had recovered his composure, Keller called his wife and told her what had happened. She suggested that he come home at once, then quickly called her brother, a lawyer. He was a man that Keller respected and liked. The brother, William Wilson, agreed to come over immediately to talk things through.

That afternoon the two men went for a walk across the fields surrounding Keller's country house. Keller was very bitter. "Imagine," he told his brother-in-law, "I've worked for that company for 15 years and done a damn fine job – and they don't even have the decency to discuss this with me."

Wilson listened sympathetically as Keller vented his rage and bewilderment. Then under gentle probing Keller conceded that his consumer buiness, while showing some growth, had not kept pace with the gains made by the company's chief competitors. It was probably only the fact that Green's division was in worse shape that had kept the heat off him.

"Given the way they have handled this," Wilson said, "don't you think they may be trying to goad you into resigning? And if you do, won't you be playing right into their hands?"

"You may be right," Keller replied, "but I have to live with myself, and I simply won't allow them to treat me like this.

"I will make them regret their action. The first thing Monday morning I am going in and giving that swine Grimsby a piece of my mind, assuming he has the courage to come to the office. Then I am going to deliver to the unions and the tax authorities some interesting information on how the company uses unrealistic transfer pricing and self-insurance premiums to move profits out of this country and into our Bermuda affiliate. Maybe I could negotiate a commission from the revenue people for information."

Wilson cautioned that such action might result in the company attempting to "blackball" him in the industry, damaging his chances of getting another job. "And you are too young to stop working even if you could afford to," he added.

"I think I am all right there," Keller said. "You know Drexel Products offered me a job at one point. In fact, they were willing to pay me a bit more, even though I didn't feel the job offered as much challenge or responsibility."

"Yes, I remember that," Wilson replied. "But that was three years ago. And as I recall you had several reservations about Drexel at that time. You said they had a record for a high turnover at the executive level and a very unsavoury reputation in the industry for pirating other people's product ideas."

"True enough," Keller said. "In fact, I was almost sure the main reason they wanted to hire me was to get some inside competitive information about Hy-tex. Given the way I feel now, nothing would please me more."

How should Wilson advise his brother-in-law?

DECISION

Side-tracked executive considers retaliatory moves against his employer

In his headlong rush to commit career suicide, David Keller is ignoring a universal rule in making any decision: do not act in anger. Worse still, his planned strategy seems to trip over nine false premises, which are, in no particular order of importance:

- Years of seniority somehow excuse poor performance.
- Shouting at the boss is a great way to "get even."
- Leaving one's job in a huff actually hurts the company.
- Betrayal benefits the betrayer.
- Vengeance works better in business than it does anywhere else.
- Verbal job offers are redeemable for the real thing.
- Wishing makes a bad job better.
- Losing a job is like missing a bus – there will always be another one along in a minute.
- The world of business is customarily fair and equitable in the first place. It simply is not so.

Keller has some difficult choices to make; anger, vengeance, self-pity and naïvety will not help. He needs realism, self-control and a strong penchant for self-preservation.

What should he do? Listening carefully to his brother-in-law, William Wilson, would not be a bad way to start. Wilson is cool, objective, weighs issues and has Keller's interests at heart.

But first Keller must simmer down, use the week-end to reflect and sort out his priorities, and discuss options further with his wife and his brother-in-law. Then, indeed, he must press for an early meeting, Monday, with group managing director David Grimsby.

At this meeting he should not storm or seek revenge – which will surely sacrifice both his job and the good references which he may need later – but discover what the staff changes really signify.

Is this development genuinely a pressure play to force Keller's resignation, or could it be based on loftier motives? If Keller concludes that he is being forced into a non-job to speed his departure, he can ask Grimsby just how much it is worth if he leaves voluntarily. Perhaps the price is right. His brother-in-law, a lawyer, could assess the generosity of an offer.

If, however, the job change is sincerely based on Grimsby's conviction that Keller can make an improved contribution at Hy-tex Enterprises Ltd., he should scrutinize the opportunity and, if all looks well, accept. It could turn out successfully for him.

But what if the planning job does not look tempting? He should still accept. Only in this way can Keller sustain his income while buying time to seek a new position on the outside.

He will need time to put out "feelers," prepare a resumé, distribute it to executive search firms, scan the "executive wanted" jobs columns, familarize himself with the market-place, assess his own value therein and pursue opportunities such as the Drexel Products offer.

By giving his new Hy-tex assignment time to jell, Keller can avoid sacrificing 15 good years of service through resignation. Even if this new assignment fails, he will have protected his salary and benefits while seeking a better job, and will also preserve benefits to which he would later be entitled should Grimsby decide to sack him. Voluntary resignation, of course, nullifies benefits.

Another possibility is that Grimsby might eventually recognize the error of changing his top-level structure. Six reporting subordinates can hardly be easier for him than two. If so, Keller might yet be happy staying on. He could find himself a hero, and be returned to his old responsibilities by a chastened Grimsby. Stranger things have happened.

Finally, a decision to accept a new assignment surely protects Keller's family from the trauma and worry of his swift, unplanned and unpleasant exit from the firm. Nor would betraying Hy-tex to tax and union officials bolster his self-respect or serve any other purpose. Such officials would hardly dignify his treachery by awarding him a commission. Moreover, what company would be willing to hire a man with such a reputation? Word would get around.

In summary, it seldom makes good sense for a man with heavy personal responsibilities voluntarily to resign a good position before he has found a challenging substitute. Perhaps in the case of a moral issue, yes. But no real moral issue is involved in this situation. Moreover, Keller is 52 years old, which cannot improve his chances of quickly finding a new position; nor can looking for a job while he is unemployed.

By moving slowly, muzzling his anger and false pride, resisting the temptation to resign and giving the new job a chance to work, while at the same time safeguarding his income, Keller best serves the interests of himself, his family and probably the company as well.

This decision was provided by Theodore O. Simpson in his capacity as a director of U.K.-headquartered outplacement consultants Sanders & Sidney Ltd., formerly the THinc. Group (U.K.) Ltd. The firm is employed by companies to help their redundant executives find new job opportunities.

How should a company wrongly committed change investment plans?

C. Y. Mahsun, general manager of ABC Manufacturing Co., makers of gear boxes, variators and reducers, gazed from his office window in Istanbul, Turkey. He had just finished a four-hour meeting with the company's officials and owners. It had been the third meeting in two months, yet still there was no consensus what to do.

The company was in a predicament because of past mistakes for which Mahsun, who had only been with ABC for one year, could not be blamed. Now it was his job to set the company on the right road at last. But how?

The sad story dated back to 1972, when the former management had decided to undertake a $9 million investment on an 8,800 square metre plant site. The object was to build a plant to produce big variators and reducers to match what seemed to be a steadily growing domestic demand.

A feasibility report on the project was duly prepared and sent to the Ministry of Industry and Technology, which would issue the indispensable "licence of encouragement".

An investment having this licence can benefit from cheaper bank loans and tax reductions. It is also exempt from customs duties provided it satisfies at least some of the criteria set by the ministry. These include that the investment should increase exports or substitute for imports and that it should be in a backward region of Turkey.

ABC got the necessary permission to go ahead. But it could not implement the project immediately because of heavy financial burdens. As a result, the last starting date for the project, set by the ministry, passed by. The project was cancelled.

Four years later, in 1976, ABC's management had resurrected the project, with slight modifications, and again submitted it to the ministry. Somewhat surprisingly, it had received the ministry's approval a second time.

The renewed project would employ 190 workers, have a sales volume of $11.2 million annually and yield a profit as high as $2 million.

Because of continuing inflation, however, the cost of the project had soared to $15.5 million. There had also been a change of location from the Marmara region of Turkey to Bilecik, a province in Central Anatolia. Marmara no longer qualified as a development area.

In September 1976, nevertheless, ABC purchased 20,000 square metres of land for $2.8 million and agreed a contract with a construction firm. It started building on a 9,000 square metre plant site.

In order to finance construction, plus the cost of importing machines and equipment, ABC borrowed a $6 million low-interest loan, as granted in the licence of encouragement. Contracts were arranged with foreign firms and by the beginning of 1977 ABC had already imported 14 machines.

The company then realized that the demand for variators and reducers for the domestic market was not as steady as had seemed likely five years previously. In order to sell the products even of existing plants, the company had to undertake contracts, generally with government enterprises, under strict financial terms.

The management, fearing the loss of government contracts, either accepted prices for current products which did not compensate for cost increases or signed delivery schedules which it had little hope of meeting.

The first thing that Mahsun did, following his arrival from another company, was to look at the investment problem. He discovered to his horror that not only was the market for big variators and reducers declining, but the existing technology was more and more being replaced by hydraulic technology.

Mahsun realized that ABC needed products where there was an assured growth market. He was on good terms with a West German gear manufacturer and persuaded it to agree to the transfer of patent rights and know-how of various gear parts, previously imported, that were used in the Turkish automotive industry. He then prepared a plan to manufacture these.

The project involved a plant size of 2,000 square metres, instead of the 9,000 square metres of the current investment, and 88 employees instead of 190. It was planned that at 75% capacity the plant would manufacture 150,000 gear parts and have a sales volume of $12.3 million and a profit of $2.5 million. But the cost of the project, at $22 million, was much higher than that of the current project.

The board of directors decided it was too costly to undertake. Autofinancing was very hard to obtain and to appeal for a loan was also very difficult, because the loan granted in conjunction with the licence of encouragement was already spent.

Meanwhile, the current project was under way but incomplete. Any changes in its context were probably not going to be approved by the ministry. Completing it, however, in Mahsun's view, would only waste more time and money. To abolish the project totally would create heavy financial problems.

Trapped by these complexities, Mahsun continued to stare through the window as the evening shadows lengthened across the Bosporus. What should he do?

DECISION

Turkish company wonders how to finance new investment

The dilemma facing C.Y. Mahsun of ABC Manufacturing Co. is not unusual in Turkey. It reflects the extremely rapid changes that have been taking place in the modern Turkish economy. Poor planning and the extremely tight money environment that has recently evolved have compounded the company's difficulties. However, the situation does not appear to be entirely hopeless. Certainly there is no reason why Mahsun should throw his hands up in despair.

He can console himself with the thought that although the demand for variators and reducers is not as big as the company anticipated back in 1972, when it first decided to build a plant, a market does exist. The state sector remains a steady, if currently unprofitable, customer.

Furthermore, even at a time of accelerated change in the economy, the State Economic Enterprises in Turkey can alter existing structural needs only at great financial and political cost. This ensures that demand for the products that ABC provides will continue for many years.

So Mahsun may conclude that, unprofitable though it may seem, the market for variators and reducers can still be attractive for a producer with good political contacts and a skilful marketing approach.

So far so good. However, it is also apparent that ABC would be extremely foolish to lock itself into an untenable position by continuing with the project to produce larger variators and reducers in its present form. Having looked at the situation calmly. Mahsun may well decide that he should slow down the project, to minimize losses, while at the same time acquiring one or more new shareholders.

The most likely candidates for shareholding will be the State Economic Enterprises themselves, since they are the major potential customers for variators and reducers. The state banks which are affiliated with that sector of the economy are another possibility. So are new entrepreneurs who are flush with cash and have good political contacts.

Obtain new capital

The fact is that despite the recent money squeeze in Turkey, a new class of entrepreneur has emerged. It is a group composed of individuals who have earned sudden, windfall (tax-free) profits from trading and speculation and who are now seeking areas of more substantial and legitimate investment. With proper guidance, such a financially sound but technically untutored shareholder can be of great use to ABC.

In other words, the company's long-term objective should be to obtain enough new capital to continue the project, thus increasing the value of its own share while at the same time reducing, and eventually even eliminating, its shareholding.

Another step Mahsun should take is to rationalize the project. He can do this by reducing its scale, researching the new hydraulic technique and its applicability, and shifting resources – such as portions of the plant site – to the new gear project, which appears to hold out hope for the future.

Incidentally, there should be little difficulty obtaining a new "licence of encouragement." The fact that the company has a licence for another, separate, project is not necessarily an obstacle,

Again, capital for the gear project can be obtained from a competent and reliable minority shareholder. Partial financing might be obtained from the Industrial Development Bank. It could also be obtained from the issue of corporate bonds.

Indeed for many companies in Turkey, the latter has become an increasingly popular, and relatively easy, means of securing finance. In cases where companies are not able to obtain bank financing, bond financing has become the only viable means of raising the necessary money.

Finally, Mahsun should ensure that the variator project and the new gear project are structured with separate corporate identities, with ABC as controlling shareholder. This will not only enhance the company's flexibility but make easier its attempts to acquire new shareholders and financing, as well as a licence of encouragement for the gear project.

This decision was provided by Mehmet Gün Çalika in his capacity as general manager and director of Istanbul-based Meban Securities.

Should trustee of foundation agree to asset stripper's takeover offer?

As Vincent Carew drove into town for a meeting of the board of Palmer Industries Ltd., he pondered what action to take over an unexpected takeover bid for the company.

Carew represented the company on the board the trustees of a charitable foundation which the founder of the company, Christopher Palmer, had set up prior to his death in 1964 primarily to make endowments in the field of health care.

Now, with the takeover bid on the table, Carew felt that his personal position was impossible. The plain fact was that what was good for the foundation was not necessarily good for the company, its directors and its employees.

Palmer had developed the U.K. company that bore his name from a small room with a single lathe into a machine tool company with sales that had reached $100 million the year he died. Since then sales had held up well although the profit performance had been uneven.

The foundation had inherited the chairman's 33% holding in the company and therefore, to all intents and purposes, possessed the controlling interest. At company board meetings the foundation, symbolized in the person of Carew, exerted a watchful, if benign, influence on the proceedings.

Carew had enjoyed the feeling of being the power behind the corporate throne; enjoyed it, that is, until a takeover bid had come suddenly from acquisition-hungry Sinclair Securities Ltd.

This was a company, frequently in the headlines, which critics of the capitalist system loved to quote as an example of unprincipled financial dealing.

Short-lived euphoria

Sinclair had offered double the prevailing market price for Palmer Industries. Carew recalled how another trustee, on hearing the news of the bid, had slapped him on the back and said: "What a windfall! Now we will be able to buy those badly needed kidney machines as well as endowing the new wing at the hospital."

Carew's own immediate reaction, in his role as trustee, had also been one of euphoria. Not only would the proposed deal boost the foundation's assets by 100%, but the share exchange involved would provide the foundation with Sinclair shares that carried a much higher level of income than the shares of Palmer Industries.

Carew's excitement had been shorter lived than that of the other trustrees, however. At an emergency meeting of the Palmer Industries board, he had read the unspoken question on the face of every other director present. They wanted to know the foundation's attitude towards the bid. And they feared the worst.

Carew had stalled, reserving his position. He was as determined as any of them, he had said, to look at the bid objectively. And after two board meetings he had to admit that the arguments against accepting the bid were persuasive and worth thinking about very seriously indeed.

First, there was the reputation of the suitor, Sinclair. There was no mistaking that the company, on past performance, was an asset stripper.

"All they want," said one Palmer Industries board member, cynically, "is to get their hands on our office block in central London, gut it and then turn it into a hotel. They'll probably turn the factory into a supermarket."

Second, in the view of a majority of board members, although Sinclair's terms were generous in relation to Palmer Industry's market value, they were not that good when related to the company's long-term potential for growth.

Against these arguments in favour of rejecting the bid, Carew had to weigh the undoubted benefits to the foundation of accepting it.

Other trustees of the foundation reminded him that he had a moral duty towards the founder and his ideals, as well as to the patients who would benefit from the kidney machines.

"I do have a moral duty to them," Carew told his wife. "But I also have a duty towards the company's employees as well as the directors. Many of them have served Palmer since they left school. Palmer is a friendly firm. Few of the employees felt the need for service contracts to protect them."

Ever since the first emergency board meeting, Carew and the board had tried to find a friendly rival that would agree to a merger, so that all jobs would be safeguarded.

Meanwhile, a number of outside shareholders had already indicated acceptance of Sinclair's offer. Time was running out, and as Carew left his car, walked through the swing doors and into the lift that would whisk him up to the boardroom, he realized that sitting on the fence was no longer possible.

He had to decide. Should he sell out the company and the other directors? Or should he decisively vote to reject Sinclair, with all its implications for the foundation?

DECISION

Trustee needs to reach decision on controversial takeover bid

T he dilemma facing Vincent Carew probably is not as bad as it seems. Further reflection, augmented by professional financial advice, which Palmer Industries Ltd. clearly has not so far sought, may lead him to conclude that the foundation's interests are synonymous with those of the company.

Time in which to reach a decision may be running out but it is not exhausted. Although some shareholders apparently have indicated acceptance of the offer from Sinclair Securities Ltd., it is clear that most shareholders are following the usual course and awaiting the board's advice before deciding what to do.

So when Carew walks into the boardroom he should not do anything dramatic. He should suggest that they all sit down and look at the facts again, urgently but also coolly and rationally.

As he well knows, in law there is no distinction between an executive and a non-executive director, or between a director representing a particular block of shares and any other director. A director has to consider the best interests of all the shareholders.

Whatever Carew may feel his moral responsibility to be, his legal responsibility is clear. It is not to the employees, executive directors or society as a whole, but to the shareholders. No matter how many trustees of the foundation advocate selling to Sinclair, Carew has every legal right to say: "No, I would be failing in my duty if I allowed it to happen."

But what about his moral duty? If he can satisfy himself, and the other trustees, that the foundation would not benefit as much as it thought, the apparent moral conflict evaporates.

Because it is a share swap and not a cash offer that is involved in the deal, the only way the foundation can acquire a large quantity of cash immediately from it is to sell some of the shares it would receive from Sinclair. But such a sale, in that kind of company, could force the share price down, which must be considered.

Carew could point out to the other trustees that share prices in any case are volatile. The 100% appreciation the foundation would enjoy on the basis of the share exchange would quickly be eroded by an decline in Sinclair's fortunes. Although the foundation needs money now to buy kidney machines, what guarantee does it have, Carew could argue, that dividends from Sinclair will be safe for the next few years?

Carew should ask the right questions about Sinclair's bid, beginning with what the level of offer is, compared with the previous market price, what is actually being offered and why Sinclair needs to pull off the deal.

The board has to consider the prospects for the enlarged company after the acquisition. Incidentally, the foundation, although it would end up with a very important stake in Sinclair, certainly would not have anything like the influence it had in Palmer Industries.

Carew may reflect that both he and the board really do not know enough about Sinclair, and its prospects, if the bid goes through. One of the first things a financial adviser would do would be to assess the quality of the bidder's own shares and perhaps say that unless there was a cash alternative to the share swap, it should not be accepted, at least not straight away.

Consider shareholders and foundation

The board, before it can give sound advice to the shareholders, needs to know:

What the assets are worth today. In other words, it should obtain an up-to-date valuation.

What the real earnings prospects are over the next few years and, therefore, what dividends the foundation might expect to receive.

What Sinclair's own position really is; for example, its credit standing.

An indication from the company's property adviser regarding the price at which the London office block could be sold, and how quickly.

After all, if Sinclair can strip this asset, surely Palmer Industries could and should do the same. The office block is not necessary to the success of the business. Its existence suggests there may have been an alarming build-up of central overheads at Palmer Industries. Almost certainly the board is now regretting not having written a higher value for the office into its accounts.

Carew may further reflect that the possibility of Sinclair shutting down the factory and turning it into a supermarket, as one board member suggests, is very unlikely. Sinclair is much more likely, having bought the total business at a very low valuation in relation to the real assets, and having sold off the office block, to sell the underlying business to somebody else in the engineering industry as a separate transaction. If Sinclair did that, at least employment in the factory would, to some degree, be safeguarded in the future.

Carew, therefore, should propose that the board takes a few more days in which to ask searching questions, accept advice and try to cut through extraneous and irrelevant issues.

Only then will it be able to recommend with confidence what should be done in the interests of the shareholders as a whole, and not the foundation in isolation.

This decision was provided by John MacArthur in his capacity as director, corporate finance, at Kleinwort Benson Ltd., a leading U.K. merchant bank.

Should office equipment firm diversify or make an acquisition?

Karl Glückner, chairman of the management board of Munich-based Tecnocrat GmbH, was holding a crucial board meeting. Tecnocrat had started out as a manufacturer of mechanical typewriters. It had moved on to electric typewriters and two years previously had decided to take a big leap into electronics by extending its product range to desktop computers and other components for automated offices.

"Gentlemen," Glückner said, "the situation we have to consider is this. Are we to go on trying to grow and diversify using our own resources, or should we make an acquisition? You all know the company I have in mind, if we decide to take that course. We also have to decide very soon whether to enter the U.S. market, where, as you know, the competition in desktop terminals is extremely fierce."

"You have all read my report," said Heinrich Gruber, the finance director. "You all know that I supported our diversification away from electric typewriters, although I did sympathize with your point of view, Hans" – he nodded towards Hans Schmidt, the head of marketing – "that we should not do anything to detract from the fine brand image we enjoy in the typewriter field."

However, he added, as his report clearly showed, revenues from typewriters continued to stagnate, due to a variety of reasons. "We do have substantial reserves, built up from the golden years," he said. "But they are not limitless, and they certainly would not cover continuing in-house research and development at escalating costs; acquiring a company that would bring us an existing distribution network in office equipment, which we now lack; and also entering the U.S. market, however we try to do it. In short, I am telling you, and the figures also prove, that we have to make a choice."

"Thank you, Heinrich," said Glückner. "I think the key thing to decide is whether we are facing a marketing or a development problem. If we acquire Office Supplies GmbH, we will be able to supplement our existing distribution channels in Germany with as many again in other EEC countries, including France and Great Britain. But we would have to make a very substantial offer, details of which are before you."

Assess technological progress

"There is also the question of back-up," said Schmidt, the marketing man. "They have the network, which we lack, for servicing the new range of electronic products now being developed."

Glückner agreed, but pointed out that there had also been developmental problems. "Your department," he said, turning to Heinz Seefelder, the director of research, "produced the Instant computer in less than 12 months, which is a very good record. However, gentlemen, you also have before you Seefelder's assessment of the technological progress in this field made by Japanese and U.S. competitors.

"We are going to have to go on running, on the technical side, simply to keep up with the competition. You recommend, Seefelder, that we establish close links with a U.S. company in this field. You spell out very clearly the technological advantages that would accrue from melding our research with theirs. But it doesn't look to me, based on Gruber's figures, that we can afford to acquire Office Supplies and also buy a stake in the U.S. company, even if they are willing to consider us as partners."

"I think they are," said Seefelder. "I have made some preliminary enquiries. Some of our own research would benefit their product line, which is not directly competitive with ours. But it would be costly."

"The U.S. company's research is aimed at developing components rather than finished products," said the marketing man. "Therefore any investment we made over there would not help us directly to market our desk computers in the U.S. I do think there is a market for us in the U.S. I expect that fact to be confirmed by a market research report I have commissioned for you to see.

A technical or marketing problem?

"But that underlines the problem yet again. We do not have the cash flow, from our existing product line, to enable us to do everything. Personally I would like to see us acquire Office Supplies while at the same time looking for a U.S. partner whose strength is on the marketing side, rather than paying for more research. After all, our research budget here in Germany has gone up by nine or ten times in the last two years. We have to draw the line somewhere."

"But our competitors are not drawing the line, that is the point," said the research director.

"The fact is," said Glückner, "that when we decided to go into the computer field we got a wild horse by the tail and now we can't let go even if we want to. But I ask again, gentlemen, in essence is our problem a technical or a marketing one? And if it is a marketing one, what relative priority should we give, at this stage of the game, to extending our distribution network in Europe and entering the market in the U.S., without which we will remain small fry?" .

The finance director interposed. "There is also the problem," he said, "that although we *think* we have a good, marketable product, with distinct advantages over other desktop computers, with improved visibility on the screen and so on, we do not *know* that it will sell. In my previous company we went out on a limb with a new product only to find the limb

280

chopped off by consumer apathy. I never want to be in that situation ever again."

"There speaks a financial man who, by virtue of his training, is not inclined to take too many risks," said the research director, tartly. "All innovation is risky."

While his colleagues were talking, Glückner was trying to make up his own mind. Where *did* the priority lie? What further facts would be pertinent to reaching a good decision? If one of the others turned to him now, and asked for his considered view, what should it be?

Company should seek a strong partner for consolidation

Glückner, the managing director, faces an important strategic decision that is likely to determine the future of his company. It is small consolation to him that his dilemma is a common one, the origins of which must be sought in past errors of judgment of both marketing and product development.

Glückner's real choice is not whether Tecnocrat should grow through acquisitions or development from within, but whether the company can envisage the future alone or not.

Tecnocrat has established a reputation for typewriters in Europe, particularly in West Germany. Its brand names have gained a reputation, with both the trade and the end-consumer, for quality and reliability.

The move to electrical typewriters was a natural development, technically not very difficult to realize. The strong brand image allowed for a premium price in the markets, of which a substantial share had been obtained during the boom period. Consequently, margins remained above average, and permitted substantial investments in research, thus opening the way to the commercialization of desk-top computers with advanced technology. This was a very big step indeed, correctly described as a big leap.

Reflect on the company's strengths

Heinrich Gruber, the finance director, reports that revenues from typewriters continue to stagnate. Is it from that source, though, that day-to-day activities, inventories and new developments have to be financed, whilst initial outlays for acquisitions have to come from retained earnings?

The acquisition of Office Supplies GmbH is essential, according to Schmidt, the marketing man, since the existing marketing and sales facilities do not meet the requirements for the distribution of the new electronic products now about to be launched, let alone for the indispensable geographical distribution within the EEC. Glückner even goes so far as to say that without an extension of the European distribution network, and a substantial presence on the U.S. market, Tecnocrat will remain small and possibly unprofitable.

It would appear that the company's philosophy has been more product than market oriented, and that the marketing side has always left a lot to be desired. So an acquisition of Office Supplies GmbH should be given serious consideration.

The envisaged investment in the U.S. would not provide Tecnocrat with indispensable marketing muscle on the American market. The U.S. company's research facilities and achievements are not certain to contribute directly, and in the near future, to an improved cash flow. Also, the financial burden for a participation in, or an acquisition of, the U.S. company would be unacceptable to Tecnocrat after a purchase of Office Supplies.

On the other hand Glückner should reflect that the company has definite strengths. These include a strong and positive brand image in the office equipment field in a number of European countries; a new product line with distinct advantages over present competition; and an innovative and aggressive research facility.

There is also a negative side, including a weak marketing structure; insufficient sales impact, physical distribution and geographic presence in Europe; and substantial capacity in the low-margin segment of electric typewriters.

Seek a willing partner

The conclusion becomes unavoidable that Tecnocrat cannot subsist under its own steam. The board therefore has little alternative but to adopt a strategy of "passive acquisition", which is to seek actively a strong partner willing to take an interest in, or even purchase, the company.

A very discreet search for a new partner can only be commenced after completion of a number of short-term strategical and tactical steps, including an in-depth appraisal of the typewriter sector. Among the questions to be asked and answered should be:

What positive contribution does the present line of typewriters make to the company and what are the future prospects?

Is there any joy to be expected from the development of electronic typewriters, or printers for the desk computers?

Should production of such products be abandoned or continued in another country? What would be the social consequences and costs?

Should and could typewriters, or parts of them, be bought in, rather than made?

The adoption of such a policy must be followed by the establishment of priorities, to be realized at short notice. Failing this, Tecnocrat would not be an attractive proposition for a possible partner.

Glückner and his associates might look for a U.S. or Japanese company, with strong products and advanced technology in the office equipment market but not as yet represented in Europe. It will certainly not be easy. But it will be much less likely to have disastrous consequences than either of the alternatives currently under discussion.

This decision was provided by Jo A. Jacobsthal in his capacity as a Dutch consultant specializing in company policy and marketing strategy, operating from Fribourg, Switzerland, in association with European Marketing Systems SA.

Can a leak of dangerous chemicals be hushed up?

As he drove away from his meeting with the minister, Sven Bronson breathed a sigh of relief that didn't really end until he was climbing the steps into his home-bound plane. Getting the agreement from the authorities to site his company's new plant in rural Denmark had occupied most of his time for months.

The problem had been critical – indeed still was, he reminded himself. Process Industrie AB (PI) had grown up from a small local engineering company, using very basic technology, to an employer of 1,500 people selling highly sophisticated process machinery. The company had also branched out into semi-automatic testing and monitoring equipment, using isotope decay techniques and toxic waste treatment.

The Swedish market had, of course, long been too small for PI even when its business had spread to Norway and Finland. Something like half its turnover was within the European community and 35% in North America. But the past 18 months had seen some unpleasant shocks in what had been a fairly stable market for PI since the mid-1970s.

The obvious fall in orders all over the world had not worried Bronson greatly; this was, after all, an expected cycle that had been allowed for. But the sudden influx of Japanese competition into the U.S. market had taken PI by surprise and the company had seen its sales there drop by 28% in three months, primarily because it could not meet Japanese prices.

In Europe, the Japanese had made less headway. Local companies had persuaded their governments, and the EEC bureaucrats, to alter the safety legislation in favour of their own products, to keep the Japanese out. But with Sweden not a member of the EEC, this had hit PI's trade, too.

Bronson had responded to the U.S. setback by bringing forward plans to build a plant in the EEC. But finding a suitable site had been a problem. Almost everywhere he went, initial enthusiasm for the venture cooled when local authorities realized that the factory would be storing large quantities of highly toxic chemicals and radio isotopes.

"We are facing a lot of opposition from environmentalists," explained one French politician. "Unless you can show that you will be creating a large number of jobs, it will be difficult for us to help you."

Finally, however, a suitable site had been found – in Denmark. The rural area chosen had a very high unemployment rate, and the 20 or 30 jobs promised by PI would make a significant impact on the prosperity of the small town nearby. Generous terms had been negotiated with the authorities for a tax holiday, and for a grant to cover the initial capital cost of the factory and the laboratory buildings. Even so, it had been a knife-edge decision.

"The main reason we are going to say yes," said the Danish minister responsible, "is PI's excellent safety record. If there was any chance of a leak of radiation from some of the chemicals you are using, then I would have to say no. If the water table in that district were contaminated, it would create enormous problems for our agricultural industry. The environmentalists would have a field-day.

"I shan't make the announcement for another three weeks," he added. "But already I have been swamped with protest letters." He pointed to a pile of letters on his desk.

Bronson had telexed the good news about the deal to his deputy, Carlson, who was waiting for him at Stockholm airport and didn't seem very happy. Bronson suddenly had that hollow feeling that something was seriously wrong.

"We have had an accident," Carlson said. "Not serious, but there has been a small leak of one of the more toxic chemicals into the atmosphere."

"*How* small!" Bronson exploded. "And what do you mean by 'the atmosphere'? The plant atmosphere or the outside atmosphere?"

"It was pretty well confined within the plant," Carlson said, giving him a quick summary of the technical details.

"Have we carried out blood tests on the employees, no matter how remotely involved?"

"No."

"Why not?"

"Because of the alarm it would cause. There is a routine test due a week next Friday. It is unlikely that anyone breathed in a harmful dose. Extremely unlikely."

"But we should warn these people now, so we can be sure," Bronson said. "After all, these chemicals can be carcinogenic."

"I know," said Carlson. "But if we do tell them, it is bound to get into the press. The Danes will hear about it and we can kiss goodbye to having a plant in Denmark."

The same thought had occurred to Bronson. The more he thought about it, the more he came to the conclusion it was highly unlikely that any harm had been done. On the other hand, if he said and did nothing, the Danes, when they finally heard about it, would be incensed.

Also there would be hell to pay when the Swedish union discovered what had happened.

How should he handle the incident?

DECISION

Company should not try to keep mishap secret

Bronson's dilemma has, unfortunately, become all too familiar in recent years. The Three Mile Island incident, at a nuclear power plant in the U.S., provided a prime example of how to handle the public implications of environmental safety problems. If we have collectively learned anything from these experiences, it must be that immediate, co-ordinated fact gathering and analysis is necessary to prevent confusion, unwarranted alarm and conflicting interpretations of the unfortunate situation.

Bronson should therefore immediately appoint a fact-finder – Carlson perhaps – to investigate thoroughly the entire incident, including the administration of employee blood tests. Also he should take personal responsibility for directing and screening all communications with those

284

involved: employees, union, press and the Danish government.

In the initial stages of this incident, it is crucial for Bronson to know the complete technical details of the situation with as much certainty as possible. What are the levels of toxicity inside and outside the plant? Have employees been contaminated and if so, to what extent? What are the specific environmental and health risks for these levels of exposure?

Once the basic facts and their consequences have been determined, the employees should be fully informed about the incident, preferably by Bronson himself.

It is important that Bronson does not hedge on the facts, however negative they may be, but clearly and directly addresses any employee questions or fears. Even if no apparent immediate harm has been done, employees exposed to the leakage of highly toxic carcinogenic chemicals should be checked for delayed or long-term effects in special health monitoring programmes.

The decision to check and inform the employees means that Bronson must "go public" on the incident. It is preferable that he take the initiative to inform the local press and the Danish government, rather than their learning of it via second-hand or distorted sources.

As far as the Swedish union is concerned, Bronson's placing of employee welfare first and foremost, in the handling of the incident, should put him on a constructive footing with the union. Any questions from the union should be answered promptly and directly.

The chance of course exists that, as a result of this incident, the Danish deal falls through. However, if the leakage proves to be minor, with no contamination of employees or outside atmosphere, the chance is greater that the Danes weigh Bronson's prompt, responsible and open handling of the situation against the risks.

If, on the other hand, the incident proves more serious than suspected, no amount of hedging or delays will prevent the truth reaching the interested external parties.

Any industry which uses potentially life-endangering processes or products, and which expects to stay in business for long, must have policies and procedures for dealing with risk assessment and risk acceptance. This applies to large corporations as well as smaller companies such as PI.

Risk assessment is essentially a scientific undertaking. It means the gathering of all possible information relating levels of toxicity in various substances to the possible effects on health and environment. Risk assessment in the form of health and environment studies should be an integral part of all new product and process development.

By contrast, risk acceptance is a societal matter. Societal stake-holders such as government, the local community and the general public ultimately determine which trade-offs are to be made between economic and ecological interests. This has to be faced although it is, understandably, frustrating for managers to be denied an operating permit while the statistical risks of smoking far outweigh those of an industrial accident.

Given our increasing levels of scientific knowledge, schooling, and concern for health and environment, industries such as Bronson's must create publicly verifiable safety policies and priorities, and communicate with their stakeholders on that basis.

This decision was provided by Deborah L. Cummings in her capacity as a U.S.-born management consultant who has worked in Africa and the Middle East and with Public Affairs Consultants in Amsterdam.

Should firm in trouble back risky new venture?

Charles Gray had been chief executive of Smoothclean Ltd., a company long involved in the business of domestic vacuum cleaners, for eight years. He had joined at a time when profits were satisfactory. However, the rising costs of raw materials, coupled with the need to be competitive with imports from the Far East, had made life difficult.

In addition, a spate of mail order selling by manufacturers offering vacuum cleaners that were highly portable, and that could be used for cleaning out lofts and other heavy duty work, had further reduced the company's sales. The intense competition had caused big inroads into profits and had led to a bout of savage cost-cutting which had included redundancies.

Gray had fought back hard, in the marketplace, but slowly and surely the company's products continued to lose ground to the competition.

He had also taken a more fundamental step. Three years previously, he had formed a subsidiary company that, while reporting to him through its own general manager and being financed by the parent company, ultimately would be expected to stand upon its own feet.

The subsidiary was charged with developing appropriate technology so that Smoothclean could move into new markets that showed a good possibility of growth, while maintaining a solid position in its traditional line of business. In particular, the subsidiary was to look at innovative uses for battery-operated motors that could be combined with lightweight metals and more efficient transmission systems to open up new market opportunities.

A blueprint in 18 months

Gray had persuaded the board to back the venture with some difficulty, as the long-serving chairman and one or two other directors had needed a lot of convincing that development money should not be spent on the existing product lines. However, after a hard fight, his view had carried the day and the plans went ahead.

To head the operations, Gray had appointed a young man called David Payne, who had trained as a metallurgist, had a fine reputation for managing research and development (R & D) departments and had served as deputy to the marketing manager of a major company. Starting with a staff of two, Payne had proved a forceful character who quickly had 20 people working for him, more than half of them with technical degrees and specialist knowledge.

At the end of 18 months, he had presented Gray with a blueprint for a unit comprising a battery-operated motor, a lightweight chassis and a highly original transmission system. It did not solve the problem of making batteries long-lived, and therefore had no potential for use in private cars. However, the unit was designed to impart 50% or 60% more acceleration and average speed to any fairly lightweight vehicle to which it was fitted.

"Where is the growth market?" Gray had asked.

"Milk floats, for one," Payne had replied.

Road transport delays caused by slow-moving, battery-powered milk roundsmen's carts had prompted the government to promise legislation that would set a minimum speed for such vehicles. Milk companies, faced with the alternative of upgrading existing battery-powered machines or scrapping them entirely, and substituting petrol-driven vehicles, were certain to opt for the former course, Payne argued, provided that development and manufacturing costs were tightly controlled. He also spelled out other possible growth opportunities.

Capital expenditure required

Of course there were snags. A lot more work was needed before a prototype, let alone a finished product, could be produced. Payne said that he needed more people, and presented Gray with a timetable for the allocation of essential money and resources. Negotiations would also have to begin with battery manufacturers; and Smoothclean would have to decide whether to manufacture its own motors or, as in the past, buy them in from outside.

Gray did three things. First, he launched an independent technical study which verified that the claims made by Payne and his people seemed justified. Second, he instituted a market study which showed that there was indeed a market for battery-powered motors which would generate superior acceleration and a higher average speed. Third, he forewarned the board that some heavy developmental, and ultimately capital, expenditure would be required if the subsidiary was to be transformed into a profit centre.

How to justify two loss-making businesses

The board's reaction was discouraging. "Our existing business has slipped from recession into near-crisis," the chairman complained. "It will be years before a new battery-motor business is viable. How are we expected to justify to the shareholders running two loss-making businesses instead of one?"

Two of the outside directors backed Gray's view that the company had no future unless it launched out into new fields. But they shared the board's general disinclination to go out on a financial limb until the world economy as a whole picked up.

Shortly before a decisive board meeting, Payne came to Gray with a proposal. "I, and five of my colleagues, are prepared to buy out the R&D subsidiary, lock, stock and barrel, and develop this idea ourselves," he said.

Gray went home to think about it. Here was an opportunity for the board to be rid of the subsidiary Payne had started, in order to make this year's balance sheet look a little better. But that would make his own position untenable, believing as he did that the long-term success of the company did not reside in vacuum cleaners. He had felt for some time that the company must diversify.

What action should he take now, with both his own and the company's best interests in mind?

Spin-off solution to new venture problem

This is a case about muddled strategic thinking, weak communications, half-hearted commitments and conflicting attitudes to risk taking.

It is also a classical case of "old" versus "new" business and the corresponding allocation of management attention, time, money and other scarce resources. Finally, it is a matter of how well a new venture fits into an old organization, and the likelihood that the venture would indeed be better off under entirely different organizational arrangements.

Smoothclean's original product line has produced a shrinking market share, profit margin and customer appeal for several years. Cost reduction exercises and sharper marketing have not reversed this trend. More drastic measures are probably called for – for example, redesigning the product line, moving production abroad or striking a cooperative deal with a competitor.

However, instead of putting more money into the old product line, Gray, the chief executive, managed with great difficulty to convince his board to put scarce development resources into a completely new business venture, involving an entirely different product line. This was a fundamental strategic decision with long-term implications. But it was never treated as such.

Although Gray carried the day when the original decision was taken, he did not do so when promising results were not forthcoming. The majority of the board members are hesitant or outright hostile. I think they have very good reasons to hesitate, although this hesitation should have been ventilated several years earlier.

A certain way to maximize risk taking in connection with diversification is to change not only the product but also the target group and distribution channel. This is exactly what the new business venture implies to Smoothclean, which seems to have few product lines and very little experience developing and marketing unrelated products.

Launching the new product also implies a switch from pure product sales to "idea selling", only later to be followed by product sales. This means changing existing patterns of thought and purchase behaviour, which takes time and money and calls for a different kind of marketing skills than those needed for selling a well-known, mature product like vacuum cleaners.

Considering all of these factors, I give the new venture no more than a 20% chance of succeeding within the framework of the old mother company. The new product will hardly aid the solution of problems associated with the basic product line, but will instead demand substantial management attention, additional funds and other scarce resources, this at a time when the company is most likely running out of time, money and patience, both at the board and at shareholder level.

This does not mean that the new product in itself is worthless. The market study, and the fact that Payne and five colleagues are prepared to put their own money on the line, are strong indications that they are on to something worthwhile. However, the best possibility for this venture to succeed is certainly away from its old parent, in a smaller, more flexible, responsive and enthusiastic environment.

To give the new venture the best possibility of success it should be moved out of the old company and financed long-term by professional risk capital, plus private funds from the entrepreneurs themselves. The development subsidiary should be completely bought out. Possibly part of the payment could be in the form of future royalties, if and when production starts. Further, if the old company could offer good assembly facilities, a normal business arrangement should be investigated but kept separate from the buy-out terms.

From Smoothclean's point of view, this solution would free capital presently tied up in the new project and make it easier to focus on its basic problem: what to do with its vacuum cleaning business. After Gray's eight years associated with shrinking market shares and profit margins, it might also be a good idea to get a new general manager. Why not a new director of corporate planning at the same time?

Gray may consider a move

With cash in hand, a likely future royalty income and possibly also a higher factory loading in the future, and no further demands for capital for completely unrelated product lines, the board seems to have an acceptable case to present to shareholders.

However, the decision in this particular case is for Gray to make. We know too little about his age, financial status, psychological set-up, attitude to change, entrepreneurial skills and capacity to absorb a blow.

Probably he would be happier with the new venture than being forced to see it disappear, while once again having to concentrate on a product line which he basically does not believe in. Since the board does not entirely trust his judgment any longer and does not support his one and only future-oriented project, this might be a logical time for him to quit.

Since Payne and his five colleagues do not have any substantial experience of general management, maybe they would welcome Gray joining them.

This decision was provided by Dr. Bo Arpi in his capacity as president of ARPI International SA, international top-management counsellors based in Brussels.

DILEMMA

Should company take the long view or go for immediate gain?

" **I**f there is more profit in military contracts," said the shareholder with the loud voice, "that is what we should go for. I have put a large slice of my savings into this company. A 3.2% return on investment is just not good enough. I want to see more worthwhile returns than this."

"So do we all," said Harry Manning, chairman and chief executive officer of Joshua Manning Co., which his father had founded. He was chairing the second annual meeting of the company since it went public. It was turning out to be a stormy affair. "I assure you, we will do what is best for the company," he added.

"Best for the company in what terms?" demanded another shareholder. "Long-term or short-term? Moral or immoral? Your father would have said it was morally wrong to pursue research to produce military hardware."

"Steer clear of death-dealing!" chanted a group waving a banner.

"I repeat," said Manning, "we will do what is best for the company. And may I stress the word 'we'. Policy is recommended to the board not by myself alone but by a five-man executive committee. All the members of that committee are with me now, on this platform. If you want to fire questions at them, go ahead."

Research for only one project

"May I say," said Philip Proctor, the director of research, "there is nothing moral or immoral about research itself. As I see it we are faced with a straight business and technical decision. It is a choice between assured military business, in the shape of an improved rocket propulsion unit, and the development of hydrogen fuel cells which would put us firmly into the energy market."

"Why not both?" a shareholder asked. "General Electric is in all kinds of business. Why not us?"

"General Electric is 100 times our size," Massing observed. "I don't want to rush into things we wouldn't be capable of doing to the best of our ability. Trying to run down two diverging paths would, in my view, be too much. It would necessitate a big injection of capital, a large extension of our research facilities and a big intake of new people."

"In other words," said a shareholder, "although you are nominally a public company, you still think like a family firm. You won't take risks."

"I wouldn't accept that," Manning said. "I can understand your feelings at our recent rather poor results. However the navy, for one, does not think that our technical performance is poor. We do have a high reputation for technological excellence. It is one that is worth preserving by not spreading ourselves too thinly."

The day after the annual meeting Manning called a meeting of the executive committee. "People are getting restless," he said. "I take it," he turned to Charles Rines, the president and chief operating officer, "that your view hasn't changed."

"No," Rines said. "Clearly, developing the hydrogen fuel cell does have attractions. But it really is rather long-term. If we go that way, we have to be prepared for lacklustre profits for some years."

"And you?" Manning looked at Proctor.

"The military option could be very rewarding," said the research director. "However, those defence contracts demand 100% dedication. The navy would want to put in their own progress chasers, their own quality control. We would no longer be masters in our own house. And we wouldn't have either the resources or the time to pursue other projects."

Vere Harmon, the marketing director, sided with Proctor. "I see much more potential spin-off, long-term, from the hydrogen fuel cell," he said. But Reginald Blake, the finance director, favoured the quicker boost to cash flow from military business.

"It's ironic," Manning thought, as he drove home that night. "When my father ran the company, he made all the decisions. Now that I work democratically with four other experienced people in a public company, I still have to make the decisions."

However, he recognized he still hadn't made up his mind. It was true he

290

had inherited from his father strong moral principles. He also knew that his dead parent would not have approved moving the company into rocketry. Those protestors at the back of the hall had included his own son, who was still at college and led an anti-nuclear movement.

But now that he was chief executive of a public company, the matter had to be decided objectively.

A contract from the navy would improve cash flow. But for how long? Only a limited number of rockets were required for an even more limited number of submarines. What happened when the contract ran down and the company had no back-up technology for other markets?

The hydrogen fuel cell would be aimed at a market that was certain to grow over the longer term. Even if energy did not become scarce it would undoubtedly become more expensive. However, the cell was not so well developed as the rocket propulsion unit. The technology could not simply be put on ice until people and resources permitted its development parallel with a navy contract. Competitors would step in.

So what *was* the decision that would most benefit the company?

DECISION

Company decides between long and short-term strategies

Will Harry Manning have the courage to do the right thing and go for what he believes to be the best interests of the company?

If the company were in dire straits financially, he would have to choose the quick solution offered by the navy contract for rocket motors. But this does not appear to be the case. The problem is one of lacklustre profits, rather than corporate life or death.

Therefore he should concentrate the firm's resources on developing the longer-term, though less immediately profitable, fuel cell technology.

True, the stockholders are restive. But if the company does a good job communicating with them, impressing upon them that the company has consciously decided to invest in future growth, they will respond positively. The constant scramble for the next quarterly earnings per share is a very definite detriment to future growth.

Retain full employment
By going for the longer-term solution, Manning will be striking a blow for employment – a subject not mentioned in the dilemma but very much on people's minds these days. Many companies have turned their minds to so many short-term solutions and activities that they have never really got to grips with long-term problems. Then they find that they have to fire people because they have finally run out of short-term opportunities.

Manning needs to differentiate clearly, in his own mind, between what is essential and what is urgent. The urgent – in this case the need to improve profits by any means available – always has the greatest visibility. The navy contract, at first sight, is highly "visible" and attractive.

The rocket project doesn't solve anything. It only postpones the problem of long-term growth – and probably worsens it, because the fuel cell technology may become obsolete during the time that the company concentrates resources on the rocket motor. So, when the navy contract expires, the company would have nothing.

This does not mean that Manning need, or indeed can, wash his hands of the rocket project entirely. He should think about licensing this advanced technology to somebody else. He could sell it outright or keep it, find a very strong subcontractor, or a number of subcontract organizations, and form a joint venture with them. The fact that the company has a solid reputation for technological excellence supports this approach.

Pursue intermediate products

An immediate step that Manning can take is to organize a task force of finance, marketing and other managers, to explore joint opportunities.

As for the fuel cell, although it is a longer-term solution this does not mean that nothing can be done in the more immediate future. Manning should pursue intermediate products and opportunities, based on the fuel cell technology that is being developed. He should insist that everyone concerned with new product development should move as quickly as possible, get into the market and have the philosophy that nothing is too small to be considered.

It doesn't matter if this does not result in any outstanding successes. More important, there will also be no great failures, for generally things that happen very fast result in small mistakes. Later, the word "mistake" can be replaced by the word "feedback".

So Manning should go for the long-term project but try to get there by a series of short-term opportunities. The company should absorb all the feedback it can get, and be adaptable enough to learn from it.

Again, Manning should get the research and marketing directors, and their managers, to work in a task force, which could include people from outside the organization, to identify the possibilities for short-term goals that are on the same broad track as the long-term goals. He should give them, say, six months to come up with suggestions. It will take them that long, anyway, to make any changes and phase into the project.

A combination of the right long-term strategy, intermediate opportunities and lateral thinking on the problem of the rocket motor could produce good results even sooner than Manning – or the disgruntled shareholders – imagine.

This decision was provided by Don Gamache in his capacity as co-founder and president of Innotech Corp., a U.S.-based consulting firm specializing in technology and marketing.

Chapter 6

Social Responsibility

As individuals, we all shoulder certain responsibilities such as not allowing our dogs to foul the pavements and not mowing down pedestrians in our motor cars. But in business, what is socially permissible can be more vague. To what extent should companies be concerned with the health of their employees, or avoiding redundancies? Those are just two of the dilemma topics tackled here.

Should company doctor name sales manager in danger of heart attack?

Yvon Rougerie, president of Aliments Laferté SA, was just filling his briefcase in preparation for going home when Michel Duhamel stuck his head round the door, "May I see you for a minute?" asked the company doctor. Rougerie readily welcomed his late guest. He always valued his frequent informal discussions with Duhamel. As an impartial outsider to company politics and the competition for promotion, the doctor had been a useful sounding board on a wide range of topics. Rougerie sometimes felt constrained from discussing with other senior executives some delicate subjects on which he had not yet made up his mind. But he had always found the doctor a wise and trustworthy confidant who could ease the lonely life of the man at the top.

But this time it was Duhamel who wanted a sounding board. He revealed that one of the three executives recently appointed to the physically taxing job of regional sales manager had a serious heart condition but would not turn down the major appointment.

Although Duhamel would not reveal which of the new appointees was at risk, it was in fact the 45-year-old Basel region manager, Réné Dorgelés, whom he had examined a month before, during the yearly check-up. Duhamel had discovered that Dorgelés had already suffered from heart tremors and was extremely susceptible to a serious, possibly fatal, attack. The new job required extended travel and was likely to produce greatly increased physical and mental stress. It would be foolhardy in the extreme, Duhamel had told Dorgelés, to accept the job in his state of health – particularly with a wife and three children.

Bound by professional ethics

"Nonsense," Dorgelés had retorted. "I'm as fit as a fiddle. All my family have had high blood pressure, and they've gone on to a ripe old age. I'm good for another 30 years yet. In any case, this is a crucial career step for me, and I'm not going to give it up for anything."

Having failed to convince the new regional sales manager, Duhamel had gone to discuss his problem with his friend, the company president. He made it clear from the start that professional ethics forbade him from revealing the name of the man. But he wanted Rougerie to suggest some way in which he might be able to persuade the stubborn executive. Rougerie pointed out, however, that since he did not know who the man was he could not advice on how he might be persuaded. He sympathized with Duhamel's plight, but suggested that while the doctor adhered to his professional principles there was nothing he, Rougerie, could do. Privately he unwittingly echoed Dorgelés' sentiments by reflecting that the regional sales manager jobs were known to be key stepping stones for future top executives in Aliments Laferté, so it was most unlikely that Duhamel would be able to persuade the new man, whoever he was, to step down.

After Duhamel had left, Rougerie considered the problem. The doctor's conscientious professionalism had been the main cause of the trust placed in him, not only by Rougerie, but also by other executives who respected his position and knew that nothing they revealed to him would get back to company management. In the past, more than one executive breakdown had been averted through Duhamel's firm intervention. In the cases Rougerie knew about, the patient had acquiesced in his making quiet arrangements to cover the man's job for a few weeks at short notice. And the company benefited from the doctor's preventive approach.

So Rougerie dismissed the possibility of insisting that the doctor give him the man's name. But he had a shrewd idea that Dorgelés was the vulnerable executive. Dorgelés smoked heavily, seemed about ten kilogrammes overweight and had the ruddy complexion that Rougerie associated with high blood pressure. But then he reflected that whether he identified the man directly or indirectly, the risk to the valuable trust placed in the company doctor would be the same, as the man would guess the reason for any change in his new appointment at this stage. And that was assuming he had correctly guessed the ailing executive's identity.

Rougerie was very concerned for the well-being of the executive in question. This worried him more than the realization that sales would surely suffer if the regional sales manager should die or be incapacitated just as he was breaking into the job. Was it worth risking an employee's health and a drop in one region's sales in order to preserve confidence in Duhamel and the company's medical programme?

DECISION

Doctor-patient confidence should be handled with care

The basic elements of Yvon Rougerie's dilemma are a threat to the state of health of one of his executives; the trustworthy position of the company doctor; and the detrimental impact on the company if Réné Dorgelés should become seriously ill.

The question arises on what ethical grounds Michel Duhamel's viewpoint is founded. On an impulse one could agree with the doctor's point of view. However, on further analysis certain flaws in his reasoning become apparent and should be examined further.

For instance, if Dorgelés were suffering from open tuberculosis or if he were a bus driver, there would be no question but that the public interest would prevail over his personal judgement. But doesn't the company have a similar duty in this case to protect the man's family?

Medical check is for a purpose
Another flaw in Duhamel's argument stems from the fact that he is the company doctor. This means he must act not just in the employee's interest, but decidedly also in the company's interest. A major aim of a yearly medical check-up is to find out whether employees are able to continue fulfilling the functions entrusted to them without risk to their health, both in their own and the company's interest.

The situation would be different if the problem had been diagnosed by

Dorgelés family doctor. In that case the doctor would have been pledged to professional secrecy, if so desired by the patient. This case is closer to that of the doctor examining an applicant for government sickness benefits: the doctor's first responsibility is to the organization.

But whereas Duhamel did not go far enough in revealing the man's name to his chief executive, he went too far in mentioning the kind of illness. He should simply have made a statement to the effect that Dorgelés was not fit on medical grounds to fulfil the functions of sales manager.

Apparently Duhamel himself wrestles uneasily with his professional code. If he were deeply convinced of his duty to maintain complete professional silence, he would not have spoken to Rougerie on the subject at all.

Policy for the company doctor
Aliments Laferté does not appear to have any laid-down policy in respect of the company doctor's function. It seems as if up to now Duhamel has always been able to act as he sees fit. An adequate policy should be laid down in consultation with employee representatives. After all, problems of this kind could have been avoided if there had been a company regulation requiring medical examination in cases of major changes in function. No doctor can have ethical objections to company medical check-ups if the employees concerned are informed in advance of the procedure and its consequences.

But without such understanding, Rougerie now finds himself in an unenviable position. If he wants the interests of the Dorgelés family and the company to prevail, he will have to persuade Duhamel that he ought to speak to the manager at risk again, telling him that he wishes to inform Rougerie of the outcome of the examination.

Avoid shaking employee confidence
If Dorgelés still refuses to allow this, Rougerie will himself have to talk to each of the three sales managers in turn, tell them the information he has, and try to find out which suffers from heart trouble. If this step is taken however, it will be practically impossible to avoid shaking employees' confidence in Duhamel. Rougerie will have to accept this consequence and, if need be, explain his viewpoint to the employee representatives. After all, the company doctor has placed him in this dilemma and Rougerie must remember his own broader responsibility.

Whether Rougerie will have to relieve Dorgelés of his new position will depend partly on his discussions with him. It may be helpful to bring Dorgelés wife into the discussion, if he agrees. If she too thinks that the risk is worth taking, maybe Rougerie can leave Dorgelés in the job.

If not, Rougerie should try to find another job that he can offer, with less stress but as far as possible equal pay and status. Possibly a staff job might provide this opportunity. Or, depending on the whole situation, it may be possible to restructure the position so that Dorgelés remains as regional sales manager but one or a number of his subordinates take over some of the travelling and other chores that could be so dangerous for him.

This decision was provided by P.L. Koppen in his capacity as chairman of Dutch-based management consultants Berenschot NV.

Should managing director investigate leak of new product design?

Leonard Crabtree was in his office at Spence & Co, a medium-sized manufacturer of electrical appliances, when his chief salesman burst in. "I thought that *we* were going to introduce something like this," the salesman said irritably, waving a new type of electrically operated can-opener in the managing director's face. "It's already on sale in the shops, and look at the name on the handle."

Crabtree looked, and frowned. The name was that of an upstart rival firm called Smethwick. The design of the can-opener was so distinctive, he though, that there was no way Smethwick could have produced the item by coincidence.

Crabtree felt that his worst fears were being realized – that possibly the wife of his own marketing director, Harold Wise, was passing on company secrets.

To the salesman he said: "I'll look into this." When the man had gone, he telephoned Charles Foster, Spence's design chief, and asked to see him as soon as possible.

While waiting for Foster, Crabtree thought back to the day, a few months previously when he had learned that Patricia Wise had taken a job as personal assistant to Smethwick's managing director. He had received that news in the most annoying way imaginable – from a rival at a trade show.

"Harry," Crabtree had said to Wise at the first opportunity, "you didn't tell me that Patricia was working for Smethwick."

Dominating wife

Wise, who was highly valued in the company but also rather temperamental, had reported that he hadn't thought it was anybody else's business what his wife did. To this Crabtree had angrily replied: "You know damn well it must be my business."

"But my wife has her own life," Wise had said, "and that is *her* business."

The brief confrontation had ended with Wise denying that he ever discussed business at home, while Crabtree had pointed out that he did sometimes take work home.

Wise had worked for Spence for eight years, and had contributed much to the firm's success. Crabtree respected his ability but suspected that probably he was dominated by his wife, who seemed to Crabtree a very ambitious woman. Crabtree had shunted the affair to the back of his mind, telling himself that if he tried to control managers' wives there was no telling where it would end.

When Foster, the design chief, arrived, Crabtree showed him the can-opener. "Who knew about our product apart from the two of us and Harry?" Crabtree demanded.

"Only a couple of development engineers," Foster replied, "and neither of them had the whole picture. As you know, this was my personal baby."

"Would Smethwick have needed our prototype to have done such a

298

good job?" Crabtree demanded.

Foster nodded. "Almost certainly," he said.

"Could either of your men have smuggled it out?"

"Not a chance. I would stake my career on that."

"You may have to," Crabtree said grimly. "Now what about Harry, did *he* take it home?"

"Yes, he did," Foster admitted reluctantly. "He took it for a few days because he wanted to identify its positive qualities for himself, to help him with his promotion campaign."

When Foster had left, Crabtree wondered what to do. He had no evidence that Patricia Wise had shown the product to her new boss. It would have been a very disloyal thing for any wife to have done. But his mind was not put at rest when his own wife informed him that it was common knowledge that the Wises' marriage was breaking up.

Should he confront Wise with his suspicions and risk an explosion which might lead to the executive's resignation?

Should he insist that his managers sign a contract saying that their wives must not work for rival firms.?

Should he employ a private investigator to look into the whole affair?

If he did nothing, he risked other breaches of confidence and of security. But if he acted too hastily, he could destroy a lot of the friendly, cooperative atmosphere that had been one of the company's great strengths.

DECISION

Company may have to consider protecting its inventions

C rabtree is in the situation of having to try and shut the door after the horse has bolted. The least that he can do now is stop other "animals" from escaping. The most is to recoup his loss through legal processes.

The very first fact that needs to be established is that the design of the Spence prototype and the Smethwick product are compatible to such a degree that the latter could only be the result of copying.

Incidentally, Crabtree might also ask himself how Smethwick could develop its product so quickly while his own product was allowed to languish so long in the development stage.

Once Crabtree decides that the Smethwick product is a copy, he must consult his company's solicitors to determine what proof is required to litigate for the theft of trade secrets, if this option is available.

If it is absolutely clear that Smethwick's product is a copy, Crabtree needs to know whether the security breach originated with Wise. He should look critically at his own security controls, if indeed they exist.

Did Wise breach any rules in taking the prototype home? If not, should adequate rules be established to prevent this sort of action taking place?

Since Wise had so little difficulty removing the prototype from the building, could other people on the staff have done the same thing with equal ease? How about Foster, the design engineer, and his two developmental engineers?

Crabtree should also take a look at Smethwick, so far as the law permits, to see whether Wise, his wife or anyone else at Spence, has a financial interest in Smethwick or any other direct ties to that company.

He should confront his marketing director face to face. No doubt Wise would explode and bluster. But there is a chance that as he calms down he might think about the situation and admit to himself that his wife had the opportunity to take the prototype out of their home.

Moreover, Wise's loyalty to the company may be stronger than his loyalty to his wife. He might not automatically resign and may be very helpful.

Crabtree should seek more facts before proceeding with any confrontations or overt action. Since the company clearly does not have an internal security manager, he should hire an outside security professional. Even at this late stage he needs someone who is skilled in collecting information and in objectively appraising it together with the company's solicitors.

I suspect that the company's top management, which is closely knit and has been deeply involved in the development of the product, is going to be too subjective to carry out a really worthwhile investigation on its own.

In addition, as the investigation proceeds, the outside professional can be developing a separate report on deficiencies in the internal controls that allow such a situation to develop. He will then be better equipped to recommend corrections.

Admittedly, his entry may cause some upset in a relatively small company. However, Crabtree can defend his decision to his colleagues by saying that it was the only fair way to handle a situation embarrassing to everyone, and of preventing a recurrence.

He can argue that hiring an outside investigator is likely to cause less harm in the long run than if he had, through lack of information, jumped to the wrong conculsion.

Many companies do make their officers and engineers sign an agreement stating that they will not reveal trade secrets. But even here there are snags if the agreement is not well thought out.

Many companies not involved in military contracts, or highly sophisticated scientific products, don't take the time to identify what company information constitutes trade secrets.

This decision was provided by Thomas B. Nagle, a former special agent with the United States Secret Service, and director of corporate security of Levi Strauss & Co.

DILEMMA

Will centralized production produce adverse public reaction?

"Parco," said Don Anzio Paz quietly, "the situation is getting worse and worse. I do not remember a time in the long history of this company when we had such bad publicity. And our sales figures are 20% down. The people are not drinking our beer because of that leak of information."

Somehow news had got out that the company was planning to close its breweries in the four provincial capital cities and would concentrate its production in a new major plant in the national capital. The story was true and the company was unable to refute it publicly. On the contrary, the announcement of the company's plans was to be released to the press by the government's ministry of industry the following week.

"I think the whole project should be cancelled," said Paz. The board would discuss just that possibility the next day.

Gideon Parco, vice-president in charge of production and planning of La Dorada SA, one of the biggest breweries and one of the largest companies in Central America, was astonished. Nearly five years of studies, consultation and planning had materialized into his most ambitious project: one large plant to be centralized in the capital of the nation, with a bottling capacity of 20 million bottles of beer monthly. This would be enough to cover the expanding demands of the country's total population and to export to neighbouring countries.

Problems of massive redundancy

But Parco's project, a result of his expertise, knowledge of the market and also of his excellent contacts with foreign investors, also meant the gradual dismantling of the four plants that La Dorada had built up over 80 years in the four provincial capitals. These plants created a source of employment, badly needed in various parts of the country.

After hearing again the technical pleas presented by Parco, Paz answered him cordially but firmly: "I know, Parco. You and your team have done a great job. I know that costs will be cut. Productivity will soar. Furthermore, I know that with the new plant we will not need to increase the price of our beer. But remember, we owe all our growth to the people. We cannot create problems of massive redundancy in these towns. Whole communities have expanded thanks to our factories. Thousands of bottles were broken in protest when *El Tiempo* leaked the news that the President of the Republic would lay the foundation stone. Now, I have information that the political pressure is so great that he will be forced to cancel his appearance at the ceremony."

"I have already told you about my project," answered Parco. "The French group which is giving us financial and technical assistance is willing to convert the old factories into centres of education for young apprentices and unskilled labour. I am sure this will placate the protesters. Also a private company in El Salvador has already agreed to buy the old equipment, eager to establish a beer industry of their own on a small scale in that country."

Government approval required

Of course, Paz was well aware that the president would be very pleased to see a new factory in the capital, which traditionally lacked industrial development. The government had initially approved the project in secret. But it was faced with a new election next year. It would almost certainly lose many votes in the provinces if the factories were dismantled. And if the radical party won, it could well ban all forms of international financial aid and participation in the country's industry. If that were to happen, the French group would cancel its backing and La Dorada would be placed in a most difficult financial position if it had to fulfil the project by itself.

Parco interrupted his thoughts: "Sr. Paz, if we abandon this project and keep our small factories going, it will be necessary to increase the price by at least 15% to meet increasing costs. That will be as unpopular as abandoning our old plants, and do not forget that the French group has approached the government with an offer to build the plant itself without exporting its earnings. It would mean our ruin."

The board was meeting the next day and Paz either had to present a case for cancelling the whole project or confirm the date and hour of the ceremony. The press expected it to be announced publicly by the government that day.

DECISION

It is not too late for
Paz to plan ahead

Evidently, Paz has not given any attention to strategy for many years. This is the real issue.

Paz knows very well that the two choices he feels are open to him are equally valid for the success of the company. But he has allowed this unfortunate conflict to emerge. Why? The answer is that he has not planned ahead.

It also appears that the production vice-president has not done any planning either during the past five years. Nor have the marketing or sales managers. Nor have the managers of the four provincial plants.

Part of the problem is a deficiency in Paz himself. It is rather late in the development of the company for him to realize that he has to take some action on something which is very difficult to accomplish.

There would be no problem now if Paz had taken earlier action. He should have been gradually expanding the company in stages. He should have expanded through acquisitions or amalgamations to ensure regular supplies of raw materials and to integrate production with distribution and marketing. He should have developed a national policy and strategy for the company within the national economy.

All of these moves were possible and viable. They still are.

There is obviously a big gap in the country's beer industry offering the opportunity for a company to expand and to increase. There is no evidence that there is a need to increase enormously the production capacity, however. The company might well consider a more modern plant but with less production capacity than the one it is now planning.

Locate in densely populated areas
It seems to me unwise for it to build a plant which is going to be expensive and runs the risk of early obsolescence. The new plant will not automatically or magically cut costs in fuel, transport or raw materials. On the contrary, although the production unit costs may be lower through increased volume and increased automation, the centralized location will raise other costs. Distribution costs in particular will be much higher.

Beer drinkers are not concentrated in certain areas nor particularly in places which have very easy access for transport. If Paz wants to control his distribution costs he will have to locate his plants in the most densely populated areas of the country. And this apparently is exactly where his present plants are situated now.

302

The stone-laying ceremony at the new plant should be postponed. This does not mean it has to be cancelled. I do not see any pressure of time since Paz does not have to confirm the ceremony right now. And the French have already been waiting patiently for five years.

I do not believe that the French group would establish a plant in central America by itself as it claims. I doubt its claim that it could promise the government to leave all its earnings in the country. It is easy enough to arrange to take earnings out of the country through the purchase of raw materials and for payment of technical assistance. And who can assure the French group that the government would not expropriate the plant?

I think that Paz should begin by concentrating all his efforts in recuperating the 20% loss in sales. That should be the top priority on the board's agenda at the moment.

The company attributes the decrease in the sale of beer to the unhappy leak of the news of the plant closures. But management should investigate whether there are not other factors causing this fall in sales. The price of rum might have gone down, for example, causing beer drinkers to switch to rum. Or it may be that people in agricultural areas have suffered a bad year, and are spending less money on drink.

Prices could be adjusted according to the market demand in various parts of the country. In Mexico in 1975, when beer prices went up, consumption in the cities went down but sales in the provinces surprisingly went up.

Once the problem of what to do about declining sales is attacked, Paz must concentrate on restructuring his organization. He needs to establish better control of operations and production. Marketing needs to be improved, with better sales promotion. At the same time he must begin to strengthen his managerial team, with fewer specialists and more people who have broader vision. His team can then devise strategies, first at regional, then national, level.

This decision was provided by Dr. Carlos Michelsen in his capacity as director of the Graduate School of Business Administration at the Institute of Technology and Advanced Studies, Monterrey, Mexico.

DILEMMA

If incentive gifts are banned will performance drop?

"Goodnight, Mr. Leek!" called out a junior buyer as the managing director walked to his reserved parking space in the car park.

"Good night ... er ..." the managing director sputtered. James Leek never could remember the names of these young buyers. They changed so often. Slightly embarrassed, Leek stared at the young man trying to squeeze a large HiLite package into the back of his car. Leek was not so much suspicious as he was curious. A man of high principles, Leek did not readily think badly of others. Still, HiLite Electronics Components Ltd. was one of the company's main suppliers. And HiLite's boxes were a familiar sight in the receiving bay.

The managing director thought again about the incident the following morning as he drove in the company car park. Leek decided to go directly to the office of the chief buyer, Thomas Cooke, and make discreet enquiries. He had no need to be discreet. Cooke was ready to discuss the matter quite openly.

"It's a gift," explained Cooke simply, "a television set from HiLite."

"A gift?" repeated Leek.

"Yes, that's right," replied Cooke. "HiLite made this special offer to the electrical goods buyer. If we doubled the order size last month and paid within ten days, they offered the product buyer a choice of gifts. I got stereo speakers from them in the same way last year."

Leek was stunned. "Does this happen very often?" he asked.

"Oh, more and more," replied Cooke. "Many companies are now making special offers of gifts for buyers. In fact I encourage my buyers to explore ways to take advantage of these special deals. Our stationery buyer last year got a two-week holiday in Spain as part of a special deal."

A question of integrity

"See here," said Leek firmly. "I do not intend to allow this company's reputation to be jeopardized by bribes."

"They are not bribes," retorted Cooke angrily. "They are legitimate sales promotion offers, made quite openly to every company. This company has saved a lot of money as a result of such deals, since bulk orders usually command a discount. What is more I do not buy anything beyond company requirements. The way prices are going up we cannot lose."

"You obviously do not worry very much about the cost of stockholding or our cash flow problems, do you?" countered Leek. "If HiLite wants to increase their sales or get earlier payments, they should offer the company a discount."

Cooke sighed. "Our suppliers say a lot of firms appreciate these offers as a means of giving their employees a tax-free bonus."

"Well, I won't have it here," said Leek firmly. "I don't want my buyers influenced by gifts..."

"I hope you are not questioning my integrity," interrupted Cooke, who was not easily impressed with Leek's self-righteousness. "I am not influenced by these gifts. They are good incentives for my buyers. They are beginning to cut down employee turnover in this department, at no cost to this company. I consider that any perquisites or buyer's commissions should be the natural reward for buyers.

"Our salesmen work on commissions, not to mention all kinds of free meals on company expenses. Why can't buyers profit from their efforts. The pay of my buyers is lower than that of any salesman. I think we contribute just as much to this company's profitability. And yet you are complaining about a buyer taking home a television."

Leek had to agree that Cooke was a good man and was running an efficient department. He had managed to keep total price increases down to 8% last year. Delivery times for crucial items had been greatly reduced despite market scarcity. But he didn't like Cooke's attitude. He felt allowing employees to accept incentives from suppliers was ill advised.

On the other hand if he demanded a stop to it, Leek thought, he might well face a revolt within the buying department and perhaps simply drive the practice underground.

Create a framework of purchasing policy regarding buyer incentives

Having brought up the subject of "buyer incentives" and the contribution of the buying department to company profitability, Leek should maintain the initiative and implement a total review of purchasing policy and operations.

There are three main reasons why Leek must stop the gifts. First, this will take the initiative from the supplier in respect of volume of purchases, prices and financing arrangements. Second, continued gifts may stimulate suspicions by other employees. Finally, stopping gifts is the only way to stimulate the *professional* development of buyers.

Provided Leek drops his self-righteous style and becomes personally involved in a participative analysis, he should be able, as have many other companies, to stop the acceptance of suppliers's gifts and commissions. At the same time the morale and performance of the total supply function can be improved by rewarding buyers through pay, personal development and job satisfaction.

Leek obviously trusts Cooke, the chief buyer, and from statistics available is not able to criticize the efficiency of his department. However, having raised doubts he should continue his discussions.

How many gifts have been accepted in the last 12 months? What is the code of practice of the national purchasing officers' association? Have the delivery times for crucial items been achieved through Cooke's long-standing personal relationship with key suppliers? At what price? Could the junior buyers achieve the same level of performance? When were order sizes and stock levels last discussed with finance and sales departments? Is the company training young buyers as purchasing managers or order clerks?

Analyse the staff rewards

Cooke's attitude should concern Leek for two reasons. Firstly, he appears to give priority to seeking out opportunities for "gifts" as an incentive and reward for the staff, including himself. Secondly, there is the question of why he has not raised the problem of the fast turnover of junior buyers with Leek. Perhaps he has with little response.

The blame cannot be placed on the junior buyer. Cooke encouraged him to seek out and accept the television set. Perhaps it will be pressure from the young buyer's wife next time. Apparently low paid, he perceives his status as lower than that of the salesmen. He sees his fellow buyers continually resigning. In this environment he perhaps sees little chance or encouragement of personal development. But if he is interested in his career he would react positively to an analysis of the sitation that allowed him to put forward his ideas.

To achieve a successful change, however, Leek will need to win the commitment and confidence of the staff. Before meeting all the buying staff Leek and Cooke need to have a thorough review of the role and key objectives of the buying department and agree a framework of purchasing policy regarding the acceptance of buyer incentives, Christmas gifts and reciprocal trading. To ensure that such a policy statement is well received, it should be presented in the context of a five-point plan to improve the development and potential reward of individual buyers and at the same time the total effectiveness of the department. The company should:

● Clarify the potential role and scope of the buying function and the need to involve other departments, such as sales and finance, in all the key decisions.

● Review the allocation of objectives and tasks between senior and junior buyers and check that levels of authority and accountability are understood.

● Specify objectives which are oriented to individual results rather than volume of work. Results objectives would include, for example, savings versus general price indices, and choice of reliable suppliers, as opposed to the number of orders processed or hours worked.

● Introduce a series of job-related training sessions beginning with the basics of value analysis. Launch a number of projects concentrating on the 20% of items that represent typically 70% to 80% of purchase value.

● Re-evaluate the relative worth of the buyer's job, paying attention to the increased demand for exploratory thinking, negotiating skills, innovation and cooperation with the company employees who use the goods that are bought.

A single incident can stimulate a major review. With the money tied up in buying. Leek can ill afford to miss the challenge.

This decision was provided by Richard Handscombe in his capacity as managing director of Urwick International NV in Amsterdam, an affiliate of Urwick, Orr & Partners based in London.

DILEMMA

Should company privileges be offered to all residents in the city?

The tropical heat hit Walther von Stolzing as he stepped from the aeroplane. The group managing director of Schwarm KG searched the airport crowd for sight of his south-east manager, Karl Szentner.

"I just don't understand how we got into this mess," he told Szentner, who had driven in from the company's main area factory located some 120 kilometres from the capital city. "We are giving employment to 2,000 workers. We are improving their welfare and living conditions and helping their families. How can the government complain because we are building a new medical centre?"

"When we announced our plans for the centre our workers were really excited," Szentner replied. "It was the local nationalist party leaders who started complaining. Suddenly the papers were full of stories about Schwarm being just another example of Western imperialism exploiting the local population. The Minister of Industry, Uy Ong, asked to meet you personally, I thought it important enough for you to come over from Düsseldorf to do so. Ong is young and a very powerful man in the government. It would be very bad for the company to upset him."

The meeting began with the preliminary courtesies, but Ong came quickly to the point. "Your policies are dividing our people," he said. "Since you set up your plant here four years ago, you have started providing free meals. You have set up a recreation centre, with sports fields and a free cinema. You have taken one of the city's best doctors. And now you want to set up a health and dental care centre, again just for your employees.

"The result is that, not only are your employees getting higher pay than the other 9,000 workers in the town, but they enjoy social and welfare benefits denied others in the community."

Von Stolzing looked sceptical. "Surely in any commuity some people are better off than others. Just remember our company is making an important contribution to your country's health and social services. By providing for our employees and their families, we are relieving the government of this burden.

"Do you believe our employees should be deprived of these privileges just because the rest of the community does not enjoy them? What do you expect us to do? Stop our benefits?"

A good public relations gesture

Ong smiled indulgently. "To begin with," he said, "perhaps the company should open its facilities to all city residents, not just employees."

Von Stolzing mopped the sweat off his brow with his cleanly pressed linen handkerchief. "See here," he retorted, "we cannot start taking on the responsibility for the whole community's welfare. We are already doing more than our share, I think. It is your responsibility to look after the community welfare, not ours."

Ong was still smiling. "Oh yes, the government has many responsibilities," he said, "such as approving plans for expansion and controlling import licences. We have let you import your components quite freely. And we have given your German managers considerable tax advantages."

Von Stolzing noted that the government was eagerly seeking more foreign investment, and his firm had recently announced plans to treble its investment there. "Surely you do not want to discourage us," he said.

Ong replied: "Ah, but your present factory uses many employees, and most of the products are re-exported. But your new plant is highly automated and will employ only a handful of people. Most of its products will be for local consumption. I wonder whether we can really afford the loss of foreign exchange it will involve.

"Besides, if you are trebling your investment in plant, why not also treble your investment in social services, and extend them to all?"

As they left the ministry, Szentner suggested: "Perhaps we could meet them part way. We could open the cinema and the sports fields to the community during working hours when we are not using them. It would cost little and would be a good public relations gesture."

Von Stolzing remained silent. He wondered whether such a move would simply whet nationalist appetites for more. He resented what he considered thinly disguised blackmail by the minister. The planned new investment would increase the company's exposure to this sort of pressure.

Should von Stolzing follow his local manager's advice, or make the counter threat to cancel his company's planned investment?

Corporate policies should compromise between home and local conditions

L ike many other companies operating subsidiaries in foreign countries, Schwarm KG has evidently paid insufficient attention to the need to "fit in". At times the company demonstrates a peculiar willingness to delude itself about low reaction to a firm that does not manifest any genuine interest in the national, rather than the company's, well-being.

It may be argued of course that any multinational company moving into a developing community will, to some extent at least, damage considerably the social fabric of the community no matter how careful, or well planned and intentioned, the entry. The pay and reward policies may produce a new rich and poor proletariat in local communities. In this instance the influence of the multinational company in the developing economy can be divisive. Uy Ong seems to be addressing this issue.

Von Stolzing appears to be faced with not one, but two problems. One is to rectify mistakes that have been made in the past. The company has paid insufficient attention to the community and its effects on it. The worker benefits have probably been far too generous.

Secondly, the company must establish a long-term personnel policy for its overseas subsidiary.

The success of a foreign company in any host country to a large extent depends on the ability of its non-national managers to assimilate the behavioural, business and cultural practices of the host country. Although "overseas management" may be similar to management of home-based operations in many ways, it is not the same thing. A manager can take for granted that he understands the environment of his home country simply because he is so steeped in it. But he cannot make this assumption in a foreign country.

Rely on local manager's advice
Unless overseas managers of companies like Schwarm are willing to make, and are capable of making, a substantial effort – and it is usually much more substantial than most realize – to absorb the culture of the country in which they are working, the exercise of management skills is likely to produce very frustrating and most unsatisfactory results.

The company must decide whether the image a foreign subsidiary should project is that of a local company or of a foreign company.

The answer appears to be some sort of compromise that will vary from country to country and at times even from industry to industry. In this compromise the ethical, human relations and forward planning aspects of management seem best based on the home country standards. The socio-economic considerations, on the other hand, should reflect the host country's standards.

In the short term I think von Stolzing must rely heavily on the advice of Szentner. The local manager will, presumably, have a much better feel of the cultural and political problems. The sharing of the recreational facilities will probably be a minimum requirement.

Since Schwarm employs some 20% of the local workforce, it cannot afford to act in a narrow "company only" manner. Von Stolzing must consider the whole community.

In the longer term Schwarm must examine, and define, a strategy for each of its overseas operations. This will dictate the corporate stance and social and economic policy. Such a strategy will call for an examination of local behavioural, business and, equally important, cultural practices.

A reasonable line to follow, I would advise, would be to adopt corporate policies which represent a compromise between what it would do at home and what local conditions demand. The long range future of any manufacturing subsidiary will depend directly on the real and effective contribution the company makes to the social and economic welfare of the host country.

This decision was provided by Ivor Kenny in his capacity as director general of the Irish Management Institute, based in Dublin.

DILEMMA

Can overburdened chairman delegate to unwilling subordinates?

"Of course I should delegate more," said Youssef Massif, the balding and portly head of Arab Automotive Engineering Co., "but people in this company are the same as in most other Middle Eastern companies. They don't *like* to take responsibility."

"Maybe you are right. But why not give it a try?" pressed Ibrahim Elrif, a visiting consultant from Egypt. After five months on loan from his university in Cairo, Elrif was now convinced that the root of most of the company's inefficiencies lay in excessive centralization at the top. Even small matters, involving expenditure of $20 or $30, were regularly passed to the chairman for approval. This buried him in administrative paperwork that left no time for more important tasks.

Having been to a school of business administration in the U.S. one or two years before, Elrif was full of the advantages of modern management techniques. He was wise enough to realize that they do not always adapt easily to foreign business environments. But he felt sure that the firm could benefit greatly from using the creative resources of all its managers, rather than relying on one overworked man at the top. "It is unlikely to do the firm any harm," he argued, "and you may find your subordinates revealing some unexpected abilities and initiatives."

Delegating 'piles of paperwork'
Massif stared long and hard at the three "in-trays" on his highly polished desk. None of the three piles of documents was less than 40 cm. high. He liked the feeling of comfortable authority that went with having all the reins in his hands. Indeed, it was the only way he could be sure everything was done to his satisfaction. Nevertheless, it would be useful not to have to tackle those piles of paperwork every day. Even if they were reduced by only half, he would have time to attend to some of the important

long-term issues which always seemed to be swept aside by the urgency of day-to-day matters. There was, for example, the whole question of modernizing the company's product range, perhaps to include sophisticated miniature electronics. Moreover, he would enjoy an occasional evening when he did not have to take work home. Right now, the constant interruptions at work made this necessary.

"All right," he declared, startling himself with the boldness of his decision, "we will see what happens."

Massif revealed the plan to his committee two days later. "From now on," he said, "you will be doing some of the work you are paid to do."

Few of the executives showed much enthusiasm. However, Elrif spent several hours with each of them. He explained how they could gain from increased authority. He agreed on what the limits of their authority should be. And Elrif reasoned that, given time to gain confidence, they would gradually ask for more responsibility. At first most of the executives greatly underrated the amount of money they should be able to spend on their own authority.

However, when Elrif made his next visit from Cairo about two months later, Massif pointed to his in-trays and said: "I told you so." They were, if anything, even more deeply piled with paper than before.

"It gets worse every week," he complained. "Look at this one. He wants to know if he can order 200 pencils!"

Massif added: "As far as I can see, they genuinely do not want to take responsibility. Even the best are continually asking me for guidelines and policy rulings on how they should run their departments."

Just then one of Massif's immediate subordinates poked his head round the door. He apologized for interrupting, then said: "We have a terrible problem on the production line. I wonder if you could spare a few minutes?" It seemed that production had been disrupted by a dispute over which department had first call on a particular batch of components. With a significant glance at Elrif, Massif sent his subordinate away with a promise to "be along in a minute".

Turning to Elrif, the worried chairman said: "That is just typical. What should I do? The last few times I've tried telling them to sort it out themselves they took days to get back to full production. And they get just as panic-stricken when the problem inevitably appears again within a matter of weeks. But if I go back to sorting out the shop-floor problems myself, I'll never get to planning this new product range."

DECISION

Clear goals and standards of performance must be set

This case represents a classic situation of a chief executive wanting to do something but being unable to bring it about because he is himself an unknowing part of the problem. What are Youssef Massif's perceptions of some of the elements of the situation?

Before even embarking on his programme of decentralization, he observed: "People in this company are the same as in most other Middle

Eastern companies. They don't *like* to take responsibility." With a start like this, self-fulfilling prophecy is almost guaranteed. Do *all* people in Middle Eastern companies not like to take responsibility? Or is he generalizing from the few to the many and supporting a stereotype in which they are trapped because no one has shown them the way out?

And how does he feel about his centralized operation? "He liked the feeling of comfortable authority that went with having all the reins in his hands." It is unlikely that this facet of his management style is unknown to his subordinates, even though he may never have stated it explicitly.

To consider other facets of his personal management style, we may look at the steps he took to introduce decentralization. He "revealed *his* plan" to his executives. He said: "From now on, you will be doing some of the work you are being paid to do." (One possible implication for an executive: "If I change my behaviour, I will be tacitly admitting that I have not been doing the work I have been paid to do.") He had Ibrahim Elrif, the outsider, spend several hours with each of them outlining the desired change: he did not do so himself. Elrif, not Massif, agreed with each of the subordinates on what the limits of their authority should be.

No clear signals given

In summary, we have here a picture of a chief executive who, although wanting to give decentralization a try in order to reduce his in-basket load and allow time for product line planning, seems to be personally comfortable with holding the reins and not being truly committed to the principle of decentralization. He even tries to delegate the bringing about of delegation to his consultant! In a superficial way, we might characterize the lack of response of the executives as a problem of resistance to change. But there is really no such thing – there is only resistance to the perceived negative consequences of change. As long as Massif does not seem to be committed to the principle of decentralization (as evidenced by his own behaviour, not his word) his executives are not receiving clear signals that this move will be to their advantage.

What is to be done? Since Massif himself is part of the problem, the only remaining change agent is Elrif (although his contributions are suspect since he seems to have acquiesced in Massif's "delegation of delegation"). Let us assume that Elrif reconsiders the situation and his own role in it.

Become a professional manager

He must, as a conscientious consultant, evaluate his own ability to affect quickly the thinking of Massif. If he feels that he is incapable he should direct Massif to an appropriate outside agency that will provide him with a useful management learning experience – preferably in the supportive company of other senior practising executives with whom Massif can share his concerns.

If he does feel personally competent, then he must help Massif to understand himself and the effect that Massif's own beliefs and values have on his behaviour and on his organization.

This situation is more than a matter of management style and behaviour. Massif must learn, through whatever resources are available, to become a professional manager. He will then be better equipped to decide *what* to do himself and then how to help others to learn also. For instance, he must work with his executives *personally* to establish limits of authority and he must work with them *in groups* as well as individually in shared problem-solving activity. The consequences of their problems are organization-wide, after all, not just personal. He should work with his team at setting goals and establishing performance standards that are understandable and mutually acceptable . His compensation plan or system of rewards and penalities must fit in with the philosophy.

This decision was provided by James L. Hayes in his capacity as president of American Management Associations Inc.

DILEMMA

Should sales director expose client firm's buyer as corrupt?

Frank Walters is district sales director for Wellington Furniture & Supply Co., a New Zealand company which has exclusive representation for several international manufacturers of business machine equipment and office furniture. He has been primarily responsible for increasing business in his territory by 20% in each of the last three years, is well liked by his clients and feels strongly that the products he represents are the best in the field.

Yet there is one account he cannot win. He has visited the Melbourne branch in Australia of Sydney-based Amalgamated Engineering Pty. at least ten times. The regional manager has always been friendly and has been unable, Walters feels, to find any fault with his sales pitch against direct competitor Linden Office Equipment Co.

Trial on a test basis
Walters has based his presentation against the firm's major competitor on three points: after-sales service; quality of products offered; and price. Yet, in 1977 Linden continued to receive all of the business from the Melbourne office of Amalgamated Engineering, valued at nearly $100,000.

When Walters asked for at least a share of the business on a test basis, the regional manager said that the chief purchasing executive at headquarters felt Wellington's equipment was of inferior quality and had directed him to buy from Linden.

After much difficulty Walters finally arranged an appointment with Amalgamated Engineering's purchasing manager, Oliver Sly. Walters travelled to Sydney to visit Sly and delivered a strong competitive sales pitch against Linden.

Sly listened with apparent interest. But at the end of the meeting he told Walters: "I only approve what the regional managers recommend. You will have to do a better job of selling to the Melbourne branch manager.He makes his own recommendations."

Not long afterwards, at a business equipment association dinner, Walters spotted Sly and his wife obviously enjoying the generous hospitality of Linden's sales director. "They went to school together," an associate explained to him, as they disposed of plates of smoked salmon.

A few weeks later, a company that Wellington represented introduced a much improved word processing system. As a result of the many meetings he had had with the Melbourne branch manager of Amalgamated Engineering, Walters knew the company was facing problems on the paperwork side of the business. Good secretarial help was difficult to find and very expensive.

Secretarial problems eased

Walters carefully prepared a proposal for the Melbourne branch manager showing how the word processing unit could solve many of his problems. He also knew that Linden could offer nothing comparable. After his presentation the Melbourne branch manager was visibly excited. "I think you have just the thing I need," he told Walters. "I'll put in a requisition for it."

Not long afterwards, Walters received a telephone call from Sly asking him to come and discuss the system. Sly explained that he was reluctant for Amalgamated Engineering to be a guinea pig in testing new equipment. Walters pointed out that a prototype of the system had been extensively tested at two U.S. companies. Sly was free to contact either of them for their comments.

Then Sly complained that the new unit would make a great deal of the Linden equipment they had recently purchased unnecessary. Walters produced figures to show that even if Linden's equipment were written off completely the word processing unit would pay for itself in three years. Nevertheless he promised to come up with an offer for the equipment that would be replaced. Within three days he had written to Sly with a full proposal, incorporating an allowance for the Linden equipment at about 10% above its resale value on the market.

Favouring an old school chum

Nearly seven weeks passed. Walters called Sly on several occasions. He got through to him only twice. Each time Sly assured him that he was seriously considering the proposal and might possibly want to extend it to other Amalgamated offices.

Walters felt that he was being fobbed off. This feeling was heightened when he heard that one of Linden's suppliers was also about to come out on the market with a new word processing system, which would be ready within three months.

Then one night Walters found himself at a small dinner party engaged in earnest conversation with Elliot Johnson, the deputy managing director of Amalgamated Engineering. The two men hit it off well. As the evening wore on Johnson remarked: "You must know Oliver Sly. I suppose he buys a lot of equipment from you. What do you think of him?"

Walters pondered his response. Should he tell Johnson of his suspicion that Sly was misdirecting purchasing operations to favour an old school chum? This might be his only hope, although a slim one, of getting the business. Or should he let the opportunity slip, believing that unkind words would find they way back to Sly?

Sales director considers denouncing buyer as unfairly biased

Walters' meeting with the deputy managing director of Amalgamated Engineering is at first sight fortuitious. However, since Walters has a proven reputation as an experienced salesman it is surprising that he is even considering telling Johnson of his suspicion that Sly might be favouring an old school colleague.

Any professional will tell Walters that this kind of remark is a certain way of both making problems for himself and losing a good deal of business. In short, he should not say a word to Johnson about his suspicions of Sly favouring the "old boy network".

Because Walters and Johnson apparently hit it off well, Walters could suggest with regret that although Sly is seriously considering buying equipment from Wellington Furniture & Supply he has not, as Johnson supposes, done so. A predominant reason for this, Walters could say, is possibly his own lack of confidence in his ability to convey to Sly the benefits of the new system.

By taking the blame himself, Walters can never be accused of criticizing Sly or of taking advantage of his social meeting with Johnson. In fact, the approach could well encourage Johnson to take up Walters' case for him, having firstly been primed on the benefits of the product.

Outweighing this argument, however, is the fact that Sly could easily retaliate by giving Walters an even more difficult time. He has the perfect excuse and opportunity to do so, since one of Linden's suppliers is due to launch a competitive product within three months.

Stop being sidetracked

One of the classic brush-offs to a salesman is for the buyer to say: "I am looking into competitive products and I'll let you know my decision after I have considered all the alternatives."

Let us now forget Johnson. Walters could suggest to his immediate boss that they both visit Sly at the next opportunity. Having introduced them, Walters could leave his boss to work on Sly. It is just possible that a new face might be more acceptable than that of Walters.

This, in turn, relieves Walters of the immediate task and allows him to get on with the job of calling on prospects who are more likely to buy. Walters, in fact, may have been sidetracked from following up these prospects. He may be trying in his attempts to get an order from Sly to impress his superior as much as to increase profitability.

The problem is not about what Walters should do to seize Amalgamated Engineering's business away from a competitor. The problem is getting Walters back on to a professional path.

Walters has allowed Amalgamated Engineering to overwhelm his attention. Even the best salesmen are vulnerable to an obsessional trap at some point in their careers, when they forget that their objective is not to win lone battles but to win the sales war.

Walters clearly wants to win the war over Linden, his competitor. Perhaps his superior should remind him that it is not necessary to wipe out your competitor to succeed over him.

Why is the superior allowing Walters to spend a disproportionate amount of time on Amalgamated Engineering? The prospect gave $100,000 of business to Linden in 1977. This, bluntly, is not a great deal of business in the office equipment industry from such an apparently significant client.

Walters is not only trying too hard to get this one prospect but is at risk of underservicing important existing customers as well as neglecting new opportunities. He has visited Amalgamated Engineering on at least ten occasions. He has spent even more time and effort travelling to and from Sydney to meet Sly, plus additional time on writing and telephone calls.

Why? To convert part of a possible but still unlikely $100,000 prospect into a customer. It is too much rod and effort to catch too small a fish.

I suggest that Walters makes his next call the last one. On that occasion he should ask Sly if he has any doubts or reservations about the quality or about the performance of Wellington's products. He should enquire precisely what improvements or changes Sly recommends so that the product becomes, in Sly's opinion, the best there is.

Ask Sly to be specific. In short, call his bluff in the nicest possible way. Sly may find himself having to admit that Walters' product is perhaps the best after all.

This decision was provided by Ken Ketteringham in his capacity as chief executive of U.K.-based Roneo Vickers Ltd., one of the largest multi-product office equipment groups in Europe.

How should department head decide which managers to sack?

As he drove home, John Pertwee was unhappy. He had just concluded a meeting with Philip Hardwick, the managing director. "John," Hardwick had said, "you know what the consultant said. We were overstaffed even before we lost the French contract. Now, cut-backs are essential. I want you to dispense with five of your people – and I don't mean shop-floor wallahs. I want your recommendations on my desk by midday Friday. That gives you two days."

Pertwee had opened his mouth to protest – then closed it again. Useless to point out that five people meant half of his managerial and supervisory staff. He knew that the parent company was cutting more.

The business of the parent, Grove (Auto) Ltd., was supplying fuel pumps, starter motors and other electro-mechanical devices to car manufacturers. A subsidiary, Grove Electronics, had been set up under Hardwick to apply microtechnology and develop new markets. Pertwee had been appointed development manager.

He had asked several long-service managers from the starter motor division of the parent company to join him. He had persuaded others to

315

give up good jobs elsewhere and join. Now he had a team of which he was proud, and who worked well together.

However, the parent company, worried by declining auto business, had engaged consultants, who looked at both companies' organization and methods and recommended staff reductions to cut overheads. About the same time the parent company had failed to get an order supplying parts for a new Ford model. Hardwick's efforts to persuade them that the electronics business still ought to be backed to the hilt had been sabotaged by the subsidiary's own failure – due to a political decision, quite outside its control – to land a contract with a French defence industry.

"I have to fire five managers out of ten," Pertwee told his wife when she asked him why he wasn't eating his T-bone steak.

"Surely you don't have to decide, John," his wife said. "Isn't it up to the personnel department?"

Only three out of six can stay

"No. I employed them, so I suppose I'll have to sack them."

"Get rid of the ones that are not so good," his wife suggested.

"They are all good. You know Harry and Charles and Graham as well as I do. Which of them would *you* sack?"

"Harry has just got a big new mortgage. It would be hard on him. Graham has enough problems already with his divorce coming up," his wife mused. "Couldn't you retire some of the older ones early?"

"The oldest is 43."

"Get rid of the younger ones, then. They have more chance of finding other jobs."

"Where?" Pertwee said. "The parent company will not have them back. The ones that joined the firm have burned their boats at their old companies. Two of them are too bright to lose anyway. Most of the others have real potential, or I wouldn't have persuaded them, less than a year ago, to relocate here. Now I have to tell them, after all the soft talk, that they are not wanted after all."

In an earlier attempt to keep overheads down, the administration of Grove Electronics personnel had been done by the central personnel department at Grove Auto – which had rubber-stamped without interfering all the appointments which Hardwick and Pertwee had wanted to make.

That fact was pointed out by Ronald Smedley, the personnel director at Grove Auto, when Pertwee saw him the following day. Smedley was sympathetic but unhelpful. "Here's a list showing what terminating each individual would save the company and what it would cost us," he said. "It is clear that terminating certain individuals would bring bigger savings. But that is up to you. What you have to do is cut around $200,000 in salaries, give or take a few hundred."

Back in his office, Pertwee pencilled in the names of two men he definitely wanted to retain, because their work was essential to the department, and two who would have to go because no jobs for them now existed following the failure to get the French contract. Those were the easy choices. Now he had to find three to go, and allow three to stay, from the remaining six.

He drew up a list of the six, writing:

Stephen Simpson. Age 31. Good development engineer. With the company 1½ years. Good team man. Married but no children. Joined at my request.

Harry Catterick. Age 38. Development engineer. Good research brain. Bit of a loner. Completes assignments ahead of time. Moved from gear division at my request. Heavy mortgage commitment.

Pertwee looked at the last remark, remembering his wife's comments. Was it relevant? He continued with the list:

Percy Somerville. Age 26. Development engineer with good marketing potential. Mixer. Well liked. Turned down alternative job to join us only last year.

Charles Peters. Age 43. Long-time acquaintance from the motor division. Able general manager. Volunteered to join me in my new job. No room for him back at the parent.

Graham Defoe. Age 35. General manager who joined from the motor division. Ambitious. Able. Good marketing brain. Marital problems (impending divorce).

Stephen Good. Age 30. Gave up a promising career to join us 1½ years ago as understudy to my production manager, whom I have already retained. Great potential. Gets on very well with shop-floor personnel yet stands for no nonsense.

Pertwee gazed at the list then added his name:

John Pertwee. Age 46. Development manager. Happier handling technical than human decisions. Can be a bit indecisive. Maybe ought to make a strong case for retaining all these people, or resign himself.

He looked at the list again, then said aloud: "Well, what do I do?"

DECISION

A redundancy policy is essential – and it's the company's responsibility

It is obvious that this company lacks any kind of clear-cut policies, or guidelines, on the procedures to be followed in the case of managerial redundancies. Indeed, there seems to be a lack of management capacity throughout the company, particularly when it comes to coordination and the allocation of responsibilities.

Thus Pertwee is told by his boss to cut his staff in half and the personnel director of the parent company tells him to save $200,000. To comply with both of these directives could mean having to arrive at entirely different solutions.

The personnel director, anyway, has no authority to give orders to Pertwee. He abdicated authority in the matter a long time ago.

How to get rid of three friends

What about the fact that 1½ years previously three of Pertwee's staff joined the new subsidiary from the parent company. Did the parent already see the bad times that were coming, and did it play the old game of palming off the fat? Managers all over the world know that game, take part in it from time to time and nobody talks about it. But where was personnel at that time? Did they go along with the idea or didn't they?

Pertwee's problem is how to get rid of three friends and, while doing so, keep up the morale of the rest. He needs time to think things through, as he is the man who will have to do the firing and explain the why and the how.

He should go to his boss, Hardwick, and insist upon clearing up two issues straight away.

First, are there any guidelines on redundancy to go by that he doesn't already know about? If there are not, he should ask his boss, or the personnel director, or the two of them together, to cough up some guidelines.

Second, he should discuss with his boss the moral obligations towards these men. Couldn't his boss bring pressure on the personnel director to accept his obligations? The face of the parent company has to be saved – if not for these men alone, then certainly for those who remain in the company.

Consider early retirement

Once Pertwee has some guidelines to consider, he can then turn again to his list of candidates for redundancy and look at their performance, and their age, in relation to considerations of early retirement, "golden handshakes" and so on.

The normal severance arrangement in such cases, in Europe, is a month's pay for each year of service. An alternative would be to keep some of the men on the payroll for a defined time while giving them the chance to find another job.

If they find a new job, some firms are willing to help, for a certain time, by supplementing their income if they have to take a drop in pay. Some firms also use outplacement consultants. By doing this, they show their concern for the man they have to release in the most practical and productive way – by helping him to find alternative employment.

Deal with grown-up people

My overall advice to the company is clear. It should not only decide what it will do, in such cases, but write it down. After all, the company is dealing with grown-up people who want to know the facts and figures and especially what is likely to happen in the future. Pertwee and everybody, headquarters and subsidiaries alike, have to know what the current facts and figures of Grove Auto's life are, what they will be tomorrow, what the future can bring and what the company intends to do to bring that future nearer.

The first thing that comes to mind is the crying need for a clear-cut policy note, a message to all involved. The managing director, or whoever is the highest authority, should have that statement made, discuss it with all the leading people involved and give them a copy.

Pertwee seems to be an excellent man, who has a great future. But he needs training in a wider managerial sense. Especially his handling of his boss should be strengthened. It is to his boss, however, that he should go now, and face that individual with *his* obligations.

This decision was provided by Paul van Ede from his outplacement bureau, van Ede & Partners, in Amsterdam. For ten years he was a member of the Dutch consultancy Berenschot NV and is a former director of personnel for a Dutch multinational.

Should an unhappy cross-border merger be abandoned?

Peter Grange, managing director of Branstein (U.K.) Ltd., based at Cowes on the Isle of Wight, was unhappy. He was involved in a merger with an Austrian company that was not working out. He had been managing director of a U.K. firm, Branston Outboard Ltd., which had sales of around $15 million, selling fuel-efficient outboard motors to small boat enthusiasts. But competition had been keen. When Branston had developed a motor which was so light-weight that it seemed adaptable to other leisure-time activities, he had started looking around for a partner who had marketing expertise – and contracts – in entirely different fields.

He had met Julian Stein, founder of a company called Steinports, and the two had hit it off immediately. Steinsports manufactured skis, bob-sleighs and sledges and had branched out into hang-gliding. It had sales of around $13 million, and had been looking for a suitable motor to develop a line of snowmobiles for export, using modified bobsleigh chassis. It also had in mind offering small power units as an option with its hang-gliders.

After protracted discussions, Grange and Stein had decided that the two companies were so compatible they should merge. Steinsports had acquired 49% of Branston, and vice versa. The company, known as Branstein, had been the outcome.

Stein and Grange had continued as joint managing directors of their respective companies, each taking it in turns to chair coordination meetings. There had been no attempt to integrate research and development. It had also been decided that the two sales forces should continue to operate separately, in the markets they knew best, until new products justified progressively moving the salesmen into a new, integrated sales force to sell in a wider field.

Difficulties in synchronizing development

Even before the merger, Grange's company had spent a lot of money developing its motor. In the two years since the merger Branston had committed itself financially to further development at the expense of keeping up with the advanced competition in the conventional outboard market. At the same time the Austrian group, initially, had energetically set about modifying its sledges, altering their centre of gravity and streng-thening the runners, to take the British engine.

However, the Austrian and U.K. companies had found difficulty syn-chronizing their development efforts and meeting agreed deadlines. Mat-ters were not helped by the appointment of Stein's nephew, Hans Offen-bach, as research and development manager of the Austrian group.

A skier and bobsleigh enthusiast, Offenbach had not been involved in the merger negotiations. Indeed, he had been completing a business degree in the U.S. at the time.

From the start, he was lukewarm about the idea of putting all the Austrian company's development effort into modifying the bobsleighs to take the new motor. "We have a fine reputation in bobsleighs and we don't want to lose it," Offenbach had said. "If we do not do some development in that area we are going to lose more ground to the East Germans than we have already."

At first, the meeting of minds between Grange and Stein overruled Offenbach's efforts to divert resources from what Grange insisted ought to be the main development effort. However, the necessary modification of the bobsleighs to take the motor continued to present tough technical problems. At least, that is, they were tough according to Offenbach, who continued to use this argument as an excuse for lack of progress.

Grange had just reached the point when he felt that he had to insist to Stein that Offenbach be moved to another job when Stein suffered a stroke. It left him totally incapacitated. The doctors held out little hope for any recovery sufficient to allow him to work again. A long-time friend of Stein, Peter Vogel, who had been the Austrian company's marketing director, took over temporarily as managing director of the Austrian company to oversee the business.

Unfortunately, Vogel did not hold the balance in the joint board discussions as Stein had done. He seemed to see it as his duty to the seriously ill Stein to back the family interests by supporting the opinions of Offenbach, who meanwhile had joined the board and taken over the job of marketing director as well as his development duties.

"It is a question of priorities," Offenbach said to Grange, explaining why he intended to divert more resources to developing the bobsleighs as bobsleighs, rather than completing the modifications. "The new products arising from the merger of our two companies are still in the future. Meanwhile, we cannot neglect our public image, which has always depended on the bobsleighs."

Grange fully realized that the Austrian end of the company could continue to thrive, if not to grow, by concentrating on its long-established and well-known products. Branstein (U.K.) Ltd., on the other hand, had put so much effort into the motor, for which it urgently needed a market, that it could not afford to return to square one. But what should he do?

One option, which he suspected would appeal to Offenbach, would be to attempt to de-scramble the merger. But where would that leave the U.K. company? Or should he attempt to reorganize the way the joint company was run. If so, how should he approach Offenbach and Vogel on that sensitive subject?

DECISION

Merger partner must weigh cost of de-merging

Peter Grange, the British managing director, made a basic error going into the merger the way he did. Because he "hit it off" with the Austrian, Julian Stein, he seems to have assumed that no problems would arise that could not be solved man-to-man, and that the merger would proceed smoothly even though his advisers no doubt pointed out the problems that could arise from a joint ownership arrangement.

Just the same, my sympathies are with Grange, who could not foresee that Stein would suffer a stroke or that his nephew, who was not even with the company at the time of the merger, would get a seat on the board. He cannot have expected, given the good relations he enjoyed with Stein, that the Austrian end of the company would not put 100% effort into developing their sledge chassis to accommodate the British motor. Equally, he could not have foreseen Offenbach's negative attitude towards the merger.

Now that there is a stalemate, Grange cannot afford to let things drift. Either he must persuade the Austrians to really contribute towards making the merger successful, or consider de-merging, or selling the total company to a third party.

Standing still leads to decline

It looks as though the British company has the most to lose by any de-merger. It has already committed a lot of money and effort to developing a motor for a different market. In the event of a de-merger, Grange may have no choice but to sell out to a bigger manufacturer in his own line of business. Having lost two years, since the merger, and a lot of money, he would find himself even further back than when he started.

Grange does not *have* to de-merge, however. Even if the Austrians favour such a step, a merger cannot be legally ended without the agreement of both partners. But he cannot allow the Austrians to go on curtailing their development effort.

He should begin by trying to make his Austrian partners more amenable. He should point out that the Austrians, too, would suffer if they backed out now. The fate of companies that stand still, and fail to exploit new markets, is to decline. The basic reasoning behind the merger is still as valid as ever, Grange should argue. All that is lacking is the will to make it work.

He should establish whether Offenbach is just being awkward or is deeply opposed to a merger which he had no part in making. There must be other executives in the Austrian company, apart from Vogel, the family friend, to whom Grange can appeal to bring influence to bear on Offenbach. In two years, he must have made some friends on the Austrian side of the firm.

Bring in an independent executive

Grange could suggest to the Austrians that they bring in an agreed, totally independent person, who might be a management consultant or an experienced independent businessman, to look objectively at the whole situation and abide by his recommendations. Quite possibly such a consultant, if he found that it was impossible to get the two parties to agree, would recommend that they sell the whole, combined operation, giving each of the partners money with which they could go their own ways. Such a solution might well appeal to a family business, which the Austrian company clearly is.

Grange could, of course, always go to law, as sometimes happens in merger disputes, and let the court decide whether the Austrians were abiding by the letter and spirit of the merger agreement. But that would take a long time, and the business could suffer further injury in the meantime.

At the same time, if Grange considers that, in the end, de-merger may become inevitable, he should start looking around straight away for a potential buyer for his end of the company – someone who could inject cash and might be persuaded to keep him on as chief executive.

The important moral of this sad tale is never to start a merger on a 50-50 basis. But if you must, there should be built into the contract a determined time clause with appropriate de-merger conditions that both parties can independently consider after an agreed period of time.

This decision was provided by Hildegard Lewis-Jones in her capacity as an Anglo-Dutch marketing and merger consultant of her company Intercontinental Market Development Operations, London, U.K.

DILEMMA

How should chief executive cope with pay anomalies?

L ars Anderson, purchasing director with PNK AB, was faced with the task of drawing up a budget for the coming year. PNK had been growing very fast and Anderson had used this as a lever to win price concessions from major suppliers. However, the sales forecast for the coming year was gloomy indeed. Anderson wondered whether inflation, coupled with decreasing buying power, might make it difficult to hit his spending targets.

He was very conscientious man and he was prepared to hold salary increases down, and even reduce his staff, if necessary. He had asked the personnel department for a printout of the personnel in the purchasing department, and their salary levels.

When he began to examine this information, he discovered that, by mistake, he had been sent a report that covered two other departments and top management. His amusement and curiosity quickly turned to anger when he discovered that the managing director was earning five times his own annual salary, and the sales director was receiving 2.5 times as much in compensation. In addition, both men had the use of company cars, which Anderson did not.

Out of line salaries
Further, in terms of people, Anderson controlled as large a staff as the sales director, and as the budget would show, was responsible for $6 million worth of annual purchases. He had never failed to keep his department costs under budget and had been complimented on this several times by the managing director, to whom he reported directly. The only solace available to Anderson was the fact that the production manager and service manager both were earning at his level.

Anderson telephoned a friend at the National Association of Purchasing Managers. His friend sent him a copy of a salary survey done by an independent consulting firm, giving comparative salary levels.

It showed very clearly that PNK was out of line with other firms in the country. On a national basis managing directors, on average, earned just over double what a purchasing executive, one level below director, was paid. The survey also showed that sales directors generally earned about 30% more.

322

Above market rate paid to salesmen

Anderson thought about the situation, discussed it with his wife and eventually went to see the managing director, Peter Jensen.

Jensen blustered, at first, about it being unethical for Anderson to confront him with figures which he should have never seen in the first place. He went on to say that he assumed Anderson felt his salary was fair because he had continued to work there and he had never brought the matter up before.

Anderson tried to remain calm. But he let slip that he imagined other managers would feel the same way if they found out. In the end, Jensen asked Anderson to let him think it over for a day or two, to give himself time to consider the matter in detail.

PNK was not a huge company. But it was the major employer in the small town where it was located. As such, it offered the best opportunity for local residents, while at the same time being able to pay much less than the going rate in larger cities. This had enabled Jensen, who was married to one of the founder's daughters, to pay himself a rather handsome salary from the family-owned company.

The firm had many competitors making basically similar products. Jensen's policy had been to pay above the market rate for his salesmen, in order to get the top people available. This policy had, so far, been successful. But it also meant that the sales manager's remuneration was very high, so that his income topped that of the most successful sales person, and was higher than was usual.

Discontent throughout the company

Jensen felt that the purchasing manager did indeed represent a bargain, considering the excellent job he did.

Other managers were earning far less than their market value, Jensen reflected. This was probably due to the fact that they were isolated in something of a backwater community. If he tried to buy Anderson off with a large increase and another of the underpaid managers discovered it, there could be a full-scale palace revolt. If he gave large-scale increases to all, in the present harsh economic climate, the firm would undoubtedly lose money.

He though of telling Anderson that if he wasn't satisfied with his pay he should leave. However, he didn't want to lose him. On the other hand, if he did nothing there was the danger that Anderson might become totally disenchanted with the company. Almost certainly he would share his information with other department heads, spreading discontent throughout the company. It was possible he might use his position to generate income from some of the firm's suppliers in the form of "kickbacks". It had been done before by other purchasing officers.

Jensen calculated how much money he could add to managerial salaries. By lowering his already depressed profit target significantly , and engaging in some cost-cutting that was sure to be unpopular, he arrived at a figure of $40,000. Although Anderson claimed that he was underpaid $20,000, Jensen believed he would be satisfied if he received a rise of about $15,000.

But there were another seven managers in roughly the same situation. Giving them the same rise would cause PNK to lose money. So should he distribute $3,500 rises to the other managers, or hold $25,000 in reserve to see whether there were any more complaints? Or should he simply hand out $5,000 a year rises to everyone, including Anderson?

Company moves towards a rational pay policy

Peter Jensen has created his own problems by not providing PNK with experienced personnel management. He must now face the problem of financing a correction of that shortcoming.

This financing should not be in the form of immediate payments to Lars Anderson or any other manager. To make significant salary adjustments on a subjective, *ad hoc* basis would risk creating other anomalies which might prove unsatisfactory.

In addition, to raise Anderson's salary beyond the normal merit and inflation limits, as suggested, could, to take an extreme but not unknown example, leave the firm open to a claim for application for the higher salary to the entire earlier period of Anderson's employment as purchasing manager. This could be done on the grounds that the company admitted underpayment by making an equity adjustment.

Instead, in working towards a solution to his dilemma, Jensen should remember that proper motivation of his managers is harder to achieve if company decisions, particularly those affecting compensation, appear to be made on a capricious, subjective basis.

Put emphasis on commissions or bonuses
Jensen, therefore, should explain to Anderson and the other managers that PNK will engage an independent compensation consultant to make a thorough study of the company's compensation methods. Such a study, which will be a one-time expense costing much less than the $40,000 Jensen has earmarked for a temporary solution, can be completed quickly, in a matter of a few weeks. It will provide PNK with information and systems needed for a permanent solution.

If the independent study shows most PNK managers to be significantly underpaid, Jensen should make every reasonable effort to give those managers whose performance has been satisfactory as great an increase as the financial situation will allow, with a commitment to reach recommended levels within a specific period. No managing director can expect to lead a company far on a policy of realizing profit by underpaying employees. It is counter-productive in the long-term.

Jensen should not be tempted to reduce any salaries which may now be above the recommended levels, to compensate for the cost of increasing others. He might consider putting more emphasis on commissions or bonuses, but any reduction of base salary, which could affect pension rights, is to be undertaken with great care.

Jensen's own salary should ideally be brought into line with the norm. But even if this is not done, non-family employees in a family-owned business often accept high salaries being paid to family members if they feel their own compensation is fair.

If Jensen acts quickly, Anderson is likely to accept that the managing director is sincere in his plan to introduce an equitable compensation plan to PNK, and will continue to work productively for the company. Once compensation is accepted as equitable throughout PNK, Jensen can fairly expect more from his managers, and will have the tools for judging performance on a sound business basis.

Leaderless personnel department

Fair pay is only one element in motivating an organization towards greater productivity and profitability. Jensen should, after this experience, see the advantages of adding an experienced personnel and industrial relations manager to his company. Normally a company with an annual materials purchase budget of $6 million is large enough in employee strength and complexity to warrant employing such a person.

It is clear that currently the company has a leaderless personnel department that is expected to do little more than keep records and try to keep secrets – the latter being perhaps an unrealistic expectation in a small, one company town. Jensen's dilemma was not created by a maverick purchasing manager but by a missing personnel manager.

This decision was provided by Russel F. Bruno in his capacity as managing partner of Frost International, a London consultancy specializing in executive search. Prior to forming Frost International, he was president of Squibb Europe, part of a U.S.-headquartered pharmaceutical company.

How should a company react to the discovery of a 'bug'?

Eric Winkler was deep in thought as he drove home. It had been a tiring week and he was looking forward to a restful weekend with his wife, Margaret, and the children.

Life as chairman of Glean Shipping had its ups and downs and the last two days had certainly been "downs". After months of secret planning, the company had been on the verge of announcing a new freight structure for many of its international liner routes, together with new lower passenger fares for its ferry services.

The market had been thoroughly researched and Winkler was confident that the changes would increase revenue by maybe 20%. This would be very useful after the mixed fortunes suffered by shipping interests in recent years.

But then, on Thursday, had come the shock. One of the company's arch-rivals, a large foreign concern, announced virtually the same freight structure. What is more, on ferry routes where they competed with Glean they proposed to undercut the new rates by another 10%. But they did not intend to reduce fares on other ferry routes.

Since there had been absolutely no announcement by Glean of its plan, this seemed to Winkler an obvious case of inside information having been leaked to the company's foreign rival. But who had betrayed what Winkler had thought to be a well kept secret?

Could it be one of his fellow directors? That was almost unthinkable.

They had met together for many years and he trusted them all.

A secretary in the office? Only the company secretary kept the board minutes. He typed up the most confidential ones himself and Winkler, who had personally appointed the secretary some years ago, would have trusted him with his life.

Something was not quite right

The board had not yet had a chance to meet to discuss the situation. But as he drove home Winkler remembered that two of the directors were returning, that weekend, from an overseas trip, and that one of them was coming to dinner on the Saturday. So the chairman turned his car round and drove back to the office to collect a briefing paper he had prepared earlier in the day.

As he left the lift on the top floor of Glean House, the cleaners were busy, the light in his own office was on and as he approached, he could see a figure through the glass door, apparently hard at work. He was about to enter when he realized that something was not quite right. The cleaner, a young man, had a roll of adhesive tape and appeared to be fixing something under the chairman's desk.

Resisting the temptation to walk straight in, Winkler moved to an adjoining office and waited until the man had left. He then entered his office and, feeling under the desk, brought out a small plastic object attached to a powerpack battery. A short piece of plastic-covered wire protruded, and the total contrivance was no larger than a cigarette lighter.

Winkler was horrified. He had read about bugging and other forms of industrial espionage, but had always assumed that it was companies dealing in secret formulae, or in the forefront of microelectronics, that were the most likely targets. It had never occurred to him that his own company's secrets might be of such interest to rivals that they would "bug" his office. At least he did not now have to worry about the loyalty of his fellow directors, he thought.

Evidence of continuing industrial espionage

At dinner the next day he made "small talk" until the coffee and liqueurs, at which point his wife excused herself and left the room. Winkler then explained the situation to his guest, Jack Hargreaves, the company's marketing director.

"I didn't want to spoil your weekend so soon after your trip," he concluded, "but I think we are going to have to re-appraise our marketing plan as a result of this leak. Then there is the question what to do about the industrial espionage itself, which evidently is continuing."

Hargreaves favoured bringing in a special investigator, or notifying the police; catching the office cleaner, or the man masquerading as the office cleaner, red-handed; prosecuting him and, if the involvement of the foreign firm could be proved, accusing them publicly of industrial espionage and trespass.

"I agree that is one option," Winkler said. "However, there are also others. If the bugging can be proved there is the possibility of legal restitution. I have spoken with our lawyer and he will have a report for the board meeting on Monday."

He paused, then added: "There is also another alternative, which we might discuss at Monday's board meeting. We could replace the bug I discovered and use it to transmit misleading information. Maybe in that way we can turn the tables on our rivals. But if we do that we'll have to do

326

it quickly, for when the cleaning staff comes in on Monday evening the man who placed the bug is going to check it out."

Hargreaves nodded. He said that personally he would favour using the device to relay misleading information. "But knowing the board as we do, Eric," he said, "they are likely to be split down the middle on whether to take legal action or try something more adventurous. It is probable that you will have the casting vote. What will you decide?"

DECISION

Shipping firm ponders how to counter espionage

Winkler's first mistake is to assume without question that the bugging of his office is connected with the reduction in ferry fares by the competing foreign firm.

This may not be the case. It could be a coincidence that the foreign firm decided to match Glean's fare reductions. Or the foreign company could have obtained its information about Glean's intentions through other means than bugging.

Realistically, Winkler has two alternatives, two courses of approach and of decision. The first assumes that there is no compulsion under the law to report to the police the use of the bug on his premises. The second assumes that there is.

Before facing up to these alternatives, however, Winkler must decide whether to call in a private investigator, or the police, in an effort to prove the connection between the bugging of his office and the actions of his competitor recently.

I would advise him to do so. Then, assuming that a private investigator does unearth a connection, he can look at the possibility of deliberately spreading misleading information, so that the competitor reaches wrong conclusions and consequently makes wrong decisions.

This may not be a bad idea. It depends, however, on the willingness of the other party to follow your lead – to react to the information you are putting out. He may not oblige.

Winkler should also beware of the legal snags of following this course of action. In some countries, obtaining information from illegal sources, or by illegal means, and using it to the disadvantage of a competitor is unlawful and therefore punishable under civil or criminal law, or both.

In West Germany, for example, the use of bugs is not permitted for any purpose. Winkler would be required to report the existence of the bug in his office so that the authorities could take appropriate action of their own, such as confiscating the device and initiating prosecutions where and when appropriate.

In using the bug to turn the tables on his competitor, Winkler could run the risk of breaking the law himself.

The two real alternatives that Winkler has, therefore, are somewhat less exciting. If he does not have to report the bug he can, in his own time and with the help of an investigator, obtain evidence and establish proof of the competitor's part in the bugging. He should also try to prove that the information obtained was actually used in the competitor's marketing decisions, though this may be difficult to establish.

Such proof, however, would constitute grounds for restitution under almost any legal system. A lot would depend upon the ability of Winkler's lawyer directly to approach the competitor with the evidence and secure an out-of-court settlement.

The other alternative, and the one which I would follow, would be to take the law into my confidence and use it. Even if the use of a bugging device is not illegal, unauthorised entry into private property almost certainly is. In the case of an office cleaner, permission for entry to a premises is granted only for the purpose of cleaning and not for any other reason.

Take six courses of action

It would be up to the police to decide whether they should set a trap and catch the cleaner red-handed, interrogate him or proceed in some other way. If consequent legal action should prove the commitment of a third party, then assuredly restitution would be a possibility.

However, no manager should be happy with taking legal action and leaving it at that. There are at least six actions Winkler could take, all of them legal, all of them necessary, all of them within his personal control, to ensure that leaks of sensitive information do not happen again.

First, he should ensure that all cleaners, and other out-of-house staff, are supervised beyond normal office hours by security personnel.

Second, he should insist that conference rooms be examined in a systematic "search and sweep" operation before any discussion involving sensitive information.

Third, he should provide monitoring services during important conferences. These would detect any electronic bugging devices in operation.

Fourth, he should have important offices and conference areas "swept" at irregular intervals.

Fifth, he should document the company's security system and train staff in the handling of sensitive information. Electronic devices are not the only way of obtaining information.

Sixth, he should employ a security professional on the staff, or an outside security consultant.

This may sound like a lot of activity to safeguard secrets which do not involve the fate of nations. But in a very competitive world, and with bugging devices getting even smaller and more sophisticated, there are not many companies that can afford the luxury of lax security.

This decision was provided by Claus J. Skupin in his capacity as a security consultant in West Berlin who served with security forces in the city for 20 years.

Should firm risk government sanctions to rescue kidnapped manager?

Wolf Frankel glanced at the bedside clock as he reached to answer the telephone. Who could be ringing at 3 a.m.?

"Herr Frankel? It's James Perez. I'm sorry to disturb you but we are supposed to report things like this immediately they happen."

Perez was the second in command in the South American country where Gasselsmann GmbH, an aluminium smelting and fabricating firm based in West Germany, mined most of its bauxite. Frankel was the firm's director of international operations.

Perez explained that Lutz Luneberger, the head of the subsidiary, had been kidnapped by terrorists.

Frankel was now wide awake. "Go and see what you can do for Frau Luneberger," he said. "I'll phone our chief of security and get him to fly out. Have someone meet him at the airport tomorrow. And keep me informed of developments."

Three days later, Perez phoned Frankel to say that the terrorists had demanded a ransom. "They want food, medical supplies and $10 million in cash or they will kill Luneberger," he said.

The security chief also came on the telephone to tell Frankel that the government of the country was proving difficult to deal with, and suggesting that Frankel himself fly out.

Taking an uncompromising line

As they drove from the airport, Perez told Frankel that a priest had been found to act as intermediary with the terrorists. "But first we have a meeting with the minister of state for security," he said.

Frankel knew the minister slightly. He was unprepared, however, for the uncompromising line the man took.

"Although you may talk with these people," the minister said, "there is no question of their demands being met. One cannot compromise with traitors and thugs. You must realize, also, that if your company gives in now, in this part of the world, it will open the flood gates. One cannot afford to be soft with terrorists."

Frankel's meetings with the intermediary were attended by a government representative whose presence inhibited free and frank discussion of the problem.

As the weeks passsed, Frankel travelled frequently between South America and the corporate headquarters in Düsseldorf. He had as many problems at home as in the field. Some members of the board took a hard line, saying the company should not pay, while others demanded speedier progress. There was also the threat of legal action by the family if the victim was killed in the meantime.

While attending one of the board meetings, Frankel received a telex from his security man saying that he had arranged direct contact with the terrorists if Frankel wanted to take advantage of it.

Frankel did. He obtained the approval of the board to offer the terrorists a ransom of $1 million if they would drop the request for food and medical supplies, which could not be delivered without the agreement of the government. The money, however, could be transferred through a Swiss bank.

Frankel flew back to South America and after a week of waiting met the terrorist spokesman secretly. At first he did not seem to be making progress, but after hours of talking the terrorists suddenly agreed to the deal as he was offering it.

Frankel was elated. However, when he got back to his hotel he received a phone call from the minister of state, who asked to see him immediately.

The minister said that he knew all about the cash deal. "In this country, nothing is secret for long. I regret that you have gone behind my back in dealing with these people. The government I represent will not allow this deal to go through. Should you attempt to proceed, we will seize your company's assets."

Frankel believed the minister was bluffing. He did not think the government could afford to alienate other international companies with interests in the country. He said as much to the minister.

"That may be," the minister replied. "But remember, we can make life very difficult for you here, from an operating point of view. You will recall, also, that next year your licence to mine and export bauxite comes up for renewal. How would you like to buy your bauxite on the open market in future?"

That night, Frankel pondered this threat. What should he do? If he paid the money he might save Luneberger's life. But if the company lost its bauxite concession it would cease to be a fully integrated aluminium concern. That could cost a lot more than the $1 million.

If, however, he did not pay, it was practically certain that Luneberger would be killed. How could he extricate both his colleague and the company at the same time?

DECISION

Government threatens sanctions if terrorist demands are met

Unfortunately Frankel and Gasselsmann GmbH have not handled this crisis in the best way. Now Frankel is faced with a confrontation with the government of the country concerned which could have been avoided.

He must tread delicately, because if he fails to deliver his end of the deal with the terrorists, it could cost Luneberger his life.

Frankel's first priority is to soften the government's position. To do that he must mobilize and bring to bear, even at this late stage, all the extensive international advice and experience, support from diplomatic channels and other commercial companies, and statistical facts on other kidnaps at his disposal.

Armed with these he can, if he really tries, demonstrate to the government that its policy of no negotiation is unenforceable and counter-productive, unless the police have already had a high success rate in dealing with terrorism.

He can also stress that the negotiations between the company and the terrorists have been conducted with the following factors in mind:

First, the safe release of the victim, while necessary on moral grounds, would also provide the security services with a very valuable source of intelligence for the future.

Second, negotiations have been conducted in a way that has played for time and sought to gain further intelligence. This intelligence will now be handed over to the police provided they agree to do nothing to prejudice the life of the victim.

Third, during the negotiations the company paid due regard to the government's requirements not to lose credibility and thus begin a rash of similar incidents.

Frankel can make the point that the details of payment still have to be worked out, giving the government further time to cope with the terrorists by other means. Moreover, Frankel should stress that the company will be keeping the exact payment details secret in order to discourage future cases, and that the company's handling of media relations, through the whole affair, has been helpful to the government.

Specialist knowledge is available

In other words, it should be possible to obtain agreement to continue negotiations, and honour the deal that has been made, provided the government is satisfied that the negotiations have been, and will be, carried out professionally and with due regard to its own interests.

During the negotiations, Frankel will probably have drawn upon the knowledge and skills of a number of other corporations that have experienced similar problems. Also there is now available to him, and others like him, a bank of specialist knowledge of facts and figures concerning other cases, which would help this case considerably.

He is probably feeling exhausted. The negotiations will have imposed a huge strain on him – for much of which he himself is to blame.

At the start of the emergency he should have recommended to the board that the company engage a firm of experts experienced in advising in this sort of situation.

The first advice from a consultant would have been to set up an adequate negotiating team on the ground, and a crisis management committee at corporate headquarters, on which consultants would serve.

No member of the corporation should actually negotiate with the terrorists. The actual negotiator, properly trained and rehearsed, will probably be a local lawyer who speaks the right language, is acceptable to the police and has the position of legal privilege.

Commission a written threat assessment

If the negotiating team had been properly structured and clearly briefed on the first day, reporting to a crisis management committee at corporate headquarters, Frankel would have been able to keep himself fresh and continue to discharge his other responsibilities.

Clearly it would have been better if the corporation had prevented the loss of its executive in the first place. Frankel may well regret that he did not address himself to that risk as he would to any other, for example the risk of an economic downturn.

Knowing the bauxite subsidiary was in terrorist country, he should have commissioned a written threat assessment. This would take into account the particular terrorist groups in the country and the political position of the company.

The threat should have been identified and analysed, evaluated, reduced if possible and either transferred, perhaps by insurance, or accepted as a risk that had to be taken, rather than ignored.

In a world in which terrorism is on the increase, the evaluation and prevention of kidnap, and other political risks, is fast becoming a science, though not an exact one.

In over 90% of real-life cases, companies have successfully negotiated the release of victims for cash ransom. Untold crisis situations have been avoided by effective crisis management planning and experience has led to a reduction in the amount of ransoms paid, and in adverse political implications for the company.

This decision was provided by a director of Control Risks Ltd., a U.K. firm which specializes in security consultancy and has advised in over 50 similar real-life cases. Because of the nature of his work, he remains anonymous.

DILEMMA

Should Japanese firm ban drinking with clients after salesman's death?

Kikuo Sugita had not particularly wanted to have another drink. But the client was ready for one and had to be humoured. Sugita could not afford to lose his order.

"Are you sure you are all right?" asked a junior colleague as Sugita stepped into the cool night air of the Ginza in Tokyo.

"I have to go home," Sugita replied. "I will see you tomorrow." The assistant had watched with some concern as the senior salesman drove away into the night.

Next morning the news of Sugita's death spread around the office. He had crashed his car into the side of a railway bridge.

Kato Toyama, the corporate personnel manager, was very upset. He and Sugita had started their careers with trading and manufacturing group Osaka-Tokyo Industries Ltd. in the same year. They had been good friends.

Cash compensation no consolation to family

Toyama spent that afternoon visiting Sugita's wife. He was acutely aware that the cash compensation the company would provide would be no consolation to Sugita's wife or his three children.

In the office the next day, Toyama began to do some research into car accidents and sick leave among the sales staff. Although only two other salesmen from the total sales force of 800 had been killed on the roads in similar circumstances over the past ten years, he uncovered a long list of minor accidents and injuries.

For example, there were 15 cases of salesmen going into hospital for more than a week as a result of car accidents. Although alcohol was not a proven factor in all these cases, the number of accidents that had

332

occurred following sales conferences and client calls disturbed Toyama. Salesmen had also taken 30% more sick leave than other workers. Because they tended to take this leave in single days, Toyama surmised that sometimes the reason must have been to recover from a hangover.

Toyama presented the results of his research at the executive meeting later that month. In taking this step, he also presented the president of the company, Iwao Saito, with a problem.

Saito listened impassively as Toyama said: "I suspect that much of the drinking we do with our clients does more harm than good. There's a moral question, too. Whether we like it or not, this company probably was indirectly responsible for Sugita's death. He didn't go drinking with the client because he wanted to, but because he knew that the company needed that important order.

Wining and dining is a part of selling

"We pride ourselves on the way in which we look after our employees. But can we truly say that we were looking after Sugita and his family?"

The sales director, Takami Moriya, said that he disagreed. "We would look after our employees less," he said, "if we ceased to be competitive. We have to sell to be competitive. I think that wining and dining is so much a part of selling that it would be very hard to put a stop to it, even if we wanted to do so."

"Just the same," Toyama insisted, "we do operate double standards within this company. Last month I had to discuss a disciplinary case with the secretary of our union. A worker in the buying department had been found drunk on the job for the third time. As you know, once someone has been warned twice, the third time he must be dismissed.

"While we were discussing the matter, a deliveryman came in and asked my secretary the way to the entertainments lounge. He was restocking it with whisky.

"The union representative asked me how we could condemn the man in the buying department for drinking when we were encouraging other employees to drink. It was hard to answer his question."

Company has some moral responsibility

"The fact remains," the sales director rejoined, "that entertaining is an essential part of a salesman's job. If he doesn't want to drink, or can't hold his drink, he should apply for a different job in another department."

"That is too easy," said Toyama. "The death of my friend Sugita has made me realize this. I propose that we no longer allow alcohol as an item on expense accounts. I have spoken with some salesmen and they tell me they would be happy not to have to drink on the job."

The president listened to all of this attentively. Ultimately they would look to him, as head of the company, to resolve the matter.

But what should he decide? Sugita, he reflected, had been known to drink a lot with clients. But he had been a star performer and noone in the company had discouraged him from drinking.

Yes, Saito thought, the company did have some moral responsibility in this matter. He himself had spoken up at public meetings about the moral responsibilities of industry. So dare he let things go on as they were?

But if, on the other hand, he cut alcohol from entertaining, he could visualize a sharp decline in the sales figures. How could he resolve the problem without a total ban on alcohol?

Proposed ban on drinking with customers threatens firm's sales

This is a dilemma between the moral issue of drinking on the one hand and maintaining customer relations by offering drinks on the other. What has to be done is to establish priority between the two.

Inherent in drinking is the resultant hangover, traffic accidents, work days lost and the lowering of the morale and health of employees. Because of the sudden loss of his dear friend, Kato Toyama is upset and does not admit that Kikuo Sugito died because he *drove* when he was drunk, rather than because he drank. He has decided to place priority on the moral issue rather than anything else.

Toyama's proposition that alcohol no longer be allowed as an item on expense accounts certainly has a point. If, as he claims, the harder the salesmen work the more drinks they have to take, there seems to be a risk that the whole sales department may turn into a group of alcoholics before very long, if they continue to be successful.

Since Toyama is the personnel manager, a position which is rather important and influential in a Japanese company, he must be heard with due respect. He is the clearing house of vital management information in the company. His opinion probably echoes the views of "unheard voices". There is no doubt that the top management of the company is expected to show its sincerity in responding to the personnel manager's proposition.

Work out a new sales directive

However, at the same time, entertaining customers is a way of life in Japan and is an essential part of doing business. The company will surely lose its competitive edge and go downhill if it stops such practices altogether. There is therefore no doubt which of the two issues has priority in the mind of the president, Iwao Saito, and of top management in general on the matter.

First, Saito should ask Takami Moriya, the sales manager, to review current marketing practices as they relate to customer relations and find out whether there is too much emphasis on drinking. He should also ask him to find out whether sick leave taken by salesmen was in fact mostly caused by excessive drinking, as Toyama was led to believe. Sugita had been known to drink a lot but perhaps most other salesmen do not have to and do not like to drink so often. Checking into these areas may identify where morale needs to be improved.

In the meantime, Saito could remind Toyama, who is still emotionally upset by the loss of his dear friend, that while entertaining customers may be an essential part of a salesman's work, it is also possible for him to serve the drinks while he remains sober. He could also suggest that the moral issue of drinking should not be confused with reckless driving.

At this point, Saito should call in both Toyama and Moriya and tell them jointly to work out a new project in order to put the sales activities on a more "healthy" line, while pushing up the sales as much as possible in order to make up for the loss of Sugita. Such a project might include the guidelines to be followed.

First, at the time of a regular medical checkup of employees, suggest that salesmen's liver and stomach functions be doubly checked to see if there are any signs of deterioration. In case any such signs are discovered, consider the steps to be followed, including job re-assignment.

Second, encourage employees to participate more vigorously in various sporting club activities sponsored by the company, such as baseball, volleyball and swimming.

Third, start a campaign to encourage safe driving among employees. In this connection, salesmen could be encouraged to use public transportation when they have to drink.

Fourth, use hire cars for senior salesmen who have to entertain more important customers.

Extend the use of the entertainments lounge
Fifth, study the feasibility of expanding and remodelling the entertainments lounge in the company so that the customers, too, can be entertained there. This has several advantages. It will bring customers to the company rather than the company going to customers, thereby realizing a saving in executive time. The cost of drinking also will be reduced to its wholesale price and it will take the drinking load off some of the salesmen by sharing the hospitality.

As Toyama resorted to the moral issue rather too strongly at the executive meeting, the president will be concerned that he might lose face at a time when he has to implement new measures. Therefore it is very important to put him in the picture from the very beginning.

By the time the next executive meeting is held, Toyama and Moriya will have worked out a plan for introducing new changes and both will be working for the common cause of improving the company's standing while caring for employee benefits as much as possible. The issue is not who wins the argument but what is best for the company.

This decision was provided by Masaaki Imai in his capacity as president of Cambridge Corp., a Japanese management consultancy and executive recruitment firm.

What action should firm take on hazardous material in new product?

Karl Schwartz, senior medical officer with Koenig AG, an industrial heating and insulation manufacturing firm in West Germany, asked to see the chief executive, Hans Weiss, and handed him a document. "It's a thesis on atmospheric health hazards produced by one of our sponsored research students," he explained. "I think you ought to read it."

"Is it urgent?" Weiss asked.

"He has researched, by chance, one of the chemicals used in our new compound for improving insulation. He suggests that surfaces impregnated with the chemical can give off fumes that may be harmful."

Weiss looked at Schwartz sharply. "*Can* give off fumes. *May* be harmful to health," he echoed. "Our own research department didn't come up with anything. You can check with them, but I think they decided that the compunds emitted only harmless fumes when sprayed on to insulating walls, screens and furnace linings."

Schwartz said that he had already shown the paper to Franz Braun, the head of research, but that he had been dismissive. "The thesis suggests," Schwartz said, "that when this chemical is heated through a certain temperature range, as it has to be when it is applied to our products, it emits small quantities of vapour that can cause a skin condition conducive to cancer."

"The student has proof, of course," Weiss said sarcastically.

"He has done experiments with rats," replied Schwartz.

"Who hasn't done experiments with rats! What's your reaction to this thesis? What do you feel about it?"

Repeat the laboratory experiment

"I think that on medical grounds we ought to look into it," Schwartz said. "I know the chemical is not on anyone's list of dangerous substances, let alone carcinogenic ones. But can we ignore this finding? I'd like your permission to repeat the student's experiments in our own laboratories. The thesis hasn't been published yet, but its findings will not be secret for very much longer."

"You have my permission," Weiss said. "But the production line on the new super insulation board has been running for six months. It has given us a real competitive edge in the marketplace. That one product has turned the company round and I'm not going to throw it all away because a research student wants to get his doctorate."

When Schwartz had left, Weiss summoned Braun to his office and asked him to read the thesis thoroughly and come back with a full evaluation within three days. When Braun reported, he avoided making any judgment on the student's thesis. But he restated that the chemical involved was an essential ingredient in the process Koenig had patented and that the search for any substitute would be lengthy, costly and probably hopeless.

Weiss was inclined to share in the general complacency. It was not until four months later that Schwartz reported that several rats which he had exposed to heavy doses of vapour from the compound containing the suspect chemical had developed incipient skin cancer. He also produced a research report from an Indian medical journal which said that the chemical was suspected of causing illness in the paint-spraying department of an electric motor manufacturer in Bombay.

Employees must be protected

"The fact remains," Braun said at an executive meeting which Weiss called, "that none of this is even remotely conclusive. I must repeat that this chemical is not on any list of dangerous substances."

"This is primarily a question of protecting our own employees," Weiss said. "One quarter of the items in our product range are now being impregnated with this compound, and as you know, social pressures on environmental health and pollution are steadily increasing."

336

He turned to the works manager of Koenig's biggest factory. "What would it cost to seal off the chemical application areas completely, install monitoring equipment and add more sophisticated extraction and filtering devices?"

"As you know," the works manager replied, "the new plant was designed to meet in every respect the environmental health standards demanded by law. But we did not believe this compound to be dangerous. To install every possible safeguard in both our plants would cost perhaps $10 million. It would also mean halting production for at least two months or possibly even longer."

"Intolerable," the marketing director butted in. "We cannot meet all our commitments to customers now. The competition is reacting to our success in the market. Stopping production would put us back five years."

"Realistically, how big is the health risk to our workers"? Weiss asked Schwartz, in a worried voice.

"However big or small," the doctor replied, "is it a risk we can afford to take at this moment."

Weiss pondered. Should he continue to market the product, as though nothing had happened, and risk serious consequences later? Or should he put in safety devices that might wreck the company's revival?

DECISION

Market-winning product may be hazardous to employees

Hans Weiss, the chief executive at Koenig AG, should not be stampeded into doing something he would later regret. To ignore the research student's report, the experiment conducted by his own medical officer and the article discovered in the Indian medical journal would be morally indefensible. On the other hand, the information that Weiss has is inadequate for him to form a considered judgment. Certainly it would not justify halting production, even for a day, at this stage.

Here is a commercial undertaking putting out a product that has changed the economic outlook of the company without breaking any health laws. But an amber light is now flashing which Weiss cannot ignore. It could turn red.

Demonstrate company action
This is a moral and medical problem that requires a lot more thought and a lot more investigation. What does Weiss really want? He does not want the company to be put out of business. But he does need to demostrate to society as a whole, and to his employees in particular, that he has taken action to try to evaluate the risks within the limits of knowledge, and that his final decision will be taken on medical, scientific and moral as well as on commercial grounds.

First, Weiss should ask his research people to investigate much more fully what work has been done on the chemical, its application and its possible harmful effects, anywhere in the world. It appears that in this respect at least, the company's research department has done an inadequate job. Already the doctor has unearthed a published paper which Franz Braun, the research head, evidently did not know existed, and which he was inclined to dismiss without further investigation. Maybe there is other evidence buried in medical and scientific literature that should have been taken into account at the earlier product-planning stage. This should be looked into.

Retain the initiative
Second, Weiss should ask his works director to provide him with detailed breakdowns to show what the costs of possible alternative production arrangements would be.

Third, he should ask Karl Schwartz to repeat and enlarge his experiments, perhaps in cooperation with an impartial external health agency, replicating more exactly the conditions under which workers apply the chemical in the factories. Both the research student and the doctor evidently conducted their experiments with rats in an environment of direct exposure of the animals to the chemical. It is not clear whether the workers at the factory are already wearing protective clothing. Perhaps experiments would show that the relatively inexpensive step of providing this protection would be an adequate solution to any health problem that exists with the chemical.

Fourth, Weiss must keep in mind the public relations aspect. Rather than trying to hush up the research student's findings, the company could gain kudos by its initiative in discovering the unpublished report and by its frankness in revealing it to the world. Weiss should encourage Schwartz to establish contact with prestigious outside medical bodies and perhaps arrange a joint investigation with one of them.

Take a moral stance
In other words, Weiss can take a moral stance and at the same time allow the uncertainty involved in such safety matters to work in the company's favour. The great problem of the safety profession throughout the world is to decide what constitutes acceptable limits and risks. It is all very well to come along and say that a chemical is dangerous. But in all probability there is a limit below which that chemical could be used with every degree of safety.

Weiss needs much more information on what research has been done, what is currently under way, what is likely to take place over the next two to three years and whether there are any other conclusions known.

Currently, the experiments with the rats are the only things that suggest the chemical may be dangerous. If, indeed, it does produce carcinogenic symptoms in rats at such an early stage, most medical people, I think, would be worried about it.

When Weiss does have the facts, it may be that there is an alternative to redesigning the factory and putting in more sophisticated and costly safety appliances. In the meantime, a positive attitude and frankness, both towards the general public and his own work-force, is the best policy.

This decision was provided by Derek Carr in his capacity as associate director and adviser on engineering and safety at Stewart Wrightson U.K. Ltd., an insurance company.

Should government directive to shed work be followed?

Ullas Premji called a conference of senior managers. He was the managing director of Eli Tractors Co., a public company making a range of agricultural equipment.

The plant was in a Far Eastern country where the policy of the government had long been to limit imports of manufactured goods and encourage local engineering industry.

Now Premji had on his desk a memorandum from the government that "strongly urged" major manufacturers to subcontract components that did not require very high precision engineering to other local manufacturing companies.

Eli Tractors was the biggest company on a fairly large industrial estate. It had been profitable. But recently, following a cut-back in government aid to farmers, business had slumped considerably.

There had been no profit in the last financial year and the previous shareholders' meeting, which was well attended, had been both vociferous and stormy.

Premji also had to cope with a militant union, and his position in that regard had not been helped by the fact that he was an active campaigner for, and contributor to, the right-wing party which was in opposition to the government.

Premji had engaged as personnel manager Akber Roy, a man of humble beginnings who was diplomatic enough to please both Premji and the work-force. He had handled the union quite well and had provided the company with a period of industrial peace.

As Premji called his executives together to inform them of the government memorandum he had a presentiment that there would be disagreement. John Righton, the production manager, said there were a number of light engineering works on the estate which could produce components for the company's harvesting machines.

Comply with request and save money

"I though this might come up," he said, pulling from his pocket a list of components with their current manufacturing costs. "You will see that some of these components are being manufactured on our own machines more cheaply than if we subcontracted them. However, as you know, many of our machine tools are obsolete and need constant attention. If we subcontract the items I have marked we can both comply with the government request and save ourselves substantial captial expenditure by not importing new machines from abroad."

Damodar Desai, the chief financial officer, puffed a cloud of smoke from his pipe. "The money we could save by not replacing the machines would make the next balance sheet look much more attractive," he said. "We can make ourselves popular with the shareholders and be patriotic at the same time."

Premji knew that at this point Roy would intervene. And the personnel manager did. "I think we have forgotten something, gentlemen," he said.

339

"Subcontracting those components is going to lose us more than 50 jobs."

"I know," said Righton. "However, the subcontractors will be able to employ more people."

"I doubt that," Roy replied. "Their machines are underemployed, which is one reason why the government wants this subcontracting. Our order will simply take up the slack. They will not need to take on more machine minders."

"That's not our problem," Desai said.

"But it is very much my problem," Roy insisted. "We cannot simply lay people off. Remember what happened when we closed a body-building section a year ago? The union took us to court and we weren't allowed to make a single man redundant. We were ordered to find them other jobs. But they are still idle on full pay.

"Not ordering new machines may help the balance sheet to look better temporarily. But what about the longer term? How many men are we prepared to carry indefinitely? Also, any further redundancies would risk a complete upset of the good relations I have built up with the work-force. Can we afford that?"

"So you have a problem," said Righton unsympathetically. He turned to Premji. "What do you think we should do?"

Premji said that first he wanted to look more carefully at the analysis of the costs of different sources of manufacture. But he realized that he faced a situation in which he would have to make the final decision on his instinctive feeling.

If he ignored the government's request to subcontract, and also put in an order for more machine tools from abroad, he would not be able to throw any crumbs of comfort to the shareholders at the annual meeting in three months' time. Since he was a known political opponent of the government, he could imagine the charges of wilful obstructionism that would be made against him.

However, if he did subcontract the components he risked a confrontation with the union and opposition from a personnel man who had greatly improved labour relations. Short-term financial gain to the company would be offset by the longer-term problem of more surplus people on the payroll. Also making people redundant would not help his political ambitions.

DECISION

Engineering plant must cut jobs or oppose government

There are two levels at which one can look at this dilemma. Ostensibly it is a question of whether Eli Tractors Co. should keep the work it has got in order to sustain the employment it has or whether it should release some work in order to create employment elsewhere.

Beyond that decision, however, there is a question of whether it is expedient to be seen to be subcontracting work as the result of pressure from an external source, in this case the government.

Encouraged by the fact that industry was "strongly urged", not ordered, to subcontract the manufacture of components, Ullas Premji, the managing director of Eli Tractors, should not do anything rash. He should take his time in reaching a decision, for where diplomacy is required, time for reflection and reappraisal can be a significant factor.

Premji's decision will be influenced by the nature and methods of the government involved. How powerful is it and how does it use its power? To what extent does Premji's firm rely on government orders?

When he sits down to analyse the situation closely, Premji probably will wonder whether there is much to be said for the scheme even from the government's point of view.

It will not increase the total amount of employment. It is really a question of shifting employment from one organization to another. The only reason why another local company would need to employ a greater number of people in order to do the same manufacturing job that Eli Tractors had done would be because it was less experienced and therefore less efficient.

So unless Eli Tractors' product is underwritten by the government, or not sensitive to price, Premji could argue that it would not be patriotic to fall in with the government's plans on national economic grounds.

If the situation in the country is such that Premji feels he cannot avoid transferring work from his company, at least he can ensure it is done in a way in which, in the eyes of his employees, as little blame as possible attaches to the company.

Perhaps it would be possible to persuade the government to replace the lost work. Premji could say to the government: "Look, it has been suggested that this work be sent to another company because of some broader view of work in the area, but it has implications for employment here. It is our intention to resist because we see no good reason for it."

Explain the government's plan
He should also take the employees into his confidence, telling them of the stand the company is taking and the reasons for it. Then, if the government persists and Eli Tractors is forced to give work to other companies, Premji is in a situation where he really cannot lose.

In other words, if the deal goes sour and the work-force objects, it will not be the company that is blamed but the government. If, on the other hand, everything goes smoothly and the employees accept the situation, at least the company will have been seen to be protecting its employees against the might of the government.

Premji's personal political ambitions are largely irrelevant in this context. Certainly it could be fatal to his chances if he were suspected of making a decision on grounds of personal ambition.

Premji should forget the political aspect and also the short-term gain of presenting the shareholders with a favourable balance sheet because money had not been spent ordering new machine tools from abroad.

He should stick with the basics, which are that Eli Tractors has been making its own components efficiently for a long time; that if the government insists on others making them it will mean new tooling, quite a large amount of learning time and other uncertainties; and that it will be on government insistence that Eli Tractors is having to suspend, if not sack, some of its productive employees.

This decision was provided by Prof. Ray Wild of Brunel University and the U.K. Henley Administrative Staff College.

Should social responsibility programme be abandoned?

Lee Rossiter, president of Vermont Foods Inc., had a problem. For three years Vermont had been running a social responsibility programme designed to give it a positive image as a forward-looking, socially aware corporation. The objective was to overtake the market share of a rival company, Interstate Products Co., which for years had been market leader in the health foods business.

However, the programme had had unhappy side-effects. These had now culminated in a demand from Vermont's personnel director, Paul Romford, that it be abandoned or severely curtailed.

The demand came at a board meeting at which Harold Filbinger, the marketing director, made a presentation extolling the success of the programme to date. As each of his slides was projected on to the board-room screen, he injected the maximum drama into his tale of how the company was increasing its market penetration.

He reminded the other board members that three years previously Vermont, which produced a range of "natural" foodstuffs for health food retailers, had 26% of the market against Interstate's 44%.

"You will recall," he said, "how we identified as Interstate's major weakness its poor reputation as an employer and social citizen. Our reputation in that area was just a little above average. Now, however, it is sky-high. I am happy to report that we are running neck-and-neck with Interstate. Each of us has 39% of the market."

Employees had three-month sabbaticals

The accolade Filbinger expected did not come. At the end of the slide presentation Romford said bluntly: "I think we should scrap the programme." He launched into his own analysis of it, beginning tactfully but then becoming outspoken about the programme's demerits. "It was an original idea to appoint social responsibility managers in every major location. Reporting to you, Harry," he said to Filbinger, "they were given a sizeable budget to spend both on internal improvements, such as recreational facilities and education grants for employees, and on local community projects such as adventure playgrounds.

"The pivot of the strategy was the programme to encourage employees to use their skills helping local charities in three-month sabbaticals paid by the company. I must remind you, however, that I was against three months from the beginning. Also, I didn't think so many people should have been sent on this programme. But I was overruled."

"The employees' response to the scheme was tremendous," Filbinger interjected. "The work they did for the charities formed the basis for an advertising campaign which, I can tell you, has been highly successful."

"We did increase our market share," Romford conceded. "However, Interstate's share did not fall as much as you expected, Harry. It was the smaller companies that lost business to our advertising campaign.

"More to the point, I want to draw the board's attention to the side-effects of this programme. Of the 44 employees who went on sabbaticals in the last two years, ten elected not to return to the company. Many of those who did come back have said, in interviews with my department, that they are no longer satisfied with the work they are doing here.

"Line managers complain about the loss of some of their best workers. Slips in quality control have occurred more often and have now resulted in a pending prosecution by health authorities which, if successful, could be disastrous to our new public image.

"I also feel," Romford continued, "that far too much time at head office is being spent administering this scheme. We have got to abandon it or at least, drastically modify it."

A high degree of demotivation noted

"Not before we have finally overtaken Interstate!" Filbinger exploded. "It would be fatal to change anything now."

"It could be equally fatal to continue," Romford insisted. "Take it from me, there is quite a high degree of demotivation among those who have returned from the programme. They are spreading a sense of dissatisfaction to the other workers.

"Recently I had to decide whether to fire an ex-volunteer who was encouraging his workmates to refuse to handle dried fruits, insisting that suppliers were under-paying their fruit pickers.

"We have got to ask ourselves whether the drawbacks are compensated by market share improvements that might have been achieved equally well by other marketing ploys."

Rossiter kept quiet as the argument raged. True, to abandon the programme could wreck the company's marketing thrust just when there seemed to be a chance of becoming market leader. But the programme's side-effects were equally intolerable.

DECISION

Social programme hits employee morale

Rossiter's problem as president of Vermont Foods Inc. is to balance the obvious gains the company has made in the marketplace against the growing losses in production.

He should not cancel the social responsibility programme, as Romford, the personnel director, suggests. To do so would expose the company to the allegation that it cynically used people, and good causes, for purely selfish ends, throwing them on the scrap-heap as soon as it was expedient to do so.

His decision should be to modify the scheme and use the opportunity to improve productivity and morale within the company, as well as to fulfil the original purpose of boosting sales. In the past, too much emphasis has been placed upon the sales objective and too little upon ensuring there is job enrichment that is in-house and lasting, rather than external and transitory.

It looks as though the hard-nosed directors of the company have simply ignored the possible impact of the programme on their own staff, or seen it as a side issue. Yet there is clearly a reservoir of goodwill waiting to be tapped, if they set out to find it.

Rossiter may well decide on a programme along these lines:

First, leave the marketing budget as it is but reduce the depth of the community activity by cutting sabbaticals from three to two months. At the same time, keep the width of the social responsibility programme.

Second, managers with social responsibility assignments should be briefed to concentrate more of their energies on in-company problems and opportunities.

Third, take the reactions of employees returning from sabbaticals seriously. Invite them to write recommendations for future action to the board and speak about their experiences at employee meetings. In other words, get them re-involved with company activities. Make them feel like very important people who have something original and useful to impart.

For example, the man who complains about the under-payment of fruit pickers may or may not have a point. The important thing is to give him the chance to state his views openly, in a group situation, rather than leave him alone to drip poison into the system.

Fourth, encourage the part-time involvement of other employees in community activities, so more feel involved in the company's good works.

Fifth, take a new look at teamwork activities in the company as a whole and how jobs that do not have the intrinsic glamour of sabbaticals can be enriched.

From the corporate image point of view, one is entitled to ask: "What is the public affairs manager, or director, doing while this debate is raging at board level?" If he exists, why is he not involved? It would be wrong for such a scheme to be adminsistered by the marketing director alone.

Also, no mention is made of the level and sophistication of market research at Vermont. The products appear to be sensitive to advertising, yet no clear link has been established, backed by research, between the socially responsible image that the company has made the cornerstone of its marketing policy and its increased market share.

Indeed, the fact that the rival company's market share dropped only 5% appears to suggest that a poor image on the social responsibility front does not matter too much. Perhaps research will show that Vermont can profitably shift some of its advertising emphasis away from social responsibility to other themes.

If I were Rossiter, I would ask Romford to draw up a long-term plan for internal job enrichment, perhaps calling in an outside consultant to advise on the type of scheme the company should try.

At the same time, Rossiter should ask the marketing director, Filbinger, to produce convincing research figures to prove that continued emphasis on social responsibility is justified. If it is not, he should gradually phase out the social responsibility campaign in the public media in favour of other kinds of advertising, perhaps placing more emphasis on quality and price.

It would be disastrous simply to abandon the programme, however. Such a move would stamp Vermont, certainly among its own employees, as a charlatan. If that were to happen, any subsequent moves to enrich jobs, cut product defects and improve morale and productivity would be an uphill task.

This decision was provided by Thomas Attwood in his capacity as managing director of U.K.-based management consultants Cargill, Attwood & Thomas Ltd.